I0876203

EXPLORING CELTIC ORIGINS

CELTIC STUDIES PUBLICATIONS
series editor: John T. Koch

CELTIC STUDIES PUBLICATIONS I
The Celtic Heroic Age: Literary Sources for Ancient Celtic Europe and Early Ireland and Wales, ed. John T. Koch with John Carey (Fourth Edition, revised and expanded, 2003) Pp. x + 440 ISBN 1–891271–09–1

CELTIC STUDIES PUBLICATIONS III
A Single Ray of the Sun: Religious Speculation in Early Ireland, John Carey (Second Edition, 2011) Pp. x + 123 ISBN 978–1–891271–18–2

CELTIC STUDIES PUBLICATIONS IV
Ildánach Ildírech. A Festschrift for Proinsias Mac Cana, ed. John Carey, John T. Koch, and Pierre-Yves Lambert (1999) Pp. xvii + 312 ISBN 1–891271–01–6

CELTIC STUDIES PUBLICATIONS VII
Yr Hen Iaith: Studies in Early Welsh, ed. Paul Russell (2003) Pp. viii + 224 ISBN 1–891271–10–5

CELTIC STUDIES PUBLICATIONS VIII
Landscape Perception in Early Celtic Literature, Francesco Benozzo (2004) Pp. xvi + 272 ISBN 1–891271–11–3

CELTIC STUDIES PUBLICATIONS IX
Cín Chille Cúile—Texts, Saints and Places: Essays in Honour of Pádraig Ó Riain, ed. John Carey, Máire Herbert, and Kevin Murray (2004) Pp. xxiv + 405 ISBN 1–891271–13–X

CELTIC STUDIES PUBLICATIONS X
Archæologia Britannica: Texts and Translations, Edward Lhwyd, ed. Dewi W. Evans and Brynley F. Roberts (2009) Pp. xii + 262 ISBN 978–1–891271–14–4

CELTIC STUDIES PUBLICATIONS XIII
Tartessian: Celtic in the South-west at the Dawn of History, John T. Koch (second edition 2013) Pp. ix + 332 ISBN 978–1–891271–17–5

CELTIC STUDIES PUBLICATIONS XV
Celtic from the West: Alternative Approaches from Archaeology, Genetics, Language and Literature, ed. Barry Cunliffe and John T. Koch (2010; 2012) Pp. xii + 383 ISBN 978–1–84217–475–3

CELTIC STUDIES PUBLICATIONS XVI
Celtic from the West 2: Rethinking the Bronze Age and the Arrival of Indo-European in Atlantic Europe, ed. John T. Koch and Barry Cunliffe (2013; 2017) Pp. viii + 237 ISBN 978–1–84217–529–3

CELTIC STUDIES PUBLICATIONS XVII
Memory, Myth and Long-term Landscape Inhabitation, ed. Adrian M. Chadwick and Catriona D. Gibson (2013) Pp. xi + 347 ISBN 978–1–78297–393–5

CELTIC STUDIES PUBLICATIONS XVIII
The End and Beyond: Medieval Irish Eschatology, ed. John Carey, Emma Nic Cárthaigh, and Caitríona Ó Dochartaigh (2014) 2 vols, Pp. xi + 944 ISBN 978–1–891271–20–5

CELTIC STUDIES PUBLICATIONS XIX
Celtic from the West 3: Atlantic Europe in the Metal Ages: questions of shared language, ed. John T. Koch, Barry Cunliffe, Kerri Cleary, and Catriona D. Gibson (2016) Pp. xii + 539 ISBN 978–1–78570–227–3

CELTIC STUDIES PUBLICATIONS XX
Celtic Religions in the Roman Period: Personal, Local, and Global, ed. Ralph Haeussler and Anthony King (2017) Pp. xiv + 522 ISBN 978–1–891271–25–0

CELTIC STUDIES PUBLICATIONS XXI
Magic, Metallurgy and Imagination in Medieval Ireland: Three Studies, John Carey (2019) ISBN 978–1–891271–28–1

CELTIC STUDIES PUBLICATIONS XXII
Exploring Celtic Origins: New ways forward in archaeology, linguistics, and genetics, ed. Barry Cunliffe and John T. Koch (2019) ISBN 978–1–789250–88–6

EXPLORING CELTIC ORIGINS

New ways forward in archaeology, linguistics, and genetics

edited by

Barry Cunliffe & John T. Koch

OXBOW | books
Oxford & Philadelphia

First published in 2019. Reprinted in paperback in 2021 and 2026 by
Oxbow Books, Oxford, UK

Paperback Edition: ISBN 978-1-78925-550-8
Digital Edition: ISBN 978–1–78925–089–3

For a complete list of Oxbow titles, please contact:
United Kingdom
Oxbow Books
Telephone (0)1226 734350
Email: oxbow@oxbowbooks.com
www.oxbowbooks.com

United States of America
Oxbow Books
Telephone (610) 853-9131, Fax (610) 853-9146
Email: queries@casemateacademic.com
www.casemateacademic.com/oxbow

Oxbow Books is part of the Casemate Group

A CIP record for this book is available from the British Library.

Library of Congress Control Number: 2018963075

Printed in the United States of America by Integrated Books International

CONTENTS

Maps, Illustrations, and Tables

ACKNOWLEDGEMENTS

The research presented in this book was supported with a grant from the Arts and Humanities Research Council (AHRC): Research Grant Proposal AH/K002600/1, funding the project 'Atlantic Europe in the Metal Ages (AEMA): questions of shared language.' Amgueddfa Genedlaethol Cymru/ National Museum of Wales and Comisiwn Brenhinol Henebion Cymru/ Royal Commission on the Ancient and Historical Monuments of Wales acted as partners in the AEMA project. Within this volume, their partnership contributions include, respectively, Figures 4.1 and 4.10, and 4.17 and 4.18. The editors thank Adam Gwilt and Toby Driver for their help in securing these images.

PREFACE

The study of pre- and proto-history has become an increasingly complex exercise involving experts from a wide range of disciplines—archaeology, history, linguistics, genetics, and a variety of other sciences. In the previous century there was a tendency for most of these disciplines to work in relative isolation except for archaeologists who had grown used to collaborating with selected scientists. Linguists preferred to practice alone, historians rarely used up-to-date archaeological evidence, while the study of ancient DNA was then barely an aspiration. Few could anticipate an integrated study of men and women who lived before written records as makers of things, speakers of words, *and* flesh and blood human beings. All this has now changed with the result that our understanding of the past is advancing at an exponential rate.

The present book focuses on a research programme, based in the Centre for Advanced Welsh and Celtic Studies at Aberystwyth in collaboration with the School of Archaeology, University of Oxford, designed to explore the origin of the Celts and of the Celtic language family. What we have set out to do here is to offer an insight into how a complex, multidisciplinary research programme is constructed and how, as it proceeds and new data becomes available, it changes direction and emphasis. This is not a bland overview of our conclusions but an attempt to capture something of the energetic debate between the researchers involved as they came to learn more of their own data and to grow in confidence in their engagements with those in other disciplines.

Research is an exciting process and those of us privileged to be involved in it live with that excitement. We hope that this volume, written by specialists who have worked closely together, will communicate something of what it feels like to be caught up in an extremely fast-moving, multifaceted debate. As the sheer complexity of the issue becomes apparent, cherished beliefs have to be modified or abandoned, and fascinating new visions begin to come into view. Two well-known truisms of how life today differs from the past are the acceleration of scientific discovery and the upward trend of longevity. In adapting to both developments, an ability we will want to carry with us into the future is to change our minds as the facts change.

Barry Cunliffe

John T. Koch

CHAPTER ONE

SETTING THE SCENE

Barry Cunliffe

OUR understanding of the past is constantly changing as new evidence emerges and the ways of interpreting that which we have fall out of and into fashion. Usually our vision accretes—it becomes more detailed and more nuanced—but sometimes the realization that traditional interpretations simply do not work anymore means that they have to be discarded and new hypotheses put in their place. So it has been with the Celts.

The Celts feature large in the popular imagination. They are so familiar that brilliant, witty comic books can be written about them—who hasn't heard of Asterix? And many people around the world are proud to speak of their Celtic ancestry. Nor are politicians slow to use selected images of the Celts for their own ends. In the years leading up to the creation of the European Union 'our Celtic heritage' was a slogan frequently misused to call up the image of a once-unified Europe. Celticness is also a concept that has been used by the people of Galicia, Brittany, Wales, Scotland, and Ireland to distinguish themselves from the centralizing attitudes of the Spanish, French, and English. 'Celtic' is a powerful and emotive concept and it is important that we try to understand the many disparate and sometimes conflicting meanings that lie within it.

Celt was a word used by Greek and Roman writers from the 6th century BC to describe the barbarian peoples of much of central and western Europe. It was a convenient, generalizing term like Scythians for those who lived in the steppe regions, and Libyans for the inhabitants of Africa. As more was learnt of these northern barbarians something of the complexity of the situation came to be understood. Caesar believed that in Gaul the Celts were one of three ethnic groupings and he was very well aware that there were many different Celtic tribes in various degrees of conflict or alliance with each other. To what extent, if at all, these disparate peoples regarded themselves as belonging to a 'Celtic nation' we will never know. But for the writers and politicians of the Mediterranean world 'Celt' became a convenient term to describe the native peoples living in the west and beyond the Alps, with whom they came into contact. While they no doubt used the name quite loosely, the alliances and intermarriages between the tribes, recorded by the classical writers, suggest a degree of closeness and it is quite likely that they would have shared a common language. The archaeological evidence also implies a degree of connectedness. From the 5th century BC onward it is possible to recognize a degree of cultural unity across a large swathe of middle Europe represented by similarities in material culture and in particular art styles. This is referred to by archaeologists as the La Tène culture, named after a deposit of artefacts found in a lake in Switzerland.

Classical writers like Livy and Polybius describe the growing tensions in trans-alpine Europe as population pressures built up only to be relieved by large migrant bands moving out of their home territories. The migrations reached a crescendo at the end of the 5th and beginning of the 4th centuries BC. One migration route led through the Alps with the incomers establishing themselves in the Po valley, while another route led eastwards along the Danube with the new settlers taking over land in the middle Danube region of Transdanubia and the Great Hungarian Plain. These migrants brought with them their La Tène culture and their language. It was from these new territories, in the comparative safety of the Po valley and the middle Danube valley, that raiding parties of Celts spread out. From the Po valley raids were mounted through the Apennines and deep into Italy, Rome itself being besieged in 390 BC. From the middle Danube raiders rampaged through the Balkans and into Greece attacking the sanctuary of Apollo at Delphi in 279 BC. Defeated by the Greeks some of the raiders moved on crossing into Asia Minor and eventually settled in the territory around modern Ankara from where they could raid the rich Hellenistic cities of the coastal regions. The first massive thrust of the Celtic folk movements was over by about 270 BC, but continuous raiding and lesser migrations continued for the next two centuries.

The scale of the migrations and their impact on the classical world of the Mediterranean meant that the threat of the barbarian Celts was ever present in the minds of the Greeks and Romans and they became a new reality when, in the middle of the first century BC, Julius Caesar led the Roman armies into Gaul. For many classical writers the Celt could be presented as the noble savage, a fierce but brave enemy to be overcome, his submission enhancing the achievement of the civilized world. It was an image reinforced in sculptural representations, most notably the famous statues of the dying Gaul and the chieftain with his dead wife, committing suicide in defeat—statues which once adorned a victory monument set up in the city of Pergamon in Asia Minor.

So, as the threat receded, the concept of the Celts as 'noble other' formed in the classical mind. In Roman literature Celts were presented as 'different from us'—they went naked into battle, they were fierce in the attack but cowardly when beaten. They were hairy, rubbing lime in the hair to make it stand up in a fearsome mane, and some had long drooping moustaches. And they got wildly drunk because they drank their wine neat, rather than diluting it like a sensible Mediterranean. This is the stuff of caricature but like all stereotypes it embodies elements of the truth.

The written accounts and the visual representations of Celts provided by the Mediterranean states were the basic sources upon which subsequent generations have built their visions of the Celts. Used with critical care this mass of observation is invaluable but we must remember that it is biased and partial. At best it reflects the lifestyles and activities one group of Celtic speakers, observed over a brief interlude in the second half of the 1st millennium BC, seen through the restricted vision of élite Greek and Roman writers.

Origin myths: the beginnings of history

The 16th century saw a renewed interest in national identity throughout western Europe with antiquaries making serious attempts to sketch out the prehistories and early histories of their countries. In France, Jean Le Fèvre published his *Les Fleurs et antiquités de Gaul* in 1532 and in Britain William Camden's *Britannia* appeared in 1586 and went on into several subsequent editions. For the early periods there was little tangible evidence for them to use but classical texts like Tacitus' *Agricola*, Caesar's *De Bello Gallico*, and Livy's *Histories* were becoming widely available introducing the classical world's vision of Britons, Gauls, and Celts to the general reader, and it was inevitable, given the vivid way in which the Celts were portrayed in the classical texts, that they should feature large in the writings of the antiquaries. But it was a Breton monk, Paul-Yves Pezron, who was the first to construct a narrative history of Europe built around the Celts. In his book *L'Antiquité de la nation et la langue des Celts* published in 1703, using gleanings from classical texts and his belief in the validity of the Old Testament, he constructed a vision of the Celts as a nation. They originated in Asia Minor, not far from Mount Ararat, where Noah's ark had landed after the flood, and were descended from Noah's grandson, Gomer. From their Asian homeland they moved west through Europe conquering Greece and finally reaching Gaul and Britain, where their ancient language, Celtic, is still spoken by the Bretons and Welsh (Pezron knew little of Ireland and Scotland). It was a confection built of scraps of history, biblical myth, and inventive imagination, powerful in its appeal not least to the Bretons and Welsh, who could present themselves as the descendants of the once-masterful Celtic race, and it was to prove influential in the subsequent development of Celtic studies.

At the moment that Pezron's book was published the Oxford antiquarian Edward Lhuyd was collecting material for his great work *Archæologia Britannica* which he planned to publish in several volumes. He was in correspondence with Pezron and was instrumental in seeing that Pezron's book was published in English in 1707. Lhuyd travelled widely to amass data for his work, visiting Brittany, Cornwall, Ireland, and Scotland, as well as his native Wales, and took a particular interest in the languages still widely spoken in these regions at the time. Recognizing the close similarities between them he named them Celtic, following Pezron's lead, and published his linguistic findings in the magisterial first (and only) volume of

Archæologica Britannica, subtitled *Glossography* in 1707. He identified two broad linguistic groupings, Irish and Scots Gaelic and Welsh, Cornish, and Breton but offered no explanation of the way in which the differences had emerged. Later, however, in the preface to the Welsh edition of his book and in letters to friends, he accepted Pezron's model and extended it suggesting that there were two invasions of Celts into Britain and Ireland: the first bringing the more archaic form of Celtic that survived in Ireland and Scotland and the second introducing the Celtic spoken in Wales and Cornwall which was similar to the Celtic of Gaul. Later scholars referred to these different groups as Q-Celtic and P-Celtic.

So it was that the traditional hypothesis, that the Celts moved from middle Europe westwards eventually colonizing Britain and Ireland, came into being. The hypothesis was to pass unchallenged for nearly three centuries, with only slight modifications. Another invasion to the south-west was proposed to explain how it was that Celtic came to be spoken by the Celtiberians of Spain. It was a pleasingly simple model—a middle European Celtic homeland, extending from eastern France across southern Germany to the Czech Republic, from which migratory movements took Celtic culture and language to most parts of Europe. Those who moved to the south and east, and impacted on the classical world, were described in vivid detail by Greek and Roman sources whilst those to the west went unreferenced.

At the time when Lhuyd was writing there was little physical evidence available to bring into the debate except for visible monuments such as megaliths and hill-forts which were immediately claimed as Celtic. But from the beginning of the 19th century a proliferation of archaeological excavations created a flood of artefacts to feed private collections and the public museums set up to satisfy the growing interest of the public. All this new evidence had to be integrated into the grand narrative and since the senior disciplines were linguistics and classics it was incumbent on the junior partners, the archaeologists, to arrange the detritus of the past which they were grubbing-up in a way that conformed to the existing model. This they did with a willing diligence.

Two excavations feature large in the growing understanding of the European Iron Age. The first was the meticulous excavation and recording of a large cemetery of about 1000 graves at Hallstatt in Austria between 1846 and 1863. This produced a massive collection of associated and well contextualized artefacts with which to compare more scattered material. The second was the discovery in 1857 of what was probably a votive deposit of weapons and other items thrown into the Lake of Neuchâtel at La Tène in Switzerland. In 1872 the Swedish archaeologist Hans Hildebrandt proposed that the European Iron Age be divided into two parts, the earlier characterized by the Hallstatt material, the later by the finds from La Tène, the divide coming at around 450 BC. These two broad periods were subsequently broken down into phases and sub-phases but the nomenclature has remained widely used since then.

In 1871, the year before Hildebrandt made his proposal, the International Conference of Prehistoric Anthropology and Archaeology held a meeting in Bologna. Delegates were taken on a visit to the excavations of the Etruscan town of Marzabotto and there saw artefacts recovered from a cemetery located towards the edge of the settlement. Those present who were familiar with La Tène material north of the Alps immediately recognized the grave finds as La Tène. Here, then, was tangible evidence of the Celts who, according to the classical texts, began to settle the Po valley around 400 BC. The Celts now had an archaeological identity. Thereafter, the advance of the Celts of the migration period was traced by the distribution of La Tène material culture. It was, of course, a very simplistic argument, at best valid only in parts. Later it led to the assumption that the appearance of artefacts, made in La Tène style, in Britain and Ireland and elsewhere represented an invasion of Celts.

By the early 20th century it was realized that the situation was far more complex and the belief grew that there may have been multiple Celtic invasions to the west, as Lhuyd had suggested for Britain. If so, some may have preceded the La Tène period. Some such hypothesis was needed to explain how it was that the Celtic language got to the Iberian Peninsula since La Tène artefacts are virtually unknown there.

By the second half of the 20th century, as the quality and complexity of the archaeological data increased, some archaeologists began to express dissatisfaction with the traditional model which required there to have been invasions to explain how it was that the Celtic language came to be spoken in the west. The simple fact was that in Britain, Ireland, and Iberia there was no convincing evidence of invasion either in the La Tène period or before that in the Hallstatt Iron Age. Nor was there anything to suggest a significant inflow of population in the preceding Late Bronze Age. Instead the evidence pointed to indigenous development but with a degree of connectivity which allowed the selective spread of artefacts and value systems through existing social networks.

In the first edition of my book *Iron Age Communities in Britain* (1974) I presented the evidence for contacts between Britain and the continent in some detail explicitly rejecting any possibility of large scale invasions of the kind that could have brought the Celtic language from continental Europe. I avoided the problem of how the language came to be spoken here simply because I had not thought it through but the implicit assumption was that Celtic was already deeply rooted in the island's prehistory well before the 1st millennium BC. Others were now also expressing doubts and by the time I came to write *The Ancient Celts* (first published in 1997) I was convinced that the Atlantic zone had played a significant role in the development of Celtic, but a cohesive evidence-based hypothesis had still to be worked out. The research that followed led to the publication of *Facing the Ocean* (2001), in which I put forward the proposal that the Celtic language had developed along the Atlantic façade over many millennia, a process that may have begun as early as the Neolithic period. Many linguists found the hypothesis difficult to accept and some still do.

1.1. A cognitive geography of the Atlantic zone as it might have been viewed by an Atlantic mariner. (map M. Crampin)

Establishing Atlantic connectivity

If, shorn of any preconceptions derived from antiquarian speculations, we consider the archaeological evidence at its face value, what stands out is the persistence of connectivity along the Atlantic seaboard of Europe over the *longue durée*. In the early Holocene, as the ice sheets retreated, the Atlantic maritime zone became one of the corridors along which human populations moved to colonize new territories. It had many attractions, not least the varied array of resources offered by the close packed ecozones—the forest edge, the river estuaries and marshes, the littoral zone, and the sea itself—which offered hunter–gatherers an abundance of choice. There is ample evidence that during this Mesolithic period coastal communities took to the sea to fish, their boats providing ease of movement for those wishing to travel. It can plausibly be argued that the arts of navigation using the stars were probably first developed by hunter–gatherers to guide them back to their home bases after long hunting and foraging expeditions. The shore dwellers, in search of fish shoals, will have honed these navigational skills (Fig. 1.1).

The introduction of farming economies to the Atlantic zone, heralding the Neolithic period, was a complex process but there is now ample evidence to show that it spread from Asia Minor, carried at least in part by new people along two routes, one by way of the Mediterranean by sea-borne enclave colonization, the other along the river valleys of middle Europe (Fig. 1.2). The spread was rapid, taking as little as 1500 years to reach the Atlantic shores. Early farming settlements, using characteristic pottery decorated with cardial shell impressions, first appeared on the coast of Portugal about 5500 BC. The pioneers had come by sea, following the Mediterranean coast, sailing through the Strait of Gibraltar to make their landfall on the Atlantic coasts of Iberia. Others, having settled on the southern coasts of France, spread into the Garonne valley eventually reaching the Atlantic coast of France facing the Bay of Biscay. Further north the spread of farming through middle Europe, characterized by distinctive linear-decorated pottery (Linearbandkeramik) reached Normandy and Brittany about 5300 BC and Neolithic farming communities were settling on the Channel Islands a century or two later. So it was that by about 5000 BC farming communities had established themselves along much of the Atlantic zone from the Algarve to the Seine valley.

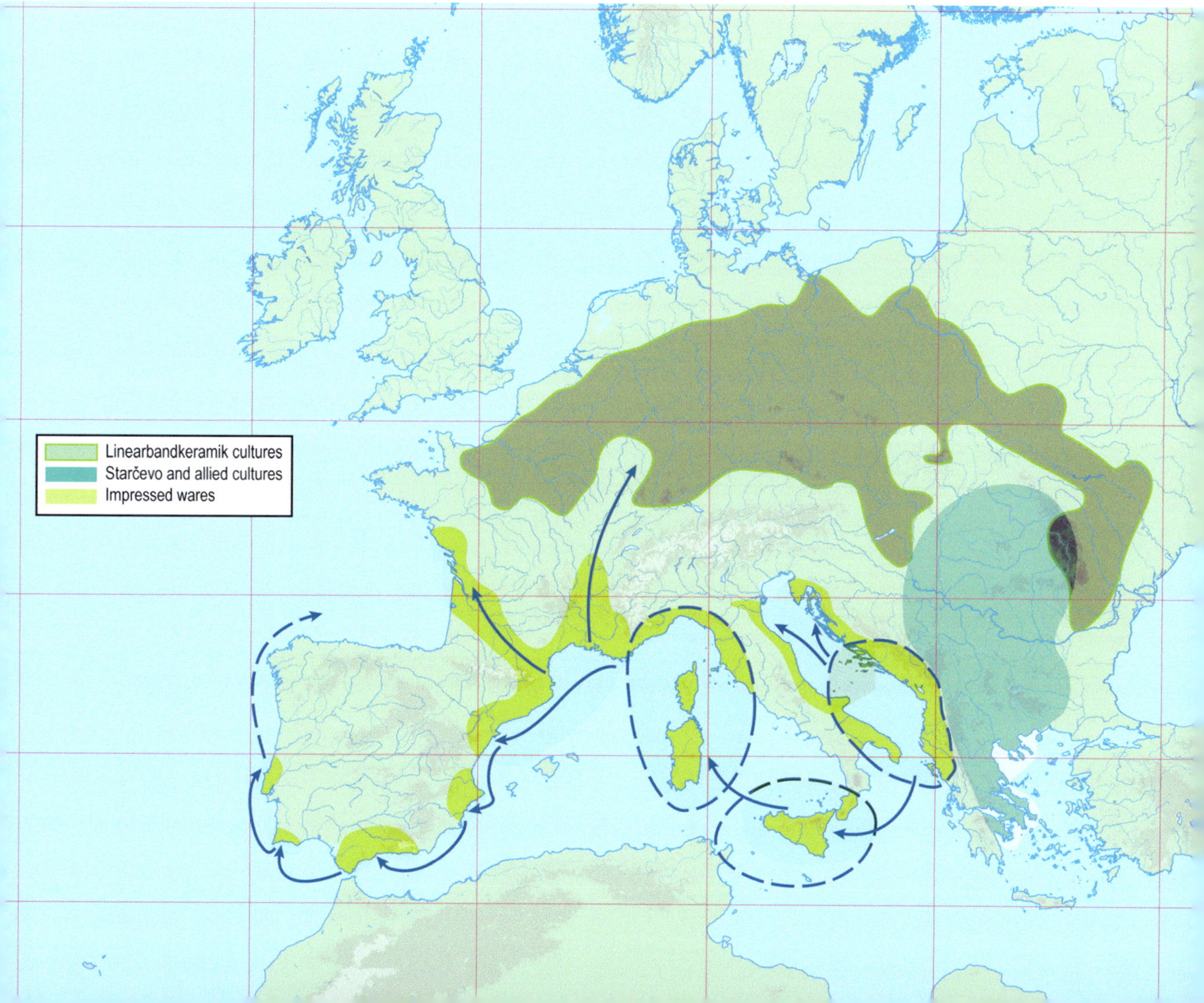

1.2. Enclave colonization: Europe in the period c. 5500–4100 BC, showing the two principal routes by which the Neolithic way of life spread through Europe from the southern Balkans, the overland spread via the Danube and North European Plain and the Mediterranean route by sea ultimately to the Atlantic coast of Iberia. (map M. Crampin)

In the millennium to follow these coastal farming communities began to develop networks of communication which gradually coalesced. One way in which this process can be traced is through the spread of a complex package of funerary rituals which saw the development of *passage graves*—stone-built grave chambers buried beneath mounds of earth and rubble but accessible by means of passages. These graves were used for multiple burials and the large stones of which they were often built were sometimes decorated with distinctive carvings or, occasionally, paintings. Some of the passages were deliberately aligned on the rising or setting of the sun of the midwinter or midsummer solstices. The earliest of the passage graves are found in Portugal and date to about 4800 BC. They were being built as far north as Brittany within a few centuries and, by the end of the 4th millennium, in Ireland and on the Orkney Islands. Although independent invention is always a possibility, the simplest way to explain this remarkable phenomenon is that the complex of conceptual ideas manifest in the architecture, art, ritual, and cosmology of these burials spread gradually northwards along the maritime networks over a period of nearly two millennia. This need not have involved long-distance journeys (though these are of course possible) since ideas and values could easily have been transmitted by short-haul journeys linking neighbouring communities. What is of particular significance here is that the transmission of these complex ideas and values over so large an area implies the development of a common language—a lingua franca.

The 3rd millennium saw a rapid expansion of connectivity throughout western Europe manifest in the Beaker phenomenon. This is a complex series of movements and interactions to which we shall return (pp. 201–3) but the part relevant to the present debate involves the development and spread of a distinctive type of pot, known as the Maritime Bell Beaker, and its associated cultural assemblages from a point of origin in the Tagus region of Portugal about 2800 BC, along the Atlantic sea routes to western France, Britain, and Ireland and inland via the river systems to the Seine and Rhine valleys and beyond (Fig. 1.3). That this was a period of enhanced mobility, of both materials and people, there can be no doubt. Commodities moving over considerable distances included copper, tin, gold, amber, and jet and it could well be argued that the desire for metals was a prime cause of this new mobility. That people were also on the move is shown by stable isotope studies of teeth but it will be the study of ancient DNA of the Beaker population that will eventually demonstrate the complexity of the folk movements underway at the time (below pp. 201–3).

The Beaker networks, by sea and overland by river, built upon those already in existence but now began to reach deep into middle Europe linking the Atlantic zone to its continental hinterland. The contribution of the Atlantic communities was considerable. It was here that copper, tin, and gold were extracted in quantity and somewhere in this metal-rich zone—perhaps in the focal region incorporating southern Ireland, south-western Britain and Brittany—bronze (an alloy of copper and tin) was first produced outside the Near East.

The need to communicate the science behind the discovery, extraction, and alloying of metal, will have demanded a common language. If the Atlantic lingua franca had begun to develop in the 5th/4th millennia then its extension into the heart of Europe could well have been during the period of enhanced mobility represented by the Beaker phenomenon.

The hypothesis, then, was that the Atlantic lingua franca developing in the 5th and 4th millennia was Proto-Celtic and that the vector for its extension into middle Europe was the Beaker phenomenon. It was during the Beaker period that the mature Celtic language developed.

Thereafter connectivity along the Atlantic façade zone continued to develop reaching a peak during the Atlantic Late Bronze Age (*c.* 1300–800 BC). This is demonstrated not only by the distribution of artefacts made at specific locations and spread widely throughout the zone but also by the acceptance of certain patterns of social behaviour across considerable distances. Standard weapon sets comprising circular shields, slashing swords, and spears were in use from Iberia to Ireland. And favoured types, like the Irish basal-looped spear heads, were exchanged throughout the zone. The carp's-tongue type of sword made in or around Huelva in south-western Spain was widely distributed in the south of the zone while, a little later, craftsmen in the vicinity of Nantes in north-western France developed a variant favoured in France and Britain (Figs 1.4; 4.2). Élite feasting also became the norm throughout the zone and is identified by the distribution of cauldrons, flesh-books for manipulating the hunks of cooked meat, and roasting spits. Other reflections of the emerging élite are the hilltop fortifications that now begin to be built. Taken together the archaeological evidence of the Atlantic Late Bronze Age suggests that, although there were regional variations, until about 900 BC the Atlantic communities shared a broadly similar value system and a material culture that differed very little from region to region. The implication is that connectivity was maintained throughout the zone during which time people communicated freely using a common language. It was during these 400 years that the Celtic language continued to develop, its regional dialects converging to form a single language comprehensible throughout. A chieftain from the Shetland Isles would not have felt out of place in the Algarve and might even have been able to join in with the conversation at the feast.

This, in outline, was the hypothesis, Celtic from the West, which was briefly formulated in *Facing the Ocean* (2001). It emerged from a consideration of the archaeological evidence uninfluenced by preconceptions derived from older models. It had the great advantage of disassociating the development of the Celtic language totally from the Hallstatt and La Tène cultures of central and western Europe. This is not to say that the Hallstatt and La Tène communities did not speak Celtic—in all probability they did—but simply that the language originated much earlier and in the Atlantic zone.

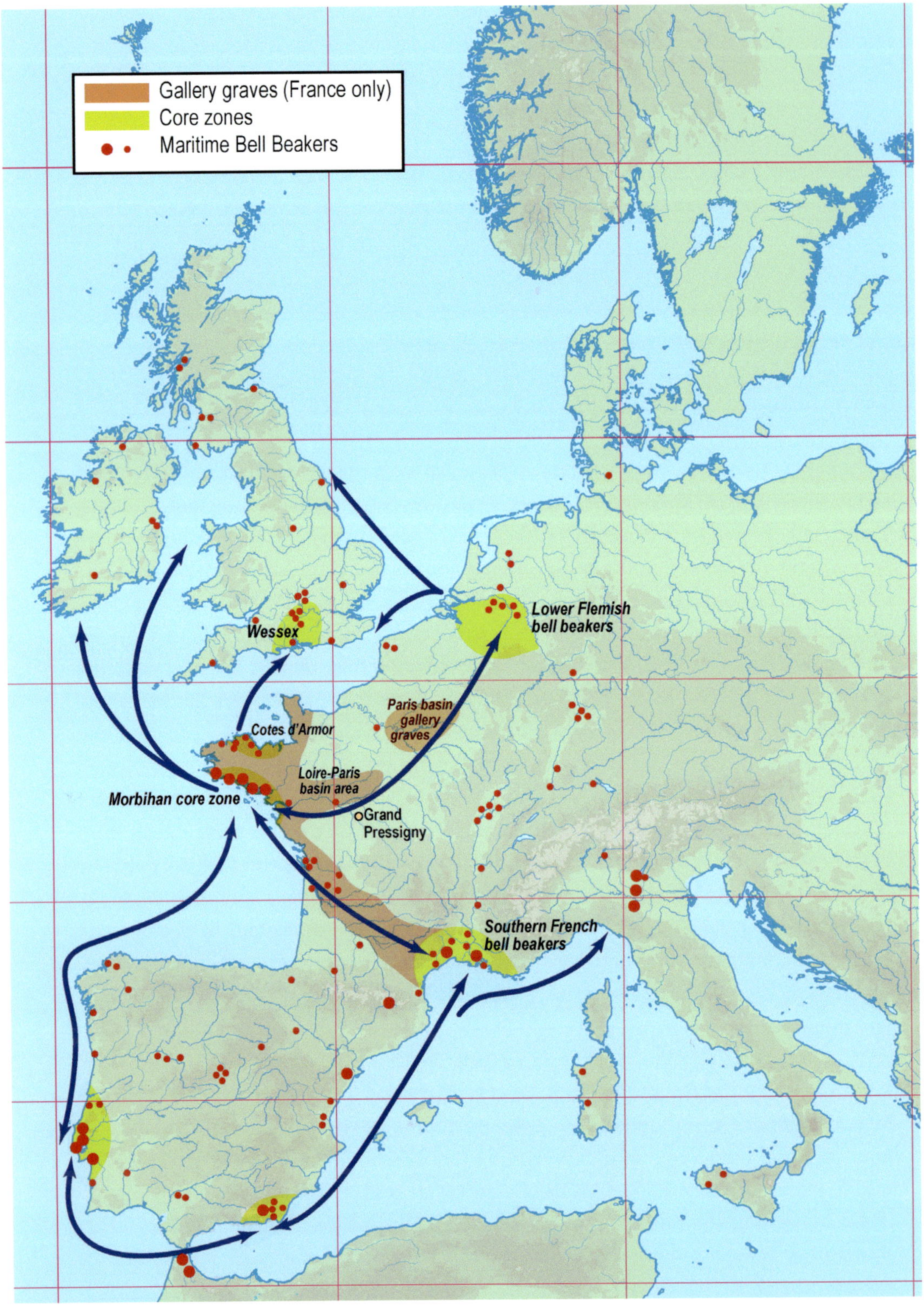

1.3. The distribution of Maritime Bell Beakers in Atlantic Europe during the 3rd millennium BC. The crucial nodes in this network were the Tagus estuary and the Morbihan, while major hinterland routes followed the navigable rivers. (map M. Crampin)

Some new evidence

In the first decade of the new millennium three new sets of evidence were published which had a direct relevance to the debate. The first was Patrick Sims-Williams' meticulous survey, *Ancient Celtic Place-Names in Europe and Asia Minor* (2006) which, for the first time allowed all the surviving ancient Celtic place-names to be mapped. This data, replotted as percentage contours by Stephen Oppenheimer, showed that by far the highest percentages occurred in Iberia, Britain, and north-western France (Fig. 1.5). A simple interpretation of the map might suggest that it was in the region of the highest survival of place-names that the Celtic language was most widely spoken and may have originated—an interpretation consistent within the Celtic from the West hypothesis. However, what the map actually shows is the place-names that survive

1.4. Late Bronze Age swords from the Río de Huelva estuary site, 10th century BC. (Museo de Huelva, photo J. Aaron)

1.5. Relative density of ancient 'Celtic-looking' place-names. (map M. Crampin, based on Sims-Williams 2006 map 5.2.)

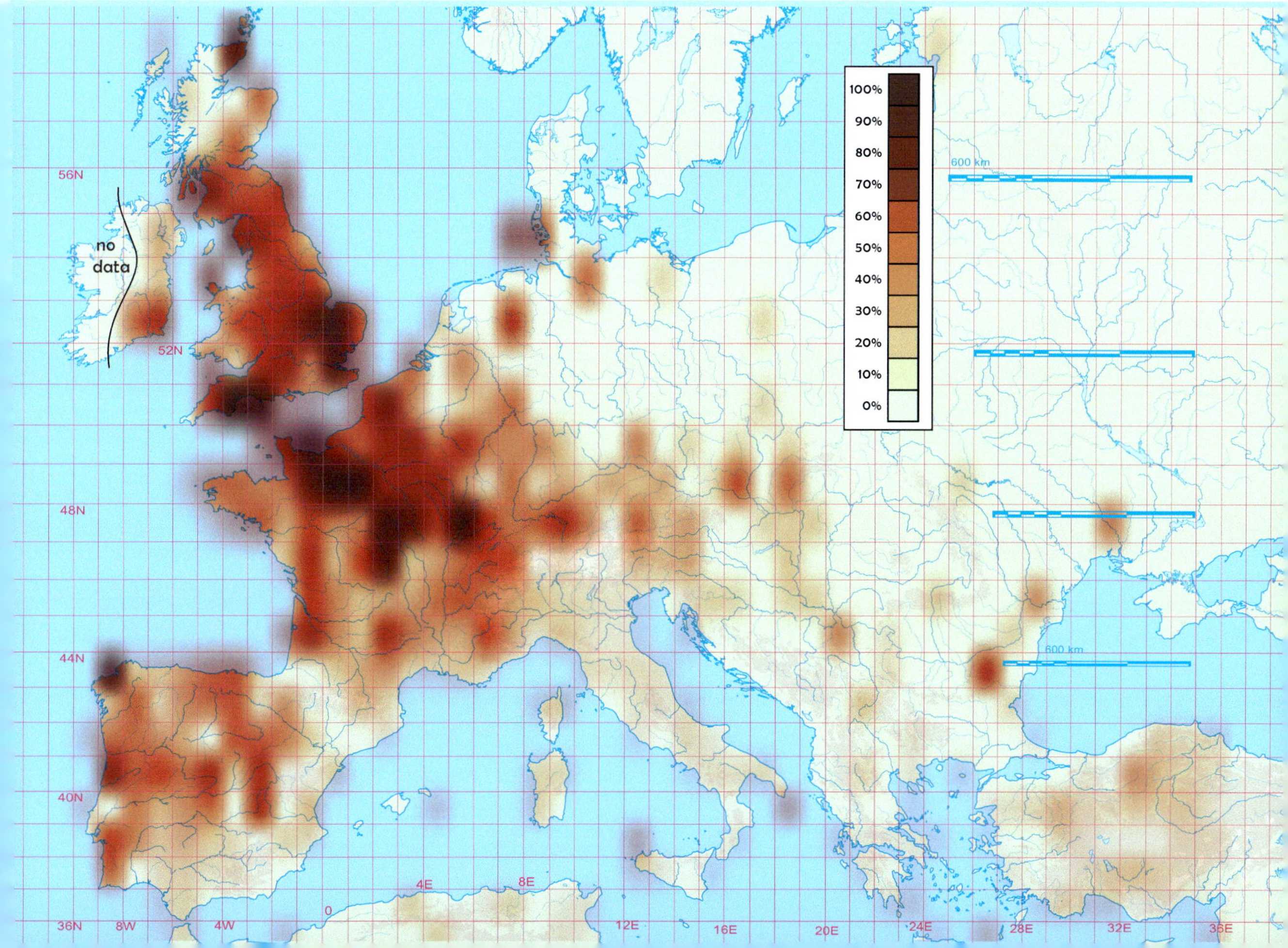

in some recorded form rather than the totality of those that once existed. There are many factors which could have affected survival, not least the effects of Romanization and the later folk movements and settlements of Germanic or Slavic speakers whose languages came to dominate. That said, the paucity of Celtic names surviving in middle Europe compared with the Atlantic zone is striking. While this evidence cannot be claimed as positive support for the Celtic from the West hypothesis it is at least consistent with it.

The second new dataset was derived from John Koch's study of a group of inscriptions found on stelae in the extreme south-west of the Iberian Peninsula. It was first published in his *Tartessian: Celtic in the South-west at the Dawn of History* (2009), in which he demonstrated that while the inscriptions were written in Phoenician script, the language used was Celtic. This was an important observation since the earliest of the inscriptions dates to the 8th century BC making them the earliest attested use of Celtic. Moreover these inscribed stelae are the latest in a tradition of carved stelae found in south-western Iberia dating back to the late 2nd millennium BC. The implication then is that not only was Celtic spoken in the region in the 8th century but that it was in all probability an indigenous language going back much earlier. The Greek historian, Herodotus, writing in the 5th century BC, was aware of the presence of Celtic speakers in the region noting that 'The Celts live beyond the Pillars of Hercules [Strait of Gibraltar] and border on the Cynetes who are the westernmost inhabitants of Europe' (below pp. 68–9; Figs 1.6; 2.4).

The third new approach to the linguistic data was introduced in a paper written by Russell Gray and Quentin Atkinson published in the journal *Nature* in 2003. Their study concerned the development of the family tree of Indo-European languages, of which Celtic is an example. Using standard vocabularies of the various language families they applied quantitative phylogenetic methods through computer modelling to arrive at new assessments of the shape of the family tree and to provide estimated dates for the formation of the sub-families. Their results opened up many new debates and have a direct impact on the question of Celtic origins. According to their analysis the Celtic language group split from the rest of the Indo-European languages of the European peninsular at an early date, estimated at about 4000 BC and that the split between the archaic form of Celtic (which used to be called Q-Celtic) and the more developed form (P-Celtic) took place much later, around 900 BC. The dates, of course, are only approximations but the implications are important—according to this analysis Celtic began to crystalize out as a distinct language family probably in the 4th millennium BC, that is, in the Neolithic period. Such revolutionary results inevitably drew criticism from traditional linguists but when the same team tested the robustness of their analysis using different datasets, subjecting them to different tests, their original conclusions held and are now supported by other workers.

The new data presented by Patrick Sims-Williams, John Koch, and the Gray and Atkinson team is entirely consistent with the Celts from the West hypothesis. What it shows is that Celtic was widely spoken in the Atlantic zone, in south-west Iberia at least as early as the 8th century BC, and that it may have begun to take on its distinguishing characteristics as early as the 4th millennium BC. This would fit well with the hypothesis which suggests that Celtic evolved as a lingua franca along the Atlantic façade of Europe to facilitate communication among the interconnected maritime communities.

Developing the hypothesis

Since Celtic is an Indo-European language it follows that its development must be consequent upon the introduction of Indo-European to the European peninsular. How and when that took place is a matter of lively debate. Until very recently there were two hypotheses in play. The first, the Kurgan hypothesis, argued that the language family was first introduced into eastern Europe from the Pontic steppe in the 3rd millennium BC by horse-riding immigrants and spread out from there. The second, the Anatolian hypothesis, saw Indo-European being introduced with the spread of farming from Asia Minor beginning in the 7th millennium BC. One branch, as we have seen, moved westward from the Balkans through the temperate forests of middle Europe while the other used the Mediterranean route. The two hypotheses are not necessarily mutually exclusive—an important caveat to which we will return to later (pp. 198–200). If Gray and Atkinson are correct in their dating then the Anatolian hypothesis best explains the mechanism by which the earliest manifestation of Indo-European reached Europe. The similarities which many linguists have argued exist between Celtic and Italic (confirmed by the Gray and Atkinson analysis) might suggest that both language families derived from that branch of Indo-European that was introduced along with the Cardial ware enclave colonization that spread through the Mediterranean to the Atlantic coast of Iberia in the period 6500–5500 BC. In the Celtic from the West hypothesis the Celtic language that eventually emerged along the Atlantic seaways as a lingua franca will have absorbed influences from other Indo-European language families encountered along the Atlantic façade and perhaps also from languages spoken by the indigenous hunter–gatherers.

Divergencies in the 1st millennium

Many linguists considering the family tree of the Indo-European languages recognize the early development of a branch which later splits to give rise to the Proto-Italic and Proto-Celtic languages. Proto-Celtic then splits to create two branches, Hispano-Celtic and Proto-Goidelic-Gallo-Brythonic: the first being the basis of the Celtic languages spoken in the Iberian Peninsula; the second giving rise to the languages spoken in France, Britain and Ireland. A later splitting of Proto-Goidelic-Gallo-Brythonic created the Goidelic branch, from which Manx, Scots Gaelic, and Old Irish eventually emerged, and a Gallo-Brythonic branch leading to Welsh,

1.6. Greek knowledge of the Celts in the age of Hecataeus and Herodotus. (map: M. Crampin)

Cornish, Breton, and Gaulish (the language spoken in Gaul at the time of the Roman invasion). The difference between the Goidelic and Gallo-Brythonic languages was, as we have seen, first recognized by Edward Lhuyd at the beginning of the 18th century and later characterized as Q-Celtic and P-Celtic. It is generally accepted that Hispano-Celtic and the Goidelic languages contain archaisms while the Gallo-Brythonic branch is more developed. This interpretation is based entirely on detailed analysis of the surviving linguistic evidence, from place-names, inscriptions, a few longer written texts, and the spoken and recently spoken languages. The question now to be asked is can the archaeological evidence be brought alongside the linguistic to enhance our understanding of what was happening to provide dates for the divergences?

We have argued above that the Atlantic Late Bronze Age was a time of complex social interactions along the entire Atlantic seaboard. In such a situation of intense connectivity one might expect the language of communication to have remained fluid—a true lingua franca. But a significant change came in the 9th century BC when Phoenician traders from the east Mediterranean began to set up trading posts, and later colonies, along the Iberian coastline attracted, principally, by the rich metal resources of the southern and western regions. One of the earliest trading enclaves was established at Huelva (possibly ancient Tartessos) as early as the 10th century. By the 9th century the Phoenicians were present along the Atlantic coast as far north as the Mondego valley and were trading further north up the coast as far as Cape Finisterre. The Atlantic coast of Iberia together with the coast of Morocco had now been brought into the Mediterranean trading sphere disrupting the old Atlantic Late Bronze Age system. In such a situation it is likely that the Celtic languages spoken in Iberia would, thereafter, have developed in isolation no longer benefitting from constant contact within the Atlantic community. This changed situation about 900 BC—*the first dislocation*—could explain the divergence between Hispano-Celtic and the rest of Atlantic Celtic.

A *second dislocation* can be identified in the archaeological record about 600 BC. Before this there is ample evidence that France, the British Isles, and Ireland were part of a complex exchange network manifest in the distribution of similar artefacts across much of the region—artefacts like the distinctive Hallstatt Gündlingen sword, horse gear, and bronze buckets, all redolent of élite exchanges. After 600 BC Ireland and northern Britain seem to fall out of the exchange network and enter into a period of isolation. This could explain the divergence of the Goidelic language family, which evolved in Ireland and Scotland (eventually to become Manx, Scots Gaelic, and Old Irish) from the Gallo-Brythonic of the rest of Britain and Gaul. While the Brythonic branch survived to become Welsh and Cornish and contributed to Breton, the Gaulish language largely died out under the impact of Romanization.

For the 1st millennium BC, then, the linguistic and archaeological evidence can be brought together in a way which relates the two principal divergencies identified by linguists to changes in connectivity recognized in the archaeological record.

The Celtic from the West hypothesis in summary

The Celtic from the West hypothesis rejects the traditional view, originating at the end of the 17th century, which sees the Celts and their language originating in middle Europe and spreading west to the Atlantic region. It argues that the Celtic language began to develop in the Atlantic zone from the Indo-European language spoken by groups of people who moved westwards in the 6th millennium BC bringing farming practices with them. What followed can be divided into four main phases:

- Establishing connectivity: 5000–2700 BC. The formation and consolidation of social networks along the Atlantic zone as the result of maritime interactions. This was the period when a distinctive Celtic language evolved as a lingua franca.
- Escalating Mobility: 2700–1700 BC. Intensification of mobility associated with the exploitation of a wide range of materials, especially metals. This is manifest in the Beaker phenomenon which saw Atlantic 'values' spread deep into middle

Europe where they interacted with new influences introduced from the steppe. This could be the vector by which Atlantic Celtic was introduced into the heart of Europe.

- Consolidation: 1700–900 BC. The development of the Atlantic Bronze Age system. During this time Celtic continued to evolve as a language spoken along the whole of the Atlantic façade, while further inland it may have developed regional variations as the result of contact with different cultures.
- Dislocation and isolation: 900 BC–present day. The fragmentation of the Atlantic system led to the emergence of regional variations of Celtic. The first dislocation occurred around 900 BC, the second around 600 BC. From the 5th century BC until the 1st migrations of Celtic speakers carried the Celtic language and La Tène material culture into southern and eastern Europe and into Asia Minor. Thereafter the advance of the Roman state and, later, the movements of Germanic and Slavic peoples in the Early Middle Ages replaced Celtic throughout much of Europe until, by the 18th century, Celtic languages were spoken only in the far west, in Brittany, Cornwall, Wales, the Isle of Man, Ireland, and Scotland.

The hypothesis, so briefly summarized here, is consistent with the archaeological evidence, from which it grows, and does help to explain some aspects of the linguistic evidence. But it must be admitted that it diverges quite widely from some traditional interpretations of the linguistic evidence. What was not in dispute was that further research in linguistics, archaeology, and genetics was needed to test the hypothesis and, in doing so, to show just how complex the process of Celtic origins really was. It was this realization that led to the creation of the 'Atlantic Europe in the Metal Ages' (AEMA) project in 2013.

Further reading

Origin Myths and Visions of the Celts

A more expanded account of the development of the concept of the Celts is given in **B. Cunliffe**, *The Ancient Celts* (Oxford, 2nd edition 2018), Chapter 1. Critical accounts of the way in which the Celts have been presented are provided by **M. Chapman** 1992 *The Celts: the Construction of a Myth* (New York), **S. James** 1999 *The Atlantic Celts: Ancient Peoples or Modern Invention?* (London), and **J. Collis** 2003 *The Celts: Origins, Myths and Inventions* (Stroud). The intellectual world in which the concept of the Celts developed is brilliantly captured in **S. Piggott** 1989 *Ancient Britons and the Antiquarian Imagination: Ideas from the Renaissance to the Regency* (London). The most thorough account of the Celts seen through the eyes of the Classical world is R. **D. Rankin** 1987 *Celts and the Classical World* (London).

Atlantic Connectivity

Prehistoric connectivity along the Atlantic façade has generated a considerable literature. The main threads were brought together in **B. Cunliffe** 2001 *Facing the Ocean: the Atlantic and its Peoples* (Oxford) and returned to in the author's later books *Britain Begins* (Oxford, 2013) and *On the Ocean: the Mediterranean and the Atlantic from Prehistory to AD 1500* (Oxford, 2017). The theme is also explored in a collection of papers brought together in **S. Oliveira Jorge** (ed.) 1998, *¿Existe uma Idade do Bronze Atlântico?* (Lisbon). Another significant contribution is **M. Ruiz-Gálvez Priego** 1998 *La Europa atlántica en le Edad del Bronce: Un viaje a las raíces de la Europe occidental* (Barcelona). The Celts from the West hypothesis put forward in *Facing the Ocean* was criticized in **G. R. Isaac** 2004 'The nature and origins of the Celtic Languages: Atlantic seaways, Italo-Celtic and other paralinguistic misapprehensions', *Studia Celtica* 38, 49–58.

Some New Evidence

Important recent contributions to the debate include **P. Sims-Williams** 2006 *Ancient Celtic Place-names in Europe and Asia Minor* (Oxford); **J. T. Koch** 2013 *Tartessian. Celtic in the South-west at the Dawn of History* (Aberystwyth; 1st edition 2009); the same author's *Tartessian 2* (Aberystwyth, 2011) and **R. D. Gray & Q. D. Atkinson** 2003 'Language-tree divergence times support the Anatolian theory of Indo-European origins', *Nature* 426, 435–9. Phylogenetic approaches have developed apace and more recent papers are cited below (p. 205).

EDWARD
LHUYD
1660-1709
IEITHYDD
HYNAFIAETHYDD
NATURIAETHWR

CHAPTER TWO

CELTIC FROM THE WEST MEETS LINGUISTICS AND GENETICS

John T. Koch

New research and a persistent idea

PICKING things up where Chapter 1 left off, the Celtic from the West idea, as formulated by Barry Cunliffe on archaeological evidence, was first published in *Facing the Ocean* (2001). Since then, it has proved of interest to researchers in two other fields—historical linguistics and archaeogenetics—and so became the focus of a sustained collaboration of cross-disciplinary research. That much is remarkable in itself. It is common for a hypothesis based in one discipline to fail immediately on contact with a second, where it can be easily invalidated or will lack explanatory power. Had incoming linguistic and genetic evidence supported the model in which a language and a genetic population formed in middle Europe then swept west to cross the Iberian Peninsula, Britain, and Ireland during the Iron Age, that is after 800 BC, there would have been no reason to look for an alternative. To understand how Celtic from the West does explain something outside archaeology, we will need first to think a bit more like linguists and then identify some milestones *en route* from the idea to the programme of research it led to.

2.1. (facing) **'Edward Lhuyd 1660–1709, Linguist, Antiquarian, Naturalist'**, bronze bust by John Meirion Morris in front of the Centre for Advanced Welsh and Celtic Studies in Aberystwyth. (photo M. Crampin)

Though endlessly fascinating, cultural identity—Celtic or any other—is an elusive and mercurial property. On the other hand, language is arguably the most scientific, measurable, and generally tractable index of Celticity. At two key points with linguistic implications, Celtic from the West differs from the prevalent Hallstatt and La Tène account of Celtic origins:

- **when:** The formative period was earlier than the Iron Age. The arrival of the Phoenicians on the Atlantic in the 10th century BC precipitated the break-up of Proto-Celtic as a unified linguistic area at the Bronze–Iron Transition.
- **where:** The formative area was west of middle Europe. The territory faced the Atlantic seaboard.

To consider the pros and cons of these two revisions for historical linguistics, the question of Celtic origins can be formulated as follows: **How, when, and where did Proto-Celtic branch off from Proto-Indo-European?**

Talk of 'branching off' means that we have a tree in mind, the Indo-European family tree, met in Chapter 1. The scientific procedure that gets us this tree is the **historical-comparative method**. Edward Lhuyd, also met in Chapter 1, was an early practitioner of this method, which is based on systematic correspondences in sound systems and grammatical features, establishing relationships between languages. For example, Lhuyd in his *Archæologia Britannica* of 1707 saw that a *p* in Welsh, Cornish, and Breton systematically corresponded to *c* in the same words in Gaelic: so Welsh *pen* 'head': Irish *ceann*.

When languages are systematically related like this, that carries historical implications: they had a common ancestor, a single undifferentiated language in the past, which evolved over time into the attested related, but separate, languages of the family. For the Romance languages (French, Spanish, Italian, Portuguese, &c.) that undifferentiated ancestor is fully attested, Latin. Proto-Celtic, the common ancestor of all the documented Celtic languages, both living and dead, is prehistoric and unattested, but the principle is the same.

Because of the historical comparative method, linguists have known for hundreds of years and with a high degree of certainty many details of prehistoric languages. For example, there is no doubt that Welsh *pen* and Gaelic *ceann* derive from Proto-Celtic **k^{w}ennom*, and that that word meant, as well as 'head', also 'hill' and 'chief'. The * (linguists call this a 'star') on **k^{w}ennom* indicates that this word does not survive in writing like this; it's a reconstruction. The same comparative procedure, repeated hundreds of times and honed since Lhuyd's day, has by now yielded about 2000 confidently reconstructed Proto-Celtic starred words.

Similarly established by systematic correspondences, it was discovered a couple of generations after Lhuyd's death in 1709 that the Celtic languages had more distant relatives, members of a larger family. These included three classical languages: Greek, Latin, and Sanskrit. The undifferentiated ancestor of all of these, that must have existed at a date earlier than any of them, is another extinct language that has long been studied and is by now reconstructed in extensive detail: Proto-Indo-European. The discovery of Indo-European is commonly recognized in words that the London Welshman, William 'Orientalist' Jones, read to the Asiatic Society in Kolkata in 1786:

> The Sanscrit language, whatever be its antiquity, is of a wonderful structure; more perfect than the Greek, more copious than the Latin, and more exquisitely refined than either, yet bearing to both of them a stronger affinity, both in the roots of verbs and the forms of grammar, than could possibly have been produced by accident; so strong indeed, that no philologer could examine them all three, without believing them to have sprung from some common source, which, perhaps, no longer exists; there is a similar reason, though not quite so forcible, for supposing that both the Gothic and the Celtic, though blended with a very different idiom, had the same origin with the Sanscrit; and the old Persian might be added to the same family.

As usually drawn today, the tree representing the Indo-European macro-family has Proto-Indo-European as its trunk and ten primary branches: Greek, Indo-Iranian (whence Sanskrit), Italic (whence Latin), Celtic, Germanic, Balto-Slavic, Armenian, Albanian, and the extinct Anatolian and Tocharian. With this tree in mind, let's go back to the question, **How, when, and where did Proto-Celtic branch off from Proto-Indo-European?** For the 'when' and 'where' of this branching, Celtic from the West gives answers different from the traditional middle European Iron Age view of Celtic origins.

In comparing these hypotheses, it is important to recognize that we are not comparing like with like. The traditional view foregrounds evidence about groups called *Keltoi/Celtae* by Greek and Roman authors and groups with La Tène- and Hallstatt-style accoutrements. These categories overlap as the Celts *par excellence*. That this probably also means speakers of Ancient Celtic languages is seldom doubted, but often merely implicit. When it loses an explicit linguistic anchor, the concept of what is Celtic becomes prone to unsafe assumptions and inconspicuous non sequiturs. For example, it does not follow that, when the La Tène style expanded into the British Isles from about 400 BC, Celtic languages were previously not spoken there, especially in the absence of other evidence as might suggest a significant in-migration at this time. Similarly, we can accept the label 'Celtic archaeology' for La Tène material, but it does not follow that all Bronze Age archaeology is by definition pre-Celtic and not Celtic.

The key point for us is that it is incorrect to assume that Celtic speech did not exist before Hallstatt and La Tène material came into use. In fact, we can be certain that it did. By 1400 BC, there are written records of Mycenaean Greek in the Linear B script and also, in cuneiform script, names and horse-training terminology from the kingdom of Mitanni in what is now northern Syria in an early form of Sanskrit. Already in these Bronze Age texts, we can see that these two Indo-European languages were different enough from each other that they could not have been mutually intelligible. Looking at the Indo-European family tree, what this means is that the undifferentiated Proto-Indo-European had ceased to exist; the branches—including Celtic—had become separate languages before 1400 BC. The sequence of branching off differs between proposed family trees, though there is universal agreement that the extinct Anatolian branch separated first. In any case, there is no possible sequencing in which Greek and Indic could be fully separate languages at a time when Celtic had yet to emerge from Proto-Indo-European. In fact, the Greek and Indic of the Late Bronze Age had already evolved past their primary branches: Mycenaean Greek was already distinct from West Greek and the 'Sanskrit' seen in the Mitanni texts was definitely not Proto-Indo-Iranian, but specifically Indic. Over the years, many linguists—including August Schleicher in 1861 (Fig. 2.1) and the influential 2002 study of Ringe, Warnow, and Taylor (Fig. 2.2)—have concluded that Italic and Celtic separated from Proto-Indo-European as a single branch, or node, which subsequently split into Proto-Italic and Proto-Celtic. Fully separate Old Italic languages are attested in the Early Iron Age. These include Old Latin by the 7th century BC, Oscan and Venetic by the 6th century BC. Therefore, undifferentiated Proto-Italic had ceased to exist before that, and Proto-Italo-Celtic earlier still, and any

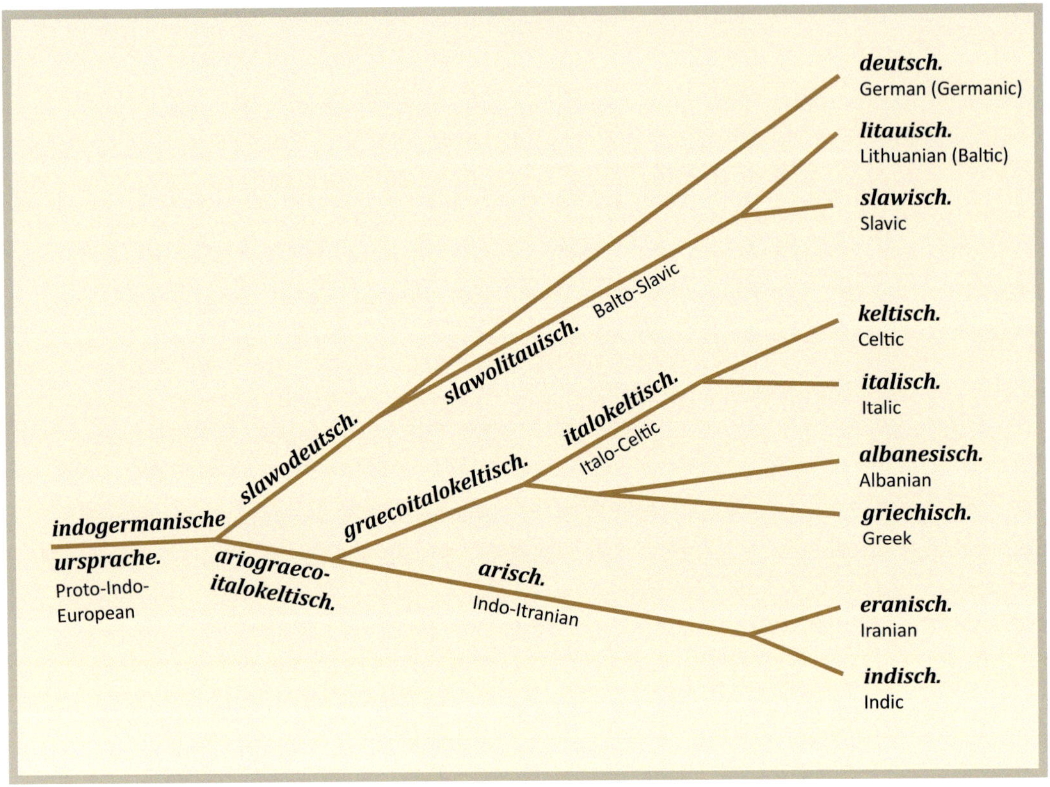

2.2. (above) **The Indo-European family tree drawn by August Schleicher in 1861** anticipated groupings universally accepted (Balto-Slavic and Indo-Iranian) or widely accepted (Italo-Celtic) today. At the time, Anatolian and Tocharian were not yet discovered.

2.3. (right) **J. P. Mallory's (2013) simplified version of the Indo-European family tree of Ringe, Warnow, and Taylor (2002)**, indicating the close assocation between Italic and Celtic.

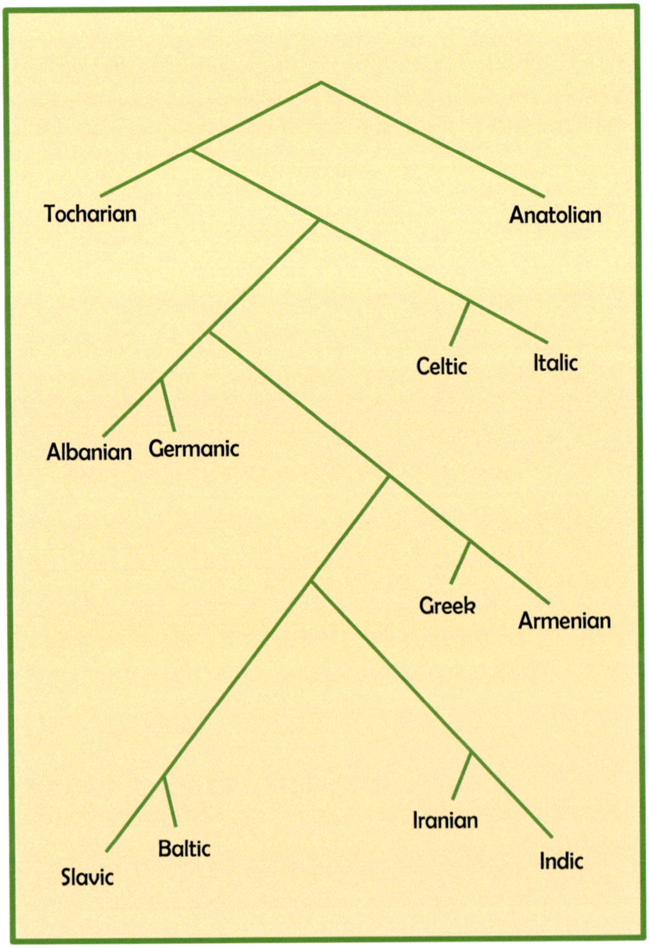

form of Late Proto-Indo-European even earlier. So it is inconceivable that the Celtic branch had not yet split off from Italo-Celtic or Indo-European when the Hallstatt Iron Age began about 800 BC.

The uncertainty over Celtic origins today recalls the upheaval in Greek studies brought by the decipherment of Linear B in the 1950s. Prior to that, the ancient Greeks had been closely identified with the classical era and Homer's archaic period a few centuries before that, in other words, the Iron Age. And that identification, of course, remains correct: Homer did speak Greek. However, by viewing classical and archaic Greece as Greek civilization *par excellence*, an assumption arose and then solidified that the very different Aegean Bronze Age civilization was pre-Greek and, therefore, not Greek. Doctrines arose that saw in the Bronze-to-Iron transformation the impact of waves of post-Mycenaean Greek-speaking invaders from the north. But the language of Bronze Age Mycenae was Greek, as we now know. There had been a different kind of Greek civilization long before the *Hellēnes* of classical times. Languages generally have life cycles longer than cultural horizons, so we should be less surprised by such discoveries.

Debate and research

There is also a hypothesis that might be called 'Celtic from the East', developed by Karl Horst Schmidt and Graham Isaac. The gist of this is that Celtic shares some grammatical features with Indo-Iranian and Balto-Slavic, and these are seen as supporting the conclusion that the Celtic branch had originally formed in the east of the Indo-European world. In 2004, Isaac published an article defending this hypothesis, critiquing both Celtic from the West and widely held views of a special and early proximity of the Celtic and Italic branches. Isaac raises several key points. He recognizes that Italo-Celtic and Celtic from the West—both of which he rejects—are compatible with each other. He queries what known model of language origin could correspond to Cunliffe's idea of Celtic emerging and evolving through contact along the Atlantic façade. Would it be a pidgin or creole or, as Cunliffe calls it, a lingua franca? The former two are surely not apt as these would entail sweeping grammatical simplification, which is not what happened when Proto-Indo-European became Proto-Celtic. As Isaac points out lingua francas commonly arise when the language of a prestigious and powerful group is adopted by their neighbours, rather than the coalescence of disparate languages interacting on more-or-less equal footing.

Thanks to strides in archaeogenetics over the last few years, we know better now than we did in 2004 what the actual situation was along the Atlantic façade at the periods in question. Two mass migrations transformed the region's population. The earlier was that of the first farmers, who had expanded from Anatolia, reaching the Iberian Peninsula by about 5500 BC and the British Isles about 4000 BC. Then, at the transition between the Neolithic and Bronze Age, about 2500–2000 BC, a second great wave brought people whose ancestors had lived on the grasslands north of the Black and Caspian Seas. In both cases, the massive influx of new people, issuing from a particular homeland, probably introduced a particular new language to the Atlantic façade. As Andrew Garrett foresaw, the probable result was a dialect continuum of shallow differentiation, retaining a high degree of mutual intelligibility between dialects. Over time, the geographical range of the Anatolian farmers and then the steppe pastoralists became too over-extended to continue to share linguistic innovations and, hence, speak mutually intelligible dialects indefinitely. But in less vast regions, such as the Atlantic façade, speakers of different dialects continued to talk to each other and so share linguistic innovations within that region, but not beyond it. Where the contact was close enough, the dialects evolved together into a branch and away from the dialects belonging to a different network, which became a different branch. At the same time, speakers of any residual languages, who had initially withstood the migration, might have found it advantageous to learn the emerging branch of their trading partners; in joining this speech community, they contributed to changing their adopted language and its evolution away from the other branches.

Another point relevant to Celtic from the West raised in Isaac's 2004 paper is the survival of non-Indo-European languages on the Atlantic façade. He names two: Aquitanian, which is either the direct ancestor of Modern Basque or its close relative, and the language of a corpus of Early Iron Age inscriptions from southern Portugal and south-western Spain, Tartessian. Aquitanian/Basque is indeed non-Indo-European and situated by the Bay of Biscay. An examination of its circumstances helps to clarify this apparent inconsistency. Looking at the map (Fig. 3.1), we see that characteristically Aquitanian place-names in *-os* have a distribution mutually exclusive with metalwork defining the Atlantic Bronze Age. The two share a sharply separated frontier on either side of the Gironde. As pointed out in Chapter 1, the most intense period of interaction along the Atlantic façade was the Atlantic Late Bronze Age of about 1300–900 BC. Since the Celtic from the West hypothesis sees this stage as the background of the consolidation of Proto-Celtic as the region's lingua franca, it predicts that a gap in the Atlantic Bronze Age should correspond to a gap in the Celtic speech area.

Geographical factors help to explain this double gap. First, the isthmus between the Bay of Biscay and Gulf of Lion is the narrowest overland route between the western Mediterranean and the Atlantic. From here, an alternative journey by sea through the Strait of Gibraltar would be the long way around. The country north of the Pyrenees is relatively flat and easily travelled via navigable rivers, leading from Aquitania to lands with other non-Indo-European languages around the western Mediterranean: Iberian, Etruscan, Palaeo-Sardinian, and Palaeo-Berber. On the Atlantic side, coastal sailing is treacherous along the Bay of Biscay, which is subject to unpredictable high waves. When sailing between western France and northern Spain, mariners often preferred a route out of sight of this coast. In other words, understanding Celtic from the West as a hypothesis that both Celtic and the Atlantic Bronze Age were outcomes of contacts along the Atlantic seaways, that hypothesis also explains why we might find neither of these in Aquitania and the Basque region (see map, Fig. 3.1).

In Isaac's paper, the language of the South-western inscriptions plays a small part, a few words: '... equally non-Indo-European [with reference to reference to Basque] Tartessian in southern Portugal.' However, as a spur to subsequent research, this was disproportionate. At the time, the Centre for Advanced Welsh and Celtic Studies in Aberystwyth was conducting a cross-disciplinary research project, 'Culture and Celtic speech', supported by the UK's Arts and Humanities Research Board (now Arts and Humanities Research Council, AHRC). Barry Cunliffe was a senior advisor in this project, with J. P. Mallory its co-investigator, and myself as principal investigator. Raimund Karl, Antone Minard, and Simon Ó Faoláin worked with me on *An Atlas for Celtic Studies* (2007), the aim of which was to bring together a large collection of mappable early Celtic linguistic evidence (place-names, group names, inscriptions) and 300 categories of archaeological evidence from the Late Bronze Age to Early Middle Ages. There was little at this stage that could be seen as a revolutionary departure from the standard view—middle Europe, Hallstatt, La Tène, &c.

Up to this time, various things had been said about the language of the SW inscriptions. A few sources might be cited to support Isaac's assignment as non-Indo-European. But many of the recent authors had recognized forms in the corpus that looked Indo-European, many of those resembled in particular names in the Ancient Celtic languages of the Iberian Peninsula. In Palaeohispanic studies (that is, research on pre-Roman Spain and Portugal), a debate arose in the 1980s and '90s over the possible classification of this Tartessian language as Celtic. A hybrid theory emerged of fairly numerous Celtic elements embedded in an unknown matrix language, which was possibly non-Indo-European.

The minimal awareness of these inscriptions in Celtic studies outside the Iberian Peninsula was remarkable. Because of their date (Early Iron Age, almost surely beginning before 700 BC), they would be of top importance for the subject if there was any Celtic in them at all. Otherwise, the oldest written Celtic is in the Lepontic inscriptions of northern Italy, which begin about 600 BC. But priority is not the main significance of the SW corpus. If, as Isaac said, their language was 'equally non-Indo-European' as Basque, that could be claimed, as he does, to falsify the Celtic from the West hypothesis. If they had Celtic content or were in fact Celtic throughout, that would be consistent with Celtic from the West and a significant complication for the standard Hallstatt/La Tène account of Celtic origins, presenting evidence contemporary with the early stage of the Hallstatt Iron Age (HaC), but over 1000km south-west of the Hallstatt cultural zone's western edge.

All of this might have seemed somewhat less unsettling had we paid more attention to what Herodotus said about the location of the *Keltoi* (Celts). This was, as pointed out in Chapter 1, 'The Celts live beyond the Pillars of Hercules [Strait of Gibraltar] and border on the Cynetes who are the westernmost inhabitants of Europe', as well as living near the source of the Danube, more neatly in accord with the usual view (below 68–9). *Cynetes* (Greek *Kunētes*) is a linguistically Celtic name and where they lived was Europe's south-western extremity, the Algarve, where the SW inscriptions are most densely concentrated.

2.5. (facing) **The western Iberian Peninsula, showing the locations of the five longer Lusitanian inscriptions**, marked with stars.
(detail of map from *An Atlas for Celtic Studies* (2007) with additions by D. S. Wodtko)

For the project assembling *An Atlas for Celtic Studies* the quandary was whether the Tartessian corpus was 'Celtic enough' to be included or not. These inscriptions were chronological, but not geographic, outliers, occurring in the part of the Iberian Peninsula where Ancient Celtic names were also found, the zone defined by place-names ending in Celtic *-briga* 'hill, hillfort, town' (map, Fig. 3.2). The degree and extent of the Celticity of their language was a subject that had been repeatedly raised tantalizingly, often with extensive supporting details, but ultimately inconclusively. A re-examination of the primary evidence for the Tartessian script and language was called for. The gist of the conclusions that I reached in that research follows.

- There was a sound linguistic basis for most of the forms in the SW corpus previously identified as Indo-European or specifically Celtic.
- Many more examples could be added to these.
- The closest and most numerous comparable forms for this material occur

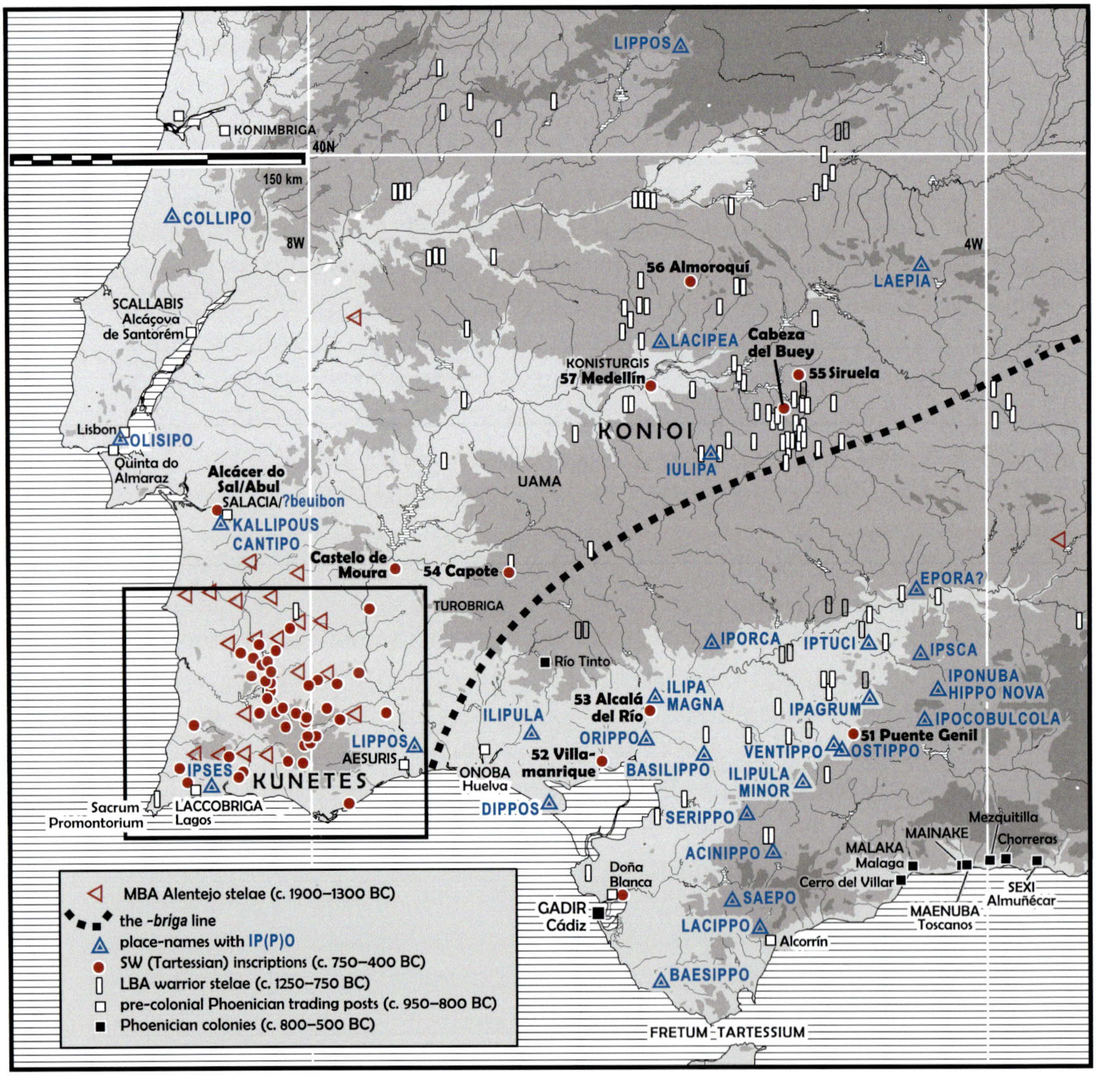

2.4. The south-western Iberian Peninsula in Late Bronze Age to Early Iron Age: stelae, place-names, Phoenician influence.
(map J. T. Koch)

A
B
BOREIOS
surely or probably CELTIC name
possibly CELTIC name
surely or probably NON-CELTIC
modern name
Phoenician settlements, 8th–7th centuries BC [§16]
north-western zone of densely distributed 'castros'
individual castros [§44]
Greek colonies [§47]
chevaux de frise defensive works [§45]
carp's-tongue swords [§123]
antenna-hilted swords [§124]
La Tène swords [§141]
LBA warrior steles [§146]
later Iron Age warrior steles [§146]
omega bridle bits [§159]
gold torcs [§173]
LBA Irish cauldrons [§190]
western Greek amphorae [§200]
LTD handled cups [§209]
Dressel I amphorae [§210]
flesh hooks & articulated spits [§213]
mints which struck Celtiberian coins [§251]
Celtiberian inscriptions [§296]
south-western 'Tartessian' inscriptions [§§16, 296]
Lusitanian inscriptions
limits of Cogotas I LBA culture [§301]
limits of Celtiberian archaeological culture c. 100 BC [§304]
-briga names [§289]
Eburo- names [§292]
-magos names [§293]
nemeton names [§294]
Sego- names [§295]
150 km
GALLAECIA
ASTURIA
VETTONIA
LUSITANI
VETTONES
CELTICI
BAETURIA CELTICA
CALLAECI
LUCENSES
KELTIKOI
Santa Tecla
Santa Luzia
Paradela do Rio
Vilas Boas
L.2.1 Lamas
L.3.1 Frágoas
L.1.1, L.1.2 Arroyo de la Luz
L.4.1 Arronches
Solance de Cabañas
Elvas
Alcácer do Sal
Trileukon Promontorium
Trileukoi Insulae
Artabris Sinus
Flavium Brigantium
Lucus Augusti
Bracara Augusta
Conimbriga
Olisipo
Ebora
Emerita Augusta
Salacia
Nertobriga
Mirobriga
Segovia
Talabriga
Langobriga
Tongobriga
Caetobriga
Lerabriga
Londobris Insula
Eburobrittium
Nemetobriga
Nemetatoi

in the indigenous pre-Roman names of the western Iberian Peninsula.

- This material resembling Palaeohispanic Celtic/Indo-European names was extensive enough—making up over a third of the best preserved and most legible 72 inscriptions—to exclude the possibility that these readings were due to coincidence or the fortuitous result of an incorrect phonetic key applied to the script. The identifiable forms did not only consistently resemble a particular language, but the particular language attested in the same region 500 to 1000 years later.
- In identifiable segments of texts, there was little to suggest a non-Indo-European matrix language, in the form of written strings longer than a couple of signs that could be compared with Iberian, Basque, or the poorly attested language of the ancient place-names in the southern Iberian Peninsula with the element *ip(p)o*.
- On the other hand, features of the SW script indicated that it might first have been adopted with little or no modification from a script devised to write a language with a sound system like that of Iberian or Palaeo-Basque, that is, a language lacking the phoneme */m/*, but having two distinct *s* sounds and two distinct *r* sounds. Since Iberian was spoken along Spain's Mediterranean coast, literate peoples from the eastern Mediterranean—Mycenaean Greeks, Cypriots, and Phoenicians—undoubtedly first met natives in this non-Indo-European zone, before venturing on to the Atlantic West.

Talking to each other

The 'Culture and Celtic speech' research project and *Atlas for Celtic Studies* that came out of it had sought to test the rather basic hypothesis that Hallstatt and La Tène type material actually occurred in the same places as evidence for Ancient Celtic languages and that this relationship would continue to hold up and strengthen as we moved to collections of data that were exhaustive rather than 'cherry-picked'. That is indeed what we found in many regions: for example, Gaul, Britain, and southern Germany. In other areas, the relationship broke down. For example, in Galatia around modern Ankara it was known from history that La Tène Celts had arrived with a Gallo-Brythonic language in the mid 3rd century BC, but once settled they adopted many elements of the Hellenistic material culture of the region. In other places, there was no good historical explanation for the discontinuity. For example, in the south-west of Ireland, there were no La Tène artefacts in the same region with the densest concentration of the ogam inscriptions recording the ancient form of the Irish language.

The biggest disconnect was in the Iberian Peninsula. There are extensive groups called Keltibēres in east-central Spain, Keltikoi in the south-west and north-west, as well as Herodotus's Keltoi also in the south-west. On the other hand, the Iberian Peninsula seems simply not to be a part of the Hallstatt and La Tène zones of the European Iron Age. In the indigenous languages of pre-Roman Spain, there is abundant Celtic linguistic evidence. The situation is more complicated than is often appreciated. 'Celtiberian' and 'Hispano-Celtic' are frequently used interchangeably; one term or the other can be found on maps spread across the entire *briga* zone (the central, western, and northern Peninsula). More accurately, 'Celtiberian' refers only to the Celtic language of the Keltibēres in the eastern Meseta.

Further west there is abundant linguistic evidence that is undoubtedly Celtic as well as peoples called 'Celts'. There is also evidence for a language or languages that are clearly Indo-European, but linguistically difficult to be classified as Celtic. An indigenous language identified in inscriptions in central Portugal and west-central Spain has been labelled 'Lusitanian'. The word for 'pig' in Lusitanian is PORCOM, which preserves Indo-European **p*, a conspicuous detail, because one defining feature of Celtic is that it does not preserve Indo-European **p*. (To avoid a common confusion: the *p* we met above in Welsh *pen* 'head' comes from Proto-Celtic **k*^{w}, as in Proto-Celtic **k*^{w}*ennom* 'head', Irish *ceann*.) So, this Lusitanian 'pig' would seem to cinch it: Lusitanian cannot be Celtic. Nonetheless, the distinguished Palaeohispanic and Indo-European scholar, Jürgen Untermann, and the distinguished Celticist, Ellis Evans—both lost to scholarship in 2013—thought otherwise. They believed that there was only one branch of Indo-European in pre-Roman Iberia, namely Celtic. To accommodate that view we must suppose that Proto-Celtic branched off from Proto-Indo-European with **p* still intact, in which case Lusitanian can be seen as an archaic dialect of Celtic in preserving this sound, while all the other Celtic dialects shared the innovation of weakening **p*. Or perhaps **p* was also weakened in Lusitanian, but not enough to suggest a different Latin letter? Further intricacies bearing on the problem of Lusitanian accumulate as a formidable crux. Moving west from a clear-cut Celtic language in Celtiberia, one finds, all the way to the Atlantic seaboard, a pattern of pre-Roman evidence that looks, on the one hand, like a gradual continuum and, on the other, more like a patchwork, in which some names are unproblematically Celtic and others must either belong to another Indo-European branch or a markedly archaic form of Celtic. Many items are clearly Indo-European, but could be either Celtic or Lusitanian. Viewed within this broader context, the Tartessian question must be understood as one facet of the labyrinth of Palaeohispanic languages.

Both the archaeological and linguistic evidence from the Iberian Peninsula falsify the Hallstatt–La Tène account of Celtic origins. If Iron Age Celts migrated *en masse* across the Pyrenees, reaching the Atlantic, we would not expect so little trace of their central-European culture and we would expect a language that closely resembled Gaulish, but showing less dialect variation than in Gaul. But in fact, the Celtic of Gaul shows less dialect variation than Hispano-Celtic. It is the Celtic from the West hypothesis that predicts what we find: no massive Iron Age culture flow from middle Europe and linguistic archaisms and diversity characteristic of long evolution *in situ* in the Iberian Peninsula. A further point—and one that became significant in setting the course for research—is that, in contrast to lack of coherence between Iberia and the rest of the Celtic world in the Iron Age, at three earlier stages evidence implies contact and sharing of complex ideas across the Atlantic façade: 1) the Megalithic

Age in the 4th millennium BC, 2) the Beaker Copper Age in the 3rd millennium, and 3) the Atlantic Bronze Age about 1300–900 BC.

As this picture became clear following the 'Culture and Celtic speech' project, the direction of the research shifted in four ways. First, the objective became testing the Celtic from the West hypothesis by assembling further collections of data. Secondly, the geographical focus narrowed from the Celtic world as a whole—from Connemara to Galatia—to Atlantic Europe with special attention to the Iberian Peninsula. Thirdly, the chronological focus deepened, going back as far as the Beaker Copper Age. The method continued to emphasize a dialogue between disciplines. As before, linguists and archaeologists worked together. A fourth change was that the cross-disciplinary programme should include genetics alongside linguistics and archaeology.

Action on this new project took place on two levels. A small team of researchers based at the University of Wales Centre for Advanced Welsh and Celtic Studies (CAWCS) in Aberystwyth collected and analysed evidence. Secondly, a series of day-long fora, open to the public, were held in which invited junior and senior researchers from the three disciplines presented new work and ideas relevant to Celtic origins. These meetings gave rise to the *Celtic from the West* series of multi-authored books. In putting together these collaborations, some contributors were invited who were sceptical, or agnostic about Celtic from the West, such as Graham Isaac, Raimund Karl, and J. P. Mallory.

The new project began with the forum 'Celticization from the West' at the National Library of Wales in Aberystwyth in December 2008. The second ('Rethinking the Bronze Age and the Arrival of Indo-European in Atlantic Europe') was held in Oxford in July 2010, the third ('Ancient Britons, Wales, and Europe—New Research in Genetics, Archaeology, and Linguistics') at Amgueddfa Cymru—National Museum Wales in Cardiff in June 2011, the fourth ('New Light on the Ancient West: Recent Work in Archaeology, Genetics, and Linguistics on Later Prehistory and Protohistory') again at the National Library of Wales in November 2012. The fifth ('Atlantic Europe in the Metal Ages—questions of shared language') was a two-day programme at Cardiff University in April 2014, and the sixth ('Beaker People, Archaeogenetics, & Celtic Origins') once again at the National Library of Wales on Hallowe'en 2015.

Working closely with Barry Cunliffe in Oxford and supported by the University of Wales and a British Academy small grant, a team of four began work at CAWCS in spring 2009. Along with researchers, this group included Martin Crampin, as a cartographer and illustrator, producing maps for the *Celtic from the West* series and drawings of the South-western inscribed stones. At this stage, this new project was called 'Ancient Britain and the Atlantic Zone', in which historical linguist Dagmar Wodtko discerned the auspicious Spanish acronym ABrAZo.

From 2009–2011, Wodtko's research included a rigorous resifting of the evidence for Lusitanian and its Western Hispano-Celtic neighbours. Two formidable challenges were thrown into sharp relief with this work: 1) to disentangle decisively Lusitanian from Celtic names and words and 2) to establish secure etymologies for enough Lusitanian words to determine sound laws and, from these, the position of the language relative to Celtic (and Italic) on the Indo-European family tree. Wodtko also developed a socio-linguistic model to explain how regions in which Indo-European and non-Indo-European communities had coexisted in later European prehistory might have gone over step-by-step to Indo-European.

Archaeologist Catriona Gibson focused on detailed comparisons between the British Isles and Iberian Peninsula in the Beaker Period and Bronze Age. This work started from the basic observation that these regions shared the Beaker Complex and, later on, Atlantic Bronze Age metalwork. Moving ahead to see how well this observation held up or required modification was in part a task of collecting more data, exhaustively rather than selectively, then bringing it all up to date in light of the most recent published and unpublished work. As standards of typological and scientific dating advanced, these give a much clearer idea about which comparable artefacts and practices (such as burial rites and deposition of metalwork) were closely contemporary in widely separated places across the Atlantic façade. The question is: under the broad labels of the Beaker Complex and the Atlantic Bronze Age, to what extent were people doing the same thing at the same time? Was the contact intense enough and the shared information complex enough to favour the use of a common language throughout the region?

From 2013 to 2016, a grant from the AHRC made it possible to expand the scope of the project. It was rechristened 'Atlantic Europe in the Metal Ages (AEMA)—questions of shared language', reflecting its evolving focus. At this stage, the Department of Digital Humanities, King's College London (now King's Digital Lab), joined as a major participant. Developer and analyst Neil Jakeman worked closely with the researchers based at Aberystwyth and Oxford to construct a complex, customized relational database. It was launched at KCL in spring 2016 as an open-access website (www.aemap.ac.uk). The goal was to make it possible for researchers inside and outside the project to exploit a large high-quality dataset more fully. The website was made flexibly interactive to enable future researchers to raise and answer new questions not yet contemplated in the AEMA project. As a Geographic Information Systems (GIS) database, the output retained the familiar format of distribution maps. The maps are generated automatically from the data by selecting any of hundreds of parameters pertaining to hundreds of sites and thousands of artefacts, toggling to compare where one or the other selected feature occurs, both occur, or neither occurs. For example, burial sites across the region may be compared according to scientific date ranges, cremation or inhumation, architectural type of the burial, age and sex of the interred, posture and orientation of corpses, typology of grave goods item by item, &c., &c. On its own, this sort of evidence will not tell us directly what language prehistoric people were speaking. But it does produce dense patterns to tell us more precisely to what degree people over a wide area were doing the same thing at the same time. In other words, this helps us to build up a well-founded picture of the extent to which people across the region were in contact and able to communicate complex ideas to one another.

In 2013, the team based at CAWCS was joined by Irish Bronze Age archaeologist, Kerri Cleary, and the philologist and ancient historian Fernando Fernández Palacios. Cleary worked closely with Gibson, collecting, inputting, and analysing data for the Beaker period and Bronze Age in Ireland, Britain, and the Iberian Peninsula. A key area of synthesis in this work was evidence for shared ideologies across the region. For example, were megalithic sites predating the Beaker Period reused in ways indicating a large zone of shared beliefs and attitudes towards the past? Religion is of course not the same thing as language, but the two do often go together.

Fernández had previously worked in Madrid on the pioneering Palaeohispanic database, *Hesperia: Banco de datos de lenguas paleohispánicas*. This background was a great asset to the AEMA project. Apart from Celtiberian, Celtic studies had never accurately identified and encompassed the Celtic of the Iberian Peninsula. The field has never completely outgrown the limitations of Lhuyd's original framework comparing Brythonic, Gaelic, and the Ancient Celtic of Gaul. In accounts of Celtic origins, Hispano-Celtic often receives a cursory treatment with an arrow shown crossing the Pyrenees in the Early Iron Age. But, as explained in Chapter 3, Palaeohispanic scholars have long recognized that the Celtic presence in Spain must go back to the Bronze Age. Down till almost the present there had been daunting barriers to any attempt to account fully for the Celtic of the Iberian Peninsula: most of the evidence was available only as local studies of uneven quality, some of it badly outdated, and much of it unavailable outside Spain and Portugal. Even if you had it all, there were gaps and unreliable readings. What Fernández contributed to the AEMA project, adding to Wodtko's earlier work, overcame these obstacles.

Nevertheless, there remains the problem of trying to use linguistic evidence of the Iron Age and Roman Period to draw conclusions about the whereabouts of languages at earlier stages. With this chronological gap, the case is circumstantial. On the other hand, we started with the recognition from *An Atlas for Celtic Studies* that there was a discontinuity between the geographic distribution of Iron Age Hallstatt and La Tène cultures and that of Ancient Celtic languages in the Iberian Peninsula. The match for the linguistic distribution was better with Beaker and Atlantic Bronze Age maps. Do these patterns hold up and come into sharper focus when we use exhaustive collections of high-quality data, rather than cherry-pick obliging points? Or do they grow blurry and inconclusive? Chapter 4 develops a new synthetic overview from the evidence assembled in the project.

Work on AEMA was also carried out in Oxford by project co-investigator Barry Cunliffe at the Institute of Archaeology and Peter Bray at the Research Laboratory for Archaeology & the History of Art (RLAHA). As Bray explains fully in Chapter 5, his research focused on metal in the European Bronze Age. The chemical 'finger prints' of ancient metal artefacts can tell us which areas were in contact: mining regions—and often specific ancient mines—and the places that metal artefacts finally ended their lives to be recovered by archaeologists. With primary metal—that is the material of an artefact produced directly from ore in a single smelting event—the task of archaeological science is straightforward. But over the course of the Bronze Age, recycled metals became more common, complicating the picture both due to the mixing scrap derived from different mines and also the volatility of some trace elements that dissipated at each successive smelting. By a sustained programme of research at RLAHA, Bray's work throws light onto the ethos as well as the industry at the heart of the Bronze Age.

As to linguistic implications, the prospecting, mining, and transformation of metals into artefacts make up a complex operational chain. Recent research has tended away from the view that this process was re-invented independently at several favourable locations; rather, people with specialist skills struck out for new lands, bringing know-how with them, a scenario consistent with the introduction of a new language along with new skills. In Ireland and Britain, copper mining and the production of copper weapons, tools, and ornaments came with the Beaker People by 2400 BC. By 2100 BC, 'pure' copper was replaced as the fabric of these artefacts with bronze, a standardized alloy of about 90% copper and 10% tin. Although tin is rarer than copper, neither element occurs widely in states that could easily be extracted and processed with early technologies. Therefore, the integrated Bronze Age economy of western Eurasia required stable long-distance exchange to ensure that large quantities of metal reached even metal-poor regions, such as Scandinavia. Finds associated with bronze weapons, ornaments, and feasting equipment show that these were high-status items and received special treatment. Once again, this is not language *per se*, but the study of Bronze Age metal provides compelling evidence for an intensity of long-distance connections and the sharing of specialized values and complex information.

In the traditional view, the hillforts of Britain, Ireland, and the western continent often figure as part of an Iron Age Celtic package, and are seen as marking an incoming warlike group taking control of the land after about 800 BC. Two projects exploring hillforts contributed to AEMA. Fieldwork by project co-investigator Raimund Karl at the University of Bangor returned mostly Iron Age dates for hillforts in north Wales, though there were also indications in the extensive excavations at Meillionydd, Gwynedd, that occupation began there in the Late Bronze Age. In contrast, seven of the eight examples of multi-enclosure Irish hillforts excavated as part of William O'Brien's project dated to the Middle to Late Bronze Age 1400–800 BC. Therefore, they coincided with the period of intensified contacts along the Atlantic façade, a period at which copper from south-west Iberia reached the Atlantic North.

Looking back now over the past ten years of research, the great difference in the pace at which linguistics, archaeology, and genetics have evolved is striking. In historical linguistics, it is common still to refer to century-old publications as standard, such as Pedersen's *Vergleichende Grammatik der keltischen Sprachen* (1909–13). In genetics, especially archaeogenetics, publications of the first decade of the 21st century now must often be set off as part of the history of ideas. At the time of the first forum, genetics was mostly limited to modern DNA and a few genetic markers. Its great potential was evident, but there was, as with historical linguistics, the problem of working out a clock to extract absolute dates. When exactly did events visible in patterns of modern populations occur? When did mutations take place and spread? For example, if the pattern in modern population genetics shows Y chromosome R1b shared widely across western Europe and especially dense along the Atlantic façade, does this reflect the movements of post-glacial hunter–gatherers, the first farmers, Beaker People, or Iron Age migrations? Around 2012, an exciting shift could be felt. There were breakthroughs in genome-wide sequencing of ancient DNA; the push was on from genetics labs for testable ancient human remains. The project received an inquiry about why Beaker People in Germany appeared to have Iberian mitochondrial DNA (this was probably a false lead, it later turned out). The date of the archaeological contexts of the samples were already known, so the genes were no longer obliged to date themselves by an elusive clock. By 2015, aDNA provided specific numbers for the dates and scales for migrations of the first farmers from Anatolia into Europe followed by Copper Age pastoralists from the Pontic–Caspian steppe.

Over the years, the project has benefited from participation of leading archaeogenetic researchers working in pioneering centres and projects: Walter Bodmer, Ellen Røyrvik, and Bruce Winney of the People of the British Isles project; Daniel Bradley and Brian McEvoy of the Smurfit Institute of Genetics, Trinity College Dublin; Stephen Oppenheimer of the School of Anthropology, University of Oxford; Mark Jobling of the University of Leicester; Wolfgang Haak of the Max Planck Institute for the Science of Human History, Jena; and the Archaeogenetics Group of the University of Huddersfield, who contribute an up-to-date overview of this rapidly unfolding field in Chapter 6 below.

The next four chapters present different kinds of new evidence coming out of research brought together in the AEMA project, leading to ideas about what this evidence means. Chapter 7 then considers prospects for the question of Celtic origins and the Celtic from the West hypothesis. The present chapter has to do with the research process, as this has now progressed for a decade. It closes with a couple of observations about that.

First, when we kicked off the first forum in 2008, it was a serious challenge for linguists, archaeologists, and geneticists to talk to each other. Underneath an obvious barrier of jargons, each discipline had basic information and theoretical principles with which professionals in other fields were no more familiar than the general public. That the effort was sustainable depended on good will and the determination of the participants to make it work. This has gradually changed. Such meetings are no longer so rare. Just to cite a few examples: the international symposium on Linguistics, Archaeology & Genetics, held at the Max Planck Institute for the Science of Human History, Jena, in 2015; the workshop on Indo-European migrations and Celtic origins: aDNA and linguistic evidence at the Internationales Wissenschaftsforum, Heidelberg, in 2016; the conference 'When Archaeology Meets Linguistics and Genetics' at Gothenburg, 2018; and the conference 'Genes, Isotopes and Artefacts: How should we interpret the movement of people throughout Bronze Age Europe?' held at the Austrian Academy of Sciences in 2018. The specialists have steadily 'upped their game' and become more adept at these dialogues. We now have a better idea how to formulate hypotheses in one discipline and test them with evidence from another. Not long ago, the wishful thought of devising a unified university course to study the human past bringing the three disciplines together would provoke the despairing question, but who would teach it? More recently, the curriculum and faculty for such a course seem not so remote from the programmes of these conferences.

A second noticeable change is that big data and scientific approaches to the evidence have increasingly come into their own in the three disciplines. Previously, it had sometimes seemed sadly as though questions such as Indo-European and Celtic origins could never really be solved, but nonetheless hypotheses would go in and out of fashion, driven by energetic personalities. These talents might be viewed positively as compelling vision or more cynically as rhetorical virtuosity coupled with academic politics. Either way, subjectivity was ascendant, and it was sometimes hard to believe that what we were doing was hard science and could lead to lasting progress. But this has changed.

Further reading

The AEMA project and its forerunners

The interactive project website (www.aemap.ac.uk) has continued to grow incrementally after AEMA formally ended in 2016. The *Celtic from the West* series gives a good reflection of the scope of the ABrAZo and AEMA projects. The present book can be seen as an extension and supplement to that series. There is a close relationship between the series and the six fora convened between 2008 and 2015. This is not a one-to-one correspondence; the books are not structured as conference proceedings: **B. Cunliffe & J. T. Koch** (eds) 2010 *Celtic from the West: Alternative Perspectives from Archaeology, Genetics, Language, and Literature*, Celtic Studies Publications 15, Oxford, Oxbow Books, paperback edition 2012, reprint 2018; **J. T. Koch & B. Cunliffe** (eds) 2013 *Celtic from the West 2: Rethinking the Bronze Age and the Arrival of Indo-European in Atlantic Europe*, Celtic Studies Publications 16, Oxford, Oxbow Books, paperback edition 2017; **J. T. Koch, B. Cunliffe, C. D. Gibson, & K. Cleary** (eds) *Celtic from the West 3: Atlantic Europe in the Metal Ages—questions of shared language*, Celtic Studies Publications 19, Oxford, Oxbow Books. An e-pamphlet relating directly to the project's basic concepts and preliminary results is **C. D. Gibson & D. S. Wodtko** 2013 *The background of the Celtic languages: theories from archaeology and linguistics*, Aberystwyth, Centre for Advanced Welsh and Celtic Studies. http://www.wales.ac.uk/Resources/Documents/Research/CelticLanguages/GibsonWodtko.pdf

The Indo-European family tree

The implications of variant versions of the family tree for Celtic from the West are discussed in two papers in the second volume of the series: **J. P. Mallory** 2013 'The Indo-Europeanization of Atlantic Europe', *Celtic from the West 2: Rethinking the Bronze Age and the Arrival of Indo-European in Atlantic Europe*, Celtic Studies Publications 16, eds J. T. Koch & B. Cunliffe, 17–40, Oxford, Oxbow Books; **C. Renfrew** 2013 'Early Celtic in the West: The Indo-European Context', *Celtic from the West 2*, 207–217. For senior Indo-Europeanist Eric Hamp's most recent Indo-European family tree, see **E. P. Hamp** (with D. Q. Adams) 2013 *The Expansion of the Indo-European Languages: An Indo-Europeanist's Evolving View*, Sino-Platonic Papers 239, Philadelphia,

Department of East Asian Languages and Civilizations, University of Pennsylvania (http://sino-platonic.org/complete/spp239_indo_european_languages.pdf). For the model of the Indo-European branches forming from a Proto-Indo-European dialect continuum, see: **A. Garrett** 1999 'A new model of Indo-European subgrouping and dispersal', *Proceedings of the Twenty-Fifth Annual Meeting of the Berkeley Linguistics Society, February 12–15, 1999*, eds S. S. Chang, L. Liaw, J. Ruppenhofer, 146–56, Berkeley, Berkeley Linguistics Society; **A. Garrett** 2006 'Convergence in the Formation of Indo-European Subgroups: Phylogeny and Chronology', *Phylogenetic Methods and the Prehistory of Languages*, eds P. Forster & C. Renfrew, McDonald Institute Monographs, 139–51, Cambridge, McDonald Institute for Archaeological Research.

Sir William Jones

For the fascinating career and diverse contributions of this remarkable, but tragically short-lived 18th-century linguist and polymath, see: **M. J. Franklin** 2011 *'Orientalist Jones': Sir William Jones, Poet, Lawyer, and Linguist, 1746–1794*, Oxford, Oxford University Press.

The Celtic from the East idea

G. R. Isaac 2004 'The Nature and Origins of the Celtic Languages: Atlantic Seaways, Italo-Celtic and Other Paralinguistic Misapprehensions', *Studia Celtica* 38.49–58; **G. R. Isaac** 2010 'The Origins of the Celtic Languages: Language Spread from East to West', *Celtic from the West. Alternative Perspectives from Archaeology, Genetics, Language, and Literature*, Celtic Studies Publications 15, eds B. Cunliffe & J. T. Koch, 153–67, Oxford, Oxbow Books; **W. Meid** 2008 'Celtic Origins, the Western and the Eastern Celts', Sir John Rhŷs Memorial Lecture, *Proceedings of the British Academy* 154, 177–99; **K. H. Schmidt** 1996 *Celtic: A Western Indo-European Language?* Innsbruck, Innsbrucker Beiträge zur Sprachwissenschaft; 2012 'Armenian and Celtic: Towards a New Classification of Early Indo-European Dialects', *Ireland and Armenia: Studies in Language, History and Narrative*, Journal of Indo-European Studies Monograph Series 61, eds M. Fomin, A. Jivanyan, & S. Mac Mathúna, 51–63, Washington D.C., Institute of the Study of Man.

The Problem of Lusitanian

The evidence for this language and the problems it presents for historical linguistics and Celtic studies are discussed in depth by **D. S. Wodtko** 2009 'Language Contact in Lusitania', *International Journal of Diachronic Linguistics and Linguistic Reconstruction* 6, 1–48; 2010 'The Problem of Lusitanian', *Celtic from the West. Alternative Perspectives from Archaeology, Genetics, Language, and Literature*, Celtic Studies Publications 15, eds B. Cunliffe & J. T. Koch, 335–67, Oxford, Oxbow Books. See also **B. M.ª Prósper** 2008 'Lusitanian: A Non-Celtic Indo-European Language of Western Hispania', *Celtic and Other Languages in Ancient Europe*, ed. J. L. García Alonso, 53–64, Salamanca, Ediciones Universidad de Salamanca; **J. M.ª Vallejo Ruiz** 2013 'Hacia una definición del Lusitano', *Acta Palaeohispanica XI / Palaeohispanica* 13, 273–91. Important ideas about Lusitanian can be found in earlier work, including **K. H. Schmidt** 1985 'Contribution to the Identification of Lusitanian', *Actas del III Coloquio sobre Lenguas y Culturas Paleohispánicas*, ed. J. de Hoz, 319–41, Salamanca, Universidad de Salamanca; **J. Untermann** 1985–86 'Lusitanisch, Keltiberisch, Keltisch', *Studia Palaeohispanica. Actas del IV Coloquio sobre lenguas y culturas paleohispánicas*, Vitoria/Gasteiz 1985 = *Veleia* 2–3, 57–76; **J. Untermann (with D. S. Wodtko)** 1997 *Monumenta Linguarum Hispanicarum IV. Die tartessischen, keltiberischen und lusitanischen Inschriften*, Wiesbaden, Ludwig Reichert.

Hillforts

For the recent fieldwork in Wales and Ireland mentioned in the chapter, see **R. Karl** 2016 'Emerging Settlement Monumentality in North Wales during the Late Bronze Age and Iron Age: the case of Meillionydd', *Celtic from the*

West 3: Atlantic Europe in the Metal Ages—questions of shared language, Celtic Studies Publications 19, eds J. T. Koch, B. Cunliffe, C. D. Gibson, & K. Cleary, 265–93, Oxford, Oxbow Books; **W. O'Brien** 2016 'Language Shift and Political Context in Bronze Age Ireland: some implications of hillfort chronology', *Celtic from the West 3*, 219–46; **W. O'Brien & J. O'Driscoll** 2017 *Hillforts, Warfare and Society in Bronze Age Ireland*, Oxford, Archaeopress.

For **Archaeogenetics**, see the Further Reading for Chapters 3 and 6.

The Celticity of the South-western or 'Tartessian' inscriptions is covered in the Further Reading for Chapter 3.

CHAPTER THREE

A CASE OF IDENTITY THEFT? ARCHAEOGENETICS, BEAKER PEOPLE, AND CELTIC ORIGINS

John T. Koch

in collaboration with
Fernando Fernández Palacios

Celtic from the West and Indo-European from the East: a dilemma?

ON first contact with the Celtic from the West idea some people hit a conceptual road block: Celtic is Indo-European, and Indo-European didn't come from the West, so Celtic didn't either. This is reminiscent of the British prime minister who said he had 'no reverse gear' or the thought that, at the end of the rail line, trains could only pile up or fall into the sea at Aberystwyth. There is no doubt that historical La Tène Celts migrated west-to-east to the Hungarian Plain, Transylvania, the Balkans, and Anatolia in the 4th and 3rd centuries BC. Why should their prehistoric forbears have been capable only of travel towards the setting sun? The key point is a linguistic one. The Celtic from the West idea is that Proto-Indo-European reached Europe's Atlantic façade and then evolved into Celtic there. There was no Celtic language before that. To imagine Celts existing before Celtic is nonsense—at least it is for linguists.

The traditional (may we call it entrenched?) Hallstatt and La Tène story of Celtic origins has always been a force fit when it came to accounting for Celtic in the Iberian Peninsula, as we will see in this chapter. By contrast, the Celtic from the West idea looks like an improvement as soon as we place side-by-side distribution maps of Ancient Celtic place-names in Spain and Portugal and metalwork characteristic of the Atlantic Late Bronze Age (ALBA; see below Figs 3.1, 3.2). However, many language and literature specialists find it hard to swallow the newer idea that there could have been a linguistic continuum on Europe's Atlantic façade for as long as the cultural continuum that can be traced from the first farmers (about 5500 BC in Iberia and about 4000 BC in Ireland and Britain) down to the earliest written Celtic of the pre-Roman Iron Age.

In part this reluctance is a spontaneous reaction to the yawning time gap between the beginning of agriculture and the written evidence. A more specific issue is once again Celtic as an Indo-European language. Many linguists have preferred the hypothesis that Proto-Indo-European dispersed from the Pontic–Caspian steppe, in what is today Ukraine and south Russia, about 5000 years ago, rather than the alternative taking it back to the first farmers who crossed from Anatolia to Europe beginning 3000 years before that. Anticipated by Gordon Childe, the steppe-homeland theory was formulated by the archaeologist Marija Gimbutas in the mid 20th century and has since been revised and extended by her student J. P. Mallory and David Anthony.

There are two main reasons that linguists tend to prefer the steppe hypothesis. The first will infuriate colleagues in other disciplines: 3000 BC simply feels about right as the necessary, but not excessive, starting date for the linguistic changes that separate the reconstructed later Proto-Indo-European and the attested languages. Most linguists, who know well the history of one or more language, have developed an intuitive sense of how fast languages can change—what is unbelievably slow and unbelievably fast linguistic evolution. For example, Greek and Sanskrit are two Indo-European languages. Both are attested by about 1400 BC. On the basis of what we know in fully documented detail about Latin evolving into the various Romance languages and similar cases, a thousand to 1500 years separating Mycenaean Greek and Vedic Sanskrit feels about right, 5000 years feels too long.

The second, more graspable reason is what is called 'linguistic palaeontology'. This means that when related languages in a family (such as the Celtic, Romance, or Indo-European families of languages) share inherited words this implies that speakers of the ancestral language (Proto-Celtic, Latin, Proto-Indo-European) had both that word and the thing it referred to. So, there are reconstructable Proto-Indo-European words for metals, wool, domestic horses, wheeled vehicles, and parts of wheeled vehicles. The Yamnaya culture on the steppe 5000 years ago had these things. The first farmers from Anatolia did not. However, linguistic palaeontology is not infallible. Loanwords between related languages can look deceptively like inherited vocabulary. For example, Swedish *vetenskap* and German *Wissenschaft* look like they derive from a Proto-Germanic word for 'science': they don't, but instead reflect ideas shared between related languages at a later cultural stage. Maybe then, the shared words for 'horse' *$*H_1ek^wos$*, 'wheel' *$*k^wék^wlos$* and *$*roteH_2$-*, 'yoke' **yugóm*, 'hub' **nobh-*, 'axle' *$*H_2eks$-*, &c., spread between the early separate Indo-European languages, but assumed forms linguistically indistinguishable from cognates, while the languages themselves had long before taken root across western Eurasia in the age of the first farmers.

To dismiss all the inherited-looking vocabulary that points towards a Late Neolithic/Copper Age stage of development for Proto-Indo-European would leave historical linguists staring into the abyss. It would deny the core of our method, which is to compare related languages to reconstruct the vocabulary, grammar, and sound system of their common ancestor. Since the time of the Welsh polymath

Edward Lhuyd, over 300 years ago, this historical-comparative method has achieved a great deal in deciphering old languages and revealing the meaning of old texts. So it does not seem to be pseudo-scientific bunk.

A modification of the Celtic from the West idea, to make it compatible with the steppe hypothesis, might be called in the present political climate 'cakeism', having it both ways. Cultural continuity of Atlantic Europe cannot be denied: traceable from the Megalithic Age, to the Beaker Period, to the Bronze Age, to the proto-historical Celtic Iron Age. But rejecting the steppe hypothesis would amount to allowing this archaeological evidence to override the linguistic on a linguistic question.

A way around the impasse would be a hybrid model in which speakers of Proto-Indo-European of steppe background boarded a cultural train already in motion in the Atlantic West, rather than derailing it. Accepting the chronological limits imposed by the steppe hypothesis—i.e. the expansion of later Proto-Indo-European from about 3000 BC—there are two episodes at which intense cultural innovation and quickening connectivity might reflect the stimulus of a new people with a new language entering Atlantic Europe: the Beaker Period (*c.* 2800–1900 BC) and ALBA (*c.* 1300–900 BC).

Contrasting with this suspiciously tricky hybrid model of Indo-Europeanization in the Copper or Bronze Age, there remains the alternative simplicity of the Anatolian hypothesis, in which the observable continuities from the Megalithic Age to the Beaker cultures to the Bronze Age to the Iron involve no inconspicuous new people and language slipping aboard, only a steady continuation of what came with the first farmers—and linguistic palaeontology be damned. As of about 2012—the eve of the archaeogenetic revolution—the matter hung on the horns of this dilemma.

A multidisciplinary approach to the human past for experts and everyone

The arrival of genome-wide sequencing of ancient DNA in recent years is a game changer. It puts us on the threshold of bringing archaeogenetics, archaeology, and historical linguistics together to understand human prehistory at a depth and level of detail previously possible only for times with written records. The fourth essential skill set is information technology, which will enable us to pick up subtle patterns and signals with sophisticated processing of big data from the three fields. It is early days, it must be emphasized. Expect the unexpected.

This sounds like fiendishly specialist stuff. Even the experts find themselves out of their comfort zones, struggling to grasp work in the other fields. But this pioneering cross-disciplinary work should also be appreciated as a way back towards a rounded view of the human past as experienced in everyone's life. The basic principle is this: **The most common way for cultural identity and a first language to be transmitted is from parent to child.** On the level of individual lives, that is the norm, a life fortunately lived in less interesting times. On the other hand, over the sweep of generations, stretching on to centuries and millennia—that is, on the scale considered in this book—this threefold inheritance often disentwines, an occurrence less usual, but not rare: a life lived in more interesting times.

In the New World, the less normal pattern falls within the historical record and living memory. For example, one of the present authors is an American. His four grandparents spoke English as their first language. Owing to the long persistence of German as a community language in the American Mid West, the two grandfathers also had that as their 'co-first language'. Two generations further back, none of the 16 great-great grandparents spoke English as their first language, though seven of them were born in the United States. This is not an uncommon linguistic family history in the New World, where the primary driver of language shift has been migration.

On the other hand, the same basic history is also common—approximately the norm—in Ireland and Wales today: first-language English speaker, patchy bilingualism in the generation of grandparents, no first-language English speakers in the generation of great-great grandparents. But in Ireland and Wales, Irish and Welsh identity have continued and migration has not been the driving force, at least not in the same way. Rather, English-speaking economic and political power and cultural influence have gradually emanated beyond England through complex networks of English-speaking social domains, which spread and were consolidated across Celtic-speaking territory.

We see, then, that the strands of an individual's genetic heritage and linguistic heritage can be pulled apart in more than one way. People might migrate to a new country where a different language is spoken and they are not numerous enough or powerful enough to preserve their old language, or simply choose not to. Or a process sometimes called 'élite dominance' can occur, in which most people stay in their country and a relatively small number of incomers, speaking a different language, hold the upper hand. In this case, change of language is usually accompanied by other significant changes in way of life.

It is important to realize with these divergent models that the genes and languages are independent systems with independent histories. When a Welsh family switches from Welsh to English, their genetic descent has not changed, but they have changed from a language that is descended from the Old Welsh spoken 1000 years ago and the Proto-Celtic of 3000+ years ago to one descended from Old English and Proto-Germanic. The history of their English is as long as anyone's, even if short in their family.

If their English today does not sound like the English of England, it is because the Welsh language of their ancestors, who learned English as a second language, and the Welsh-speaking ancestors of others in their community have affected the local English. Hiberno-English and Wenglish are not the results of Irish and Welsh genes on the English language, but the legacy of a generation or generations of bilinguals who learned Irish or Welsh in infancy and then later English as a second language after the phonetics and syntax of their first language had already been 'hard-wired' into their mature brains.

In a community undergoing language shift, the impact of the previous language can affect subsequent generations who never spoke it, but learned the new first language (English, in the present example) from bilinguals who never sounded like native speakers of their second language. The effect can continue for generations. This is why first-language Welsh speakers often expect monoglot English speakers from south Wales to speak Welsh. Their English sounds like that of Welsh speakers. The usual linguistic cues can be so strong that the Welsh speaker sometimes refuses to believe that the South Walian doesn't understand Welsh at all.

The incomplete education available in the disadvantaged communities of the Celtic west was one contributing factor in the formation of Wenglish and Hiberno-English. But it was not the only factor. To speak English in the south Wales coalfield was an economic necessity. However, to speak English like an Englishman was not only unnecessary, but could be seen as a betrayal of the community, leading to ridicule and ostracism. On the other hand, Wenglish could function economically like standard English while also simultaneously functioning as a badge of group identity like Welsh.

In moving back from the era of living memory to Celtic origins in deep prehistory, we will want to bear in mind these concepts of genes, identity, and language passed from parent to child most of the time in those less interesting times, but disconnected some of the time in more interesting times. We will also want to remember that there is more than one sort of circumstance—with and without migration—in which people might learn a second language and pass it on as a first language to their children. We should remember also that a language or group identity usually changes somehow when adopted by a people to replace the language or identity of their grandparents.

The dog that didn't bark

Genome-wide recovery of aDNA now reveals mass migration coming out of what is today Ukraine and south Russia during the 3rd millennium BC. These movements reached the Siberian Altai, central Asia, northern and central Europe, and parts further west, including Britain and Ireland. Some researchers see this evidence as confirming the theory that the homeland of the Indo-European languages was in this Pontic–Caspian steppe region, from which it expanded by migration during the Copper Age, so about this time.

The genetically confirmed migrations thus far correspond fairly neatly to four of the ten primary Indo-European branches: east-to-west—Tocharian, Indo-Iranian, Balto-Slavic, and Germanic. Further west, near the Rhine, upper Danube, Alps, and British Isles, DNA from the steppe is now found heavily present in the genomes of individuals associated with the archaeological phenomenon known as the 'Beaker' Complex. These are lands that emerge—when written records begin in the pre-Roman Iron Age—speaking Celtic languages.

How is our present focus on Celtic to be teased out against this unfolding population history of western Europe? Although based on only four individuals—three of whom were close relatives found in a single cist burial alongside McCuaig's Bar on Rathlin Island—Cassidy et al. 2016 succeeded in throwing potentially decisive light on the problem. Their fourth sample was a Neolithic woman buried alongside the Giant's Ring, a megalithic henge at Ballynahatty near Belfast. She is dated 3343–3020 cal BC. Like most of Europe's early farmers her ancestry goes back to Anatolia. But her genes also included a smaller proportion derived from the hunter–gatherers of western Europe, indicating that her forbears had reached Ireland along the east-to-west Mediterranean route and not up the Danube through central Europe. She did not have steppe ancestry.

On the other hand, the three men from Rathlin did, at double-digit percentages. The Neolithic portion of their background differed from that of the Ballynahatty woman, more probably having spread west through central Europe. In other words, if these four individuals are representative of the ancient Irish gene pools of their eras—a significant 'if', considering the small number of samples—there was a sharp break between the Middle Neolithic and Early Bronze Age. The intermediate turning point that comes to mind is the arrival of the Beaker Complex and metallurgy. Both occur, new to Ireland, about 2400 BC at the Ross Island copper mine near Killarney, County Kerry. From Ross Island itself, there is one Beaker-period human bone, a tibia found to be unusable for aDNA testing by the GeoGenetics lab in Copenhagen.

The Rathlin men (dated to 2026–1534 cal BC) had R1b Y chromosomes characteristic of ancient Western Indo-European areas and western Europe today, including Ireland quite heavily. Their genomes also anticipated the modern Irish population in other ways. They had genes determining blue eye colour, tall stature, and the genetic defect haemochromatosis (iron build up), lactase persistence (allowing cow's milk to be digested as an adult), all common in Ireland today. It is this genetic continuity with the present-day Irish population that led Cassidy et al. to the conclusion that the Rathlin men are likely to have spoken the Indo-European that evolved into Celtic, then Gaelic, *in situ*.

At this point, readers familiar with the traditional account of Celtic origins will sense a disturbing silence. This 'dog that didn't bark' is the apparent lack of similarly transformative events datable to the Late Bronze Age (*c.* 1300–800 BC) or the Iron Age (*c.* 800 BC–AD 100). These are the periods at which the traditional model envisions speakers of Ancient Celtic migrating westward from Urnfield/Hallstatt/La Tène west-central Europe. Is it still necessary to think of Celtic expanding west to reach the Atlantic at this time? Does such a third migration—after that of the first farmers from Anatolia and that of Indo-Europeans from the steppe—explain anything anymore? A genetic type that has been plausibly linked with Indo-European elsewhere has now been found coming into Ireland heavily at the Neolithic–Bronze Age Transition (about 2400–2100 BC) with not much population change afterwards until historical times. As the case for an Iron Age invasion evaporates, is there any good reason to think that the Indo-European that came to Ireland 4000 years ago was other than the Indo-European that became Gaelic? *Sláinte!*

The puzzle of Celtic in the Iberian Peninsula

Is it settled then? A done deal? Is the steppe hypothesis of Indo-European origins no longer a hypothesis, but now a proven fact? Can the alternative model of language dispersal with the first farmers out of Anatolia in the 7th millennium BC be safely consigned to the dustbin of the history of ideas? As Jim Mallory observes in 'Clouds over Indo-European Homelands', data points have an annoying habit of becoming harder to connect with straight lines as they become more numerous. The block-buster archaeogenetic papers of 2015 were based, between them, on a total of a few hundred aDNA samples, thinly spread over vast territories and time spans. In the coming years, we can expect thousands and then tens of thousands of sampled individuals from later prehistoric Europe, and at densities of genomic coverage greater than what's been possible so far. Already alongside the initial signal that the steppe hypothesis is broadly on the right track we see loose ends and frayed edges, and we will want to pay special attention to these as more data of higher quality becomes available.

To start with, the steppe component is not effectively a genetic prime integer, an isolated population going back to the Ice Age. Rather, it's a mixture of two older populations, at a ratio of about 50:50—one gene pool identified as 'eastern hunter–gatherers' and a second from the south Caucasus and Iranian Plateau. This second population was not related to those first farmers who spread from Anatolia into Europe, but had also adopted a way of life with domesticated animals at a similarly early date. Proto-Indo-European did not abruptly arise—like Athena from the head of Zeus—on the eve of the great steppe migrations in 3000 BC. It somehow evolved out of the speech of the eastern hunter–gatherers and/or that of the Caucasian/ Iranian group. In other words, be alert to the possibility that something like an archaic Proto-Indo-European existed south of the Caucasus before the steppe component and its language spread widely across Europe and deep into Asia.

A second loose end more directly relevant to our Celtic focus is the puzzling picture presented by the aDNA data thus far obtained for Beaker People. At the time of the great Copper Age population movements now seen as an Indo-European expansion, the western half of Europe came to be dominated by a recurrent package of culturally significant items known as the Beaker Complex. Its defining components included the namesake drinking vessel and the bow and arrow as the weapon of choice. Although their burial rites usually differ from those of their Neolithic predecessors—reflecting a new focus on the individual—Beaker People often continued to use and modify the earlier megalithic monuments distributed across western Europe.

The first form of the Beaker phenomenon appears about 2800 BC on the lower Tagus, near modern Lisbon. From there, it spread to other parts of the Iberian

Peninsula. It then expanded rapidly along the Atlantic and Mediterranean coasts of France towards Brittany and reaching the western Alps by 2550 BC.

The curious fact, which preoccupies the present chapter, arises in the Beaker aDNA study of Olalde et al. 2018. The steppe component—unmissably large in most Beaker individuals sequenced from southern France, northern Italy, central Europe, and Britain—is wholly absent from the genomes of 24 of the study's 32 Iberian Beaker people, including all 5 from Portugal. The disparity is not subtle. Olalde et al. calculate the population replacement in Britain between the Neolithic and Beaker Period at 90%!

As explained above, the four samples from Ireland in Cassidy et al. 2016 similarly imply a major break—from a genome without the steppe component to genomes with it—between the Neolithic Ballynahatty woman and the three Early Bronze Age Rathlin Island men. But for Portugal and Spain, the Beaker People of the Olalde et al. study had mostly Iberian Neolithic and pre-Beaker Copper Age ancestors, so ultimately descended from the first farmers who spread from Anatolia along the northern Mediterranean plus some western hunter–gatherer admixture.

For many researchers, the circumstantial case of Haak et al. and Allentoft et al. for identifying steppe ancestry with Indo-European speech is compelling. In the light of Olalde et al., that would now also imply that the Beaker phenomenon began amongst non-Indo-Europeans in the Iberian Peninsula and was then embraced as an ideology and cultural identity by Indo-Europeans north of the Pyrenees. In other words, it looks like Indo-Europeans in west-central Europe switched teams.

The Beaker way held practical advantages for steppe people as they moved west. With a lifestyle that took shape near the Atlantic surf pounding central Portugal, Proto-Beaker communities knew how to negotiate this coast and its great estuaries. Before they acquired these skills, groups speaking Indo-European could not dominate lands by the western ocean.

It is more economical if we don't suppose that two distant and unrelated groups—Indo-Europeans from the steppe and non-Indo-European Proto-Beaker People on the lower Tagus—were simultaneously seized by explosive expansionism. The Olalde et al. study finds no genetic evidence for Beaker groups migrating out of Iberia into central Europe. But the implications of maternal aDNA discussed in Chapter 6 below are not clearcut in excluding this possibility. A study by Jocelyn Desideri of the tooth shape of 1200 individuals from Beaker burials indicates that those from southern France and western Switzerland had Iberian ancestry. But the case for Iberian origin based on dental morphology does not extend to Desideri's Beaker remains from the Czech Republic.

The genetic heterogeneity of the Beaker People is not altogether surprising. Cultural differences have long been recognized between the users of the earliest 'Maritime Bell Beakers' on the Tagus and the later form of the culture once it had come into contact with Corded Ware groups along the Rhine and upper Danube and in the western Alps. Steppe antecedents were obvious in the burial rite of the latter, but not the former.

A
B
C
D
E
F
G
1
2
3
4
5
6
56N
52N
48N
44N
40N
36N
8W
4W
0
4E
8E
12E
16E
300 km
300 km
Atlantic
LBA II
c. 1000 BC
metalwork depositions Bronze Final atlantique 2 (Milcent 2012, pl. 81)
Atlantic BA cauldrons and buckets (Gerloff 2010, plates 144–51)
Iberian inscriptions, NE script (Hoz 2011, mapa 1.1; Gorrochategui 2013, fig.1)
Meridional (SE) Iberian inscriptions (Hoz 2011, mapa 1.1)
place-names in *-os*, *-osse*, *-oz*, *-otz*, *-ués* (apud Gorrochategui 2013, fig. 4)
Atlantic Bronze Age II (cf. Harrison 2004, fig. 2.1)
Mediterranean sailing routes (Aubet 2001, fig.40)
RHAETIAN
PALAEO-BASQUE
ETRUSCAN
IBERIAN
PALAEO-SARDINIAN
PALAEO-BERBER
Hío
Baiões
pre-colonial Tartessos (tršš)
Huelva

Linguists could see an obvious correspondence in the big picture: the distribution map of the Beaker phenomenon as a whole (below Fig. 4.4) and that of the Ancient Celtic languages (above Fig. 1.5) are unmistakably similar. Basically this is western and central Europe for both. But the overlap is not perfect. If we leave aside the historically documented Celtic migrations to eastern Europe and Asia Minor, all lands with attested Ancient Celtic languages previously had Beaker material, but not all Beaker territories became Celtic speaking. For example, there were Beakers in Sardinia, which had an indigenous non-Indo-European language before the Romans arrived and is now often cited in genetic studies as having a modern gene pool resembling that of Europe's first farmers, specifically for its dearth of the steppe component.

More to the present point, there were Beakers in the western Pyrenees and on the Mediterranean side of Spain, that is, in parts of the Iberian Peninsula where non-Indo-European languages were spoken in pre-Roman times. One could argue that the 'out of Iberia' Proto-Beaker People spoke Indo-European nevertheless, but they somehow failed to impose their language on these areas. However, now that we know that the Proto-Beaker People

3.1. (facing) **Atlantic Bronze Age metalwork shows a geographical distribution that is directly inverse to that of evidence for non-Indo-European languages near the western Mediterranean**: Palaeo-Basque/Aquitanian, Iberian, Etruscan, Rhaetian, Palaeo-Sardinian, and Palaeo-Berber.
(map J. T. Koch)

3.2. Zones of pre-Roman Indo-European and non-Indo-European names in the Iberian Peninsula: the dashed green line shows the divide, pointing out group names with 'Celt-' and the diagnostically Celtic *-briga* 'hill, hillfort, major town', contrasting with non-IE *il(t)i*. Some IE (mostly Celtic) outliers are shown in green.
(map J. T. Koch)

were not genetically related to (other) Indo-European-speaking populations, such an argument would be despite the evidence.

For the Bronze Age, the Portuguese aDNA recovered by Martiniano et al. 2017 contains the steppe component, at lower levels, but notably with characteristic R1b paternal lineage. This Y chromosome occurs in the genomes of three men found in deep 'hypogaeum' burials near the lower Guadiana, a great navigable Atlantic-facing river. These three date to the Middle Bronze Age, about 1740–1430 BC, roughly half a millennium after the end of the Beaker Period. Over 100 further samples tested by Valdiosera et al., at the Max Planck Institute in Jena and at Harvard's Reich Lab, confirm this result. This combined evidence shows a new genetic type with steppe ancestry became common during the Iberian Early Bronze Age, between 2500 and 2000 BC. It rarely appears at levels higher than 15%, but sustained that level through the Middle and Late Bronze Age. Of the Iberian Bronze Age males with steppe ancestry, 90% carried the R1b Y chromosome. In contrast, Szécsényi-Nagy et al. found no detectable change between the Iberian Neolithic and Bronze Age mitochondrial DNA (i.e. the DNA passed down the female line).

What these statistics tell us is that the newcomers were mostly men and that these men and their sons and their sons' sons, &c., were uncommonly successful in producing offspring with indigenous Iberian women. This same pattern was found in samples from various parts of the Iberian Peninsula, including individuals from the Early Bronze Age El Argar culture in south-east Spain, which was a non-Indo-European-speaking region in early historical times. This evidence implies the following situation in Spain and Portugal towards the beginning of the Bronze Age: there were two widespread groups—a larger, but more static group whose ancestry went back to south-west Europe's first farmers, and an expansionist minority with paternal ancestry from the steppe. Social inequality favoured males of Yamnaya ancestry in most regions, possibly all regions. David Reich sees Iberia as 'the most striking example' of such a disparity.

Thinking as linguists, these details imply unrelated languages coexisting in the same territory. At the generation of the R1b founders, these were men born beyond the Pyrenees and probably speaking Late Proto-Indo-European as their first language. They arrived in Iberia and produced children with women born there and probably speaking a non-Indo-European first language. What did subsequent generations speak: Indo-European, non-Indo-European, or both? Basic sociolinguistics tells us that the language or languages that survived in various areas amongst various communities were determined by which of the available choices was more useful, more prestigious, and perceived to be most advantageous for children's future. For Indo-European to persist, indigenous women learned it as adults, or their children grew up bilingual, or both. The scenario was then repeated over successive generations, as R1b spread with Indo-European.

Turning to the map of pre-Roman place-names of the Iberian Peninsula (Fig. 3.2), we do not find Indo-European and non-Indo-European names evenly mixed across the Peninsula. Rather, a well-defined line (the '*briga* line') separates Indo-

European evidence, most of it specifically Celtic, in the west, north, and centre, from non-Indo-European along the Pyrenees, and Bay of Biscay, and Mediterranean. The last had been the territory of the El Argar culture in the Early Bronze Age. There are a few Indo-European outliers, most of them specifically Celtic, south and east of the *briga* line. Some examples are shown on the map (in green): *Ebura*, *Segida*, *Saguntum*, &c. These probably stand witness to an earlier, more fluid situation. In the rest of this chapter, we will look at linguistic and archaeological evidence and try to explain how we get from a migration of R1b men permeating, though thinly, the entire Iberian Peninsula in the Early Bronze Age to the stark divide of the *briga* map.

Most people will not think of Spain and Portugal as particularly Celtic countries. Only in Galicia have ideas about Celtic identity made their way into popular thinking. A lot of this deficit is due to the way Celtic studies evolved from its beginnings. Edward Lhuyd's discovery of the language family in his *Archæologia Britannica* of 1707 rested on a comparison of the Gaelic and Brythonic languages of his own day (Irish, Scottish Gaelic; Welsh, Breton, and Cornish) with what could be gleaned of the language of ancient Gaul as preserved as isolated names and words in ancient Greek and Latin texts. Evidence from the Iberian Peninsula was not part of Celtic as it was discovered or rediscovered 300 years ago. And so it remained for centuries. Even in the 20th century, handbooks that are still essential today—such as Lewis and Pedersen's *Concise Comparative Celtic Grammar* and Thurneysen's *Grammar of Old Irish*—do not include Hispano-Celtic. In these standard works, 'Continental Celtic' is synonymous with Gaulish, treated as a single language. Little more than this was possible before the discovery of the first long Celtiberian inscription from Botorrita in 1970.

Nonetheless, historians have long been aware of Celts in ancient Hispania. The classical authors identify peoples called *Keltoi* and *Keltikoi* in the south-west of the Peninsula, *Keltikoi* also in the north-west, and *Keltibēres* 'Celtiberians' inland in the eastern Meseta. Before the Second World War the Catalonian, subsequently Mexican, archaeologist Pere Bosch-Gimpera realized that these Hispanic Celts were a problem for the standard account of Celtic origins. The prevailing thinking put both Celtic ethnogenesis and expansion into the 1st millennium BC, the Iron Age. It still does. This doctrine involves a particularly close identification between the Celts and the La Tène art style of the later Iron Age. La Tène expanded beginning in the 5th century BC from its core zones along the Marne and middle Rhine and Bohemia. The style reached Britain and the northern half of Ireland afterwards. As Bosch-Gimpera saw, La Tène was stylistically irrelevant for the Hispano-Celts, and too late. They had to go back to the Bronze Age. He envisioned two Celtic waves into Spain emanating from the central European Urnfield cultures during the Late Bronze Age—about 1200, then about 900 BC.

The standard view has not moved on much over the intervening 80 years. Outside of Spain and Portugal, one finds a familiar map of the Celtic homeland with a shaded area coterminous with the zone of the earliest Hallstatt Iron Age, Ha C1a, in the 8th century BC, near the source of the Danube in present-day south Germany. For archaeologists working in Spain and Portugal, the Urnfield LBA is usually viewed as Celtic.

But even before the aDNA evidence, there was a problem with Bosch-Gimpera's theory. This has become more and more evident as the Palaeohispanic languages have become better known. The Urnfields of the Iberian Peninsula are in Catalunya, which is not where any Ancient Celtic language is attested, but rather the zone of hundreds of inscriptions in the non-Indo-European language known as Iberian. Similarly, taking an overview of the ancient place-name evidence, the Catalonian Urnfields lie inside the zone where the term referring to an important town was the non-Indo-European *ili* or *ilti*, rather than the widespread Celtic *briga*. The latter name element originally meant 'high place' or 'hill', and then 'hillfort' and simply '(important) town' (*'berg'* > *'burg'*).

The wealth of Hispano-Celtic linguistic material is today more evident. Some of this is in the form of continuous statements in Celtic, providing regular vocabulary—verbs, nouns, adjectives, &c. But more proper names survive. As well as the diagnostically Celtic *briga*-names, there are many other Hispano-Celtic place-names, also group names and gods' names. The largest category is personal names. Amongst these, we find a few dozen popular names and name elements that recur in inscriptions across the *briga* zone. There are variations over time and space, but overall it appears that a single stable system for naming individuals in Celtic was widely established. This stability implies a degree of time depth. *Medu-genos*, a compound of Celtic elements meaning 'mead' and 'born', is one example of this Hispano-Celtic stock of personal names. The same name occurs in Brythonic and Irish. Therefore, we can conclude that this compound already existed and was used as a name in Proto-Celtic, the prehistoric language that was the ancestor of all the attested Celtic languages.

We may know that *Medugenos* is 'mead'+'born', but what does 'mead-born' mean? Mead and words related to Proto-Celtic **medu-* carry a lot of ideological significance in Celtic traditions. For example, the most formidable female character in Early Irish literature is Queen Medb of Connacht, the worthy rival of the super-hero Cú Chulainn of Ulster. Her name is derived from Proto-Celtic **Meduā*, which is simply the feminine form of the adjective meaning 'intoxicating (with mead)'. One recurrent idea in Irish and other traditional Celtic literatures is that a woman, or goddess, offers a hero an intoxicating drink signifying his destiny to be king. At the Romano-British cult site in Thetford, Norfolk, MEDVGENVS was equated with FAVNVS in the Bacchic cult of drunken ecstasy. In the Welsh elegies of *Y Gododdin*, the heroes feasted for a year at court at Din Eidyn (Edinburgh) on mead before fighting the battle where most of them were killed at Catraeth, now Catterick, Yorkshire. Their fate is poignantly described as *talu medd* 'paying for mead'. The poems call these men *meddfaeth* 'mead-nurtured'. Their relationship to the court poet is described by the words *câr* 'friend, kinsman' and *cyfaill*, which today means simply 'friend', but originally meant 'one nurtured together, foster-brother'. Was such formal mead-sharing once seen as a warrior's rebirth into the new family of comrades?

Text Box 3.1. Proto-Celtic ***Medu-genā**, ***Medu-genos**, personal name, 'mead-born' < Proto-Indo-European **medhu-* 'mead' + **ĝenH$_1$-* 'give birth, beget, be born'

¶CELTIBERIAN REGION. **mezukenos abokum turo** (Botorrita, Zaragoza); **mezukenos loukanikum** (Botorrita, Zaragoza); **mezukenos elazunos tirtukue ailokiskum** (Botorrita, Zaragoza); **mezukenos akikum memun** (Botorrita, Zaragoza); **mezukenos turanikum** (Botorrita, Zaragoza); **mezukenos tirtobolokum** (Botorrita, Zaragoza); **mezukenos kalisokum** (Botorrita, Zaragoza); **turos retukenos statulu mezukenos koitina tueizu uiroku munika koitu koitina** (Botorrita, Zaragoza); **arkanta mezukenoskue abokum** (Botorrita, Zaragoza); **MEDVGENVS RVFINVS D[** (Riba de Saelices, Guadalajara); **ANO MEDVGINVS AVITIAMI** (San Esteban de Gormaz, Soria).

¶CENTRAL REGION. **MEDVGENVS CARPA+[---]** (Puebla de Montalbán,Toledo).

¶WESTERN PENINSULA. **MEDVGENA TERE[NTI] FIL.** (Salamanca); **MEDVGENA CAI F.** (Salamanca); **MEDVGENAE ARRONIS F.** (Fariza, Zamora); **MEDVGENVS CESARONIS EX GENTE CILVRNIGORVM** (Gijón, Asturias); **MEDVG[ENVS]** (Jerez de los Caballeros, Badajoz); **C. LABERIVS MEDVGENVS** (Messejana, Aljustrel, Beja); **C. LICINIVS VERVS MEDVGENI F. C[L]VN.** (São Salvador dc Aramenha, Marvão, Portalegre); **CAVNVS MEDVENI** (Plasenzuela, Cáceres); **MEDVCEA MEDVENI F.** (Ponte da Barca, Ponte da Barca, Viana do Castelo); **MEIDVENA** (San Cristovo de Cea, Ourense); **MEARVS MEIDVENI F.** (Malpartida de Plasencia, Cáceres); **MEIDVENVS ANDAMI** (Abertura, Cáceres); **TALTICO MEIDVENI F. LANCIENSI OPPITANO** (Nuñomoral, Cáceres); **RVFVS MEIDVENI** (Valdeobispo, Cáceres); **TANGINVS MEIDVENI F.** (Idanha-a-Velha, Idanha-a-Nova, Castelo Branco); **CVMELIVS MEIDVENI F.** (Región de Lamego, Viseu), **[M]EDIGENVS** (Mérida, Badajoz); probably **SEX. IVLIVS LVPVS GAL. MEDVC[-- F.]** (Jerez de los Caballeros, Badajoz).

¶OTHER CELTIC LANGUAGES. Latinized Ancient Brythonic DEI FAV MEDVGENI, DEI FAVNI MEDIGENI, DEI FAVN[ ] MEDIGENI (inscribed silver spoons, Thetford treasure, Norfolk); Ogam Irish (genitive) MEDDOGENI, Old Irish *Midgen*; Old Welsh place-name containing personal name *Porth Medgen*.

The Pan-Celtic god Lugus

That much of the Iberian Peninsula was not only richly Celtic linguistically, but also belonged to the Celtic world culturally, is shown by evidence for the god Lugus. One challenge facing anyone trying to study the religion and mythology of the Celts is that pagan gods are not found with the same name across the various Celtic-speaking lands. There are only a few divine names that occur in more than one Celtic language (especially if we disallow the fairly recent separation of Irish and Scottish Gaelic). Therefore, forms of the name *Lugus* have a unique importance, as this god is well known in Hispano-Celtic, Gaulish, Gaelic, and Brythonic. The plural is also found in Gaul, in an inscription consisting merely of the nominative LVGOVES.

In the medieval Irish Mythological Cycle, Lug is the leading figure in the *Túath Dé* 'Tribe of the Gods', later called *Tuatha Dé Danann*. In the elaborate 9th-century tale 'The Battle of Moytirra' he prevails as the omnicompetent master of all crafts as conveyed also by his epithet *Samildánach* 'equally endowed with many arts'. The protagonist of the Fourth Branch of the Mabinogi is named *Lleu*, the Welsh cognate of *Lugus*. In that tale, he receives this name in an episode in which he makes gold-ornamented shoes. An intriguing parallel was recognized by Sir John Rhŷs in 1892 in a dedication commissioned by a guild of shoemakers (*collegium sutorum*) in the Celtiberian town Uxama Argaela, invoking the divine *Lugoues*: **LVGOVIBVS SACRVM L. L(...) VRCICO COLLEGIO SVTORVM D. D.**

Antonio Tovar drew attention to the long Celtiberian inscription in Roman script from Peñalba de Villastar: **ENIOROSEI | VTA · TIGINO · TIATVMEI | TRECAIAS · TOLVGVEI | ARAIANOM · COMEIMV || ENIOROSEI · EQVOISQVE | OGRIS OIOCAS · | TO·GIOAS · SISTAT · LVGVEI · TIASO | TOGIAS.** Although there is no agreement about what the whole text means, most see both instances of **LVGVEI** as meaning 'to, for [the god] Lugus'.

Tovar also drew attention to Roman Period inscriptions from the northern and western Peninsula, which again call upon the Lugoues as a group, as at Uxama. These include **LVGVBO ARQVIENOBO C(AIVS) IVLIVS HISPANVS V.S.L.M.** and **LVCOVBV[S] ARQVIENI[S] SILONIVS SILO EX VOTO**. In these two examples, the Lugoues' byname *Arquien-* begins with the element that is common as the Palaeohispanic personal name *Arquius* 'archer, bowman', to which we'll return below. *Arquien-* is probably a compound with a second element **-genos* 'born from' with loss of *-g-*, a common occurrence in Western Hispano-Celtic, as in **MEDVGENVS** (Aljustrel, Beja) versus **CAVNVS MEDVENI** (Plasenzuela, Cáceres). The god's multiforms in the Iberian Peninsula include feminine examples: **LVGGONI ARGANTICAENI** and **LVGVNIS / DEABVS / AVR(ELIVS) CEL(ER) / V.S.L.M.**

In the personal names with *Lugu-*, the 5th-century Irish LUGUDECCAS and similar forms have been explained by Jürgen Uhlich as meaning 'serving the god Lug'. Gaulish **LVGVDECA(E)** and Hispano-Celtic **LVGVADICI** seem to be this same name. Therefore, 'serving the god Lug' had been a name in the prehistoric common ancestor of the Celtic languages, Proto-Celtic.

During the 1980s, significant progress was achieved on the decipherment of the South-western or 'Tartessian' inscriptions of the Early Iron Age, notably with the pioneering work of J. A. Correa. Beginning as early as the 7th century BC and probably the 8th, the SW corpus is the earliest indigenous writing in the Iberian Peninsula, in fact anywhere in Europe west of the Etruscans in central Italy. Correa identified several probably Celtic elements in the SW corpus, most of which have won wider acceptance in subsequent scholarship. Especially relevant to the present study is what was, until September 2008, the longest known SW inscription, J.1.1 'Fonte Velha 6', reading: **lok^{o}ob^{o}o niirab^{o}o t^{o}o aŕaia/i k^{a}alt^{e}e lok^{o}o/n ane naŕk^{e}e k^{a}ak^{i}iśiin/ k^{o}olob^{o}/o ii t^{e}e·ro-b^{a}ar/e (b^{e})e t^{e}a/siioonii**.

Text Box 3.2. Proto-Celtic ***Lugus**, god's name

¶CELTIBERIAN REGION. **LVGOVIBVS SACRVM L. L(...) VRCICO COLLEGIO SVTORVM D. D.** (Osma, Soria); **ENIOROSEI | VTA · TIGINO · TIATVMEI | TRECAIAS · TOLVGVEI | ARAIANOM · COMEIMV || ENIOROSEI · EQVOISQVE | OGRIS OIOCAS · | TO·GIOAS · SISTAT · LVGVEI · TIASO | TOGIAS** (Peñalba de Villastar, Teruel); **DIBVS M[.] LVCVBO** (Peña Amaya, north of Burgos); **LVGVNIS / DEABVS / AVR(ELIVS) CEL(ER) / V.S.L.M.** (altar in Atapuerca, Burgos).

¶CENTRAL REGION. Personal names **[A]TTA LVGVA CARAECICVM EBVRENI VXOR** (Narros del Puerto, Ávila); **VALERIO ANNONI LVGVADICI F. VXAMENSIS** (Segovia, Segovia).

¶WESTERN PENINSULA. **LVGVBO ARQVIENOBO C(AIVS) IVLIVS HISPANVS V.S.L.M.** (Liñarán, Sober, Lugo); **LVCOBO / AROVSA(ECIS) / V. S. L. M. / RVTIL[IA] / ANTIANIA** (Lugo); **LVCOVBV[S] ARQVIENI[S] SILONIVS SILO EX VOTO** (Sinoga, Rábade, Outeiro do Rei, Lugo); **BANDE LVGVNO** (Vale de Prazeres, Fundão, Castelo Branco); **LVGGONI ARGANTICAENI** (Villaviciosa, Oviedo); **lok^{o}ob^{o}o niirab^{o}o t^{o}o aŕaia/i k^{a}alt^{e}e lok^{o}o/n ane naŕk^{e}e k^{a}ak^{i}iśiin/k^{o}olob^{o}/o ii t^{e}e·ro-b^{a}ar/e (b^{e})e t^{e}a/siioonii** ('Fonte Velha 6', Bemsafrim, Lagos, Portugal); personal names **CVM LVGARIO SEPTANII F. / LVGARIVS SEPTANII F.** (Vila Nova de Gaia, Pontevedra); **LVGVA CADDECVN** (La Remolina, León).

¶OTHER CELTIC LANGUAGES. Gaulish LVGOVES (Avenches [Aventicium], Switzerland); Old Irish *Lug*; Welsh *Lleu*; Gaulish personal names D M IVL(IAE) LVGVSELVAE VXORIS (Périgueux); ELVONTIV IEVRV · ANEVNO OLICNO · LVGVRIX ANEVNICNO (Genouilly); NAMNIA SVLLA LIVI LVGAVN[I] A(AVLI) LIVI VIND[I]LICIANI LIVIVS LVGAVNVS POSVIT (Bordeaux); LVGIOLAE (Paris); LVGISSIV[S (Trier); D M LVGVDECA(E) PIAE(?) C[O]NIVG(I) GRAT(A)E [ET] GRAECINO FILI[S] PO[S(VIT)] (Bourbonne-les-Bains); Ogam Irish personal names MODDAGN[I] MAQI GATTAGN[I] MUCOI LUGUNI (Windgap, Waterford); COVAGN[I] MAQ[I MU]C[OI] LUG[U]N[I] (Castlekeeran, Meath); VEQIKAMI MAQI LUGUNI (Knockshanawee, Cork); [..]CANAVVI MAQ L[UGU]N[I] (Knockshanawee, Cork) = Old Irish *Luign;* LUGUQRIT MA[QI] QRITT[I] (Reask, Kerry); LUGUQRIT[TI MAQI] [ADDI]LONAS (Kilcaskan, Cork); --]ECC MAQI L[UGUQ]RRIT (Kilcoolaght, Kerry) = Old Irish *Luccreth*; VELITAS LUGUTTI (Crag, Kerry), compare Old Irish *file*, gen. *filed* '(high-ranking) poet' and *Luigtheg*, genitive *Luigthig*; CATVVIRR MAQI LUGUVVE[C] (An Drom Loiscthe [Dromlusk], Kerry); LUGUVVECCA MAQI[-- (Áth an Charbaill [Aghacarrible], Kerry) = Old Irish genitive *Lugech*, *Lugach*; LUGUDECCAS MAQI [...MU]COI NETA-SEGAMONIAS DOLATU BIGA-ISGOB[... (Ardmore, Waterford); [CU]NAMAQI LUGUDECA MUC[OI] CUNEA (Kilgrovan, Waterford); LUGUDUC MAQI MAQIOC[--]CI[-- (Kilcullen South, Cork); NETTAVROECC [KOI] MAQI MUCCOI TRENALUGGO (Donaghmore, Kildare) = Old Irish *Luguid* or *Lugaid*, genitive *Luigdech*; TTRENALUGOS (Montaggart, Cork) = Old Irish *Trianlug*; Brythonic personal names *Louocatus* AD 509 x 521, Old Welsh *Louhelic*, *Loumarch*, Old Cornish *Loumarch*, *Leumarch*, *Leucum*, place-name *Lugu-ualium* > Old Welsh *Cair Ligualid* 'Carlisle'.

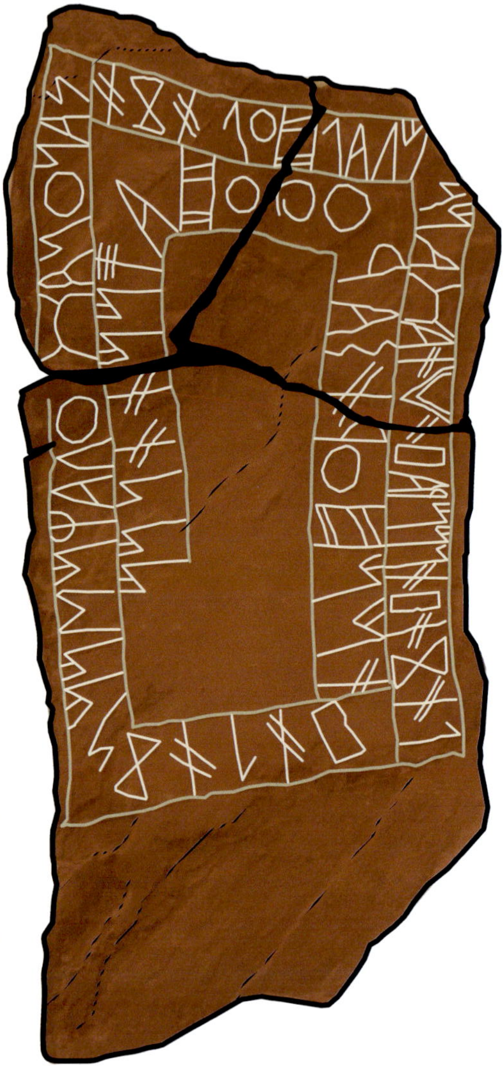

3.3–4. The large SW inscription of 'Fonte Velha 6' from the Early Iron Age necropolis of Bemsafrim, Lagos, south Portugal, 6th or 7th century BC, 136 x 73 x 15cm. The site is located near Sagres, at the extreme south-west of the Iberian Peninsula. The text begins at the outside on the lower righthand corner and then spirals inwards, anticlockwise.
Transliteration: **lok^{o}ob^{o}o≡niirab^{o}o t^{o}o aŕaia | i k^{a}alt^{e}e lok^{o}o | n ane naŕk^{e}e k^{a}ak^{i}iśiin | k^{o}olob^{o} | o ii t^{e}e·ro-b^{a}ar | e (b^{e})e t^{e}a | siioonii**
Tentative translation: 'To the divine Lugoues [and] to the chief men to *araia* (= ?"the ploughed land"), in the grove (i.e. necropolis), a burial deposition/urn [*logon*] rests within—and invoking all the *Eχskingoloi* "heroic ones"—it has carried [the offering/deceased] away, so they will give [benefit].'
(Museu Municipal Figueira de Foz; Museu da Escrita do Sudoeste, Almodôvar; photo J. Aaron; drawing M. Crampin & J. T. Koch)

Correa compared its opening words **lok^{o}ob^{o}o niirab^{o}o** with **LVGVBO ARQVIENOBO** and similar paired gods' names from the Roman Period inscriptions cited above. He explained **lok^{o}ob^{o}o** as the dative plural of the Celtic god's name *Lugu-* and derived **niirab^{o}o** from Proto-Indo-European root √*ner-* 'man, hero, leader', which also occurs as the ancient group name *Nerii* in Galicia. These explanations have been widely accepted. Correa also explained that the written form **lok^{o}ob^{o}o** was probably pronounced */lugubo/* in light of the fact that **u** was wholly absent from the 72-sign text. This impressive inscription probably dates to the 6th or 7th century BC, thus several centuries earlier than any other attestation of *Lugu-*. It also shows that the god had been worshipped as a group (like the *Lugoues* in Switzerland) as early as this and using a formal diction essentially like that found formulaically in inscriptions of the Roman Period, such as **LVGVBO ARQVIENOBO**.

3.5. Geographical distribution of forms of the name *Lugu-* in the Iberian Peninsula, as mentioned in the text.

(map F. Fernández & J. T. Koch)

The Archers

From the beginning of the Proto-Beaker package on the lower Tagus about 2800 BC, its most prominent culturally loaded material expressions included archery equipment. This emphasis on the high-status warrior as bowman sets the Beaker People apart from Copper and Bronze Age societies with steppe antecedents and likewise heroic traditions in early Indo-European languages, where the emphasis was on hand-to-hand combat between single champions facing each other at close quarters, like Achilles and Hector in the Iliad. As shown by Needham, the Beaker package—and its warrior as bowman ideology—had a distribution mutually exclusive to that of the era's fearsome hand-to-hand weapon, the halberd. These antithetical warrior concepts alternated as patchworks across Ireland, Britain, France, and the Iberian Peninsula.

Archery for hunting had existed amongst Mesolithic hunter–gatherers and Neolithic farmers. Does its special place in Beaker ideology reflect a conservatism, harking back to concepts of manhood in an earlier age? Of the 28 Beaker-related anthropomorphic stelae of Petit-Chasseur in western Switzerland, four include prominent representations of bows. These carvings have antecedents about 2000 years earlier in Atlantic Europe at the beginning of the megalithic age, when bows, resembling the Petit-Chasseur representations, were carved on upright stones in Early Neolithic passage graves at Gavrinis, Ile Longue, Barnenez, Runesto, and Kerioned in Brittany, Le Déhus on Guernsey, and one of the menhirs arrayed at Vale Maria do Meio, near Évora, in southern Portugal.

But there was probably more than a tenacious Stone Age idea sustaining Beaker archery. Like the mounted archers who later swept off the steppe to devastating effect, we may simply be seeing the triumph of a more effective weapon. A skilled archer with well-made equipment could neutralize opponents 30 metres away and come away wholly unscathed. The Tyrolian iceman Ötzi was killed by a bow and arrow about 3200 BC. As both reality and heroic ideal, hand-to-hand combat often involved serious injury to the victor, who might never recover.

Ireland, Britain, and parts of Gaul abandoned archery in the Middle Bronze Age. This is a perplexing development in the evolution of military technology. That shift was possibly not completely rational but ideologically driven. In other words, the idea of the heroic swordsman defeated the idea of the archer.

In south-west Europe archery persisted through the Bronze Age. In this region, archery had been iconic since the Early Neolithic. Here the Beaker phenomenon began and its roots were deepest, and steppe ancestry slightest.

In 1891, Sir John Rhŷs recognized that the Palaeohispanic name *Arquius* was Celtic and meant 'bowman, archer', being derived from the Western Indo-European word for bow and arrow: Latin *arquus* and *arcus* 'bow, arch', Gothic *arhvazna* 'arrow', also English 'arrow'. As we now know better than Rhŷs, *Arquius* was an extremely popular name across the *briga* zone. There is also an example from the SW inscriptions of the Early Iron Age: clearly legible **aark^{u}uio** begins an inscription from the Algarve.

As the bow and arrow ceased to be used in Britain and Ireland in the 2nd millennium BC, it is not surprising that Gaelic and Brythonic didn't keep the old word. Middle Irish *boga* and Welsh *bwa* are derived from Old Norse. Old Irish *saiget* 'arrow', Welsh *saeth*, and Middle Breton *saez* are from Latin *sagitta*. A different inherited word for 'bow' is seen in Middle Welsh *gwarac* 'bow, crooked stick, yoke, loop, handle, half circle, curve' corresponding to Middle Breton *goarec* 'bow, arch'.

In the Iberian Peninsula, on the other hand, bows and arrows are one of the recurrent motifs of the Late Bronze Age warrior stelae, where they occur together with other items of the high-status warrior's panoply: shields, spears, swords, helmets, chariots, brooches, mirrors, combs. At this stage, the images clearly represent powerful reflex bows with a pronounced double curve. Bronze arrowheads that had come into use probably increased effectiveness against leather armour of the Late Bronze Age (1300–900 BC). Bows are also represented on the Middle Bronze Age Alentejo stelae (1800–1300 BC). Archaeologists generally agree that the bow and arrow survived from Beaker times in south-west Europe, rather than being

Text Box 3.3. Proto-Celtic ***arkʷios** 'archer, bowman'

¶CELTIBERIAN REGION. **L. ARQVIVS [L. F.] GAL. CO[NT]V[CI]ANCO** (San Esteban de Gormaz, Soria); **A(VLO) M() MVNERIGIO ARQVI F.** (Calderuela, Soria); **L. VALERIVS L. F. ARQVOCVS** (Peñalba de Castro, Burgos).

¶CENTRAL REGION. **ARQVIO** (Ávila); **FL[ORIN]A LIBERTA ARQVIOCVM** (Alcalá de Henares, Madrid).

¶WESTERN PENINSULA. **ARQVIVS CANTABR(I)** (Braga); **ARQVIVS VIRIATI F. Ɔ ACRIPIA** (Braga); **[A]RQVIVS CANTAB[RI---]** (Braga); **APIL[VS] ARQV[I]** (Dume, Braga); **C. IVLIO CILIO ARQVI** (Santa Cruz de la Sierra, Cáceres); **ARQVIA HELENA** (Condeixa-a-Velha, Condeixa-a-Nova, Coimbra); **ANTONIVM ARQVIVM, EX GENTE VISALIGORVM** (Astorga, León); **ARQVIVS CLEMENS GIGVRRVS** (Puente de Domingo Flórez, León); **S. ARQVI(VS) CIM(---) L(IBERTVS)** (Carriça, Maia, Ourense); **VALERIE ARQVI (F.)** (Yecla de Yeltes, Salamanca); **AETVRAE ARQVI F.** (Valença, Viana do Castelo); **CAMALA ARQVI F. TALABRIGENSIS** (Estoraos, Ponte de Lima, Viana do Castelo); **ABRVI ARQVI APIOBICESIS** (Taroquela, Cinfães, Viseu); **AMBATO ARQVI F.** (Villalcampo, Zamora); **ARQVIO TALAI F.** (San Pedro de la Nave, Zamora); **IEMVRIAE ARQVI F.** (Villalcampo, Zamora); **APLONDVS ARQVIAECVS SVRNAE F. MIROB(RIGENSIS** (Garlitos, Badajoz); **AMBATI ARQVICI** (Barruecopardo, Salamanca); **[H]ERCVL[AN]AE ARQ[VI]C(I) F(ILIAE)** (Salamanca. ¶DIVINE NAMES: **LVGVBO ARQVIENOBO C. IVLIVS HISPANVS V. S. L. M.** (Liñarán, Sober, Lugo); **LVGOVBV[S] ARQVIENI[S] SILONIVS SILO EX VOTO** (Sinoga, Rábade, Otero del Rey, Lugo); ¶S.W. INSCRIPTIONS. **aarkᵘuio**, the opening sequence of inscription J.7.6 ('Ameixial 2', Loulé, Faro).

¶OUTSIDE THE *BRIGA* ZONE: **STATVIVS ARQVIO** (Monteagudo, Navarra).

The well attested series **ARCIVS**, &c., is most probably a variant of **ARQVIVS**.

¶CELTIBERIAN REGION. **ARCEA ALTICON ALEONEI FILIA** (Lara de los Infantes, Burgos); **ARCEA [---] AMBATI F.** (Lara de los Infantes, Burgos); **ARCEA [---]AVCA AMBATI TERENTI F.** (Lara de los Infantes, Burgos); **ARCEAE DESIIAE CADAECI F.** (Lara de los Infantes, Burgos); **[A]RCEAE DESSICAE PAT[ER]NI F.** (Lara de los Infantes, Burgos); **ARCEA ELANIOCA PATERNI F.** (Lara de los Infantes, Burgos); **ARCEAE LONGINAE C. F. (MATRI)** (Lara de los Infantes, Burgos); **ARCEA PLANDICA MATICVLA(E) F.** (Lara de los Infantes, Burgos).

¶WESTERN PENINSULA. **ARCIAE MO[---]** (Meixedo, Bragança); **ARCIVS EPEICI F. BRACARVS** (Vila da Feira, Aveiro); **TAVRVS ARCI F. AMMICIVS** (Villar del Rey, Badajoz); **ANIVS ARCI** (Idanha-a-Velha, Idanha-a-Nova, Castelo Branco); **ARCIVS** (Idanha-a-Velha, Idanha-a-Nova, Castelo Branco); **[CAE]NIVS ARCI** (Idanha-a-Velha, Idanha-a-Nova, Castelo Branco); **L. SVLLA ARCI F.** (Idanha-a-Velha, Idanha-a-Nova, Castelo Branco); **TERTVLA ARCI F.** (Idanha-a-Velha, Idanha-a-Nova, Castelo Branco); **TOVTONI ARCI F.** (Idanha-a-Velha, Idanha-a-Nova, Castelo Branco); **ARCIVS** (Ponte da Barca, Viana do Castelo); **ARCISSVS ARENIER(I) F.** (Cáceres); **MEDAMVS ARCISI F. CASTE[L]LO MEIDVNIO** (Cadones, Celanova, Ourense).

3.6. SW inscription of 'Ameixial 2' (J.7.6), Loulé, south Portugal, probably 6th or 7th century BC, 99 x 53 x 4cm. The text begins at the lower righthand corner and then spirals inwards, anticlockwise. Transliteration: **aark^{u}uioriou⟨t^{i}⟩b^{e}a:i :elurear[| uii** . In the SW corpus, it is common for identifiable Celtic names to begin the text. Breaks between words are not usually shown. **aark^{u}uio** could be a complete name meaning '[grave] of Arquius (of Archer)' or it could be the first element of a compound name, like the gods' name **ARQVIENOBO**.

(Museu Nacional de Arqueologia, Lisbon; drawing M. Crampin)

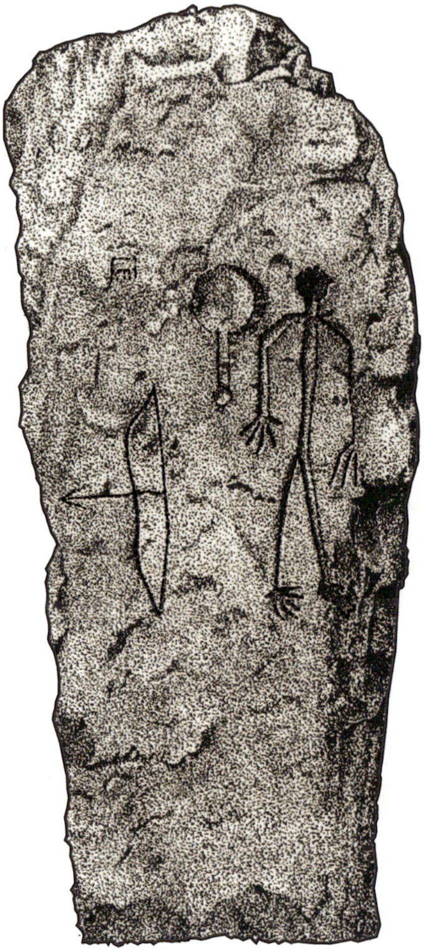

3.7. (right side of page) **Late Bronze Age warrior stela from Montemolín (Marchena), Seville, Spain**, showing a human figure, mirror, comb, and bow and arrow, 135 x 37 x 27cm.

(drawing J. T. Koch after Harrison (2004) p. 297)

reintroduced from somewhere else. So for linguists it is interesting that a Western Indo-European word meaning 'archer' was such a popular name in the Iberian Peninsula after the bow had gone out of fashion as a weapon and status symbol in the neighbouring parts of Europe. Is **Ark^{w}ioi* what the Beaker People called themselves? Or is it what their Bronze Age descendants called themselves once they had come to speak Indo-European?

The Hispano-Celtic place-name *Arcobriga* probably also contains Western PIE **H$_{a}$érk^{w}os* 'bow and arrow'. The second element of *Arcobriga* we have met already. It's a Celtic word meaning 'hill, hillfort'. We know of three places in the ancient Iberian Peninsula called *Arcobriga*. The location of only one is certain, Monreal de Ariza in the province of Zaragoza, within the ancient Celtiberian region. An impressive hill overlooks the ruined Roman town there, although the expectation that this hill had been the site of a pre-Roman hillfort has not been borne out. Viewed from the site of the ancient town, the silhouette of the hill on the horizon, especially when this is compared with

3.8. Bow and arrow from the LBA warrior stela from Montemolín, Seville (see 3.7) superimposed on a view of the prominent hill at Monreal de Ariza (Arcobriga), Zaragoza, Spain, viewed from the ruined Roman town.

(Source: http://aeternitas-numismatics.blogspot.co.uk/2012/03/la-ciudad-celtibera-de-arcobriga.html)

the images of bows from the Late Bronze Age stelae, leaves little doubt that the place-name means '[reflex] bow-shaped hill'.

Indo-European, non-Indo-European, and Celtic

When someone learns a second language in childhood (say ten years old or younger, at any rate before puberty), learns it fully, and continues to use it frequently afterwards, they will usually sound like a native. With a language learned later in life, even if used every day and with impressive competence, there will usually be some residual non-native giveaways. Mostly, what the competent adult masters will be the vocabulary and morphology (that is, the suffixes, prefixes, and other changes of the forms of words that express their grammatical relationships). What betrays the adult learner will be word order and pronunciation. The latter is what is called a foreign accent. This universal pattern is the result of the parallel evolution of two complex self-organizing systems: the human species and natural language. The learner learns what has to be learned to survive: the vocabulary and morphology of language must be mastered to convey information. But one can usually get by with an approximation of the sound system and unidiomatic word order carried over from one's mother tongue. Human beings work this way because languages work this way and vice versa.

People called *ieithgwn* in Welsh (which means literally 'language hounds', people endlessly fascinated by languages) often discover that the Celtic languages have features in common with non-Indo-European languages. Over a hundred years ago, the Welsh polymath (and *ieithgi*), Sir John Morris-Jones, recognized parallels in the syntax of Welsh and that of Ancient Egyptian and the Semitic languages, such as Hebrew and Arabic. The idea was not altogether new in 1900, but Morris-Jones took it out of the realm of antiquarian pseudo-science and doctrines of the British Israelites. His work began the 'Hamito-Semitic' substratum theory of Celtic, which remains credible for many linguists today. The claimed substratum features are mostly in word order. For example, it is most normal in Irish and Welsh for the verb to begin its clause, which is uncommon in most Indo-European languages, but widely found in the Hamito-Semitic macro-family (which is today more often called 'Afro-Asiatic'). As usually framed, the hypothesis supposes that Britain and Ireland spoke a language (or languages) that were typologically similar (or even genetically related) to Afro-Asiatic before Indo-European arrived. When the new language was introduced, enough first language Afro-Asiatic(-type) speakers survived and learned Indo-European as a second language that speech habits from their mother tongue eventually transformed the syntax of Insular Celtic.

There has always been a problem with the theory formulated in this way. An Afro-Asiatic(-type) language with effects this pervasive and persistent in Britain or Ireland would be expected to have left additional traces. So where are they? Today there is another new problem. Olalde et al. find a population with a large steppe component—virtually indistinguishable genetically from the Beaker People on the lower Rhine—coming to Britain and replacing the Neolithic population at a rate of 90%. That is not an auspicious context for the language of the indigenous pre-Beaker inhabitants to have left an enduring impression. Coming mostly from one compact region along the lower Rhine, the Neo-Beaker settlers probably spoke only one language. Keeping the culture from their homeland, they did not change to emulate the indigenous British Neolithic people. Therefore, if these settlers spoke the Indo-European that became Celtic, a pre-Beaker substratum big enough to transform the word order of this incoming Indo-European has yet to be detected. This is not to say that Brythonic and Gaelic show no influence from one or more non-Indo-European language, but, so far, the archaeogenetic data does not show this mixing occurring as the Beaker Complex entered the British Isles in the second half of the 3rd millennium BC.

By the Roman Period, some individuals from south-east Britain show a reduced steppe component. One possible explanation for this shift is as a resurgence of marginalized survivals from the Neolithic. Limited resurgences of Neolithic ancestry occurred in other parts of Bronze Age Europe. Similarly, hunter–gatherer admixture had increased between the Early and Middle Neolithic. Such patterns indicate a prolonged time lag between the arrival of a new dominant group and the effects of interbreeding with a marginalized indigenous population. Migration in the Iron Age into south-east Britain from a neighbouring country, with the exception of Iberia, would not explain the decrease in the steppe component, and it is unlikely that mass movement between Iberia and south-east Britain took place at that time. The biggest post-Beaker intrusion was the post-Roman Anglo-Saxon settlements known to history, contributing about 35% to the gene pool in lowland Britain.

A second substratum theory has to do with consonants. It involves the whole Celtic branch, rather than just Gaelic and Brythonic, and non-Indo-European languages found in direct contact with Celtic across a wide area in historical times. The key sound change, often used to define the emergence of Celtic from Proto-Indo-European, is the weakening of IE **p*. In most positions, the sound was then usually lost completely. In recent years, several linguists have come to the view that this weakening occurred due to contact with the *p*-less non-Indo-European language of ancient Catalunya and Valencia, Iberian.

North-west of the country of ancient Iberian, towards the western Pyrenees and Bay of Biscay, there is another non-Indo-European language, one that has survived to this day, Basque. What Basque was like 2000 years ago can be recovered with some certainty by comparing the few surviving ancient inscriptions, the modern Basque dialects, and the development of Latin loanwords of the Roman period. There are also about 500 inscriptions of the Roman Period preserving names of the Aquitanian language, spoken to the north of the modern Basque country. Aquitanian was either the same language as Palaeo-Basque or an extremely close relative. Like Iberian, Palaeo-Basque/Aquitanian lacked *p*. In fact, the sound systems of Iberian and Palaeo-Basque/Aquitanian appear to have been very similar. One of the great unresolved questions of historical linguistics is whether Iberian and Palaeo-Basque/Aquitanian form a language family or had become similar as neighbours in prolonged contact, which is a common development. The concept 'Vasco-Iberian' can be used here, allowing that it could mean either a language family or typological language area.

The system of what are called the 'stop' consonants, which are formed through a complete stopping of the breath flow, were as follows in late Western PIE (that is, in the so-called 'Centum' group of languages):

p	**t**	**k**	**k^w**
[b]	**d**	**g**	**g^w**
bh	**dh**	**gh**	**g^wh**

The Proto-Celtic system of stop consonants was much simpler than its ancestor, and also simpler than its Western Indo-European neighbours, Proto-Italic and Proto-Germanic. It had only seven members, rather than twelve.

_	**t**	**k**	**k^w**
b	**d**	**g**	**g^w**

To get there, PIE */g^w/ became */b/, and then */b d g/ merged with */bh dh gh/ as */b d g/, as well as the loss of */p/.

The great Basque linguist Koldo Mitxelena (1915–1987) reconstructed the consonant system of Palaeo-Basque as follows.

fortes:	_	**t**	**c**	**ć**	**k**	**N**	**L**	**R**
lenes:	**b**	**d**	**s**	**ś**	**g**	**n**	**l**	**r**

For the question of Celtic origins, the first key point about this is that an adult who spoke Palaeo-Basque as his or her first language would find Centum PIE relatively difficult to pronounce. The five consonants eliminated between PIE and Proto-Celtic (*p*, *bh*, *dh*, *gh*, and *g^{w}h*) did not occur in Palaeo-Basque. In other words, these were five problems that the first-language Palaeo-Basque speaker did not have in learning Proto-Celtic rather than PIE.

A second key point about the Palaeo-Basque consonant system is the systematic opposition of strong and weak articulations, fortes and lenes. This was not a feature of PIE, but it occurs in all the medieval and modern Celtic languages. This is the basis of the 'lenition' and other so-called 'consonant mutations' characteristic of Celtic grammar: for example, Welsh *tŷ* 'house', *ei dŷ* 'his house' = Irish *teach* and *a theach*. As a phonetic development, the fortis-lenis opposition must go back to Ancient Celtic, before it came to be revealed in writing or functioned in grammar and syntax as it has since the early Middle Ages. It is not certain whether a fortis–lenis opposition had also been a feature of the Iberian language.

None of these phonological developments—loss of *p*, *bh dh gh* merging with *b d g*, and a system of strong and weak consonants—is highly unusual in the languages of the world. *p* was also lost in the Armenian branch of Indo-European, for example. But it is striking and probably significant to find these features together in both Palaeo-Basque and as innovations in the Indo-European branch attested on both sides of Palaeo-Basque, namely Celtic. The transfer of these features to the Indo-European that (thereby) became Celtic would be understandable in a socio-linguistic situation in which native speakers of Palaeo-Basque (or similar) learned Proto-Indo-European as adults. Recall now the lives of indigenous women who produced children with R1b men in Early Bronze Age Iberia. As would be expected, many did not successfully acquire new sounds. The resulting learner's speech was passed on to the next generation because the adult learners were numerous within their community their speech was not stigmatized, but emulated as representing the preferred group identity, and/or the declining language died out gradually with prolonged bilingual interaction. Over successive generations, what began as 'my foreign mother's funny accent' became 'the way we talk'.

In spreading far from the homeland—crossing natural obstacles and then settling in new environments—the Indo-European speech community became geographically over-extended. It then became impossible to maintain the regular long-distance contacts necessary to preserve a high degree of mutual intelligibility over the whole speech area indefinitely. Therefore, one reason that the Celtic branch split off from Proto-Indo-European was purely mechanical and value neutral.

A second key factor is that it now appears likely that groups with steppe ancestry in what became Celtic western Europe adopted the ideology, beliefs, and to a large extent the identity of a non-Indo-European group from Atlantic Europe. 'Beakerization' of groups with steppe background in western Europe resulted in separating them culturally from the rest of the Indo-European world. But as one door shut another opened. They henceforth shared a common cultural space with a non-Indo-European group, a road west. It also affected their language through deep and prolonged interaction with the original non-Indo-European language of the 'out of Iberia' Proto-Beaker People. These linguistic effects include simplification of the PIE consonant system, such as loss of **p*, and acquiring a systematic phonetic opposition of strongly and weakly articulated consonants. From the time of their Beaker conversion, they would probably want to speak differently—as well as acting and believing differently—from the 'un-Beakerized' Indo-Europeans. They could do this either by learning to speak the language of the Proto-Beaker People or speaking Indo-European so as to sound more like Proto-Beaker People who had learned Indo-European as adults. The latter course put them on the linguistic path leading from Proto-Indo-European to Proto-Celtic.

The Beaker enigma

Haak et al. 2015 and Allentoft et al. 2015 felt like an exhilarating flash of clarity. A theory of the origin and dispersal of Proto-Indo-European, that had already gained many adherents without any genetic evidence at all, found confirmation. Mass migrations had come back to archaeological modelling, having been revealed coming from the right place (the Pontic–Caspian steppe) to at least some of the right places, at the right time (Copper Age to Early Bronze Age). Cassidy et al. 2016 brought the expectation that this clarity might soon include the Celtic west. The big break separating the gene pool of the woman from the Giant's Ring and that of the three men from McCuaig's Bar signalled a new population with a sizable steppe component becoming predominant close to, if not precisely at, the Beaker Period. For Britain, at least, Olalde et al. 2018 confirmed this expectation emphatically, with their 90% replacement of the Neolithic population by Neo-Beaker People from the Netherlands. Combining this evidence for a great transformation in the 3rd millennium BC with that for greater genetic continuity from then to the present, the traditional assumption of Celtic migrations into the British Isles during the Iron Age is now in doubt.

But when the Beaker and Celtic worlds are filled in to include the Iberian Peninsula with Olalde et al. 2018, Martiniano et al. 2017, and Valdiosera et al. 2018, the clouds of ambiguity roll back in. The steppe component surfaced less dramatically and later there. There are various clues that something more anciently western—not off the steppe—was involved.

The challenging complexity of Celtic and Atlantic Europe is not altogether exceptional in the ancient Indo-European world. One of the leaders of 20th-century Celtic studies was Myles Dillon (1900–1972). He was an influential authority when he proposed that the Indo-European that became Celtic arrived in Ireland with the Beaker People. That idea never completely went out of contention and, as we see, is back after recent aDNA results. Another of Dillon's durable ideas was presented in his posthumous *Celts and Aryans* (1975). There, he argued that certain Indo-European linguistic and cultural inheritances survived especially well in detailed parallels in these two branches. Though this idea had significant impact on Celtic and Indo-European studies, it found barely polite reception in India.

Archaeogenetics now puts the Indo-Celtic parallel back in the frame. Both the Indo-European of Atlantic Europe and that of south Asia coexist in their regions with indigenous non-Indo-European languages that have survived to the present day. Dravidian and other non-IE families still thrive in south Asia. In south-west Europe, non-Indo-European Basque survives with Berber nearby in north Africa. In ancient times, the lands near the western Mediterranean were also home to non-Indo-European Aquitanian, Iberian, Palaeo-Sardinian, Etruscan, and Rhaetian (see map, Fig. 3.1).

Silva et al. 2017 and Narasimhan et al. 2018 find steppe DNA including the R1a Y chromosome (the eastern counterpart of R1b) unevenly distributed in the near two billion modern population of south Asia (Pakistan, India, Bangla Desh, Sri Lanka, Nepal, and Bhutan). There is more of it in Pakistan, in the north of India, amongst speakers of Indo-European languages, and amongst the higher Hindu castes. The genetic clock points towards the Early Bronze Age as the period when this component arrived in south Asia. Diverse maternal DNA reflects more ancient migrations. Overall, it appears that the migration event that links the gene pool of south Asia to other Indo-European-speaking populations was not on the scale of population replacement. The modern population structure implies that between about 2000 and 1600 BC foreign men entered the north-west and produced children with indigenous south Asian women and that the resulting group were expansionist and spoke an Old Indic language, more-or-less the attested Vedic Sanskrit.

Comparative evidence also reflects an inherited Indo-European institution of an age grade of young warriors, who had not yet attained wives, property, or adult status. This group lived on their kindred's margins, hunting and fighting. As proposed in Kristiansen et al. 2017, some at least of the Indo-Europeans who came from the steppe and founded the Corded Ware cultures (CWC) in northern Europe were probably organized as these male-only warbands. These groups seized the lands and women of indigenous Neolithic Europeans, as implied by CWC aDNA.

Their steppe descent is stronger and more homogeneous in the paternal genome, the maternal DNA more diverse. In a study of the X chromosomes of 16 individuals of Late Neolithic to Early Bronze Age date, Goldberg et al. 2017 concluded that the movements from the steppe to central Europe at this stage spanned many generations and that almost all comprised single men, rather than family groups. However, Lazaridis and Reich of Harvard argue for a migration into central Europe including more steppe women.

Whether the movements into central Europe were mostly family groups or male warbands, Goldberg et al.'s view of migrations over many generations might explain a linguistic phenomenon. Widely across Indo-European-speaking territory—and most densely in that bounded by the Baltic on the north, the Alps and Carpathians on the south, the Rhine on the west, and Don on the east—a stock of 'Old European' (*alteuropäisch*) river names recur. Most linguists agree that these reflect an early stage of Indo-European. Most of these river-name roots survive as regular vocabulary in Baltic (the IE branch to which Lithuanian belongs). But the linguistic characteristics of Old European do not agree exactly with any attested branch. If migrations from the steppe had in fact continued for centuries, the speech of the homeland would have changed. And we'd look for linguistic layering to distinguish the earlier from later incomers.

Speaking in general, the story of the IE expansion is clearer in the north than in the south. This is no accident. DNA is better preserved in colder climates. Furthermore, south of the Pontic–Caspian steppe in the 3rd millennium BC was a zone containing complex, metal-using societies, some inhabiting large defended settlements. Such societies were not so easily overwhelmed. But they offered opportunities for infiltration by young unmarried warriors. Unless we are today lucky enough to get hold of viable genetic samples from precisely the right place and the right time, such élite incursions might prove elusive—turning up only centuries later as an aggressive Y chromosome, where it had not washed out altogether.

Indo-Europeanization, Beakerization, and Celticization

Even before the genetic diversity of the Beaker People was known, archaeology strained to interpret the cultural fusion of CWC and Beaker cultures in central Europe—in the Alps and along the Rhine and upper Danube (below Fig. 4.13). This new evidence, coupled with the inferences linking the steppe component and Indo-European, might now help to explain these processes. During the 3rd millennium BC, the Yamnaya culture on the steppe and CWC in northern Europe were aggressive and successfully expansionist warrior societies. In light of their dearth of steppe ancestry, it is a reasonable hypothesis that the Iberian Proto-Beaker People did not speak an Indo-European language.

It can be seen from the comparative evidence of literatures, laws, and kinship systems that Proto-Indo-European society was patriarchal, patrilocal, patrilineal, and exogamous. In other words, inherited status and property were reckoned through the male line. The men remained in their ancestral group and married women from outside it. The spread of the R1b and R1a Y chromosomes in the 3rd millennium—more rapidly than anyone had previously imagined—is understandable as a result of this Indo-European social structure.

In describing the spread of the Beaker phenomenon out of Iberia, Volker Heyd writes that '... an expansionist drive—almost missionary in appearance—became the dominant element'. The Beaker expansion and its fusion with Indo-European groups north of the Pyrenees—with genetic results as now known—make sense allowing a leading aspect of recruitment or proselytizing. The same orientation in ideology and social organization is probably reflected in the continuation of collective burial rites in south-western Europe as opposed to the single burial rites on the steppe and areas with people of ultimate steppe origin. It is possible, then, that owing to their complementary differences these two warlike groups were not fated to hostile confrontation, but could coalesce when they met.

The story of the R1b/R1a expansion and that of the early Indo-European literatures seems to be that a male outsider could not join Indo-European society by adopting their ideas and marrying an Indo-European woman. On the other hand, the missionary quality and genetic diversity of the Beaker People implies that the reverse had been possible. An Indo-European (R1b) man could join Beaker society by mastering Beaker archery, partaking in the communal drinking ritual, and marrying a Beaker woman. When this happened, the Beaker culture expanded, but Indo-European society also expanded. The Beaker initiate had not renounced his patrilineal kin group. Rather, Beaker society became Indo-Europeanized as Indo-European society became Beakerized. The Beaker way, with its metallurgical know-how and strong warrior aspect, was compatible with the Indo-European value system.

North of the Pyrenees, in places where Indo-European groups outnumbered Beaker groups, Indo-European men could seek out the Beaker way of life and advantageous unions with the hybrid Neo-Beaker women at the next generation. From the perspective of the Beaker side, it was also advantageous; they had a recruit. The reverse—an 'out of Iberia' Proto-Beaker man marrying into Indo-European society—was not advantageous, as he and his male relatives had no recognized status. Over a few generations, the trend would be for the Beaker culture to continue to spread, in its Indo-Europeanized form, while R1b Y chromosomes dominated and distinctively Iberian autosomal DNA was rapidly diluted.

Rasmussen et al. 2016 offers a possible explanation for the turnover of population in northern Europe between the Neolithic and Bronze Age, and this might also explain the apparent drastic transformations in Britain and Ireland at this stage. That study detects the plague bacterium in the aDNA of the 3rd millennium BC. It is possible, therefore, that the greater advantage clearing the way for Indo-Europeans of ultimate steppe origin was immunity rather than cultural intolerance enabled by military prowess. As islands, Britain and Ireland were probably more isolated during the Neolithic and thus less likely to develop immunities to new infectious diseases.

On the strength of the results in Olalde et al. we can see that the situation on the Iberian Peninsula in the 3rd millennium BC was different. The steppe component was thinner on the ground. Enough samples from enough regions have been returned for us to expect the main outlines of this picture to hold up. However, archaeology leads us to expect some élite steppe influence at an early date. Volker Heyd draws attention to what appears to be elements of steppe ideology in an extraordinarily rich burial of the Pre-Beaker Copper Age at Valencina de la Concepción (2875–2700 cal BC). Beneath a large barrow, the inhumation burial of a crouched male showing several parallels to Yamnaya and Corded Ware chieftain burials of the same period, including red pigment, a flint dagger, and paired sandal-shaped objects, one of gold and one of ivory. The site, in the province of Seville, sits beside the Atlantic-facing,

3.9. A Middle Bronze Age stela from Lugar de Pedreirinha, Santa Vitória, Beja, Portugal, 90 x 68 x 12cm, c. 1500 BC, depicting a sheathed rapier, warrior's belt, and enigmatic anchor-shaped object (as frequently prominently represented in these Alentejano stelae). (Museo 'Rainha D. Leonor', Beja; image J. Aaron)

then navigable lower Guadalquivir. Long-distance contacts with this place involved seafaring.

Geographically Valencina de la Concepción is not far from the three Middle Bronze Age men with R1b Y chromosomes from south Portugal analysed by Martiniano et al. It is also near the region of the MBA cist burials, in which Alentejo stelae with steppe affinities were found (Fig. 2.4; Fig. 3.9). These stelae from south Portugal of the period 1800–1300 BC resemble, in their symbolic weaponry and belts, Copper Age anthropomorphic stelae found with cist burials under kurgans in the Yamnaya culture of the steppe and associated Kemi Oba culture on the Crimean Peninsula. These stelae of the Pontic region have been recognized as reflecting early Indo-European iconography. The visual similarity is striking, and the burial practices are parallel in that the stelae have often been replaced, turned face down as lids capping burial cists. The chronological gap is great between the Alentejo stelae and suspected prototypes near the Black Sea. Further study of the iconography and dating evidence for rock art associated with Beaker sites and later megalithic burials in the western Iberian Peninsula will probably illuminate a chain of development through the intervening centuries. These include anthropomorphic stelae closing entrances to collective tombs of the 3rd millennium BC along the middle Tagus in western Spain at Lagunita, Alconétar, and Cañamero. These represent figures with weapons suspended from belts, a widespread type in the Copper Age, possibly traceable to the anthropomorphic stelae of the steppe.

Dirk Brandherm has recently shown that the MBA Alentejo stelae (about 1800–1300 BC) use a burial rite that was revived in the same region in the Early Iron Age (about 750–450 BC), at which time the stelae involved are the 'Tartessian' inscriptions with recognized Celtic names. The common features include cist burials in slab-lined rectangular boxes, circular or subcircular pavements over the cists, sometimes with pavements of new burials overlapping older ones, and the stelae themselves (originally made to stand upright) later reset face down as cap stones over the cists. Several of these recurring features, including the replacement of the stela face down over the burial cist, are found also with the Copper Age anthropomorphic stelae under kurgans on the Pontic steppe.

It is also from the south-west of the Peninsula that some of the earliest evidence for Celtic occurs in classical literature. In the Histories of Herodotus written in the mid 5th century BC, we have an account King Arganthonios of Tartessos, a kingdom probably centred on the coastal town of Huelva. His implausibly long reign ran notionally from about 625 to 545 BC, and his name is based on the Celtic word for 'silver' *arganto-*, as also found in the divine epithet of the **LVGGONI ARGANTICAENI** 'Lugu- goddesses beautiful in silver' mentioned above. A phenomenal abundance of silver in the neighbourhood of the Río Tinto mines was the chief source of wealth of Tartessos. In two rather repetitive accounts Herodotus wrote that Celts lived in this area.

> §2.33. For the Nile does, after all, flow from Libya—indeed it bisects it—so my own conjecture, based on analogy between what is apparent and is unknown,

would be that its length is equivalent to that of the Ister ['Danube']. That river, which splits Europe in two, has its source at the city of Pyrene, in the land of the Celts [Keltoi], who dwell beyond the Pillars of Heracles, and are the neighbours of the Cynetes [Kunēsioi], the people who live closer to the setting sun than any other in Europe. (trans. Holland 2013, 121)

§4.49. . . . the Ister ['Danube'] flows through the whole of Europe: its source lies in the land of the Celts [Keltoi], a people who live further from us and closer to the setting sun than any other except for the Cynetes [Kunētes], and only after the Ister has flowed through the whole of Europe, and reached the very edge of Scythia, does it empty into the sea. (trans. Holland 2013, 281)

The Kunētes, who lived in the Algarve, also had a Celtic name, based on the word meaning 'dog, hound, wolf'. **Kū*, **kuno-* was a common metaphor amongst the early Celts for a hero, for example Cú Chulainn, superhero of the Irish Ulster Cycle of tales, who earned his name as the human guard dog of the smith Culann. Essentially the same group name as *Kunētes*, Welsh *Cynwydion*, identified the war-band of Dark Age Strathclyde.

Text Box 3.4. Proto-Celtic ***arganto-** 'silver'

¶CELTIBERIAN REGION. **arkato-bezom** plausibly 'silver mine' [argã^{n}tobeδom] (K.0.7, find spot unknown); **arkanta mezukenoskue abokum** (K.1.3, III–11 — Botorrita, Zaragoza); **arkanta loukanikum** (K.1.3, III–12 — Botorrita, Zaragoza); **arkanta teiuantikum tirtunos** (K.1.3, III–21 — Botorrita, Zaragoza); **arkanta toutinikum** (K.1.3, III–44 — Botorrita, Zaragoza); **arkanta ailokiskum** (K.1.3, III–53 — Botorrita, Zaragoza); **arkanta** (K.1.3, IV–20 — Botorrita, Zaragoza); **[T]OVTONI ARGANTIOQ(VM) ABALI F.** (Palencia); **SEMPRONIA ARGANTA** (Saelices, Cuenca); **ARGANTO MEDVTICA MELMANIQ(VM)** (Riba de Saelices, Guadalajara).

¶CENTRAL REGION. **LVCRETIA ARGANSA** (Valdenebro de los Valles, Valladolid).

¶WESTERN PENINSULA. **FLACCVS ARGANTON(I) MAGILANCVM MIROBRIGENSIS** (Garrovillas, Cáceres); divine epithet of the **LVGGONI ARGANTICAENI** (Villaviciosa, Asturias) the exact equivalent of the Early Breton woman's name *Argant-ken* 'beautiful in silver' (Cartulary of Quimperlé, AD 1126).

¶OTHER CELTIC AND INDO-EUROPEAN LANGUAGES OUTSIDE THE IBERIAN PENINSULA. Gaulish ARGANTODANNOS 'officer of silver, overseer of currency, moneyer' on the coins of the Lexovii and Meldi (cf. SW **k^{a}aśet^{a}ana** 'tin-/bronze minister' (J.53.1)), place-name *Arganto-magus*; Cisalpine Gaulish (Vercelli) ARKATOKO⟨K⟩MATEREKOS/ ARGANTOCOMATERECVS, Old Irish *argat, aircet*; Old Welsh *argant*, place-name *Lıcat Arganhell* < Ancient Brythonic **Argantillā*, Middle Welsh *ariant, aryant*; Old Breton *argant, Argantan, Arganthael, Argantlǫn, Argantlouuen, Argantmonǫc*, Middle Breton *archant*, ModB *arc'hant*; OC *argans*, OC personal names *Arganteilin, Argantmoet, Arganbri*; Hittite **ḫarki-*,**ḫarkant-* (Vanséveren 2012); Latin *argentum*, Sanskrit *rajatá-*, Avestan *ərəzata*, Old Persian *rdata*.

Considered alongside the genetic evidence of Martiniano et al., Valdiosera et al., the Reich Lab, and Max Planck Institute, the dense Hispano-Celtic linguistic evidence across the *briga* zone raises an important question. The steppe component was weaker in the Iberian Peninsula than in west-central Europe, Britain, and Ireland. But Indo-European—the same very specifically developed form of Indo-European, Celtic—became established in all these places. Therefore, is it really only the paternal ancestry—i.e. the R1b Y chromosome—that is relevant for the spread of this language? If there was such a straightforward equation, that would simplify the task of tracking the spread of Indo-European and its branches. We could forget about the mtDNA and the 45 other chromosomes, and the women. It would also tell us something significant about the social organization of early Indo-European-speaking societies. As well as being tenaciously patrilineal, patrilocal, and exogamous, these societies would have strongly favoured the language of fathers and resisted passing the language of foreign mothers on to their descendants. If this were the case to an extreme degree, identical longer-term linguistic outcomes would eventually come to pass in countries where there had been massive inflow of family groups of steppe origin and countries where only a small group of males of steppe origin gradually spread through a larger population, marrying non-Indo-European women over successive generations. As well as cultural bias favouring the language of the father's kin, practical consequences of Indo-European patrilocal exogamy were in play. A typical Proto-Indo-European founder community comprised men who were close relatives, thus speaking the same first language, and women from diverse outgroups, hence languages different from that of both the men and each other.

But in fact, there does not seem to be a simple one-to-one correspondence of R1b/R1a and Indo-European. 87.1% of modern Basque men are of the same R1b-M269 haplogroup as the three Middle Bronze Age men tested from south Portugal. The Iberian Bronze Age samples of the Harvard and Max Planck studies show that the steppe component and R1b were not confined to the *briga* zone. Similarly, R1a is common amongst the non-Indo-European Dravidian speakers of south Asia. It seems, then, that the Indo-European kinship system did not so strongly disfavour bilingualism and sometimes did not even ensure the survival of the paternal language at all. Where greatly outnumbered, incoming Indo-Europeans might retain political dominance and patrilineal inheritance, while adopting the language of their wives and neighbours, as being of more practical advantage for themselves and their children. One is reminded of the powerful Anglo-Norman families who linguistically went native in Gaelic Ireland, likewise the Bronze Age kingdom of Mitanni, speaking their region's non-Indo-European Hurrian language, but retaining Indic for names of their kings and gods and chariot terminology.

It is likely that factors other than paternal ancestry explain the genetic diversity of the lands that spoke Ancient Celtic languages, or, to put it the other way around, the Celtic linguistic unity across genetically diverse western Europe. Archaeological distribution maps throw light on this problem by showing the regions of the Beaker network that continued in contact during the post-Beaker Bronze Age. In the Early

3.10. Geographical distribution of names with Celtic *arganto-* 'silver' in the Iberian Peninsula.

(map F. Fernández & J. T. Koch)

Bronze Age, we see widespread changes of beliefs and practices entering the Iberian Peninsula by sea from the north, as discussed in another chapter of this book:

> It is only in the centuries after 2200 BC that a discernible transformation in burial ideologies is noted in these regions, indicated through the marked increase in individual burial; 200 years or more later than its acceptance in Wiltshire and Dorset, for example. Burials were now generally crouched inhumations in stone-lined cists or in pits, sometimes covered by small mounds (*mamoas*), and most were accompanied by grave goods that included Beaker-derived pots, along with bracers and daggers, demonstrating continuity with Beaker traditions. Examples include the cist burials of As Antas in Galicia which contained a bronze dagger and Ciempozuelos or late Beaker bowl, and Pera Gorda in the Tagus estuary, which was also accompanied by a dagger in addition to two Palmela points. What is intriguing is that this single cist burial tradition may have been influenced by existing practices already established further north in other parts of Atlantic Europe, such as Ireland and north-eastern Scotland, perhaps highlighting new spheres of interaction now flowing from north to south.

In the circumstances described above, the Bronze Age contacts with Britain and Ireland (and probably also Brittany) would have continued to favour

Indo-European consolidation in the post-Beaker Early Bronze Age of the western Iberian Peninsula. As reflected in metal chemistry and typologies of metalwork, these regions were again linked during the Atlantic Late Bronze Age (1300–900/800). In the Iberian Peninsula this network extended as far south as the key terminus of Huelva, which was probably the Tartessos known to the Greeks and source of the wealth-laden 'ships of Tarshish' of the Old Testament.

The intensity of contacts across Atlantic Europe through the Late Bronze Age implies that the Indo-European languages of the region would have continued to share innovations, maintaining Proto-Celtic as the regional lingua franca with a high degree of mutual intelligibility. The interaction was also sufficiently intense during the Atlantic Late Bronze Age for a levelling out of uneven degrees of substratum influence from the non-Indo-European speech of south-west Europe. As communities with Beaker backgrounds, their substratum was probably always the same non-Indo-European language, although varying in degree between localities. The late survival of this linguistic commonality is consistent with the similarity of the attested Ancient Celtic languages. By 900 BC, Phoenicians from Tyre had displaced mariners of the Atlantic North as the dominant sea power at Huelva. This ended the Atlantic Bronze Age in all of Spain, except Galicia, and most of Portugal (see Chapter 4); it probably ended Proto-Celtic as the lingua franca of Atlantic Europe.

Looking at the distribution map (Fig. 3.1), it is striking that the characteristic ALBA metalwork types shun the Pyrenees and Aquitaine. One can see an inverse relationship between ALBA metalwork and surviving non-Indo-European languages. In other words, there were cultural and economic reasons that Celtic was not a sufficiently useful language—despite the R1b Y chromosome—where the Basque language prevailed instead. The shape of the *briga* zone suggests that the stronger Indo-European stream came from the north by sea, bypassing treacherous sailing along the Biscay coast.

Ancestry and people of the past

The Beaker People were of diverse origin. Most of the Proto-Beaker People of the Iberian Peninsula had no steppe ancestry. In the light of the patterns of mass migration revealed by Allentoft et al. and Haak et al., it is therefore doubtful that these Proto-Beaker People spoke Indo-European. The Neo-Beaker People, who coalesced in west-central Europe and then spread to Britain and Ireland, had substantial steppe ancestry and so, by the same reasoning, more probably did speak Indo-European. Both subgroups shared elements of a common culture, ideology, and identity that had originated amongst the presumed non-Indo-European Iberian group. Many from both subgroups also shared a linguistic destiny: the lands they had inhabited in the Copper Age, and their descendants in those lands, spoke languages of the Celtic branch of Indo-European at the beginning of written records. The aim of this chapter has been to reflect on what this changing picture means for the question of Celtic origins.

In historical times it is common for people with very different genetic backgrounds to share important elements of culture, ideology, and identity. Spheres for which this generalization applies include religion and nationality. Many recognize as their group's founding fathers and mothers figures they know have no blood relation to themselves. Some people are unaware that their ancestors changed religion or group loyalty. Parents sometimes withhold this information if they think it would harm their children's chances for social advancement.

The modern exploration of the early traditional literatures of Ireland and Wales often assumes a simpler situation, that the genealogical ancestors of the poets and authors were also the source of their identities and traditional ideas. Anything else could usually be attributed to known texts in Latin.

Two facts, that may no longer be facts, conditioned much of the thinking about the native strand of early Irish and Welsh literature. First, the languages of these literatures were believed to go back to Celts who had migrated from the European mainland during the Iron Age. For this reason, what Irish literature had to say about the Irish Iron Age might be valid cultural evidence—a *Window on the Iron Age* as Kenneth Jackson memorably put it—even if the characters and incidents were fiction. Second, because Irish and Welsh were Indo-European languages, it was expected that they would preserve ideas about heroes, gods, the supernatural, social values, &c., that came from Proto-Indo-European ideology. A methodology resulted in which parallels were expected in Homer, Norse mythology, the Indian Rig Veda, and so on.

These assumptions also led to the negative expectation that early Irish and Welsh literature could have nothing factual to tell us about Ireland and Britain during the Bronze Age or before. But medieval Irish literature does have a lot to say about what happened in Ireland before the Iron Age. Numerous Irish tales focus on the country's *síd* mounds. When these can be located in the landscape, they are, when not natural hills, megalithic collective tombs. Newgrange (*Síd in Broga,* Modern Irish *Brú na Bóinne*), dating to about 3000 BC, is the most famous.

In the traditional scheme of Irish legendary history, the Gaels, that is, the Gaelic-speaking Irish, arrived from Spain and took over about 1700 BC. The previous inhabitants were the *Túatha Dé Danann*. The TDD were the denizens of the *síd* mounds, to which they were confined after relinquishing control of Ireland's surface world to the Gaels led by Míl Espáine. The story is summarized in the opening of the Ulster Cycle tale, *Mesca Ulad* 'The Intoxication of the Ulstermen':

> When the sons of Míl Espáine came to Ireland, they outsmarted the Túatha Dé Danann. Míl's son Amairgen Glúnmár made the division of Ireland, for he was a king-poet and a king-judge. He divided Ireland in two. And he gave the side that was under Ireland to the Túath Dé Danann & the other side to the sons of Míl Espáine [that is] to his own kindred.
>
> The Túath Dé Danann went into the hillocks & *síd* dwellings, as the *síd* places under the earth had been pledged to them...

The assumptions that conditioned 20th-century interpretations of these traditions must change. It now appears more likely that the language that became Gaelic has a continuous history in Ireland since the 3rd millennium BC and that key elements of the founders' culture had first evolved amongst a non-Indo-European people in the megalithic zone of Atlantic Europe.

As Catriona Gibson has recently shown, a shared feature of the Beaker cultures in Britain, Ireland, northern France, and the Iberian Peninsula was the reuse of megalithic monuments. The ways they were reused in these lands were closely parallel, reflecting similar ideas. Single burials were inserted at the margins and entrances to collective tombs, which were often then sealed off or somehow blocked.

As we now know from Olalde et al., the Iberian Proto-Beaker People were genetically similar to the megalith builders of their region, as well as those in pre-Beaker Britain, Ireland, and Brittany. Viewed as gene pools, the Proto-Beaker People were the descendants of the Atlantic Megalithic People. In their genetic ancestry, the Neo-Beaker People who came to Britain and Ireland from the lower Rhine region were different. But in their behaviour and attitude towards the megalithic past they were not so different. The practices by the Beaker subgroups of both ancestries aimed to control and contain the power of the Megalith People and their monuments. Ritualistic reuse symbolizes the end of an earlier age and its people and mastery by new people in a new age. The aggressive expansion of the R1b Y chromosome shows that the Indo-Europeanized Neo-Beaker People were in no doubt about their personal genealogies. But their broader conception of the human past—what might be thought of as their cultural ancestry—was shared with the probably non-Indo-European Proto-Beaker People with an Atlantic Megalithic past.

ACKNOWLEDGEMENTS

Dan Bradley, Volker Heyd, Jim Mallory, David Reich, and Martin Richards read drafts of this chapter and provided invaluable feedback. The collections of linguistic data here, particularly the Palaeohispanic names in the text boxes and maps, are mostly the work of Fernando Fernández. The overall interpretation offered is that of John Koch.

Further reading

Archaeogenetics

It was only about 2013 when full-genome sequencing of ancient DNA became feasible enough to drastically improve our understanding of the origins and relationships of ancient populations and prehistoric migrations. An excellent and accessible introduction to this 'archaeogenetic revolution' is **D. Reich** 2018 *Who We Are and How We Got There*, Oxford, Oxford University Press. For a lucid and concise overview, see **I. Lazaridis** 2018 'The evolutionary history of human populations in Europe', https://arxiv.org/abs/1805.01579v1 [q-bio.E]. Milestone articles with implications for Celtic origins include: **M. E. Allentoft, ... K. Kristiansen** 2015 'Population genomics of Bronze Age Eurasia', *Nature* 522, 167–72; **P. de Barros Damgaard, ... E. Willerslev** 2018 'The first horse herders and the impact of early Bronze Age steppe expansions into Asia', *Science* 10.1126/science.aar7711; **L. M. Cassidy, ... D. G. Bradley** 2016 'Neolithic and Bronze Age migration to Ireland and establishment of the insular Atlantic genome', *Proc. National Academy of Sciences USA* 113/2, 368–73; **A. Goldberg, T. Günther, N. A. Rosenberg, & M. Jakobsson** 2017 'Ancient X chromosomes reveal contrasting sex bias in Neolithic and Bronze Age Eurasian migrations', *Proc. National Academy of Sciences USA* 114/10, 2657–62; **W. Haak, ... D. Reich** 2015 'Massive migration from the steppe was a source for Indo-European languages in Europe', *Nature* 14317; **V. Heyd** 2017 'Kossinna's smile', *Antiquity* 91, 356, 348–59; **E. R. Jones**, et al. 2015 'Upper Palaeolithic genomes reveal deep roots of modern Eurasians', *Nature Communications* 6:8912; **I. Lazaridis & D. Reich** 2017 'Failure to replicate a genetic signal for sex bias in the steppe migration into central Europe', *Proc. National Academy of Sciences USA* 114/20, E3875–E3877; **M. A. Lipson, ... D. Reich** 2017 'Parallel ancient genomic transects reveal complex population history of early European farmers' bioRxiv preprint first posted online Mar. 6, 2017; doi: http://dx.doi.org/10.1101/114488; **R. Martiniano, ... D. G. Bradley** 2017 'The population genomics of archaeological transition in west Iberia: Investigation of ancient substructure using imputation and haplotype-based methods', *PLoS Genet* 13(7): e1006852 https://doi.org/10.1371/journal.pgen.1006852; **I. Mathieson, J. Krause, R. Pinhasi, ... D. Reich** 2018 'The genomic history of southeastern Europe', *Nature* 555, 197–203, doi:10.1038/nature25778; **I. Olalde, ... D. Reich** 2018 'The Beaker Phenomenon and the Genomic Transformation of Northwest Europe', *Nature* 555, 190–196 doi:10.1038/nature25738; **V. M. Narasimhan, ... D. Reich** 2018 'The Genomic Formation of South and Central Asia', bioRxiv preprint first posted online Mar. 31, 2018, doi: http://dx.doi.org/10.1101/292581; **S. Rasmussen, ... E. Willerslev** 2015 'Early Divergent Strains of *Yersinia pestis* in Eurasia 5,000 Years Ago', *Cell* 163, 571–82; **M. Silva, ... M. B. Richards, & P. Soares** 2017 'A genetic chronology for the Indian Subcontinent points to heavily sex-biased dispersals', *BMC Evolutionary Biology* 17:88; **A. Szécsényi-Nagy**, et al. 2017 'The maternal genetic makeup of the Iberian Peninsula between the Neolithic and the Early Bronze Age', *Scientific Reports* 2017, 7:15644; **C. Valdiosera, ... M. Jakobsson** 2018 'Four millennia of Iberian biomolecular prehistory illustrate the impact of prehistoric migrations at the far end of Eurasia', *Proceedings of the National Academy of Sciences* Mar 2018, 115 (13) 3428–3433, doi: 10.1073/pnas.1717762115.

The Beaker People and Europe in the Copper and Early Bronze Ages

The Beaker phenomenon and Early Bronze Age cultures that followed it are now, if anything, even more challenging subjects than ever as a result of unresolved complexities raised by the 'archaeogenetic revolution'. These are some important recent examples of our evolving understanding: **K. Cleary** 2016 'Burial Practices in Ireland during the Late Third Millennium BC: connecting new ideologies with local expressions', *Celtic from the West 3: Atlantic Europe in the Metal Ages—questions of shared language*, Celtic Studies Publications 19, eds Koch, Cunliffe, Cleary, Gibson, 139–78, Oxford, Oxbow Books; **J. Desideri** 2011 *When Beakers met Bell Beakers. An analysis of dental remains,* British Archaeological Reports International Series 2292, Oxford, Archaeopress; **A. P. Fitzpatrick** 2013 'The Arrival of the Bell Beaker Set in Britain and Ireland', *Celtic from the West 2: Rethinking the Bronze Age and the Arrival of Indo-European in Atlantic Europe*, Celtic Studies Publications 16, eds J. T. Koch & B. Cunliffe, 41–70, Oxford, Oxbow Books; **C. D. Gibson** 2016 'Closed for Business of Cultural Change? Tracing the re-use and final blocking of the megalithic tombs during the Beaker Period', *Celtic from the West 3*, 83–110; **R. J. Harrison & V. Heyd** 2007 'The Transformation of Europe in the Third Millennium BC: the Example of 'Le Petit-Chasseur I + III' (Sion, Valais, Switzerland)', *Prähistorische Zeitschrift*, Band S, 129–214; **V. Heyd** 2013 'Europe 2500 to 2200 BC: Between Expiring Ideologies and Emerging Complexity', *The Oxford Handbook of the European Bronze Age*, ed. A. Harding, H. Fokkens, 46–67, Oxford, Oxford University Press; **K. Kristiansen, ... E. Willerslev** 2017 'Re-theorising mobility and the formation of culture and language among the Corded Ware Culture in Europe', *Antiquity* 91/356, 334–47; **S. P. Needham** 2016 'The lost cultures of the halberd bearers: a non-Beaker ideology in later third millennium Atlantic Europe', *Celtic from the West 3*, 40–81.

The steppe (or 'Kurgan') hypothesis of Indo-European origins

The following are accessible presentations of the leading theory of the origin and dispersal of the Indo-European languages: **D. W. Anthony** 2007 *The Horse, the Wheel, and Language: How Bronze-Age Riders from the Eurasian Steppes Shaped the Modern World*, Princeton, Princeton University Press; **D. W. Anthony & D. R. Brown** 2017 'Molecular archaeology and Indo-European linguistics: Impressions from new data', *Usque as radices: Indo-European studies in honour of Birgit Anette Olsen*, Copenhagen Studies in Indo-European 8, eds B. S. S. Hansen, A. Hyllested, A. R. Jørgensen, G. Kroonen, J. H. Larsson, B. N. Whitehead, T. Olander, & T. M. Søborg, 25–54, Copenhagen, Museum Tusculanum Press; **V. G. Childe** 1926 *The Aryans: A study of Indo-European origins,* London, Kegan Paul; **M. Gimbutas** 1981 'The Three Waves of the Kurgan People into Old Europe, 4500–2500 BC', *Anthropologie et archéologie: le cas des premiers âges des Métaux. Actes du Symposium de Sils-Maria, 25–30 septembre 1978*, Archives Suisses Anthr. Générale 43, 2ed. R. Menk, A. Gallay, 113–37; **J. P. Mallory** 1989 *In Search of the Indo-Europeans: Language, Archaeology and Myth*, London, Thames and Hudson; 2013 'Twenty-First Century Clouds over Indo-European Homelands', *Journal of Language Relationship* 9, 145–54.

The theory of Celtic origins in Atlantic Europe

The launching point of the Celtic from the West idea is **B. Cunliffe** 2001 *Facing the Ocean: The Atlantic and its Peoples 8000 BC–AD 1500,* Oxford, Oxford University Press. The case that the Celtic branch of Indo-European formed in Atlantic Europe and before the Iron Age is explained in these more recent publications: **B. Cunliffe** 2010 'Celticization from the West: the Contribution of Archaeology', *Celtic from the West. Alternative Perspectives from Archaeology, Genetics, Language and Literature*, Celtic Studies Publications 15, eds B. Cunliffe & J. T. Koch, 13–38, Oxford, Oxbow Books; 2013 *Britain Begins*, Oxford, Oxford University Press; **J. T. Koch** 2013b 'Out of the Flow and Ebb of the European Bronze Age: Heroes, Tartessos, and Celtic', *Celtic from the West 2: Rethinking the Bronze Age and the Arrival of Indo-European in Atlantic Europe*, Celtic Studies Publications 16, eds J. T. Koch & B. Cunliffe, 101–46, Oxford, Oxbow Books.

Some precocious 20th-century ideas of Celtic origins

The following publications represent important milestones or turning points in 20th-century Celtic studies: **P. Bosch Gimpera** 1942 *The Two Celtic Waves in Spain*, Sir John Rhŷs Memorial Lecture 1939, *Proceedings of the British Academy* 26, London; **M. Dillon** 1975 *Celts and Aryans: Survivals of Indo-European Speech and Society*, Simla, Indian Institute of Advanced Study; **M. Dillon & N. K. Chadwick** 1967 *The Celtic Realms*, New York, New American Library; **K. H. Jackson** 1964 *The Oldest Irish Tradition: A Window on the Iron Age*, Felinfach, Llanerch, 1999, first published, Cambridge, Cambridge University Press; **A. Tovar Llorente**, 1980–2 'The God Lugus in Spain', *Bulletin of the Board of Celtic Studies* 29, 591–9.

Irish origins

Ireland's prehistoric past can be pursued through archaeology, Irish tradition, the Irish language, or synthesis of these. The following studies demonstrate this breadth of approaches: **J. Carey** 1990/91 [1993] 'Time, Memory, and the Boyne Necropolis', *Proc. Harvard Celtic Colloquium* 10/11, 24–36; **J. P. Mallory** 2016 *In Search of the Irish Dreamtime: Archaeology and Early Irish Literature*, London, Thames & Hudson; **W. O'Brien** 2004 *Ross Island: Mining, Metal and Society in Early Ireland*, Bronze Age Studies 6, Galway, National University of Ireland; **J. Uhlich** 2002 'Verbal governing compounds (synthetics) in Early Irish and other Celtic languages', *Transactions of the Philological Society* 100/3, 403–33.

Rock art and funerary stelae

This under-researched area offers a window onto the movement of ideas, people, and potentially languages in later prehistory: **D. Brandherm** 2016 'Stelae, funerary practice, and group identities in the Bronze and Iron Ages of SW Iberia: a moyenne durée perspective', *Celtic from the West 3: Atlantic Europe in the Metal Ages —questions of shared language*, Celtic Studies Publications 19, eds Koch, Cunliffe, Cleary, Gibson, 179–216, Oxford, Oxbow Books; **P. Bueno Ramírez, R. de Balbín Behrmann, R. Barroso Bermejo, E. Cerrillo Cuenca, A. González Cordero, & A. Prada Gallardo** 2011 'Megaliths and stelae in the inner basin of the Tagus river: Santiago de Alcántara, Alconétar and Cañamero (Cáceres, Spain)', *From the Origins: The Prehistory of the Inner Tagus Region*, BAR International Series 2219, eds P. Bueno Ramírez, E. Cerrillo Cuenca, & A. González Cordero, 143–60, Oxford, Archaeopress; **S. Cassen, L. Lescop, V. Grimaud, P. Alvim, P. de Jersey** 2015 'Sites de passage. La représentation de l'arc au cours du Ve millénaire d'après les stèles de Bretagne, des Îles Anglo-Normandes et ae l'Alentejo', *Death as archaeology of transition: thoughts and materials: papers from the II International Conference of Transition Archaeology: Death Archaeology 29th April–1st May 2013*, British Archaeological Reports International Series 2708, eds L. Rocha, P. Bueno Ramírez, & G. Branco, 95–125, Oxford, Archaeopress; **P. Corboud** 2009 'Les stèles anthropomorphes de la nécropole néolithique du Petit-Chasseur à Sion (Valais, Suisse)', *Bulletin d'études préhistoriques et archéologiques alpines* 20, 9–97; **M. Díaz-Guardamino**, 2010 Las estelas decoradas en la Prehistoria de la Península Ibérica, Madrid, Universidad Complutense de Madrid; **D. Y. Telegin & J. P. Mallory** 1994 *The Anthropomorphic Stelae of the Ukraine: The Early Iconography of the Indo-Europeans*, Journal of Indo-European Studies Monograph 11, Washington, D.C., Institute for the Study of Man.

'Old European' (*alteuropäisch*) river names

The new light thrown onto prehistoric Europe's settlement history by the archaeogenetic revolution has brought back into focus the subject of an ancient layer of widespread river names, apparently predating the formation of the attested Indo-European branches. Most of the research has been in German. Amongst the following titles, Kitson's paper includes a good introduction to the subject in English:

H. Bichlmeier 2013 'Analyse und Bewertung der sprachwissenschaftlichen Standards aktueller Forschungen traditioneller Art zur ‚alteuropäischen Hydronymie' aus der Perspektive der heutigen Indogermanistik', *Namenkundliche Informationen* 101/102, 397–437 (online unter: www.namenkundliche-informationen.de); **P. R. Kitson** 1996 'British and European River-Names', *Transactions of the Philological Society* 94/2, 73–118; **H. Krahe** 1964 *Unsere ältesten Flußnamen*, Wiesbaden, Otto Harrassowitz; **W. P. Schmid** 1998 'Das baltische Zentrum in der alteuropäischen Hydronymie', *Baltistica* 33(2), 145–53.

The Atlantic Bronze Age

Studies of Bronze Age metalwork show that contacts continued in the post-Beaker period, linking the British Isles, north-west France, and the western Iberian Peninsula, and that they intensified greatly between 1300 and 900 BC: **D. Brandherm** 2007 'Algunas reflexiones sobre el bronce inicial en el noroeste peninsular. La cuestion del llamado horizonte "Montelavar"', *CuPAUAM (Cuadernos de Prehistoria y Arqueología de Universidad Autónoma de Madrid)* 33, 69–90; **S. Gerloff** (with J. P. Northover) 2010 *Atlantic Cauldrons and Buckets of the Late Bronze and Early Iron Ages in Western Europe: With a Review of Comparable Vessels from Central Europe and Italy*, Prähistorische Bronzefunde II, 18, Stuttgart, Franz Steiner; **P.-Y. Milcent** 2012 *Le temps des élites en Gaule atlantique: chronologie des mobiliers et rythmes de constitution des dépots métalliques dans le contexte européen (XIIIe–VIIe av. J.-C.).* Presses Universitaires de Rennes.

The Celticity of the South-western or 'Tartessian' inscriptions

The evidence, first recognized by Correa, that a Celtic language was contained in Early Iron Age inscriptions from southern Portugal and south-west Spain has more recently been explored in greater detail: **J. A. Correa Rodríguez** 1992 'La epigrafía tartesia', *Andalusien zwischen Vorgeschichte und Mittelalter*, eds D. Hertel & J. Untermann, 75–114, Cologne, Böhlau; **T. Kaufman**, *Notes on the Decipherment of Tartessian as Celtic*, Journal of Indo-European Monograph Series 62, Washington DC, Institute of the Study of Man; **J. T. Koch** 2013 *Tartessian: Celtic in the South-west at the Dawn of History*, Celtic Studies Publications 13, Aberystwyth. Revised & expanded edition, first edition published 2009; 2018 *Common Ground and Progress on the Celtic of the South-western (SW) Inscriptions*, Aberystwyth, Centre for Advanced Welsh and Celtic Studies, e-book.

Ancient non-Indo-European languages of western Europe and the Hamito-Semitic hypothesis

The theory that the Celtic languages reflect contact between Indo-European and non-Indo-European languages goes back over a century to Sir John Morris-Jones and remains credible. The following include studies of the history of Basque, a non-Indo-European language known to have been in contact with Celtic: **J. Gorrochategui Churruca**, 2013 'Linguistique et peuplement en Aquitania', *L'âge du Fer en Aquitaine et sur ses marges. Mobilité des hommes, diffusion des idées, circulation des biens dans l'espace européenà l'âge du Fer. Actes du 35e Colloque international de l'AFEAF (Bordeaux, 2–5 juin 2011)*, Aquitania Supplément 30, eds A. Colin, F. Verdin, 17–32; **S. Hewitt** 2016 'The Question of a Hamito-Semitic Substratum in Insular Celtic and Celtic from the West', *Celtic from the West 3: Atlantic Europe in the Metal Ages—questions of shared language*, Celtic Studies Publications 19, eds Koch, Cunliffe, Cleary, Gibson, 407–30, Oxford, Oxbow Books; **L. Michelena [Koldo Mitxelena]** 1977 *Fonética histórica vasca*, 2nd edn. (first published 1961), Donostia–San Sebastián; **J. Morris Jones** 1900 'Pre-Aryan syntax in Insular Celtic' (Appendix B), *The Welsh People*, eds J. Rhŷs & D. Brynmor-Jones, 617–41, London, T. Fisher Unwin; **R. L. Trask** 1997 *The History of Basque*, London, Routledge.

Milestone works of historical–comparative Celtic linguistics

In purely linguistic studies, the story of the Celtic languages and their descent from Proto-Indo-European has been remarkably stable, undergoing incremental and evolutionary, rather than revolutionary, change, since the time of Edward Lhuyd over 300 years ago. Characteristically, standard handbooks have tended to outlive their authors: **H. Lewis & H. Pedersen** 1989 *A Concise Comparative Celtic Grammar*, 3rd edn. Göttingen, Vandenhoeck and Ruprecht, first published 1937; **E. Lhuyd** 1707 *Archaeologia Britannica, Giving some Account of the Languages, Histories and Customs of the Original Inhabitants of Great Britain: from Collections and Observations in Travels through Wales, Cornwal, Bas-Bretagne, Ireland and Scotland. Vol. I. Glossography*, Oxford, The Theater; **J. Rhŷs** 1891–94 'The Celts and the other Aryans of the P and Q groups', *Transactions of the Philological Society*, 1891–94, 104–31; **R. Thurneysen**, 1975 *A Grammar of Old Irish*, trans. D. A. Binchy & O. Bergin, rev. and enlarged edn., Dublin, Dublin Institute for Advanced Studies, first published 1946.

Primary sources for Celts in the west and Tartessos

Primary written evidence for the both the Celts and the kingdom of Tartessos in Atlantic Europe is found in the Histories of Herodotus, and recent archaeological evidence from the town of Huelva in south-west Spain is now seen as confirming that this was the urban core of Tartessos: **P. M. Freeman** 1996 'The Earliest Greek Sources on the Celts', *Études Celtiques* 32, 11–48; 2010 'Ancient References to Tartessos', *Celtic from the West: Alternative Perspectives from Archaeology, Genetics, Language and Literature*, Celtic Studies Publications 15, eds B. Cunliffe & J. T. Koch, 303–34, Oxford, Oxbow Books; **F. González de Canales, L. Serrano, & J. Llompart** 2006 'The precolonial Phoenician emporium of Huelva, *ca.* 900–770 BC: A résumé', *BAbesch (Bulletin Antieke Beschaving, Annual Papers on Classical Archaeology)* 81, 13–29; ***Herodotus****: The Histories*, trans. T. Holland, 2013, London, Penguin; **J. T. Koch**, 2014 'Once again, Herodotus, the Κελτοί, the source of the Danube, and the Pillars of Hercules', *Celtic Art in Europe: making connections. Essays in honour of Vincent Megaw on his 80th birthday*, eds C. Gosden, S. Crawford, & K. Ulmschneider, 6–18, Oxford, Oxbow Books; **A. Mederos Martín** 2006 'Fenicios en Huelva, en el siglo X a.C., durante el reinado de Hîrãm I de Tiro', *Spal* 15, 167–88.

CHAPTER FOUR

CONNECTIVITY IN ATLANTIC EUROPE DURING THE BRONZE AGE (2800–800 BC)

Kerri Cleary & Catriona Gibson

Summary

THIS chapter explores a two-thousand-year time period during which key technological innovations paired with associated social and ideological developments reflected the fluctuating interconnectivity of Atlantic Europe. Archaeologists have identified these through specific changes in the sets of material evidence uncovered, and, viewing them from different geographical scales of analysis, are able to explore questions of connectivity. The approach taken by the Atlantic Europe and the Metal Ages project was to collate a diverse range of evidence attesting to long-distance contact and interaction, comprising artefact types, such as pottery and metal objects, and their associated contexts, including burials, hoards, settlements, and ritual sites.

From the later Neolithic onwards (*c.* 3300 BC), there is increased evidence for the spread of more widely shared ideologies and technologies, as indicated by the extensive distribution of specific architectural styles, object types, and artistic motifs. Comparable megalithic architecture in the form of passage graves and later, open-air monuments such as timber or stone circles and henges suggest that many regions of Atlantic Europe became more closely connected. Integral elements of the associated belief systems active during this time included geometric motifs decorated on stones in megalithic contexts, and a distinctive ceramic style known as Grooved Ware, which was first adopted in Orkney or mainland Scotland, spreading southwards, reaching Ireland and southern England by around 3000/2900 BC. The widespread adoption of this geometric or Atlantic style of decoration has been linked to the increased importance of the sea as a means of communication. These supra-regional connections (the Atlantic 'maritories') indicate that rather than being on the periphery, these areas of western Europe were closely linked from an early stage, not only for the transfer of knowledge and ideologies, but also for the movement of people, animals and objects.

After *c.* 2700 BC these networks of interaction become both more intensive and extensive. It has long been postulated that this occurred in tandem with the inception of metal (initially copper and sheet gold, followed by tin bronze). Throughout Europe, this connectivity is most clearly manifest in a shift towards a new rite of single burial, and the widespread adoption of a new ceramic style: the Beaker. The Beaker pot, a vessel with an S-shaped profile and distinctive impressed banded decoration, originated in central Portugal around the Tagus estuary. It is known as the Maritime style, as it initially had a predominantly Atlantic coastal distribution. From there this pottery style spread north and east into central Europe, in connection with metal supply and exchange. A pre-existing single-grave tradition, commonly known as the Corded Ware culture, had emerged in the middle Rhine *c.* 3000 BC from where it radiated outwards to most of continental Europe. Around 2500 BC the social and ideological traits associated with both of these 'cultural' packages effectively collided in a fusion corridor between the middle and lower Rhine (below Fig. 4.13). It was in this region that the Corded Ware vessels merged with the Maritime style to create a new Bell Beaker form decorated with twisted cord motifs, and known as All-Over-Ornamented (AOO) or All-Over-Corded (AOC). It was also at this juncture that the rite of single burial was adopted into the Beaker Complex, and a standardization in body orientation in accordance with sex was established. This had already been evident in the Corded Ware Complex, but the ways in which Beaker males and females were aligned now changed in these Rhineland regions. While males continued to be buried on their left sides and females on their right, they were now aligned north-south rather than east-west. It is also only around this time that a more eclectic set of grave goods accompanied the burials, including objects associated with hunting, combat, and personal adornment. Items such as stone bracers (wristguards), daggers, arrowheads, and v-perforated buttons, often made from non-local materials, became increasingly common. This so-called consolidated Beaker phenomenon was now adopted and adapted throughout parts of western Europe in diverse ways; it was interleaved with various regional traditions and had different durations of popularity. To some extent this may have been influenced by the availability, access to and supply of metal ores.

By around 2000 BC many Atlantic seaway zones had begun to express a range of regional burial traditions, with associated pot styles. In Britain this development is referred to as a 'fissioning' horizon, i.e. one where there was a fragmentation of the supra-regional Beaker network. A series of novel, yet perhaps disparate, burial traditions now unfolded. In southern regions of Britain, north-west France and, to a lesser extent, north-west Iberia, a number of seemingly 'élite' or high-status burials emerged, accompanied by a lavish array of exotic objects. At the same time in Ireland, similar objects were not chosen for deposition with the dead, but instead were placed within hoards or singly in water contexts, perhaps as votive offerings. Along with burials however, the tradition of burying objects of gold and bronze in the ground or water increased markedly from the river Douro in Portugal northwards.

Towards the middle of the 2nd millennium BC, there are further developments in the social, economic, and ideological concerns of these communities. Landscapes

4.1. Late Bronze Age shale boat from Caergwrle, north Wales.

(© National Museum of Wales)

became more intensively managed through the creation of field systems and associated roundhouse settlements. Organized, divided landscapes are not ubiquitous in all Atlantic regions, and have only been identified in parts of Britain and Ireland and across the Channel in Brittany, and the Low Countries. In western Iberia, small settlements also began to emerge, but were more connected to cattle pastoralism, and associated with extensive droveways traversing the landscape rather than bounded fields. One more widely recognized change throughout western Europe is that by the Middle Bronze Age there is no longer a strict division between domestic and funerary space. In addition, types of pots accompanying or containing human remains compared to those from domestic contexts become indistinguishable. Cremation practices were now favoured over inhumation in most regions, and by *c.* 1200 BC there was a significant decrease in the formality of the burial record. This coincides with two further trends: a decline in the visibility of the grave architecture, and an increase in the fragmentation and disarticulation of human remains compared to the previous pattern, usually retaining whole bodies. Furthermore, the dead were now placed in a variety of places, including

4.2. Selection of bronze weapons and tools from the estuary find at Huelva, on the south-western coast of Spain.

(photo taken in National Museum, Madrid © Catriona Gibson)

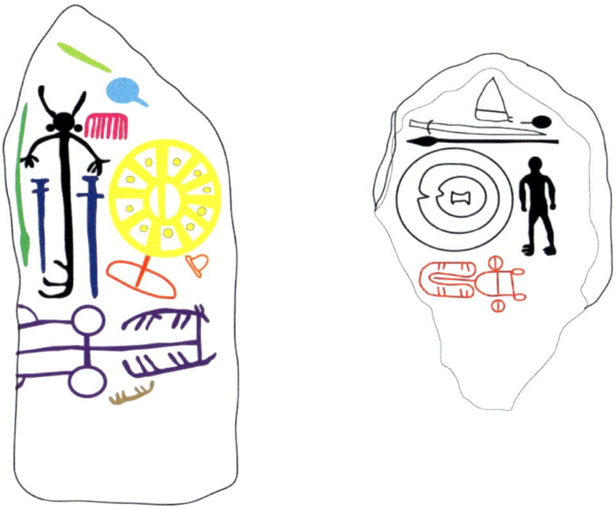

El Viso I, Córdoba

Zarza de Montánchez, Cáceres

4.3. Wheeled vehicles depicted on Late Bronze Age stelae from Spain.

(© Catriona Gibson)

domestic spaces (such as entrance postholes of roundhouses, associated storage pits, and enclosing ditches).

Around the transition between the Middle and Late Bronze Age, palisaded and ditched enclosure settlements become more common. An augmentation in defensive sites is evident in the emergence of hilltop enclosures and hill-forts during the Late Bronze Age, reaching an apogee towards the turn of the 1st millennium BC. Few of these early examples have substantial evidence for settlement, and many may instead have been communal gathering places, additionally functioning as exchange centres with extensive storage facilities. These are impressive and monumental sites, frequently encircled with several defensive circuits; they would have required a considerable labour force to build. It is also feasible that they were closely connected with the various strands of exchange and trade, including that of metal.

At this time, in tandem with the decreased visibility of burials, there is an inverse pattern in the deposition of metalwork, where hoards containing weapons, tools, and ornaments become much more prominent; in several regions such as southern England and Brittany, as many as several thousand objects might be contained within these hoards. The metal objects were often decommissioned in similar ways throughout the Atlantic regions. For example, both swords and spearheads were deposited in wet locations in a broken or warped state.

This synopsis has outlined the principal sets of evidence that will now be explored in more detail to tease out and interpret the ebbs and flows of connectivity and changing networks of interaction throughout Atlantic regions between the Late Neolithic and Late Bronze Age. One aspect that helps us comprehend how the shared characteristics between different regions of Atlantic Europe came about is the potential routes and means by which prehistoric travel through land- and seascapes was possible (see Text Box 4.1).

Text Box 4.1. Traversing the seas, travelling the land

Voyages in prehistory were undertaken by different people for a multitude of purposes—colonization, creating and maintaining social contact and exchange, fishing and hunting expeditions, fleeing hostilities, participation in ritualized journeys, and so on. When we think about how people were connected at this time we must consider the means by which they were able to travel and transport belongings, which may have included animals. In prehistory, water undoubtedly provided the most efficient way to move over long distances. Much debate has surrounded the types of boats used and the level of seafaring and navigational knowledge required to sail the Atlantic coast. It has been suggested that a seven- to nine-day open-sea crossing from Brittany to Ireland in a paddled vessel would have been possible, although this might have involved intermediate stopovers in south-west Britain or the Isles of Scilly. Similarly, the main route from north-west Iberia directly to Brittany may have been predominantly in open-sea conditions, where possible avoiding the dangerous Bay of Biscay coastline. Most journeys, however, probably involved travelling along the coast within sight of land and landfalls in the form of natural harbours and tidal rivers, such as along much of the coast of south- and north-western Iberia, Brittany, the English Channel, Irish Sea, and the western Isles of Scotland. Furthermore, with the exception of the south-eastern part of the Bay of Biscay, many offshore islands could have been used for intermediary stops. Accessing these 'corridors of communication' along the Atlantic seaways would have required navigating several interlinked sections of coastline that also connected with overland routes along major riverways (e.g. the Tagus, Loire, and Thames).

By 2800 BC almost any type of raft and boat could have been built and used on inland waterways, but only those with propulsion and steering, such as sails, paddles and oars, would be suitable for seafishing and coastal voyages. From the earliest times hide or currach boats, and possibly paired logboats, were used at sea. The oldest plank boats in Europe, dating from the Early Bronze Age onwards, have been discovered in Britain, and include examples from North Ferriby and Kilnsea on the Humber estuary, along with the famous Dover boat, yet only the latter has definitive evidence of sea worthiness. Offshore artefacts recovered from the seabed, such as in the mouth of the Odiel River opposite Huelva, the English Channel and North Sea areas have traditionally been interpreted as the result of shipwrecks, or 'trade interrupted', although some at least may also represent Bronze Age depositional practices (see below) in a marine context. The Langdon Bay assemblage, recovered approximately 500m offshore and 3km from the site of the Dover boat, consists of some 360 Middle–Late Bronze Age tools, weapons and ornaments and is believed to represent a combination of cargo, ship's equipment and personal possessions of the crew and passengers. Stylistically, the objects may attest to a diverse range of origins from Brittany in the west to northern Germany in the east, while metal analysis identified at least three different source areas on the continent. The Sotteville-sur-Mer gold twisted torcs, dredged up by a trawler 5.5km off the Normandy coastline, are deemed to be a later Bronze Age shipwreck of Irish origin.

Although the deposit of over 400 bronze objects, mostly weapons of Atlantic origin, found at Huelva in southern Spain was re-interpreted as a ritual deposit rather than a shipwreck, it still hints at

Text Box 4.1 (continued)

the importance and intensity of maritime trade in the Late Bronze Age. Many of the sword blades were deliberately warped and broken prior to deposition, and its discovery at the significant junction of the Odiel and Tinto rivers suggests that these may represent a series of votive offerings to ensure safe onwards travel, or give thanks on a successful return (above Fig. 1.4, Fig. 4.2). To continue these journeys after arrival on the mainland may have required the transfer of people, animals and goods into smaller vessels, perhaps rafts and logboats, to utilize river arteries. Wheeled carts may also have been used, possibly drawn by oxen or horses, depending on the terrain and available resources. Evidence for early cattle traction in the Atlantic façade has been suggested by the discovery of an Early Bronze Age wooden yoke from Loch Nell in Argyll, Scotland and rock art depicting scenes of horse-riding from the south-western coast of Galicia has been dated to the transition between the 3rd and 2nd millennia BC. Cheek-pieces and bridle-bits of antler and bronze, such as those from Heathery Burn in Northumberland, north-east England, Easter Essenside in Selkirk, Scotland, and Moynagh Lough in Ireland indicate that horse-riding was practiced in Britain and Ireland by the Late Bronze Age, if not earlier. In addition, many depictions of wheeled vehicles are noted on Iberian Late Bronze Age stelae, which exhibit uncanny similarities with examples engraved on Scandinavian rock art.

Ancient routeways in the form of man-made sunken lanes (holloways) are known across southern England, western France, and northern Spain. On several, such as the South Downs Way in Wessex, or the Offa's Dyke Path along the Welsh-English border, hundreds of Early Bronze Age barrows, representing linear cemeteries along the routeways, suggest they had early origins. These are sometimes referred to as 'barrow roads' and may have an antiquity of 4000 years or more. In addition, direct evidence for prehistoric trackways has been uncovered in the Irish midlands, and boggy regions in Britain, particularly the Somerset wetlands, where waterlogged conditions have preserved paths constructed of brushwood, hurdles or planks.

The 'Beaker package'

Introduction

In comparison to what both preceded and succeeded it, the emergence and spread of the Bell Beaker phenomenon from *c.* 2800–2100 BC is generally epitomized as the first time large swathes of Europe from Hungary in the east to Ireland in the west adopted a comparable suite of object types, though often with regional twists. The spread of this so-called 'Beaker package' is most evident in the burial sphere, and along with the eponymous Beaker pot, other grave goods included arrowheads, bracers, daggers, and ornaments. In many countries, such as Poland, Hungary, England, and Scotland this development was accompanied by a gradual change from collective to single burial rites, traditionally thought to mark a profound departure from the previous Neolithic traditions and implying a new shared ideology in the way that death was expressed, one that celebrated personal rather than group

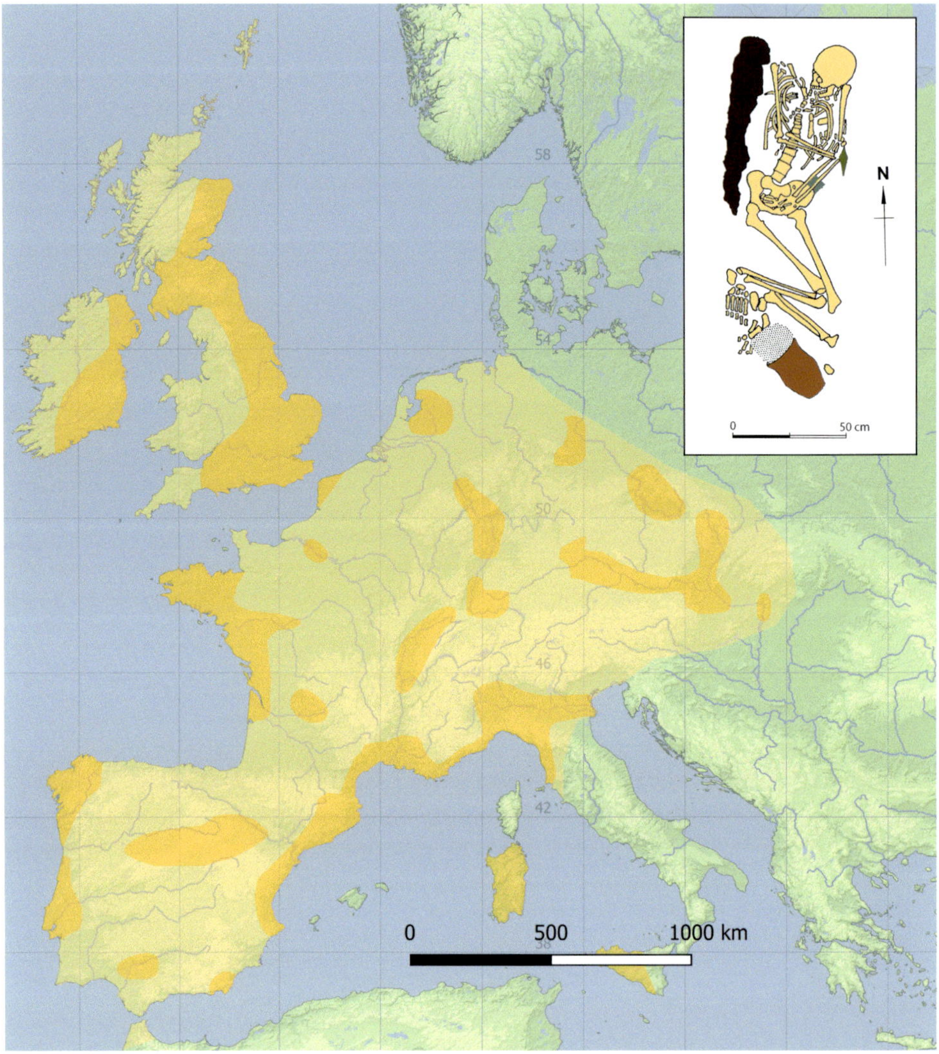

4.4. Distribution of Bell Beaker phenomenon (darker orange shading marks principal Beaker concentrations) and an example of a 'classic Beaker burial' from Barnack, Cambridgeshire.

(after Donaldson 1977, 209)

identity. In many parts of Europe the burial evidence implies the widespread adherence of rites and rules governing the way that the body was arranged and oriented. Less discussed, however, are Beaker-using areas, such as Ireland and western Iberia which did not systematically follow these conventions.

As early as 1912, the Beakers were interpreted as representing a classic example of an ethnic group or 'race' of migrants, but by the 1970s interpretations focused on the adoption of a desirable 'symbolic' or 'ceremonial' package rather than a spread of people. In the last few years, several important research projects have employed novel scientific techniques including oxygen and strontium isotope and ancient DNA (aDNA) analyses (see Chapter 6) that lend detail to the 'human' dimension of this phenomenon, and the types and scales of mobility involved. Both techniques are employed in different ways; the isotope compositions in tooth enamel can provide information about where an individual spent their childhood, while aDNA can provide a longer but temporally less precise view, from genetic kinship to entire population histories. The recent Beaker People project aimed to determine the extent to which the movement of people was bound up in the spread of the Beaker package from the continent across Britain. To achieve this it analysed the strontium and oxygen isotopes of over 260 skeletons dating between 2400–1500 BC. The results indicated that just over a third of all individuals (equally males and females) had probably moved during their lifetimes, however this was mostly small-scale or regional. There was no suggestion of an initial mass immigration of male warriors or entrepreneurs from the continent, rather movement involved small groups of people or lone individuals. Notable exceptions to this rule include the Amesbury Archer and some of the Boscombe Bowmen, who may have travelled to the Stonehenge region from the Alps and Wales or Brittany respectively. A middle-aged male from Bee Low, in the Peak District, may also have migrated there from continental Europe.

A recent flurry of aDNA studies has to some extent contradicted the conclusions from the isotope analysis of Beaker-date burials. Several separate studies have employed data from over 350 individuals dating to 3900–1200 BC. Preliminary results suggest that so-called steppe genes from central Eurasia were introduced to Europe during the 3rd millennium BC and this steppe ancestry appears to have quickly spread to central Europe, Italy, southern, and Atlantic France, Britain and Ireland, replacing Britain's Neolithic gene pool within a few hundred years. These studies assume this westward mobility of genes occurred in tandem with the introduction of the 'Beaker package' and have led to a resurgence of migratory explanations for the spread of the Beaker phenomenon. Understandably these initial conclusions have been grabbing the headlines, particularly when they have implied the almost complete removal of the indigenous population of Britain in a relatively rapid timeframe. It should be noted, however, that the datasets used to identify these patterns are still rather small, and the results drawn may change in

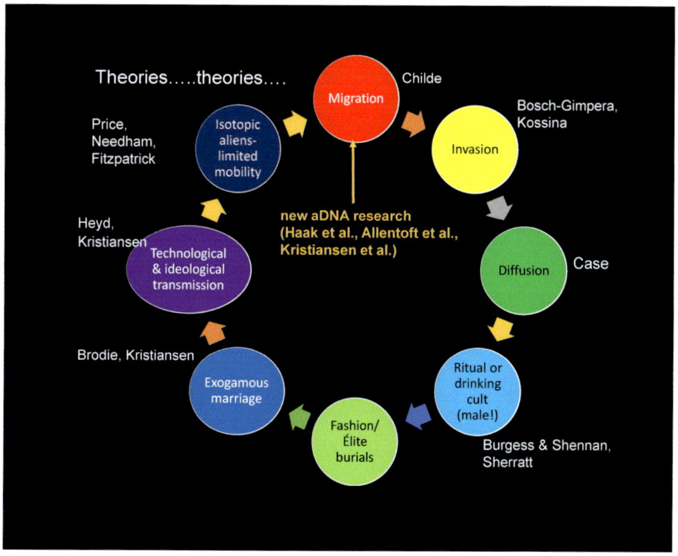

4.5. Cycle of interpretations for the Bell Beaker phenomenon.
(© Catriona Gibson)

the light of further research. For example, the analysis of aDNA from 37 Beaker-associated burials from Iberia has shown that their genes have very little affinity to those of the Beaker-using individuals from north-western and central Europe, leading to more questions about the connections between mobility and Beakers. Overall, in just over a century, interpretations of the Beaker phenomenon have now swung full circle from invasion to diffusion to changing ideologies and fashions back to migration and possibly invasion again!

Iberian Beakers

As already mentioned, the earliest known Beaker pots come from the Tagus estuary in central Portugal, dating to *c.* 2800–2700 BC, making the lack of standardized Beaker burial in western Iberia all the more intriguing. As we will see below, the Beaker cultural package did not become fully formed or adopted in Iberia until several hundred years after its emergence, partly as a result of Corded Ware influences from the east. If the widespread and relatively rapid adoption of the Beaker package was bound up with the desire for metal, particularly copper, tin, and gold, perhaps this influenced the lack of its wholesale adoption not only in Iberia, but also in Ireland and parts of France. Exploitation of copper ores was already established across the Iberian Peninsula and regions within France (e.g. the Paris Basin) and Ireland (see below) prior to the adoption of Beakers. Early mining sites dating from about 3000 BC onwards are known throughout Spain and include Cabezo Juré in Huelva and El Milagro and La Profunda, both in Asturias. As there was an abundant supply of minerals, any attempts to control and dominate supply would have been difficult. These sites generally comprised informal workshops and small temporary settlements, and production was likely undertaken on a domestic level, possibly on a seasonal basis. Some larger, fortified settlements with internal workshops such as Zambujal, Leceia, and Vila Nova de São Pedro, situated in the Tagus estuary, imply that in certain cases, copper production was more intensively controlled and specialized. In the last decade or so, the number of Chalcolithic ditched-enclosure sites known in western Iberia has increased on an exponential scale, mainly due to large infrastructure projects and aerial photographic analysis. Many of these sites were also likely involved in small-scale copper production.

Unlike Britain, where Beaker burials were almost exclusively in flat graves, stone-lined cists, and later under small barrows, greater diversity is evident in Iberian early Beaker burials. Many were placed in earlier megalithic monuments—either through continued use or re-use and enlargement of their chambers. Most individuals were found partially or fully disarticulated, indicating a persistence of Neolithic burial rites. Occasionally complete crouched inhumations were placed in discrete cists inserted into chambers and accompanied by personal grave goods, but these tend to be later in date (post-2200 BC). Other funerary contexts include pits and underground tombs (hypogaea) associated with a variety of body treatments and manipulations. Some of the larger hypogaea show continuity in use spanning the Late Neolithic to the Early Bronze Age (1000 years or more), and witness both inhumation and cremation practiced simultaneously, as at Carrascal and Perdigões, both in central Portugal. Accompanying grave goods, such as pots, weapons and ornaments, are like the human remains, generally fragmentary. The variety of funerary treatments suggest that a similarly wide range of burial ideologies and rituals were held during this time.

Irish Beakers

Between 2450 and 2200 BC, Beakers were the only pottery type used on the island of Ireland, although the majority of these vessels have been recovered from settlement contexts and, as in western Iberia, there was a lack of standardized Beaker burial. Only a small number of early, continental-style Beakers (AOO or AOC), are known and the same is true of Atlantic-style Maritime Beakers. Indeed, the insular hybridization of Bell Beaker pottery, combining elements from the early Atlantic tradition with those of north-western Europe and Britain, occurred very soon after the first appearance of these pots, before 2400 BC. For example, both Irish-styled Beakers and International vessels have been found together at the Hill of Rath and Faughart, in County Louth and Dunboyne, County Meath. A few late-style Beakers also occur and probably extended in use to overlap with a new ceramic, the Bowl Tradition, beginning 2200/2150 BC, representing an insular adoption of the individual burial rite and contemporary with the main *floruit* of later Beakers in Britain (see below).

Burials directly associated with Beakers in Ireland are scarce and it appears that people did not feel the need to use these new-style pots as grave goods, or indeed any of the other items from the so-called Beaker package, such as v-perforated buttons, stone bracers, copper tanged daggers/knives, gold lunulae and discs, the majority of which similarly occur in non-funerary contexts. Where Beaker-period burial has been identified, collective rather than individual burial generally predominated. Many were cremations rather than inhumations, and burial in older megaliths and megalithic cists with cairns was practiced, as well as the re-emergence of megalithic building in the form of wedge tombs, which appeared across the island in the period 2540–2300 BC. Evidently the need to continue pre-existing burial rites practiced from at least the Middle Neolithic onwards initially out-weighed the desire to adopt the 'Beaker individual burial rite'.

The emergence of these wedge-shaped gallery graves at this time is a particularly interesting phenomenon; some scholars have favoured external influences, from regions such as north-west France, others have seen them as a purely indigenous re-invention of earlier monuments, and still others have argued for a combination of the two. These wedge tombs have also been linked to a larger group of contemporary monuments found in Ireland and other Atlantic regions, including Wales, northern England and Scotland. Known as stone circles, these embodied widely shared

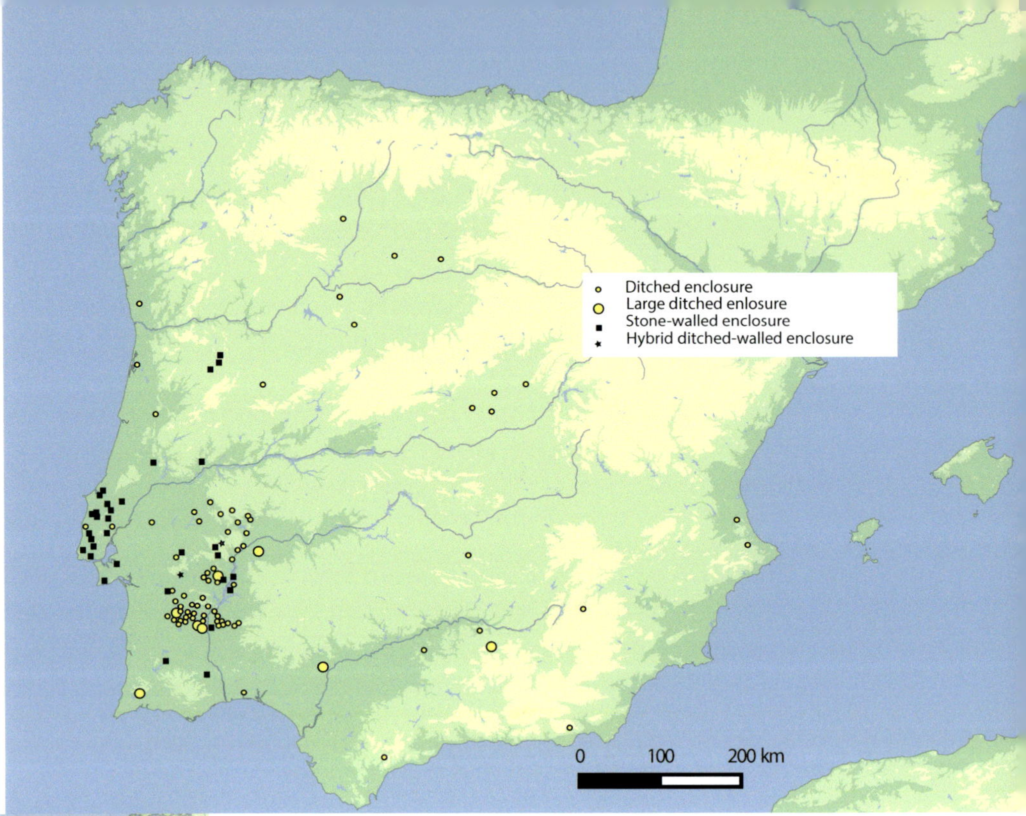

4.6. (right) **Distribution of Late Neolithic–Chalcolithic enclosures in Iberia.**

(© Catriona Gibson from AEMA database)

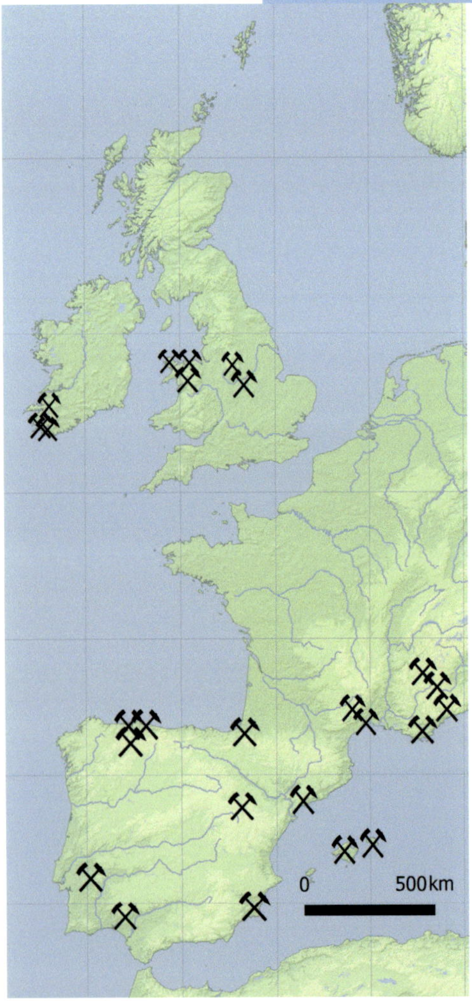

4.7. (lower left) **Distribution of prehistoric copper mining sites/ districts.**

(after O'Brien 2015, fig. 1.10)

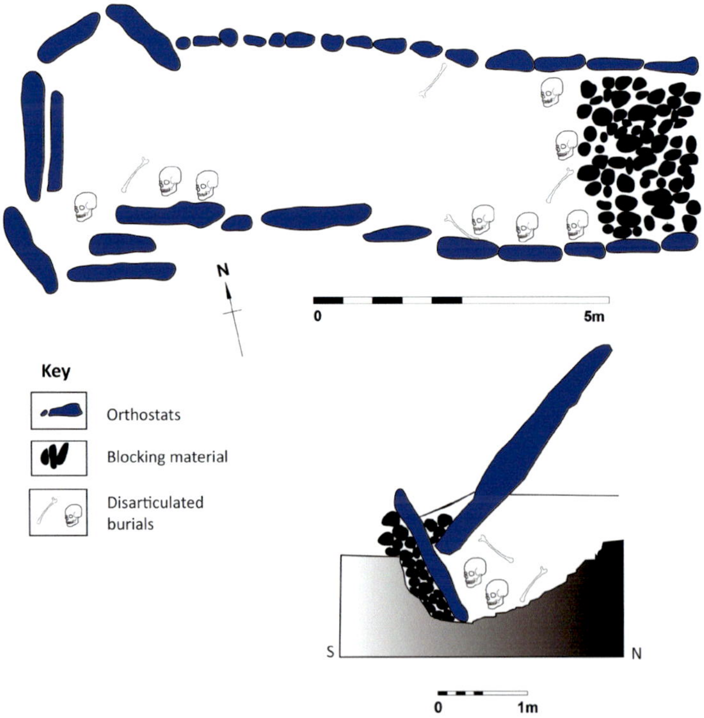

4.8. (lower right) **Disarticulated Beaker burials in Neolithic megalithic tomb at Monte Abraão, Sintra, Portugal.**

(© Catriona Gibson; after Leisner 1965, fig. 36)

ideas and common characteristics; the occurrence of cup-marks, quartz and other coloured stones, associations with fire and sometimes burials, and recurring south to south-west orientations, linked to either the setting sun or movements of the moon. This ideology is also evident in other practices at this time, including the wedge tombs, which generally open to the west and align on the setting sun (see below).

By the middle of the 3rd millennium BC Ireland also held an important role in the earliest copper metallurgy; the extraction of copper ores at Ross Island in County Kerry was underway from at least 2400 BC and the mines remained active until *c.* 1900 BC, most likely on a seasonal or part-time basis. The archaeological excavation indicated that the earliest mining techniques were introduced as an already developed expertise, leading to speculation that the know-how must have come from the continent, with similar metallurgical practices underway in Atlantic France, south-eastern France, Iberia, and northern Italy. The metal exploited was primarily used to make flat axeheads, but also daggers and halberds: items that were exchanged across Ireland into parts of England, Scotland, and Wales, such as the three flat bronze axes found on the slopes below Moel Arthur hillfort in Denbighshire. Of the British and Irish copper objects analysed to date and assigned to the period before *c.* 2200 BC, over 70% have a Ross Island ore fingerprint. Throughout the later 3rd millennium the smelting undertaken in Ireland was relatively sophisticated, and this expertise in the mechanical attributes of copper, including the ability to re-melt and re-model, ultimately permeated outwards, widely occurring in Britain after 2200 BC (see Chapter 5).

4.9. Recent excavation of a wedge tomb on Roughan Hill, County Clare, Ireland.

(© Ros Ó Maoldúin, The Irish Fieldschool of Prehistoric Archaeology, NUIG)

British Beakers

The earliest Beakers in Britain are from southern England—specifically Wessex—dating between 2420–2340 BC. Rather than exhibiting inspiration from Atlantic regions (Maritime style), the majority of these Beaker pots tend to be decorated with twisted cord motifs, representing the AOO or AOC styles that originated in central Europe, developing out of the Corded Ware traditions. While they are almost always found in funerary contexts, in contrast to other Atlantic regions including western Iberia, Ireland, Brittany, and the Paris Basin, they are more often found as single burials. These tend to relate to deep pits, and inhumations were often placed in wood-lined graves or coffins, occasionally covered by small mounds or barrows. The burials were predominantly oriented roughly north-south and individuals were in crouched positions; the males were regularly placed on their left sides and the females on their right, a gender-linked convention adhered to in other European regions where the single burial tradition was also adopted. While grave goods were often restricted to one or more Beaker pots, and perhaps a flint tool or knife, some individuals were accompanied by a variety of objects that may attest to an eclectic range of origins. For example, the adult male buried in a timber-lined grave at Chilbolton, Hampshire, was adorned with two pairs of gold ear or hair ornaments, and a necklace of gold and shale beads, while a bronze dagger and a strike-a-light made from iron pyrites had been placed near his feet.

In Scotland, specifically along the west coast and in the north-east, Beakers appear about 100 years later than Wessex (*c.* 2340–2250 BC) and radiocarbon dates support their gradual spread from south to north. While individuals were also interred in simple pit graves or stone cists, they were generally oriented east-west and this divergence from the north-south alignment may reflect different burial ideologies. In Yorkshire the majority of burials were also oriented east-west, and perhaps as Beakers spread northwards, new sets of cosmological practices and religious beliefs associated with the rising and setting of the sun were reinforced, such as through motifs on mobile objects (see below). Solar ideologies had already been established in some Atlantic regions since the Neolithic, including the Atlantic coast at the well known sites of Maes Howe in Orkney, Bryn Celli Ddu in Anglesey, and Newgrange in Ireland. Early graves were generally focused in the Highlands and Islands in the north and west of Scotland, with a rapid dissemination into the fertile southern lowlands. Although most of the early burials were accompanied only by pots, as at Sorisdale, in the Inner Hebrides, or Upper Largie, in Argyll and Bute, one of the potentially earliest Bell Beaker burials in northern Britain was the well-furnished Kirkhaugh cairn in Northumberland, and like the Amesbury Archer, the grave goods included a pair of gold basket ornaments and a cushion stone (thought to form part of a metalworking tool kit). In both instances, the individuals interred were considered to be precocious metalworkers from abroad who spread this innovative technology more widely across Britain.

Text Box 4.2. All that glitters .... gold objects of adornment

A variety of gold objects are strongly associated with the 'Beaker package' and continued in use into the Early Bronze Age. Amongst the earliest gold objects in Britain and Ireland are ear or hair ornaments, known as 'basket ornaments'. These can be distinguished by two style-regions; a predominantly Iberian distribution and a British distribution, the latter is typified by the Amesbury Archer grave assemblage and is believed to be an insular response to the Iberian style. These objects are contemporary with or slightly earlier than the earliest gold flat discs (also known as sun-discs), which date to 2400–2200 BC and probably represent adornments for clothing. Examples of these early discs are known from the already mentioned Banc Ty'nddôl in Wales, Kirk Andrews on the Isle of Man, several sites in southern England (Wiltshire, Oxfordshire and Kent), Ireland (un-provenanced), Moëlan and Belz in Brittany, and Cabeceiras de Basto in northern Portugal. A slightly later date of 2200–1900 BC has been attributed to many of the Irish-style discs that are contemporary with gold lunulae. The latter objects appear to have evolved out of the primary Beaker tradition and represent large, crescent-shaped neck ornaments, with three examples of the Classical style also found in Cornwall, which has recently been postulated as a source of raw gold. Outside of Ireland, lunulae of the Provincial style dominate, with examples known from northern Britain, southern Scotland, north-western and western France and Belgium, with lunula-type ornaments also known from Denmark and northern and western Iberia, such as at Allariz in Galicia (possibly from a funerary context in a dolmen). While lunulae are rare in Iberia, gold diadems or neck-chokers are more frequent and generally found in funerary contexts, rather than deposited in isolation in the ground as the lunulae are in Ireland. Examples include Agolada in Galicia and São Bentos in northern Portugal, the former diadem accompanying an adult female inhumation. Gold diadems or long sheet-gold bands dating to the Beaker period are also known from Armorica, with single examples known from County Cavan in Ireland and near Winchester, Hampshire, in southern England.

There are very few earlier Beaker finds from Wales, and while some early Beaker pots are known in Anglesey, these tend to come from the re-use of chambered tombs (such as Tŷ Newydd). Cremation is also more commonly practiced than inhumation in western Wales. In addition, like in Ireland, Beakers are rarely found complete, and are usually represented by Maritime-decorated style sherds, suggesting Atlantic influences. Examples are known from the Erglodd and Copa Hill copper mines in Ceredigion. Very close to the latter site, at Banc Ty'nddôl, a probable flat grave contained a decorated gold 'sun-disc', that has Irish or Iberian affinities (see Text Box 4.2), generally associated with the north-westerly movement of the 'Maritime Bell Beaker set'.

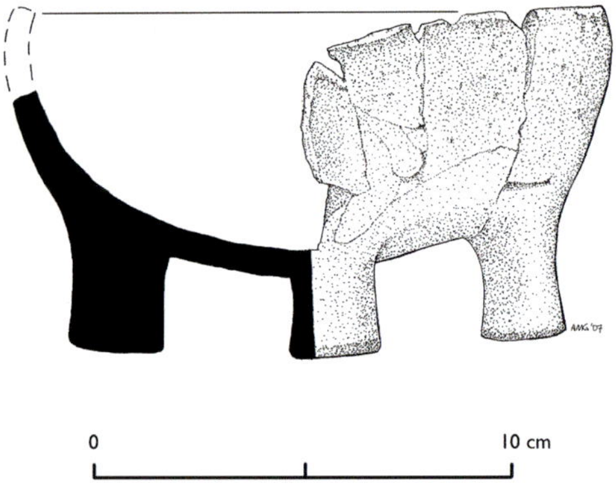

4.10. (above left) **Early Bronze Age sun-disc from Banc Ty'nddôl, Ceredigion, Wales.** (©National Museum of Wales)

4.11. (upper right) **Gold lunula from Ireland.** (after Eogan, 1994, fig. 11)

4.12. (mid-page right) **Near-complete ceramic polypod bowl from a pit at Newtownbalregan, County Louth.** (illustration by Alva McGowan, reproduced with permission from Irish Archaeological Consultancy Ltd.)

Adopting and adapting the Beaker package

Archaeologists are now realizing that the uptake of the Beaker package varied from region to region not only in terms of what was adopted, but also in the timing of its spread. In some areas, it was long-lasting, emerging in central Portugal in the 29th century BC and enduring for the following 700 years, although evolving throughout that period. In other areas, such as north-east Scotland, Beakers were short-lived and only became common in the 24th century BC, falling out of fashion by the 20th century BC, if not before.

This diversity over a large geographical area can be exemplified by things like regionally distinctive Beakers, preferences for different styles of stone bracers and the adoption (or not) of artefacts such as polypod bowls or Palmela points. Palmela points, or copper-alloy tanged projectiles, are principally known from central Portugal, in the Tagus estuary, and from there spread to France with two main concentrations—one along the Atlantic coastline between the Gironde and the Gulf of Morhiban and a second cluster along the Mediterranean coast. In the case of stone bracers, broadly two style-regions are evident: two-holed types have a more Atlantic-Mediterranean

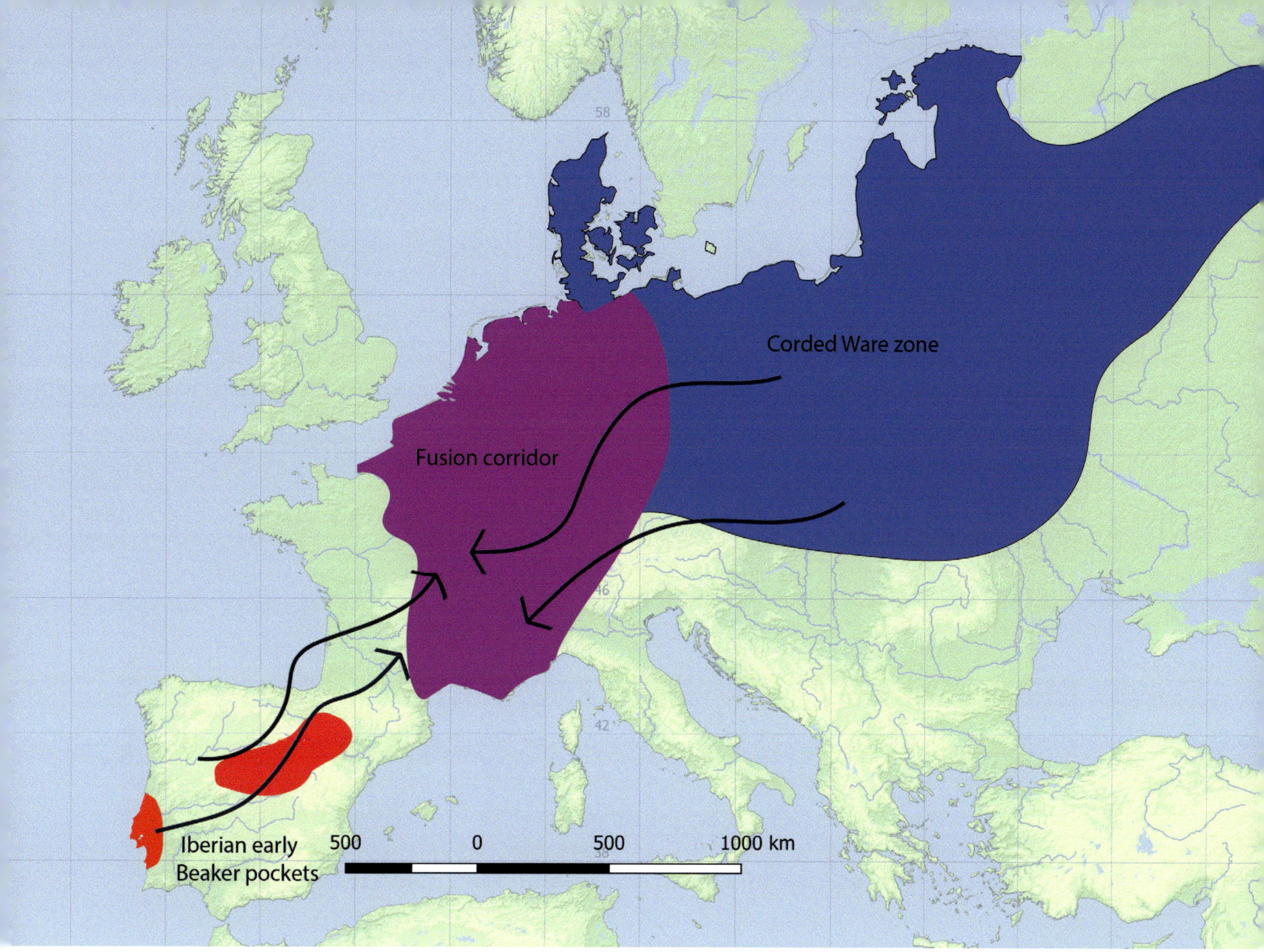

4.13. Merging of Corded Ware and early Beaker traditions.
(© Catriona Gibson)

distribution and are the dominant type found in Ireland (although straight-sided variants are also found in central Europe), and four-holed types are most frequent in central Europe, but also appear in significant numbers in England and Scotland. On the other hand, polypod bowls, widely occurring in northern and central Europe and believed to have affinities with a more eastern Bell Beaker and Corded Ware influence, have also been found in the Netherlands and southern France. Sixteen polypod vessels are known from Ireland, six of which are wooden, while there are just four from England, with a predominantly north-eastern distribution.

The successful transmission of other knowledge sets at this time included copper sourcing, metalworking technologies, and perhaps also languages. Evidently throughout the Atlantic region the varied reactions to the Beaker package indicate that the new ideas, technologies and innovations accompanying Beaker pots were not imposed on the communities that adopted the vessels; rather they were selected, often adapted and interleaved with existing regional traditions. In some areas, such as parts of England and Scotland where Beaker adoption was more standardized, perhaps the new

4.14. **Solar motifs on a gold sun-disc and the bases of a Beaker pot and Irish Bowl Food Vessel.** (after Clarke 1970, fig. 191; Cahill 2015, plates 2 & 5)

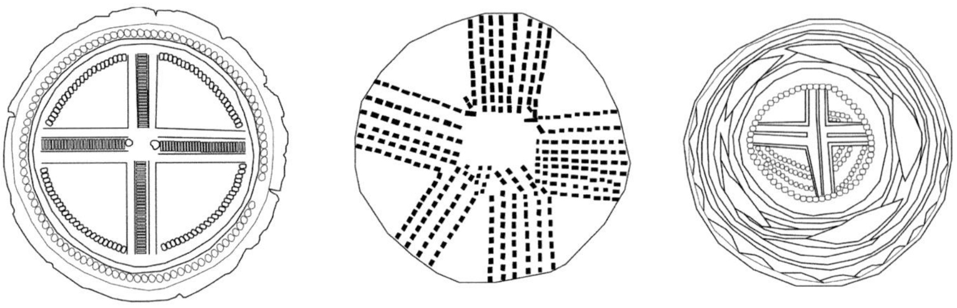

Text Box 4.3. Solar and lunar ideologies

Alongside the burial evidence already presented, an array of iconographical evidence for the Beaker period and Early Bronze Age also hints at potential connections in shared ideologies throughout parts of Europe. It can be argued, for example, that solar and lunar symbols occurred more widely on portable objects, such as pottery, personal ornaments, burial stelae and rock art. The cruciform, laddered, and zig-zag motifs on gold discs (see Text Box 4.2) found in Ireland, Britain, France, and Iberia, have been suggested as representing the sun in forms that are visible to the naked eye, particularly at sunrise and sunset. A similar range of motifs, such as 'sunburst explosions' or star motifs, can also be seen in the decoration on pots when viewed mouth downwards from a vertical position, such as many Beaker vessels from Britain and Iberia, Bowl Tradition vessels from Ireland, and on the slightly later miniature vessels or accessory cups, as well as many jet buttons.

As the name suggests, the gold lunulae have a crescent moon-shape and can also be linked to this celestial symbolism, and many are decorated with geometric patterns comparable to that on Beaker pottery. Ireland has the most significant concentration of gold lunulae in Atlantic Europe, and seems to be the main centre of production. More recently it has been argued that they represent solar boats, in particular because of the association of some (Coggalbeg in Ireland and Cabeceiras de Basto in northern Portugal) with pairs of gold discs. This connection between boats and sun symbols is also documented on ceramics from Los Millares in southern Spain and the Caergwrle bowl from Wales (in the shape of a boat decorated with possible sun motifs), as well as Scandinavian rock art.

The gold diadems more frequent in Iberia are also often decorated with incised zigzags. Solar representations are also found on anthropomorphic idols, schist plaques and decorated menhirs and stelae, dating from the Late Neolithic to the Beaker period (e.g. those from the Almendres cromlech in central Portugal or the Peña Tú cluster in Asturias), where lunulae and sun motifs are sometimes engraved together. Decorated schist plaques from central Portuguese megalithic tombs also include a number of anthropomorphic designs where the human eyes are depicted as suns.

ideologies and symbolic systems that the Beaker objects represented reinforced a more collective identity, with continental inspiration.

In summary, a fully-formed Beaker Complex was only consolidated in southern Atlantic regions through the merging of Corded Ware and early Beaker traditions, the effects of which gradually trickled through to the other regions. The initial spread of Beakers along Atlantic coastlines from western Iberia to western France and Ireland lacked the emphasis on single burial rites and individual grave goods; instead collective Neolithic traditions continued. That England and Scotland adopted a more fully-fledged version of the Beaker package perhaps indicates that this was a result of different spheres of influence from central Europe. These different rates and types of adoption highlight the varied and multiple strands of interaction in Atlantic Europe at this time.

Earlier Bronze Age: cross-channel connections (post-2200 BC)

From 2200 BC onwards there is more diversity in social, material, and ideological practices in some areas, but also continuity and augmentation in others. In Britain, this is generally referred to as the 'Beaker fissioning horizon', when there was a rapid mutation in the pot style, associated grave goods, and their embedded meanings, but there is also evidence of a fusion of some old and new funerary practices such as individual burials in cists in eastern Scotland, Ireland, and north-west Iberia. The resultant situation is rather complex, with regional pockets of polymorphism and diversity that contrast with other zones of relative homogeneity and increased standardization.

Western Iberia

It is only in the centuries after 2200 BC that a discernible transformation in burial ideologies is noted in these regions, indicated through the marked increase in individual burial; 200 years or more later than its acceptance in Wiltshire and Dorset, for example. Burials were now generally crouched inhumations in stone-lined cists or in pits, sometimes covered by small mounds (*mamoas*), and most were accompanied by grave goods that included Beaker-derived pots, along with bracers and daggers, demonstrating continuity with Beaker traditions. Examples include the cist burials of As Antas in Galicia which contained a bronze dagger and Ciempozuelos or late Beaker bowl, and Pera Gorda in the Tagus estuary, which was also accompanied by a dagger in addition to two Palmela points. What is intriguing is that this single cist burial tradition may have been influenced by existing practices already established further north in other parts of Atlantic Europe, such as Ireland and north-eastern Scotland, perhaps highlighting new spheres of interaction now flowing from north to south. It could even be posited that the Middle Neolithic Linkardstown-type cists in Ireland acted as a precursor to the sub-megalithic cists associated with Beaker activity in western Iberia.

4.15. The rite of cremation was fashionable during the Neolithic and the Bronze Age.

(© Ken Williams)

Ireland

At about the same time in Ireland, Beakers were in decline in favour of a new decorated ceramic style, known as Bowl Tradition pottery, and often referred to as Irish Bowl Food Vessels. Single crouched inhumation burials also became more common and were accompanied by these Bowls and occasionally other grave goods indicative of Beaker use elsewhere, such as v-perforated buttons. Many of these burials were placed in cists and pits, but older megaliths also continued to be re-used for burial alongside the newer wedge tombs. It is notable, however, that the use of cists and the rite of inhumation had a relatively short period of popularity during the beginning of the Early Bronze Age, lasting only a few generations until the decades around 1850 BC. In contrast, the rite of cremation remained fashionable from the Neolithic right through the Bronze Age.

Alongside the Bowl Tradition pottery, further styles in the form of Vase Tradition pottery soon emerged, and a closer examination of these vessel types within their cross-Channel context suggests considerable two-way relations between Ireland and regions of Britain. Elements of Irish Bowls, for example, can be seen on vessels from Scotland, with notable concentrations along the western coast and in the east-central region, and further clusters in south-eastern Scotland, northern England, such as the Tyne Valley in Northumbria, and the Isle of Man. Influences also flowed in the opposite direction, with some Irish Urns closely resembling southern British and Welsh vessels, which may have related to wider changes in social and cultural networks from *c.* 2000 BC, particularly the shifting emphasis from Irish to Welsh copper sources. Other Cordoned Urns represent another distinctive Irish-Scottish concentration, with a few examples also known in northern Britain and the Isle of Man.

The widespread adoption of tin bronze in Ireland dates to 2150/2000 BC, when axes, daggers and halberds continued to be the dominant metal forms. These objects were widely deposited in natural places, mainly rivers and bogs, both in hoards and singly. Hoards ranged in size from two to 25 objects, with the number of items per hoard decreasing as the Early Bronze Age progressed. Alongside this decline in the size of hoards, acts of single object deposition were steadily increasing, and continued to do so into the later Bronze Age. Comparable to trends across western Europe, weapons were usually deposited singly in wet contexts, especially rivers, but more nuanced patterns have also been observed, for example metal axes and subsequently spearheads towards the end of the Early Bronze Age, had a significantly lower rate of river deposition.

In contrast to élite burials underway elsewhere, such as in Wessex and Armorica (see below), Irish graves were generally not selected for the

4.16. Bronze Age barrow in barrow cemetery grouped around site of Neolithic long barrow, north of Maiden Castle in Dorset, south-west England.

(© Kerri Cleary)

deposition of luxury gold- and metal-work. Perhaps with the exception of a small number of copper and bronze awls, other objects remained comparatively sparse, for example, just 15% of the known daggers/knives were placed in funerary contexts. One notable exception was towards the end of the Early Bronze Age, in association with Cordoned Urn pottery, when some three quarters of known razors were deposited in graves, after which time the practice ceased and razors all but disappeared from the archaeological record only to re-appear again in small numbers in Late Bronze Age hoards.

The emergence of Early Bronze Age barrows and a cross-Channel maritory

In many parts of Europe, the Early Bronze Age coincided with the emergence of the barrow tradition. This was a time when burials became highly visible once again, through the construction of large mounds made from earth, turf, and stone. From the turn of the 2nd millennium these were built on an impressive scale throughout many regions of Britain, Ireland, France, and northern Iberia, sometimes organized into extensive linear barrow cemeteries. Tracts of landscapes were in effect transformed into monumental 'barrowscapes'. Individuals were often sequentially buried in pits or layers within their mound deposits, and some barrows contained over 20 individually placed interments. The earlier barrows were associated with inhumation burials, often accompanied by derived Beakers or Food Vessels and occasionally an assortment of other objects that exhibit continuity with Beaker traditions. Towards the end of the Early Bronze Age, cremation became the predominant burial practice, and the cremated remains were often placed within a new style of pot, known as the Collared Urn. Barrows are particularly numerous in the chalklands of Wessex and Yorkshire, and in the former area, include over 100 lavish or 'high status' burials. They form part of a distinctive set of burials known as the 'Wessex culture', which was at its height between 2000 and 1700 BC. Its focus has traditionally been held to lie between south-western Britain and Armorica in north-western France, where several barrows contained a similar range of exotic grave goods. The exchange of these objects made from amber, jet, tin, gold, shale, and faience has been argued to indicate the emergence of a high-status and specialist cross-Channel 'maritory'.

Alongside the famous and oft-discussed gold- and amber-rich burials of Bush Barrow and Upton Lovell, both in Wiltshire, and Clandon in Dorset, there are other well-furnished barrow graves such as that of an elderly female at Preshute in Malborough. She was buried with two bronze knife-daggers, a shale and amber necklace, a gold-encased shale disc, and a gold-bound amber pendant in the shape of a halberd placed behind her head. A second amber halberd pendant also accompanied an adult female, this time a cremation in a Collared Urn from Double Dykes near Bournemouth, alongside several amber beads and two gold cones.

Across the Channel in Armorica, similarly rich burials under barrows include Brun Bras, where an inhumation was buried with a beautiful silver cup, three bronze daggers, and two gold studs, and Crugel, where grave goods included four bronze daggers and two gold studs. These high-status burials in south-west Britain and Armorica attest to the importance and intensity of cross-Channel exchange networks, and the range of exotic goods exchanged reflect the shared social and funerary ideologies that they were bound up with. In addition, there is also some evidence that the influence of these élite burials reached across the Irish Sea towards the end of the Early Bronze Age. A Wessex-type gold bead cover from Mucklagh in County Offaly accompanied the cremated remains of a child and an adult (possibly female) placed in a pit with a burnt and broken antler awl, melted copper pieces, and charred cattle bones. A connection to the Wessex region can also be reiterated by a number of other artefacts, including two striking finds from County Cork: an amber dagger pommel found with Encrusted Urn sherds at Liscahane and 'mitre-shaped' amber beads and a herringbone decorated plaque of gold found in association with an inhumation at Knockane. Similarly in County Meath, a composite necklace of jet, amber, bronze, and faience beads with strong links to contemporary examples in Wessex, was associated with the inhumation of a young male placed in a Neolithic passage tomb at Tara. Isotopic analysis on this individual ruled out that he grew up on the chalk of Wessex, and also that he was raised locally; his place of birth thus remains a puzzle.

There is also a series of well-furnished burials in north-west Iberia, implying that Galicia and northern Portugal may have been sporadically plugged into these maritory networks during the Early Bronze Age. Although only a few 'rich' burials are known in comparison to Wessex, at least 15 examples were accompanied by high-status items. For instance the barrow at Cicere, in Galicia, contained several gold objects including a bracelet and two diadems, and at Quinta da Agua Branca, in north Portugal, an adult male was accompanied by a rich panoply of objects that included a bracer, diadem, and two spirals all made from gold, and a bronze dagger. What is intriguing about these burials is that they seemingly represent a fusion of two funerary traditions. While some of these high-status individuals were buried under barrows, others were placed in stone-lined cists, implying a mixture of influences from the 'Wessex-Armorican' sphere, on one hand, and Ireland and Scotland, on the other.

Middle Bronze Age

Settlement, society and economy

In southern Britain, as well as Ireland and western Iberia (see below), evidence for the domestic arena greatly increases from the Middle Bronze Age, with a focus on settlements and associated field systems, droveways, and pastoral routes. In many parts of lowland Britain, landscapes become reorganized and divided up through the creation of extensive co-axial field systems, with associated groups of post-built roundhouses. Settlements tended to be small, and were often nestled within field

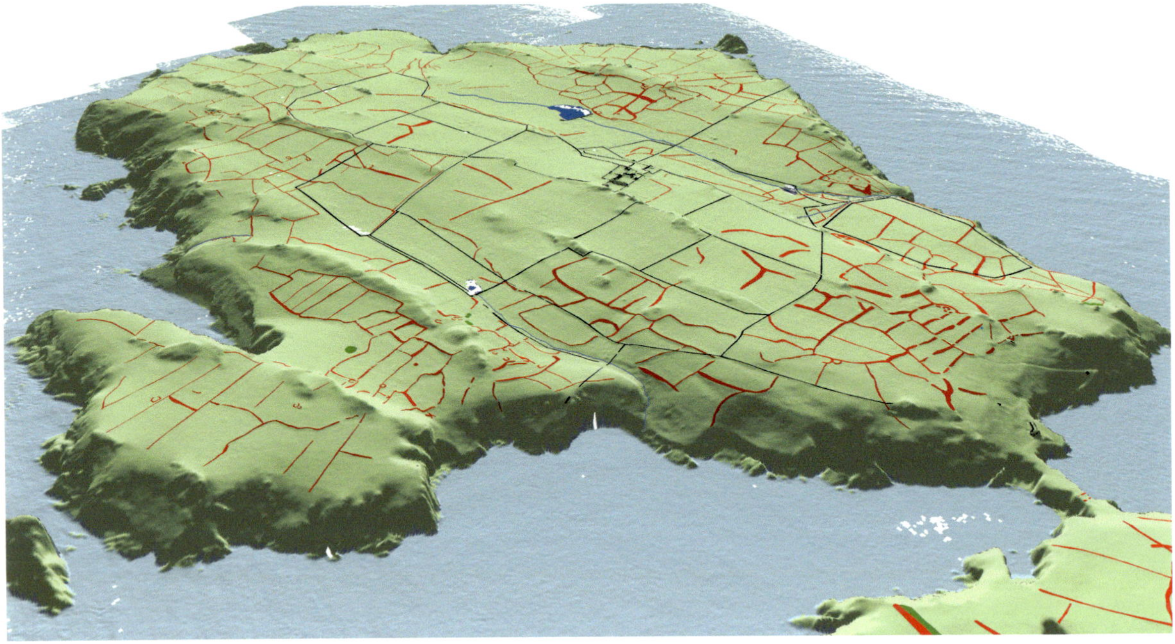

4.17. 3D Lidar digital surface model of co-axial field system on Skomer Island, off the coast of Pembrokeshire in west Wales. (© Royal Commission on the Ancient and Historic Monuments of Wales)

system or enclosure boundaries. Some well-preserved examples of these can be witnessed in Dartmoor or along the South Downs Way in Sussex, at Plumpton Plain, Blackpatch, and Itford Hill, and hundreds of hectares of connected field systems have been excavated in the middle Thames Valley in west London. At the same time, the burial record becomes less prominent; the Early Bronze Age barrow tradition is replaced by flat urned or unurned cremation cemeteries (known as Deverel-Rimbury), sometimes spreading out from earlier mounds. Far fewer burials are known than in preceding periods, and other than pots, grave goods tend to be restricted to occasional metal items such as pins or razors (often burnt on the pyre). The lack of defended settlements (e.g. hillforts) and the general dearth of rich burials could imply that social groups were less hierarchical and more pacifistic in nature; however, this is also the time when many new types of weapons, particularly long rapiers, spearheads, and short swords, enter the archaeological record on an impressive scale. These are usually found as single deposits or in small hoards, in both wet and dry land contexts, and include the rapier hoards of Larkbeare, in Devon, and Buphen Fen, in Essex, both from bogs.

In Ireland, communities were similarly settling the landscape through the construction of roundhouses, often with ancillary buildings, and activity areas centred on external hearths and pits. The frequency of enclosing or demarcating these sites with ditches and palisades also increased during this period, but still remains relatively low at around 35% of known sites. While the kind of extensive linear earthworks and field systems evident across southern Britain at this time have yet to be identified in Ireland on the same scale, that is not to say that such agricultural organization was not being practiced. The control and management of landscapes was clearly practiced from an early date, as evidenced by surviving stone-wall field systems in the west of the island, from the Neolithic and Early Bronze Age complexes at Céide Hill in north Mayo and the Coolnatullagh Valley in the Burren, County Clare, to the possible Middle Bronze Age field system at Slievemore on Achill Island. Further survey and analysis, particularly of uplands and preserved landscapes, may yet yield additional evidence and indeed traces of field systems surviving as ditches only have been uncovered in recent years during excavations in the lowlands, such as those at the later Bronze Age sites of Killeany in County Laois and Skreen in County Meath. By the beginning of the Middle Bronze Age a domestic variant of a previously funerary pottery vessel (Cordoned Urn) had developed and as elsewhere, there was a decline in visible burial practices. Other traditions must have been adopted alongside the continued, albeit lesser, use of cremation. Burials were increasingly placed in simple pits, often as 'token deposits', and either unaccompanied or in association with a plain, bucket-shaped vessel style that was also used at settlements and which was increasingly deposited as fragments rather than a complete pot. Although the copper exchange networks dominant in the Early Bronze Age were in decline from the Middle Bronze Age, evidence for exchange across the Irish Sea can still be seen. In Wales, for example, Irish-style palstaves have been recovered from Anglesey and Caernarfonshire, and the Pigeon's Cave hoard from the Great Orme contained a late palstave and two Irish gold lock rings. Alongside these perhaps low-level connections there were also insular developments, such as two broadly contemporary spearhead traditions on both sides of the Irish Sea; kite-shaped spearheads in Ireland and leaf-shaped spearheads in Britain.

Until fairly recently, settlement evidence for the Middle Bronze Age in western Iberia remained rather elusive, and there was even a suggestion of a significant population decline during this time, or that groups became increasingly mobile, building only temporary and ephemeral settlements. Developer-led excavations in particular have now altered this picture to some extent, leading to the identification of a number of domestic sites, often sealed under deep deposits of alluvium or colluvium. Many of these sites were situated in low-lying fertile valleys and tended to be small and undefended. They give the appearance of hamlets or villages, often with no more than three or four stone-built houses. A further development is a much closer spatial association between the domestic and funerary spaces. Cist cemeteries were often paired with settlements, with a distance of less than a few hundred metres separating them, as at Atalaia and Horta do Jacinto, both in central Portugal. Circular and rectangular stone cists held crouched inhumations that were rarely accompanied by more than a single pot. While these settlements were not associated with field systems, an exceptional number of old droveways called *carreradas* or *cañadas* are known; these weave for nearly 160,000 kilometres across a wide range of landscapes in Iberia. Objects recovered along these paths indicate that their origins go back to the Middle Bronze Age at least. These finds include short swords and daggers placed at river fording points, like at Puentecesures in the river Ulla, and ornaments deposited in rocky crevices, such as the gold bracelet from the foot of the Sierra de São Mamede in Portalegre. In addition, a diverse range of engraved stelae and statue-menhirs dating from the Early Bronze Age onwards have been found along these ancient paths, as at Corgas and Ribeiro do Carvalhal in the Sierra da Estrela, or Talavera de la Reina in the foothills of Barranca del Águila in Toledo. These may have acted as prehistoric boundary or territorial markers, or as signposts that provided links between fertile valleys and more mountainous pastures.

During this time there appears to be a dislocation of Iberia from Atlantic connections, with regions becoming more inward-looking evidenced by restricted styles in pottery and metalwork. In particular, Iberian metal objects included double-looped palstaves and there is a marked drop-off in deposits of bronze tools and weapons in comparison to preceding and later periods. A variety of local ceramic types emerge, such as Penha and Proto-Cogotas traditions in northern Portugal and the Meseta respectively. The majority of bronze objects deposited relate to single axes/palstaves, but occasionally ornaments made from precious metals were also deliberately placed in significant locations in the landscape, such as the gold bracelets from Alcobaça in cental Portugal or the gold torcs from Forno in northern Portugal. The reasons for the interruption in interaction networks between Iberia and other Atlantic regions may have partly been the result of exploitation of copper in other areas and in particular increased exchange in metal between central Europe and northern parts of Atlantic Europe during the Middle Bronze Age. There is also considerably more recycling of bronze, as indicated by chemical analysis of metal objects in western Europe between *c.* 1600–1200 BC (see Chapter 5).

Other factors, however, may also have had a part to play in these changing spheres of interaction. There is evidence for more intensive pastoralist economies during this period, indicated not only by the extensive creation of track and droveways, but also the increased representation of cattle bone in faunal assemblages from domestic sites. A greater reliance on cattle would have resulted in more mobile and transhumant social groups, and this may have impacted upon the long-distance connections of previous periods, resulting in their subsequent fragmentation. Certainly the greater variety of regional pottery styles and diversity in other socio-cultural practices, such as in burials and associated ideologies, would support the idea of a reduction in extensive spheres of connectivity throughout Atlantic Europe.

Coeval with a more universal adoption of cremation, a new arena of display emerges. From the Middle Bronze Age onwards, and dramatically increasing in scale and intensity during the Late Bronze Age, assemblages or 'hoards' of metal objects are deposited in the ground or under water. This practice of hoarding may be seen as a substitute for grave goods to some extent; again it signals a common characteristic throughout many parts of Atlantic Europe, and indeed also central Europe.

The 'Atlantic Bronze Age'

Introduction

From the late 1930s the concept of a connected 'Atlantic Bronze Age' developed, incorporating the coastal zones of western Europe, from Scotland in the north to Portugal and western Spain in the south. The height of this complex occurred *c.* 1150–950 BC when the Atlantic seaboard became reconnected through trade and exchange networks. Metal analysis has indicated that in Britain during this time there was a growing reliance on imported continental metal, such as evidenced by the Langdon Bay cargo from Dover and the Salcombe find from Devon. Thus the exchange of objects and raw materials throughout Atlantic regions was now very much back on the agenda, contrasting markedly with the apparent regionalization of the Middle Bronze Age. Along with the movement of metals, it is likely that other, perhaps less tangible, things were also spread, adopted and adapted over these far-flung regions. For instance similarities can be discerned not only in Late Bronze Age metalworking traditions, but also in the settlement and funerary spheres. In many Atlantic regions, there was a significant increase in hillforts and hilltop fortifications from around 1300 BC and from around the same time onwards burials further decrease in visibility.

Changing burial traditions

As mentioned, in the Early Bronze Age funerary evidence often suggests an emphasis on the demarcation of place through the construction of prominent monuments in the landscape, and grave goods frequently accompanied the dead. In parts of Britain, Ireland, Armorica, and Iberia, medium and large cemeteries were created either in barrow clusters or extended cist or pit necropolises, implying that constructing and maintaining links between lineages and ancestors were significant. By the Late Bronze Age throughout almost all parts of Atlantic Europe these connections were broken and there was a general move from monumental to less visible burial contexts; in addition the funerary arena was no longer the appropriate domain for the deposition of metal objects. When found, most Late Bronze Age burials are unaccompanied and they are rarely in large cemeteries; more often they occur singly or in small groups, although a few were still associated with ring-ditches, and others re-used megalithic tombs. In some places this change was already underway by the Middle Bronze Age and a clear regional example has already been demonstrated by the so-called razors in Ireland, which although found in burials until *c.* 1600 BC all but disappear only to re-appear again in the Late Bronze Age, but only in hoards.

The general scarcity of funerary evidence has long been taken as a shared characteristic of the Atlantic Bronze Age. Although increased radiocarbon dating in recent years has helped identify a number of Late Bronze Age burials, particularly those without grave goods, there are still relatively few compared to earlier periods,

4.18. Late Bronze Age and Iron Age hillfort at Llwyn Bryn-Dinas, above the Tanat valley in Powys, Wales. (© Royal Commission on the Ancient and Historic Monuments of Wales)

suggesting that after death many people were buried in ways and in places that remain archaeologically invisible. Pots tended to be the only objects that accompanied the dead, and these are usually the same styles as those used in domestic contexts, indeed some have residues that suggest they may even have been used for cooking. In other words, objects were no longer made specifically for the funerary domain. There was also a notable increase in secondary mortuary practices, such as defleshing and removal of parts of the corpse, as well as the processing of cremated bone through crushing or pounding. The deposition of token amounts of bone in whole vessels, or more commonly with vessel sherds, also became increasingly common, particularly in Britain and Ireland.

It can be argued that the worlds of the dead and the living were being brought into even closer proximity than in the Middle Bronze Age. Examples include cist burials found adjacent to hilltop settlements, such as Nora Velha in southern Portugal, cremations incorporated into roundhouses, as at Broom in south-east England, Cloghers in south-west Ireland, and Los Tolmos do Caracena in north Spain, and human remains in pits or under house floors at settlement sites such as Cladh Hallan in the western Isles of Scotland and Lough Gur in southern Ireland. Throughout Atlantic regions, death no longer appears to have been used as a tangible marker of display in the landscape and this occurs in tandem with settlements becoming more visible, being sited on hilltops and often comprising monumental earthworks. In Iberia, large and heavily fortified examples include Castro de Santa Luzia and Castro de São Romão in north Portugal and Senhora da Guia, Azougada, and Corôa do Frade in central Portugal. These are first occupied just before the turn of the 1st millennium, and continue in use until the Early Iron Age. This is perhaps comparable to Ireland, where excavated hilltop enclosures such as Haughey's Fort in County Armagh and Cashel in County Cork, have construction dates in the late 2nd and 1st millennia BC, with an apparent collapse of hillfort culture by the 8th century BC. In Britain hillforts, such as Rams Hill or Uffington in Oxfordshire, emerge slightly later, closer to the transition to the Early Iron Age, but in contrast to Ireland, often remain active until the end of the Late Iron Age.

Metal deposition

Due to the dramatic rise in deposition of metal objects during the Late Bronze Age, much of the Atlantic Bronze Age research traditionally concentrated on hoards and metalwork typologies, rather than the funerary or domestic spheres. During this time, metal objects were seemingly thought about, used, and decommissioned in similar ways over extensive regions. This can be highlighted through focusing on Late Bronze Age swords which were deposited both complete and fragmented in the case of single finds, but when from hoards the majority were fragmented. Closer examination of each region does, however, also reveal significant differences in the ways they were treated and placed.

In Iberia the rules for the deposition of swords (predominantly leaf-shaped and Huelva styles) appear to have been quite loose; many were recovered as part of multi-piece assemblages with a mixed range of object associations and from wet locations, although they were also deposited singly. The majority were placed in rivers, particularly along the Guadalquivir and its tributaries, with a smaller number found on hillsides, caves, or rocky crevices. While the swords are sometimes complete, they are also often bent, warped, or even burnt, and thus seemingly decommissioned and destroyed before deposition. Many hoards with swords are also known from dry contexts and several highly fragmented examples have been recovered from settlement contexts, such as the hillfort of Senhora da Guia, Baiões, in central Portugal.

By contrast, in Ireland 90% of the locally developed styles of Late Bronze Age swords occur as single finds, but the vast majority similarly come from wet contexts, and they are predominately complete objects with little or no damage. The French and British carp's-tongue swords are slightly later in date—mid-10th to earlier 9th century BC—and over time more coherence seems to emerge in the depositional choices. There is a shift towards dry contexts and swords are frequently accompanied by more uniform object associations of spearheads and socketed axes, and this increasing standardization may imply that exchange alliances throughout

Atlantic regions were becoming further consolidated. Although Iberia seemingly initiated some of these long-distance exchanges, by the 10th century, parts of Spain and Portugal became detached from Atlantic spheres of connection, and instead were realigned with a different 'maritory', and drawn into Mediterranean networks. The exception to this is north-west Iberia which remained very much Atlantic in character and where non-functional axes or 'axe-ingots' (perhaps representing standardized units of metal or even 'currency') were deposited in large numbers; a situation paralleled in Brittany. For example, at Samieira in Galicia, over 170 complete almost identical Late Bronze Age axes weighing over 92 kg were deposited under a large boulder very close to the coast. Breton hoards include the massive axe-ingot deposits of Ergué-Armel where 169 similar axes were found in a pot, and Saint-Hélen which contained a staggering 500 axes. These axe hoards were generally found close to the coast, accentuating long-distance maritime exchanges.

Commensal activities and feasting

One component of Late Bronze Age metalwork that highlights the changing spheres of interaction within Atlantic regions relates to feasting. A number of deposits contained objects specifically associated with commensal activities and these fall into three main types: cauldrons, flesh-hooks, and articulated spits. The former two categories are usually coupled with stewing or boiling meat (or perhaps drinking alcoholic beverages), while the latter one is associated with roasting meat. Notably, the two sets form geographically discrete clusters. Although flesh-hooks and cauldrons or buckets are rarely found together in the same contexts, their spatial distributions roughly overlap.

Articulated spits

Only one articulated spit has been recovered from either Britain or Ireland, and this exception was found at Saltwood in Kent. It survived as a fragment within a larger scrap hoard suggesting that it may have been displaced from its original area of use for later recycling. In both central Portugal and western France there is an overlap of the spit and flesh-hook traditions, although with a notable lack of spits in north-western Brittany. A few spits are known from western France, such as at Challans, but the majority come from Iberia, particularly central Portugal and form part of a Mediterranean rather than Atlantic tradition. The majority of these spits were found in a slightly broken or totally fragmented condition and nearly half were single finds, rather than from hoards. With the exception of one cave deposit, all the Portuguese spits came from hillforts, and perhaps after a final feasting event they were deliberately decommissioned and consigned to the ground.

Cauldrons, buckets, and flesh-hooks

This distinction in deposition contexts can also be seen in the use of cauldrons, buckets, and flesh-hooks. No cauldrons and only three flesh-hooks have been found south of the river Tagus in western Iberia; instead the latter have concentrations in Brittany, Ireland, and south-east England. All of the Iberian cauldrons have been recovered from dry contexts, mainly hillforts situated in the mountainous regions near the Atlantic coast. At some sites they formed elements of house foundation deposits or hoards just outside settlements, as at Castillejos in the north Meseta.

In stark contrast, the majority of Irish, and to a certain degree northern British, cauldrons, were purposefully deposited at wet, perhaps isolated locations—such as the cauldrons placed in bogs at Hattenknowe, in Peebleshire Scotland, or Castlederg in County Tyrone, Ireland. Indeed it is possible that uninhabited landscapes were specifically slected, thereby removing the cauldrons from their spheres of use and into liminal, perhaps more neutral, locations. While two intact cauldrons come from north-western Spain, both from deep copper mines and possibly suggesting a ritual or feasting connection to mining activities, all of the other Iberian examples were deposited in highly fragmentary states, generally deliberately broken and often burnt or warped. Where cauldrons have been retrieved from dry contexts in Britain they are also always in an incomplete state and almost always have contextual associations with settlements, such as the cauldron fragments found in a pit outside the ramparts at Cadbury Hillfort in Somerset. Again this is in contrast to Ireland, where nearly 70% of the cauldrons were largely intact.

Thus towards the end of the Late Bronze Age, parts of western Europe became entangled within two distinct interaction spheres. North-western Iberia, western France, and the British Isles became increasingly enmeshed within an Atlantic network, while central and southern Portugal engaged with contemporary Mediterranean circuits. The feasting elements highlight this re-orientation through the two different sets of commensal eating practices of stewing or boiling (Atlantic) and roasting (Mediterranean) meat. To some extent these may have been linked to separate ideologies, although here the distinctions between 'Atlantic' and 'Mediterranean' spheres are more blurred. As stated above, in Iberia, France, and parts of southern England, cauldrons from dry contexts were deliberately broken up, perhaps to remove their potency after a specific ritual, or to dramatically commemorate a highly charged feast by sacrificing the associated object. Those from wet contexts in southern Britain, however, were almost always deposited in an intact state. This is in keeping with evidence from Ireland and northern Britain where such feasting equipment is predominantly found complete in isolated deposits, generally in bogs or rivers. Many of these cauldrons were extensively repaired and patched up, as in the cases of Portlegone II in County Antrim and Cardross in Argyll and Bute, indicating use over a protracted period of time and suggesting that the memory of previous feasting events was perhaps important in future rituals. Ultimately, however, there was also a need to remove these cauldrons from the community, but it seems that it was equally important that they were deposited whole.

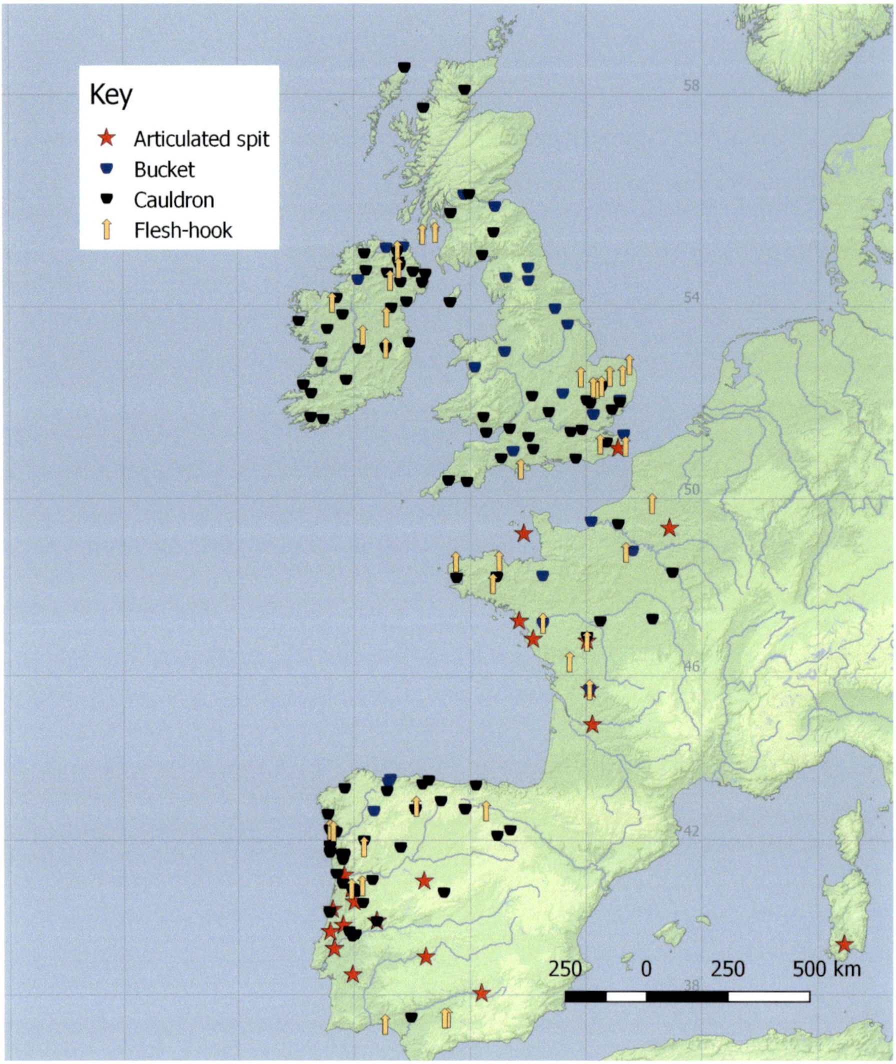

4.19. Distributions of feasting equipment: cauldrons, flesh-hooks, and articulated spits.

(© Kerri Cleary & Catriona Gibson from AEMA database)

Discussion

Traditionally, a key archaeological indicator for long-distance interaction and exchange is change, and this is often taken as relating to the introduction and spread of novel technologies, material culture, and ideologies. Periods that are subject to greater visible transformation and sharing of certain innovations and material styles in the archaeological record tend to be considered times when regions were more connected. If taken at face value, one could suggest that the Beaker and Late Bronze Age periods are two highly intensive periods of long-distance interaction, while in the Early Bronze Age where supra-regional connectivity began to wane, and the Middle Bronze Age seemingly became a time of increasing regionalization.

In the Late Neolithic the main evidence sets come from monumental complexes such as henges, timber and stone circles, and the re-use of megalithic tombs. While most of the activity seems to be locally and regionally focused, there are hints of more extensive spheres of interaction, as indicated by certain widely shared architectural and object types, such as chambered cairns and stone axes. During the Beaker period, the archaeological focus shifts predominantly to the burial record, where funerary customs, grave goods, and ideologies indicate a more 'internationally' connected world. As already outlined, however, there are many local takes on Beaker practices and for a range of different reasons, the 'Beaker package' was not universally adopted throughout all of Atlantic Europe. By the Early Bronze Age, burials continue to form the main visible category of archaeological evidence, and while it is often accepted that this is a time when the 'pan-European' networks of the preceding period break down, this chapter demonstrates that the emergent picture is more complex. The adoption of the cist burial appears to be a unifying trend that connects parts of Ireland, Scotland, and western Iberia, and this may highlight new connections, stimulated or initiated from northern regions. In addition the cross-Channel maritory identified from the richly furnished burials under monumental barrows in Wessex and Armorica likely extended its influence to Galicia and northern Portugal, where similarly high-status burials are known.

Moving on to the Middle Bronze Age, settlements, field systems, and associated small inconspicuous cemeteries rise to the fore in the archaeological record, but grave goods are often reduced to a pot of regional rather than supra-regional style. These categories of evidence provide fewer clues for identifying supra-regional interaction, and may have affected our ability to discern wider exchange networks. This leaves archaeologists concentrating on the metalwork, where typological considerations of various hoard deposits imply this was a time of increasing fragmentation and isolation throughout Atlantic regions. Metallurgical analysis tells us that increased recycling of bronze was dissipating the need for intensive metalworking exchange; however, some perhaps smaller scale interactions can still be demonstrated such as the occurrence of rapiers with Breton features in eastern and southern England.

By the Late Bronze Age the evidence-sets change again. Settlements and communal gathering places become more visible, through the emergence of large, complex defended hilltop enclosures and hillforts. In addition, the deposition of metal objects in watery and below-ground locations rises on an incremental scale, and many of the tool, ornament, and weapon categories exhibit more coherence throughout many Atlantic regions; the ways in which metal objects are deposited also highlight both regional similarities and differences.

The interaction networks during the Bronze Age were complex and interleaved, subject to various ebbs and flows throughout the extensive time-frame under discussion. This chapter has begun to tease out some of the principal patterns in these Atlantic regions. During the Beaker and Early Bronze Age, Ireland and Iberia were connected through Atlantic exchange systems. Ireland was also closely linked to regions in Scotland and, to a lesser extent Wales. Sporadic interaction between these regions and western Iberia may also be detected in gold objects and cist burials, yet the various strands of evidence indicate that flows of interaction were complex. While the initial Beaker influence may have spread gradually northwards from central Portugal, by the Early Bronze Age multi-directional spheres of interaction were very much in evidence, with halberds and cist burials suggesting a dissemination of other sets of practices from Ireland and Scotland southwards. England and Scotland were initially plugged into different interaction networks, and the introduction of Beakers was likely from central Europe. After a period of relative insularity and detachment in the Middle Bronze Age, Atlantic networks became reformed on an increasingly intensive scale, during the first half of the Late Bronze Age. It was only when southern parts of Iberia became more closely realigned with Mediterranean trade networks towards the end of the Late Bronze Age that this period of coherency and integration once again began to fracture.

These supra-regional connections indicate that rather than being on the periphery, these areas of western Europe were closely linked from an early stage, not only for the transfer of knowledge and ideologies, but also the movement of people, animals, and objects. These archaeologically visible networks of connectivity have important implications for research into the nature and types of communication that they facilitated, including the sharing and dissemination of different languages.

Further reading

Useful general overviews for the Bronze Age, including a specific focus on the Atlantic regions include **A. Harding**, *European Societies in the Bronze Age* (Cambridge, 2008); **J. T. Koch & B. Cunliffe** (eds), *Celtic from the West 2: Rethinking the Bronze Age and the Arrival of Indo-European in Atlantic Europe*, Celtic Studies Publications 16 (Oxford, 2013); **A. Harding & H. Fokkens** (eds), *The Oxford Handbook of the European Bronze Age* (Oxford 2013); **J. T. Koch, B. Cunliffe, K. Cleary, & C. D. Gibson** (eds), *Celtic from the West 3: Atlantic Europe in the Metal Ages—questions of shared language*, Celtic Studies Publications 19 (Oxford, 2016).

Regionally specific accounts include **R. Bradley**, *The Prehistory of Britain and Ireland* (Cambridge, 2007); **B. Cunliffe**, *Britain Begins* (Oxford, 2012); **M. Herity & G. Eogan** *Ireland in Prehistory* (London, 1989); **J. Waddell & E. Shee Twohig** (eds), *Ireland in the Bronze Age* (Dublin, 1995); and **M. Cruz Berrocal, L. García Sanjuán & A. Gilman** (eds), *The Prehistory of Iberia. Debating Early Social Stratification and the State* (London, 2013).

Late Neolithic, Grooved Ware and megalithic monuments

A useful introduction to subject of Grooved Ware is **R. Cleal & A. MacSween** (eds), *Grooved Ware in Britain and Ireland* (Oxford, 1999), and for the development and spread of megalithic monuments and art see **E. Shee Twohig**, *The Megalithic Art of Western Europe* (Oxford, 1981); **C. Scarre** (ed.), *Monuments and Landscape in Atlantic Europe: Perception and Society during the Neolithic and Early Bronze Age* (London/New York 2002); **A. Sheridan**, 'Going Round in Circles? Understanding the Irish Grooved Ware 'Complex' in its Wider Context', in H. Roche, E. Grogan, J. Bradley, J. Coles, & B. Raftery (eds), *From Megaliths to Metals* (Oxford, 2004), 26–37; and **C. Scarre** 'Rock of Ages: Time and Tempo in Megalithic Monuments', *European Journal of Archaeology* 13/2 (2010) 175–93.

Traversing the seas, travelling the land

Much has been written on prehistoric travel, and a most useful introduction is **B. Cunliffe** *Facing the Ocean: The Atlantic and its People* (Oxford, 2001). Useful summaries on prehistoric boats are **S. McGrail**, *Ancient Boats in North-West Europe* (London, 1987); **P. Clark** (ed.), *The Dover Bronze Age Boat in Context: Society and Water Transport in Prehistoric Europe* (Oxford, 2004); and **S. Needham, D. Parham, & C. J. Frieman**, *Claimed by the Sea: Salcombe, Langdon Bay, and other Marine Finds of the Bronze Age* (York, 2013). Other pertinent articles on boats and sea travel include **K. Muckelroy**, 'Middle Bronze Age Trade between Britain and Europe: A Maritime perspective', *Proceedings of the Prehistoric Society* 47 (1981) 275–97; R. **Callaghan & C. Scarre**, 'Simulating the Western Seaways'. *Oxford Journal of Archaeology* 28/4 (2009) 357–72; and **R. Bradley, A. Rogers, F. Sturt, F. and A. Watson**, 'Maritime Havens in Earlier Prehistoric Britain', *Proceedings of the Prehistoric Society* 82 (2016) 125–59. For evidence of horse riding and wheeled vehicles, see **S. Piggott**, *The Earliest Wheeled Transport: From the Atlantic Coast to the Caspian Sea* (London, 1983); **R. Fábregas Valcarce & C. Rodríduez-Rellán**, 'Walking on the stones of years. Some remarks on the North-west Iberian Rock Art', in P. Skoglund, J. Ling, & U. Bertilsson (eds), *Picturing the Bronze Age* (Oxford, 2015) 47–63; and **R. Brunning & C. McDermott**, 'Trackways and Roads across the Wetlands', in F. Menotti and A. O'Sullivan (eds), *The Oxford Handbook of Wetland Archaeology* (Oxford, 2012) 359–84

The Beaker 'package'

Much has been written on Bell Beakers, and comprehensive overviews include **R. J. Harrison**, *The Beaker Folk* (London, 1980); **F. Nicolis** (ed.), *Bell Beakers Today: Pottery, People, Culture, Symbols in Prehistoric Europe* (Trento, 2001); **M. Allen, J. Gardiner, & A. Sheridan** (eds), *Is there a British Chalcolithic? People, Place and* *polity in the later Third Millennium* (Oxford, 2012); **J. Czebreszuk** (ed.), *Similar but Different: Bell Beakers in Europe*' (Leiden, 2014); and **M. P. Prieto Martínez & L. Salanova** (eds), *The Bell Beaker Transition in Europe: Mobility and Local Evolution during the 3rd Millennium BC* (Oxford, 2015). Some interesting interpretations regarding the spread of the Beakers are **C. Burgess & S. Shennan**, 'The Beaker Phenomenon: some Suggestions', in C. Burgess & R. Miket (eds), *Settlement and Economy in the Third and Second Millennia* (Oxford 1976) 309–31; **S. Needham**, 'Isotopic Aliens: Beaker Movement and Cultural Transmissions', in M. Larsson & M. Parker Pearson (eds), *From Stonehenge to the Baltic: Cultural Diversity in the Third Millennium BC* (Oxford, 2007) 41–46; and **M. Vander Linden**, 'What Linked the Bell Beakers in Third Millennium BC Europe?', *Antiquity*, 81 (2007), 343–52.

Recent research on tracing mobility through isotope analysis can be found in **M. Parker Pearson**, 'Beaker Migrants. Force? Or Fantasy?', *British Archaeology* 150 (2016) 30–35; **M. Parker Pearson, A. Chamberlain, M. Jay, M. Richards, A. Sheridan, N. Curtis, J. Evans, A. Gibson, M. Hutchison, P. Mahoney, P. Marshall, J. Montgomery, S. Needham, S. O'Mahoney, M. Pellegrini, & N. Wilkin**, 'Beaker People in Britain: Migration, Mobility and Diet', *Antiquity*, 90/351 (2016) 620–37; and **P. Díaz-del-Río, A. J. Waterman, J. T. Thomas, D. W. Peate, R. H. Tykot, M.I. Martínez-Navarette, & J. M. Vicent**, 'Diet and Mobility Patterns in the Late Prehistory of Central Iberia (4000–1400 cal BC): the Evidence of Radiogenic ($^{87}Sr/^{86}Sr$) and Stable (^{18}O, ^{13}C) Isotope Ratios', *Archaeological Anthropological Science* (2017), Doi: https://10.1007/s12520-017-0480-y. For follow-up reading on aDNA studies see **W. Haak et al.**, 'Massive Migration from the Steppe was a Source for Indo-European languages in Europe', *Nature* 522 (2015) 207–11. http://dx.doi.org/10.1038/nature14317; and **I. Olalde et al.**, The Beaker Phenomenon and the Genomic Transformation of Northwest Europe', *Nature* (2017), bioRxiv 135962; doi: https://doi.org/10.1101/135962

Mining and metallurgy

Early copper mining and metallurgy is also a well-explored subject. Further reading on copper exploitation includes **W. O'Brien**, *Ross Island. Mining, Metal and Society* (Galway, 2004); **W. O'Brien**, *Prehistoric Mining in Europe, 5500–500 BC* (Oxford, 2015); and **S. Timberlake** 'Copper Mining, Prospection and the Beaker Phenomenon in Wales—the significance of the Banc Tynddol sun disc', in J. T. Koch, B. Cunliffe, K. Cleary, & C. D. Gibson (eds) *Celtic from the West 3: Atlantic Europe in the Metal Ages—questions of shared language*, Celtic Studies Publications 19 (Oxford, 2016) 111–38. For analysis of metals see **B. Rohl & S. Needham**, *The Circulation of Metal in the British Bronze Age: the Application of Lead Isotope Analysis* (London, 1998); **P. J. Bray & A. M. Pollard**, 'A New Interpretative Approach to the Chemistry of Copper-alloy Objects: Source, Recycling and Technology', *Antiquity* 86/333 (2012), 853–67; and **J. Ling, Z. Stos-Gale, L. Grandin, K. Billström, E. Hjärthner-Holdar, & P.-O. Persson**, 'Moving Metals II: Provenancing Scandinavian Bronze Artefacts by Lead Isotope Analyses', *Journal of Archaeological Science* 41 (2014) 106–32.

Adopting and adapting Beakers

The diversity expressed in the Beaker package can be traced through the following articles. For bracers see **H. Fokkens, Y. Achterkamp, & M. Kuijpers**, 'Bracers or Bracelets? About the Functionality and Meaning of Beaker Wrist-guards', *Proceedings of the Prehistoric Society* 74 (2008) 109–40; and **A. Woodward & J. Hunter**, *An Examination of Prehistoric Stone Bracers from Britain* (Oxford, 2011). With regards to polypod bowls see **T. G. Manby**, 'Skeuomorphism: Some Reflections of Leather, Wood and Basketry in Early Bronze Age Pottery', in I. Kinnes & G. Varndell (eds), *Unbaked Urns of Rudely Shape*, (Oxford, 1995) 81–88; and **H. Case**, 'Bell Beaker and Corded Ware Culture Burial Associations.

A Bottom-up rather than Top-down Approach', in **A. Gibson & A. Sheridan** (eds), *From Sickles to Circles: Britain and Ireland at the Time of Stonehenge* (Stroud, 2004) 201–14. For weapons see **S. Needham**, 'The Lost Cultures of the Halberd Bearers: a non-Beaker Ideology in the Later 3rd Millennium Atlantic Europe', in J. T. Koch, B. Cunliffe, K. Cleary, & C. D. Gibson (eds) *Celtic from the West 3: Atlantic Europe in the Metal Ages—questions of shared language*, Celtic Studies Publications 19 (Oxford, 2016) 40–82.

Gold objects

Further reading for goldwork includes **J. J. Taylor**, *Bronze Age Goldwork of the British Isles* (Cambridge 1980); **B. Armbruster & B. Comendador Rey**, 'Early Gold Technology as an Indicator of Circulation processes in Atlantic Europe', in M. P. Prieto Martínez & L. Salanova (eds), *The Bell Beaker Transition in Europe: Mobility and Local Evolution during the 3rd millennium BC* (Oxford 2015) 140–50; and **S. Needham & A. Sheridan** 'Chalcolithic and Early Bronze Age Goldwork from Britain: New Finds and New Perspectives', in H. Meller, R. Risch, & E. Pernicka (eds), *Metals of power —Early Gold and Silver. Papers from the 6th Archaeological Conference of Central Germany* (Halle, 2014), 903–32. With regards to solar and lunar ideologies, consult **F. Kaul**, 'Bronze Age Tripartite Cosmologies', *Praehistorische Zeitschrift* 80 (2005) 135–48; **M. Cahill**, 'Here Comes the Sun…', *Archaeology Ireland*, 29/1 (2015) 26–33; and **M. Cahill** 'A stone to die for', *Archaeology Ireland*, 30(3), (2016), 26–29.

Early Bronze Age diversity and cross-channel maritories

Recent interpretations on the development of Early Bronze Age cultural complexes are given by **S. Needham**, 'Transforming Beaker Culture in North-West Europe: Processes of Fusion and Fission', *Proceedings of the Prehistoric Society* 71 (2005) 171–217; and **P. Clark** (ed.) *Bronze Age Connections. Cultural Contact in Prehistoric Europe* (Oxford, 2009). For further work on high-status Early Bronze Age burials, a comprehensive account for southern Britain is provided in **A. Woodward & J. Hunter**, *Ritual in Early Bronze Age Grave Goods: An Examination of Ritual and Dress Equipment from Chalcolithic and Early Bronze Age Graves in England* (Oxford, 2015). For other areas of Atlantic Europe useful accounts include **S. Needham**, 'Power Pulses across a Cultural Divide: Cosmologically Driven Acquisition Between Armorica and Wessex', *Proceedings of the Prehistoric Society* 66 (2000) 151–207; and **D. Brandherm**, 'Algunas reflexiones sobre el Bronce Inicial en el Noroeste peninsular: La cuestión del llamado horizonte "Montelavar"', *Cuadernos de Prehistoria y Arqueología de la Universidad Autónoma de Madrid* 33 (2007) 60–90.

Some of the more accessible regional accounts for the diversity evident in the Early Bronze Age of Atlantic Europe include **B. Ó Ríordáin, & J. Waddell**, *The Funerary Bowls and Vases of the Irish Bronze Age* (Galway, 1993); **A. Brindley**, *The Dating of Food Vessels and Urns in Ireland* (Galway, 2006); **K. Becker**, 'Transforming Identities—New Approaches to Bronze Age Deposition in Ireland', *Proceedings of the Prehistoric Society* 79 (2013) 225–65; **C. Burgess**, *The Age of Stonehenge* (London 1980/2001); **S. Needham, C. Bronk Ramsey, D. Coombs, C. Cartwright, & P. Pettit**, 'An Independent Chronology for British Bronze Age Metalwork: the Results of the Oxford Radiocarbon Accelerator programme', *Archaeological Journal* 154 (1998) 55–107; **A. Sheridan**, 'Towards a Fuller, more Nuanced Narrative of Chalcolithic and Early Bronze Age Britain 2500–1500 BC, *Bronze Age Review*, 1 (2008), 57–78; and **P. Vázquez Liz, L. Nonat, & M. P. Prieto Martínez**, 'Dynamism and Complexity of the Funerary Models: the North-west Iberian Peninsula during the 3rd–2nd Millennia BC., in M. P. Prieto Martínez & L. Salanova (eds), *The Bell Beaker Transition in Europe: Mobility and Local Evolution during the 3rd Millennium BC* (Oxford, 2015) 195–210.

Middle Bronze Age

In the Middle Bronze Age, the focus of archaeological research switches from the funerary domain towards landscapes, settlements, and metalwork. Further reading for these spheres can be found in **J. Barrett & R. Bradley** (eds), *Settlement and Society in the British Later Bronze Age* (Oxford 1980); **B. O'Connor**, *Cross-Channel Relations in the Later Bronze Age* (Oxford 1980); J. Brück (ed.), *Bronze Age Landscapes. Tradition and Transformation* (Oxford, 2001); **D. Yates**, *Land, Power and prestige: Bronze Age Field Systems in Southern England* (Oxford, 2007); and **H. Schubart**, *Die Kultur der Bronzezeit im Südwesten der Iberischen Halbinsel* (Berlin, 1975).

Atlantic Late Bronze Age

Research on the Late Bronze Age of Atlantic Europe has traditionally focused on the metalwork evidence. This includes **C. Burgess & I. Colquhoun**, *The Swords of Britain* (Munich, 1988); **G. Eogan**, *The Hoards of the Irish Later Bronze Age* (Dublin, 1983); **A. Coffyn**, *Le Bronze Final Atlantique dans la Péninsule Ibérique* (Paris, 1985); **S. Needham & S. Bowman**, 'Flesh-hooks, Technological Complexity and the Atlantic Bronze Age Feasting Complex', *European Journal of Archaeology* 8/2, (2005) 93–136; **S. Gerloff**, *Atlantic Cauldrons and Buckets of the Late Bronze and Early Iron Ages in Western Europe* (Stuttgart, 2010); and **D. Brandherm & M. Moskal-del-Hoyo**, 'Both Sides Now: The Carp's Tongue Sword Revisited', *The Antiquaries Journal* 94 (2014) 1–47.

CHAPTER FIVE

CHEMISTRY AND BRONZE AGE METALS IN ATLANTIC EUROPE: FLOWS OF IDEAS AND MATERIAL

Peter Bray

Pioneers and polymaths

IN 1686 Robert Plot (1640–1696) wrote in his *The Natural History of Staffordshire*:

> It is plain that all those places [...] were sometime visited by the Roman militia, and were places of some action. And so for the same reason the parish of Ilam, where was found near the spring call'd St. Bertram's Well, an instrument of brass, somewhat like (only larger than) a lath-hammer at the edg [sic] end, but no so [sic] on the other [...] which I take to have been the head of a Roman Securis with which the Papae slew their sacrifices, notwithstanding it have no eye for the manubrium to pass through, the securis itself sometimes only stuck through it as may be seen at many places amongst the Roman antiquities of Bartolus and Bellorius...

Though we now know this artefact to be an Early Bronze Age axe, the effort to classify and explain ancient metal artefacts has been an organized pursuit for centuries. Museums, field archaeology and the physical sciences have always been closely united in these efforts. The career of 'the learned Plot', as he was nicknamed by his illustrious Royal Society colleagues, is just one excellent example. In 1683 he was simultaneously appointed the first Keeper of the Ashmolean Museum of art and antiquities in Oxford, and the first professor of the nascent science of chemistry at the University. This was a remarkable achievement that underlines the connections between different branches of enquiry during the European Enlightenment.

This chapter continues the story of chemists' work on early metals in Atlantic Europe. To do this we must also discuss broader changes in how archaeologists thought about metal and technology in ancient societies, as well as the changing techniques utilized by scientists to engage with these questions. Modern archaeometallurgy has become an exciting mixture of cutting-edge material science, experimental reconstructions of ancient techniques, chemical analysis of artefacts, social archaeology, and conceptual models. The complete range of skills can no longer be contained in one modern-day Plot, no matter how learned.

In the 18th and 19th centuries the tools and frameworks that modern archaeologists continue to use were slowly developed. The most famous of these, the three-age system, was based on a sequence of materials reflecting a series of stages of human society: stone, bronze, and iron. This idea has deep roots in European thought, stretching back beyond the *Works and Days* of Hesiod (*c.* 7th century BC) and *De Rerum Natura* of Lucretius (*c.* 99–55 BC). For these ancient writers, changes in the material assemblage reflected the decline of mankind from a golden age, or alternatively the rising up of humanity from a state of barbarism. Rather than rely on these general arcs of change, scholars such as Christian Thomsen (1788–1865) at the National Museum of Denmark began to order systematically the large amounts of archaic objects that were being recovered during farming or building work. By paying careful attention to the shapes (typological class) of objects, their associations in burial, and the layers or strata they were recovered from, Thomsen and others could demonstrate the broad validity of the Stone Age, Bronze Age, and Iron Age sequence. Beyond this, regional and local patterns emerged of distinctive styles of metalwork, which allowed much finer gradations of the Bronze Age to be defined. The detailed typo-chronological study of different artefact types across Europe continues to this day. Despite the principles being laid down in the 19th century, this work continues to be at the heart of our understanding of chronology, local identity, contacts between societies, and metal technology.

Less well known is the important chemical work that was underway at the same time that the three-age system was coalescing. In many ways these pioneer scientists were following the same approach as their museum colleagues, often trying to classify chemical types and alloy sequences within ancient bronzes. Many of the early scientists working on archaeological material will be familiar, such as Humphrey Davy (1778–1829) who completed a study of Roman pigment, or Michael Faraday (1791–1867) who first discovered the use of lead glazes in antiquity. Ancient metals were often at the heart of these early experiments, and, as with the development of object-typology studies, the conceptual tools they developed are still in current use. In fact, it is fair to say that the study of the composition of ancient metal is one of the longest ongoing chemistry experiments in the world.

Two studies from this period stand out as setting the tone for almost the whole history of chemical archaeometallurgy. In the mid-19th century many of the key concept of the 'Provenance Hypothesis' had been derived and put into action. Jan Wocel (1803–1871), Professor of Archaeology and Art History at the University of Prague, and Karl Göbel (1794–1851) Professor of Chemistry and Pharmacy, University of Dorpat, both argued that by comparing chemical compositions of different societies they could demonstrate the age and source of the material. Wocel working on the composition of Czech Iron Age metal artefacts concluded that the presence of zinc in the alloy demonstrated contact with the Roman Empire. Göbel came to similar conclusions by comparing large amounts of chemical composition data from excavated artefacts in the Baltic with those from secure Greek and Roman contexts.

The principal metals and alloys (the mixture of two or more metals) were known from contemporary industry and also key historical texts. Pliny the Elder's *Naturalis Historia* and the standard early modern work on mining and metallurgy *De Re Metallica* by Georgius Agricola directly informed research. Early archaeometallurgists were therefore very familiar with the fact that mixing the metals copper, tin, lead, and zinc produced a wide range of alloys (Fig. 5.1):

Binary: Bronze (copper, tin), Brass (copper, zinc)
Ternary: Leaded Bronze (copper, tin, lead), Gunmetal (copper, tin, zinc)
Quaternary: Leaded Gunmetal (copper, tin, zinc, lead)

There were also specific mixtures of metals that had special properties such as the high-tin bronze used for mirrors called speculum (*c.* 33% tin), or the slightly different bronze (*c.* 25% tin) that is named bell-metal due to its hardness and attractive sound when struck. These alloys were identified through practical experience and had been in use long before modern chemistry or industry.

By the mid 19th century scientific archaeometallurgy had already moved beyond the one-off analysis of ancient objects and towards the systematic collection, comparison, and demonstration of group chemical patterns. Patterns were seen as representing a time-period (for example brass from the first centuries AD), an identifiable named group (the Roman Empire) and place (western and Mediterranean Europe). It is worth quoting in full the definition of the 'Provenance Hypothesis' as it stood by 2001 in the work of Mark Pollard, Professor of Archaeological Science, University of Bradford. The direct conceptual threads running back to Wocel and Göbel are clear.

> We can determine the source of the material from which an object was made if:
> 1. Some chemical (or isotopic) characteristic of the geological raw material(s) is carried through (unchanged, or predictably relatable) into the finished object.
> 2. This 'fingerprint' varies between potential geological sources available in the past, and this variation can be related to the geographical source of the raw material. Inter-source variation must be greater than intra-source variation.
> 3. Such characteristic 'fingerprints' can be measured with sufficient precision in the finished artefacts to enable discrimination between competing potential sources.
> 4. No 'mixing' of raw materials occurs (either before or during processing, or as a result of recycling of material), or that any such mixing can be adequately accounted for.
> 5. Post-depositional processes either have no effect on the characteristic fingerprint, or some satisfactory allowance can be made.
> 6. Any observed patterns of trade or exchange of finished materials are interpretable in terms of human behaviour.

The analytical procedures changed radically, the amount of data and archaeological details also drastically improved, but the underlying conceptual framework of 'chemical provenance' ties together the next hundred years of our story.

The systematic collection of metal composition patterns always occurred alongside the work of archaeologists studying the shapes and cultural associations of the artefacts. Dozens of regional and country-wide specialists extended out the typo-chronological work begun by pioneers such as Thomsen. In retrospect this approach has been termed the Culture-Historical school, as collections of similar looking objects were seen as defining specific cultures with fixed time spans. Monumental works such as Sir John Evans' (1823–1908) *The Ancient Bronze Implements, Weapons and Ornaments of Great Britain and Ireland* united the antiquarian work of earlier centuries and offered a new synthesized model of prehistory that continues to be referenced. Interestingly, Oscar Wilde's physician father Sir William Wilde (1815–1876) created one such scheme for Ireland. The Early Bronze Age assemblage contains flat axes and simple daggers, in the Middle Bronze Age the axes shape changes to that of a palstave (an axe with deep flanges allowing the secure fastening of a split handle) and daggers lengthen to be called rapiers. While in the Late Bronze Age axes become fully socketed and the leaf-shaped sword became dominant, effective for slashing as well as stabbing. Of course there are a wide range of other artefact types within the record, and the dating of these objects continues to be refined, however the overall *relative* sequence is still valid and is in current use.

Industrialization of Data

A significant jump forward for scientific archaeometallurgy was the introduction of new instrumental analysis techniques to the field. In the 1920s and 1930s optical emission spectroscopy (OES) gave archaeologists access to large amounts of affordable, relatively accurate (close to the 'true' figure as determined by known standards) and precise data (a result within a low spread of possibilities). Formerly, relatively large samples were required for laborious 'wet' chemical approaches; the chemical composition being determined by dissolving the sample in acids, precipitating each element out of solution separately, and weighing the resulting solids.

OES works by a very different approach that is based upon the behaviour of elements on a sub-atomic level. The atom consists of a dense, positively charged, nucleus and orbiting negative electrons. Each element has a unique number of protons in its nucleus (29 for copper, 50 for tin, and so on), and a corresponding arrangement of orbiting electrons that fall into well-defined shells. In optical emission spectroscopy the ground-up sample of metal is volatilized through a powerful electric spark and emits light. The wavelengths of this emitted light can be split by a prism and recorded on photographic plates. Each element in the sample produces a characteristic set of lines on the plate because of their distinctive electron structure. Beyond identifying the elements in the sample, their different weight percentage can be determined by comparing the varying intensity of the recorded lines to known standards. Importantly the entire composition of an artefact could be quickly ascertained all at once through sparking a small sample. Essentially a chemical analysis production line could be set up that reduced costs.

Though OES may appear to be a more complicated procedure than just dissolving a section of the artefact, it actually revolutionized how scientists could investigate ancient materials. Now museum curators could be persuaded to part with small amounts of metal drilled from huge numbers of artefacts, and during the mid 20th century co-ordinated programmes of analysis started in earnest. In a break with the 19th century pioneers, the formerly close links between the chemists and archaeologists became increasingly strained, while both groups were actually attempting to answer similar questions. We hope that describing two large-scale projects, all of which made extensive use of OES, will explain this apparent contradiction. Loosely described as the Austrian and Stuttgart Schools, their approaches to data collection and interpretation demonstrate the range of concerns held by archaeometallurgists at the time.

In their contemporary review of the dramatic new wave of scientific analyses of Bronze Age metal archaeologists Waterbolk and Butler noted that the different teams tended to work from their local strengths. The Austrian team, led by Pittioni, working mostly in the rich mining region of the Alps naturally focused on the variation in the metal-bearing minerals. Conversely, the series of Stuttgart SAM projects (*Studien zu den Anfängen der Metallurgie, Studies on the origins of metallurgy*), that were based further north, aimed to understand variation in the huge collections of recovered metal objects housed in the museums of Europe. Unfortunately, despite being initially recognized as complementary projects, each working within local circumstances, the debates over the results of their work quickly became acrimonious. Heated discussions over which is the sole correct way to interpret the chemical data from early mining and metallurgy continue to this day.

To simplify, Pittioni used a presence-absence approach to the data. For him the crucial distinguishing mark of the various mineral systems used in antiquity were the different combinations of metals brought together in the rocks. If you look at any table of minerals, they all tend to have the textbook definition of their composition, for example:

Tenorite: CuO
Malachite: $CuCO_3.Cu(OH)_2$
Tennantite: $Cu_{12}As_4S_{13}$
Tetrahedrite: $Cu_{12}Sb_4S_{13}$

Real ores deposits however tend to be complex mixes of various elements, with metals often substituting for others in the dominant mineral structure. This is commonly seen between arsenic (As) and antimony (Sb) for example, which tend to form ranged tennantite-tetrahedrite series. Pittioni and the 'Austrian School' hoped to cut through complex variations in the precise *level* of the chemical elements being found in the artefacts, in order to focus on the signal of *combinations* preserved from the mine.

The details of the ore-formation process are important to interpreting the chemistry of archaeological copper-based objects. The common occurrence of low levels of arsenic in early bronze can mean very different things if that arsenic is found with accompanying nickel, or found alone. Arsenic may end up in the final metal from a wide range of sources, but the combination of arsenic-antimony-silver is more rare and can help identify the source region or even a particular mine.

Meanwhile the SAM project, based in Stuttgart, focused on creating huge amounts of chemical data and then mathematically analysing the chemical variations within their collection. To this team the precise level of the various chemical elements was the key to identifying the source of copper and bronze. By current standards of funding, access to objects, and permission to take samples, the SAM project is astonishing. It was a sustained effort, stretching more than a decade that touched upon practically all the major European collections of Bronze Age metal. As its name suggests, *Studies on the origins of metallurgy* mostly sampled Copper Age (Chalcolithic) and Early Bronze Age artefacts, while also collecting published data from other contemporary scholars. If you visit the Early Bronze Age galleries in most European capitals today it is often possible to see the distinctive filled-in drill holes created by the SAM project. In total over 30,000 artefacts were sampled for analysis by optical emission spectroscopy (OES). Most modern curators will cringe at the thought of that volume of destructive sampling. The position of the drill holes within the objects also reveals the confidence and access of the scientists. It is remarkable to researchers today that they usually drilled into the middle of the axe face, or through the centre of the dagger. Nowadays it is typical policy to take solid samples rarely if alternative techniques are available, and only if the question really demands that level of intervention. Even under these circumstances only broken edges or concealed faces tend to be sampled.

Mark Pollard refers to this era as the field's 'heroic age' of boldness and self-assurance. Faith that scientific approaches would open new insights into past technology cut across all sections of the archaeological world, from curators, period specialists, through to laboratory technicians and mathematical modellers. With only a few pilot studies having been completed, in particular the work of W. Witter and H. Otto, the SAM project was a dramatic intensification of the application of chemistry to ancient metallurgy. The underlying provenance concept was still intact, unchanged from the days of Wocel and Göbel, but the volume of data now available would quickly outstrip the ability of archaeologists to detect patterns by hand. The SAM team's confidence in their scientific approach was so great that much of the interpretation of their data was passed to statistical modellers.

The volume of chemical data created by the series of related SAM projects presents both a mathematical and a philosophical challenge. It is important to bear in mind that there is not a universally accepted method by which to interpret any structure or shapes within the composition figures. All the research groups during the 1950s and '60s agreed on two main signals: one from the mine and the other from deliberately adding tin to make bronze. After stripping away the alloying elements,

Pittioni's team focused upon *combinations* of other elements, in small amounts, to reveal patterns reflecting the mine. SAM instead took the view that our knowledge about Bronze Age mining will always be lacking, therefore the precise *level* and *distribution* of elements in the assemblage of finished objects must be emphasized. Certainly, the intensive exploitation of ore sources by modern industrial methods can obscure some Bronze Age activity.

What is an appropriate way to reconstruct a mining signal, if we cannot be sure we can check the chemistry from identified prehistoric mines? Klein, the statistician on the project, proposed a method to identify statistically recurring groups of uniform composition. In effect he decided what the mathematical shape of an ore source would look like chemically, and then tried to find this shape within the data statistically. Based on a small pilot study of Bronze Age copper ingots, it was decided that the chemical pattern created by a source would create a shape that is described as a log-normal distribution. This is a very common pattern found in the natural world and is related to the more widely familiar bell curve, but with the fat part of the curve pushed towards lower levels, and a long drawn out tail stretching up to higher levels. Klein was trying to untangle mathematically the whole chemical dataset into groups that showed the repeating off-centre bell curve shape, trusting that that one shape represented the underlying archaeological reality of metal extraction.

For the SAM project and their supporters, the mathematical sieving of the data into repeated clusters was a remarkable success. Rather than trying to cope with an overwhelming mass of data, filling several large volumes of fine print, they could now identify a series of groups, each with a characteristic signature. To explain this complex procedure to archaeologists they drew a branching decision diagram, which explained the thresholds of each group. You begin with the 'Total Population' of all the chemical composition sets that were produced by OES. Then all the objects that contain more than 0.08% bismuth are split off from those that contain less. The next step for the high-bismuth objects is to split them into high-arsenic (C1), over 0.64%, and low-arsenic groups. For the high-bismuth (>0.08% Bi), low-arsenic objects (less than 0.64% As), the final factor was determined to be the amount of antimony in the object: less than 0.5% defined group C3, more than 0.5% defined group C2.

The advantages of summarizing these complex steps into one clear diagram will be quickly appreciated. From the vast amount of time represented by the Early Bronze Age (*c.* 2200–1600 BC), its thousands of metal artefacts, dozens of mines, and the range of technological processes, SAM abstracted twelve chemical groups: C1, C2, C3, A, B1, B2, E01, E00, E11, E10, F1, and F2. The industrialization of chemical analyses that had threatened to outstrip the ability of archaeologists to interpret them had been brought back to a human-scale challenge. Pittioni's approach of combinations of elements was now firmly replaced in the debate by intense discussion of SAM clusters.

After the groupings were defined, the SAM programme plotted where objects made from each group of metal were deposited, in which periods, and in what forms. It was immediately obvious that some of the groups clustered in particular regions, for example C2 is present in very high levels in the first half of the Early Bronze Age just north of the Alps in central Europe. Also some regions showed clear splits in their object assemblages, with Italian axes famously being made of very low impurity metal, while the daggers contain a great deal of arsenic. They felt that their aim had been achieved, that through statistically sifting the available data repeating workshops of metal production had been identified. By the early 1970s scholars such as Edward Sangmeister were confident that these chemical groups represented Bronze Age hotspots of the accumulation of raw material and the production of finished objects.

The changing character of technology and material in archaeology

The great chemistry projects of the post-war period need to be understood alongside the debates on technology from the wider archaeological world. Dealing with the scientific data was both a mathematical and philosophical question. The answers are not straightforward. What structure does the data contain? By what process should we investigate those patterns? And how can we link those patterns to understanding the nature of technology?

We saw above how metal artefacts have taken on a series of roles within archaeology. Their characteristic shapes have been used to distinguish the peoples and periods of the past. This effort of classification and linking, typo-chronology, continues to this day and is a fundamental archaeological tool. Though all archaeologists can identify the major classes of metal object, we all rely on a small band of specialists who can identify obscure nuances of shape and decoration and link these to time and place. Without this expertise long stretches of the Bronze Age would be an undifferentiated mass. With them, we can carefully identify regional traditions, the style of individual craftspeople, shifts in production technology, and choices made in the past.

For many decades material culture, the objects and technology employed in the past, were the simple, straightforward building blocks of archaeology—challenging and complicated to learn, but straightforward in their interpretation. Christopher Hawkes (1905–1992), Professor of European Archaeology at the University of Oxford, famously summarized this point of view in his Ladder of Inference model, published in 1954. The question is a fundamental one: how easy is it to identify secure knowledge about the past? How do we know what we know, and when do our inferences become tenuous and unsafe? Material culture was seen by Hawkes and his contemporaries as the firm base of a ladder, arguing that it is relatively easy to infer the meaning, place, and purpose of objects and technology due to their functional and common-sense place in life, particularly when compared to the top rungs: political relationships, social organization, and spiritual life. This is a powerful model of how we should go about archaeology, building carefully from the known to the unknown, while being explicit about the steps being taken.

Hawkes' philosophical worldview passed directly into his interpretation of the Bronze Age *and* his relationship to scientific investigation. For example, Hawkes argued in 1959 that iron's superiority over bronze allowed the invasion and colonization of southern Britain:

> Hallstatt adventurers were moving in—aliens to the country and its metal merchants. They were roving and spying out the land. They had bronze gear of their own; but what was more, they had come already knowing iron. [...] Lowland Britain could be colonised outright. Neither their Urnfield forerunners nor the remnants of older folk, with no use of iron nor near resource of bronze, could long prevent it. By the middle sixth century the colonists were coming.

Here metal sits, relatively simply, as a fundamental factor of change. Our modern appreciation of hardness, sharpness, and toughness being linked to shifts in the past.

There are also links in that paragraph to the work of Gordon Childe (1892–1957, Professor of Archaeology at Edinburgh, then Director of the Institute of Archaeology, London), who argued in a famous concept that archaeological ages could be seen as technological stages, with iron as the next phase of 'development' after bronze. The argument largely rests on iron's apparent practical advantages; it is far more common than the rare resources of copper and tin oxides, and has superior mechanical properties, especially when alloyed with carbon to make steel. However iron is harder to win from its oxides and therefore requires more sophisticated smelting technology, thus appearing later in the archaeological record.

Childe and Hawkes were central to the development of British prehistory studies and both had deep links with archaeological science; sharing the view that all academic disciplines should be brought to bear on the past. Childe was a founding member of the Ancient Mining and Metallurgy Committee of the Royal Anthropological Institute, created in 1945. Hawkes, in 1952, helped found the first dedicated archaeological science department in Britain, the Research Laboratory for Archaeology and the History of Art (RLAHA), University of Oxford. Both men serve as prime examples of fruitful dialogue across specialisms and were just as remarkable polymaths as their predecessors from 250 years before, such as Robert Plot. Realizing a dedicated term was required to describe the application of science to archaeology, Hawkes proposed 'archaeometry', the 'measuring of the past', which still enjoys widespread use in the name of journals and conferences.

Clear connections exist between the Ladder of Inference concept, and the philosophical underpinnings of the SAM analytical projects and their contemporaries. For the chemists in the 1960s the bottom rung of interpretation was identifying repeating shapes in the data. The SAM team believed that the chemical levels for a related group of archaeological objects would fall into the log-normal, off-centre curves, whence they built up more complex archaeological interpretations. However, this assumption of the shape of Bronze Age chemistry was based on themes from modern metallurgical processing: consistency, repeatability, purity, markets, and design. These are chemical versions of Hawkes' assertion that material culture can be assigned, relatively common-sense functional roles in life. Of course, this is still a challenging process, but one that is more accessible than spiritual or political life.

The term 'process' has gone into and out of fashion within archaeology. During the 1960s and 1970s it came to define the dominant academic framework for studying the past: 'Processualism'. Growing out of debates about 'functionalist' material culture, it tried to explicitly use the 'hard' sciences of biology, chemistry, and physics to understand the past. This often went beyond just applying analytical techniques and there were efforts to identify laws of behaviour, and rules of how these processes would be preserved in the ground. Again, there was a clear relationship between chemical analysis of metal objects and the wider philosophical atmosphere. The rules for identifying repeating structures in large lists of numbers, such as the decision tree used by SAM were attempted for areas of life, such as the breakage rate of ceramics, or the production costs of glass vessels. In fact, the progress and statistical clarity of SAM and other projects were sometimes looked on with jealousy by other archaeologists who wished to create law-based archaeology. Part of describing the 1950s and '60s data explosion as 'heroic' is that chemists were in the unaccustomed role of being at the forefront of archaeological interpretation and policy.

The heroic phase did not last long as there were intense debates over whether the variety of human experience could be, or should be, reduced to formulas and laws. The reaction to the most strident Processualist theoretical positions was strong, and termed (not very imaginatively) as Post-Processualism. From the mid 1980s up to the present time, subjectivity, negotiation, fluidity of roles, and individual experience were emphasized by many archaeological thinkers. Crucially for this story, objects and technology were to be active parts of this nuanced and complex debate. It is important to note that, throughout these theoretical machinations, excavations, typo-chronology, museum curation, analytical programmes, and model building continued. How much the 'high-theorists' of Post-Processualism had impact on other archaeologists is debatable, but they certainly had influence over the academy, many university departments, and some funding opportunities.

To caricature the current working environment, material culture is seen as an *active* participant in society and life. Objects are still used as representing places and time periods through typo-chronology, but also participate on all the other rungs of human experience. Indeed, archaeologists more commonly use metaphors of webs, networks, and meshes when trying to explain the connectivity and complexity of the past. Technology is no longer seen as a common-sense solution to functional problems, but an inextricable part of political, spiritual, and social life. To create objects, to use them, and to understand them requires the establishment and maintenance of social rules, procedures, and beliefs. We can extend the idea further to conclude that as we make and use objects they are simultaneously making us. Key texts include the marriage of anthropology, history, and economics in Arjun Appadurai's *The Social Life of Things*, and Chris Gosden's linking of museum studies, anthropology, and archaeology in *The Cultural Biography of Objects.*

These powerful and exciting ideas led to a plethora of terms, all of which emphasize a slightly different aspect of the principle that technology is a social act. We therefore read of technological dramas, perfomativity and display, the agency of things, intrinsic influences of material properties, materiality and thingness theory. Objects have individuality, biographies, life courses, social relationships, and concerns. For the concerns of this chapter, this change in thought on material culture poses a tremendous challenge. Archaeology has moved away from static concepts of metal use, which seemed to share the aims of 1950s and 1960s scientists. Previously we could only map the source of metal, identify its mechanical properties, and thence track the 'development' of technology through clear stages. Could we now use the same datasets and scientific tools to explore complex, socially embedded technologies, the products of which hold agency in the formation of societies? The answer to this question is a tentative yes, but archaeological scientists and their colleagues have only just begun to tackle how it can be done.

Challenges to provenance models for metallurgy

The SAM project promoted a flurry of debate and further research. Their methods and conclusions continue to be cited and debated to this day, and most archaeological libraries hold their large and intimidating published volumes. Supporters immediately began to use the geographical hotspots of particular SAM chemical groups to infer metal production centres in Bronze Age Europe and the trade of material out of them. This work continued to be a good fit with prevailing fashions of archaeological interpretation through the 1970s, which aimed to find the underlying processes and rules of technology.

If we return to the six-fold Provenance Hypothesis outlined above, Sangmeister and others felt that they had demonstrated that distinct patterns passed from the ores into metal objects and that this structure showed the archaeological reality of Bronze Age metal sources. Through using patterns more nuanced than combinations of elements, as Pittioni proposed, they thought they could differentiate more precisely between mining regions. Finally, SAM argued that by concentrating on strong signals from the beginning of European metallurgy, they would be able to avoid problems of wide-scale recycling, mixing and metal alteration. This interpretation still receives support today from influential archaeometallurgists such as Ernst Pernicka, a student of Sangmeister, who re-ran the SAM statistical analysis to confirm their groupings.

Almost immediately however the SAM group received criticism from a number of directions and spheres of expertise. Metallurgists were concerned over some of the elements chosen to define their chemical groups. In the first arrangement of chemical sets bismuth (Bi) was the first split on the classification 'decision tree'. In other words, the whole European Early Bronze Age chemical assemblage was first divided into the objects that did or did not contain 0.08% bismuth. John Charles and others objected to this on the grounds that bismuth tends to segregate within the microstructure of copper. This slight accumulation between the microscopic grains of copper metal, can makes it hard to determine securely the real bismuth content of the sample. Coupled with the very low 0.08% threshold that SAM held as significant made bismuth an insecure classificatory building block.

The variation of chemical composition was at the heart of a broader critique of the SAM classification approach led by Ronald Tylecote (1916–1990). Widely seen as the founder of modern scientific archaeometallurgy, Ronnie was equally at home in the laboratory, trench, or on survey. His ability to blend and communicate this range of sources made him one of the most influential scholars to work in this area, and his books such as *The Early History of Metallurgy in Europe* quickly became standard references.

Tylecote's interest in how to interpret the chemical composition of ancient bronze began with his doctoral research on the oxidation of copper, which he undertook in the early 1950s. Fire refining is a standard technique for increasing the purity of smelted copper, which may include lots of unwanted material left from the ores and furnace. The copper is refined through cycles of being molten in an oxidizing atmosphere, during which more vulnerable elements burn off, leaving the relatively un-reactive copper behind. Tylecote combined his interest in this process with his work on ancient metals in a series of experiments with Hugh McKerrell. They wished to test if melting, hammering, and recasting typical Bronze Age metal would alter its chemical composition. First they took arsenic- and antimony-rich copper and repeatedly melted their samples in a furnace from which all oxygen was excluded. Though molten, there was no reaction with the gas surrounding the metal and therefore no change in the chemical composition. When the experiment was repeated in normal air, which contains around 20% oxygen, they saw consistent drops in arsenic and antimony. Their conclusion was that this oxidative loss seriously threatened the SAM approach to understanding metal chemistry and put into question whether the provenance of copper could be securely identified.

Tylecote and McKerrell's demonstration that the chemistry of copper alloys could change through use essentially rediscovered common knowledge amongst metal casters. From the Victorian period to the present day there are a series of practical manuals and workbooks which track how the ingredients into a melt would alter during casting. These records, kept for example by the *Institute of Foundrymen,* are important pragmatic guides to maintaining quality and consistency when using copper-alloys under modern conditions. They carefully follow how much tin and zinc may be expected to oxidize out of bronze and brass; and remind archaeologists that the reuse of metals can change their chemical composition. To these foundry records we can now add detailed thermodynamic calculations and laboratory experiments to our models of how copper alloys behave when used.

At the heart of the mathematical approach of the SAM project was the assumption that chemical patterns were locked into the prime copper produced inside the smelting furnace. Assuming that the European chemical database contains a series of regular curves that can be isolated using statistics, appears out of place in a world where the normal use and reuse of metals would alter this structure. The SAM clusters are even further threatened when we consider that copper alloys from different sources may be easily mixed together, blending their patterns of tin, and also combining the low levels of arsenic, antimony, silver, and nickel that are often found in Bronze Age copper. Lastly, archaeological understanding of material culture had moved from a static world, where metal axes or daggers represented blocks of time or regions, towards a complex, mixed situation where individual things had power, biographies, and networks of influence. These individual stories do not mesh well with a limited number of mathematical defined clusters, each of which is assumed to represent a separate metalworking tradition.

From the 1980s on, the post-processual approach continued to gain ground. As outlined above, this stressed the individual power of things, complex negotiated histories, and technology as a blend of social choice and material laws. In its more extreme interpretations this actually harmed several of the building blocks for understanding early metals. The chemistry of objects, and even science as a whole, was sometimes seen as detrimental to the effort of writing social stories. Compared to the post Second World War enthusiasm, intensive programmes of chemical analysis and typo-chronology had gone out of fashion.

Despite these critiques, the collection of chemical data did continue, though never reaching the levels seen in the 1960s and '70s. This work employed new techniques particularly the electron probe microanalyser (EPMA) and scanning electron microscopy—energy dispersive spectrometry (SEM-EDS). These entail firing focused beams of electrons onto a sample, which knock out the electrons closest to the nucleus. Electrons from further out fall down to fill these vacancies, at the same time giving out energy in the form of an X-ray. The exact energy level of these emitted X-rays vary slightly for each element and are very well understood, therefore the overall composition of a sample can be deduced from the X-ray spectrum recorded by a detector.

The new chemical datasets produced in the 1980s and '90s were often treated differently to those of the 'heroic' large-scale projects that preceded them. Following the criticism of mathematical frameworks and the contemporary archaeological desire to tell local, individual, stories, we see a number of descriptive historical schemes. One of the most influential was produced by the prolific analyst Peter Northover, who was commissioned to investigate and interpret chemically the Bronze Age collections of the National Museum of Wales. Mostly using the extremely accurate microprobe method, Northover produced several hundred analyses, which he then placed into a series of groups. Known as his alphabet scheme, groups A to G cover the Early Bronze Age of Wales (*c.* 2200 to 1500 BC). Rather than dictate a repeating chemical shape or mathematical clusters for these data, he simply noted recurring patterns and combinations of elements, then listed these from most common (A) to least (G). This aims to reflect the structure of that area and time period, without relying on a rule about what a prime source 'should' look like. 'A' metal therefore contains arsenic (As), antimony (Sb), and silver (Ag), with sub groups within the set: 'A1' As>Sb>Ag, 'A2' where antimony is highest, and 'A3' where the levels for the three elements are roughly equal. In his work Northover often wrote of the 'A' source, or 'F' source, and was followed by other scholars debating recurring patterns of chemistry. This included

Stuart Needham's discussion of the distribution of 'Bell Beaker metal', his name for copper containing small amounts of arsenic and nickel, which is commonly found in western European artefacts from the late 3rd millennium BC.

In many ways this approach appealed to other branches of archaeology, it was straightforward, descriptive, and was based upon a detailed understanding of one small region. It avoided the level of criticism of the SAM cluster framework as it did not have an inflexible mathematical approach to attack. The letters A to G simply *were* the pattern and could be followed across a landscape and across time. However, in many ways this was an unsatisfactory solution. Classifying repeating patterns by eye seems to retreat back to pioneers such as Pittioni, Coghlan, and Case, while ignoring the potential for metals to be mixed and altered by use and reuse. As scientists, are we limited to analysing and categorizing rather than engaging with the dynamic social questions of how materials were used and understood in the past?

Beyond provenance: People and processes hidden in the data

This brings us to the current state of research in this area. As with much of archaeology there is a plethora of traditions, methodologies, and concepts all being applied concurrently. Perhaps it will take more distance, but there is not one easy term like 'New Archaeology' or 'Post-Processualism' as a catch-all phrase for current research methods. Working within this variety, the rest of this chapter describes research undertaken by the current author at RLAHA in Oxford and how it aims to merge several of the chemical, theoretical and archaeological threads outlined above.

Distilled down to its essence, our approach builds on the history of the subject. Ronnie Tylecote was concerned that the practical use of metals would obscure any hope of finding structure within the chemical sets, due to the chemical changes caused by melting and working. However, rather than limiting us to analysing objects and listing categories, these effects actually allow us to engage directly with the idea of object lifetimes, recycling, agency, and social technology.

The exact chemical behaviour of molten copper alloys may appear to be a world away from discussions of how objects help create social networks. However if we move our concern from pursuing a clean provenance signal towards understanding the complex character of a messy signal, then we approach a more realistic understanding of early metal. Though it looks precise and well defined, the long columns of chemical data are not preserving a 'true' fingerprint of the mines. Instead they are a complex proxy for the mines *and* a host of other effects including people choosing to reuse objects, melt and mix objects, refine metal, alter the surface, change the colour or hardness of metal, and so on. These social processes can be imprinted on the broader chemical structure due to the slight chemical shifts that Tylecote and others found in lab experiment (arsenic loss due to melting in an air atmosphere for example) and that others knew through practical experience in foundries and workshops. Rather than obscuring information by hiding a provenance signal, these effects actually enhance our understanding of past metal use, and allow us to approach the human, social stories that archaeologists want us to investigate. The minerals in the ore can create a chemical baseline for an assemblage of metal, which can be altered in further melting, working, retention, and mixing. Crucially, all of the impurity elements in copper behave in their own particular way. Arsenic and antimony are very vulnerable to being lost through oxidation in air, meanwhile nickel and silver are very stable under melting and are not lost. These trends can be used in combination to understand more about how metal was really being used in the past.

Under this approach archaeological chemists can take part in theoretical debates: Were bronze objects kept for several generations and recast into new shapes? Which objects were special and retained in their old forms? When did people begin to mix objects from several sources and how did this alter the perception of metal? Can we trace the 'hidden' metal which was recast as part of trade and exchange? Was recycling an economic or ritualized process? Of course, these aims and methods are part of a longer tradition of scientists working closely with archaeologists. In the same way that the early development of chemistry was intimately tied to the rise of academic archaeology, and Hawkes' vision of technology overlapped with the 1960s aims of provenance, similarly our work aims to blend with current thought on how to characterize the interaction of people and things. These links are no accident and represent how different areas of archaeology have always fed off each other and provoked new work.

The chemical data cannot be seen as containing one provenance story; but instead have several layers, perhaps partially erased, overwritten, and twisted, which in the study of early texts would be called a palimpsest. How can it be best untangled and what is a useful new framework for its interpretation? Most of the chemical schemes or typologies focused upon, mathematically or otherwise, highlighting recurring clusters of data. Therefore we have the SAM Klein groups with their artificial curves of elements, or Peter Northover's alphabet scheme. These already assume that clusters are 'correct', that the data will bunch and that these represent copper mines and specialized workshops producing finished copper-alloy objects. What we use instead is an open, universal 'copper space' concept. We wish to imagine all the possible places that a copper-alloy chemical analysis could sit and then see what shapes and patterns are created. This then uses the laboratory and practical experiments to interpret the structures created. For example we imagine the three main alloying elements, tin (to make bronze), zinc (to make brass), and lead (added to other alloys to make them easier to cast), as defining a box (Fig. 5.1). Where a collection of chemical data sits within that box helps explain that selection's alloying approach. We can compare the high-leaded bronze of Late Bronze Age Britain, with the tin bronze use of the Middle Bronze Age. Did the tin levels have a distinct shape in that space (high or low, tight or diffuse, patterned or chaotic) that reveal something about access to materials in each period?

The deliberately added alloying elements, tin, zinc and lead, therefore make eight different areas of the box, including copper which has none of these metals added to it. The same principle can be followed to define an open space for understanding the small amounts of 'impurity' elements that often go from the ore to the copper during smelting. Remember it is from the structure and changes within these elements that we hope to infer the history and 'social life' of the metal. One thing that all analytical teams tend to agree upon is that four elements are most useful for this work, as they are relatively commonly found in the copper alloys, and at levels that are easy to detect. Plotting four elements, arsenic, antimony, silver, and nickel unfortunately cannot be done in three dimensions, therefore we have to use a schematic image of the 4-D 'copper impurity space' (Fig. 5.2). I hope that it is clear that 16 different regions now open up in space, and again we are interested in the shapes created by the analysis of an assemblage of metal. That assemblage could be any grouping of objects—by style, period, region, burial method, shape, decoration, weight, and so on. Figure 5.3 lists the constituent parts of each of these 16 regions, defined by arsenic, antimony, silver or nickel being present (above 0.1%) or absent. As mentioned earlier, arsenic is particularly vulnerable to being lost through oxidation while the metal is heated or molten, antimony too tends to be lost. Nickel and silver levels are resistant to change, as they are less reactive than the copper in which they are mixed.

This idea of an open space, within which the chemical patterns can be interpreted, allows large amounts of data to be compared quickly. This means that, with caution, the chemical character of widely separated regions, or differing time periods can be easily contrasted. If we were just aiming to find tight clusters in each period, then a grouping scheme for Early Bronze Age Europe, for example SAM, is pretty meaningless to help interpret Shang Chinese Bronze (*c.* 1600 to 1050 BC). However it is feasible to compare these two regions within a universal 'space' concept that makes no assumptions about clusters.

This accumulation and comparison of data has to be done with some caution, however. Each analytical technique has defined uncertainties based on the exact mechanism used to deduce the chemical composition of the sample, and also on the set-up of the machine and laboratory conditions that day. Adding to that, human error, corrosion in the sample, potential lack of calibration, and poor record keeping will mean that any trends in the data have to be carefully checked to make sure they are actually associated with archaeology rather than the analyst. Within the set of data for Roman coinage, for example, there is a potentially interesting pattern for nickel, which seems to come and go with meaningful regularity. However, when these patterns were compared with the analyst it was clear that one particular laboratory set up was recording nickel that was actually absent.

If our concept of chemical space helps ground the analytical data and make it meaningful, a second framework is required to link the metallurgy with wider archaeology. Particularly popular is the concept of object biographies, wherein things have influence, agency, lifetimes, and life events stretching over time. The interaction of biological agents (people and animals) and non-biological agents (objects, materials, landscapes, and so on), create networks of influence and patterns that, we hope, get recorded in the archaeological record. Scientific metallurgy is becoming increasingly good at recognizing the 'life events' of objects and helping place them into wider meshes of social interactions. Alongside the chemical arguments sketched out above, there are a series of other techniques that also help describe how metal was a part of complex social interactions in prehistory. Unfortunately these are beyond the scope of this chapter but include lead isotope analysis, metallographic examinations, use-wear analysis, developing technological *chaînes opératoires*, and ceramic analysis (particularly of crucibles and moulds). All of these biographical fragments, events, or factoids (again the nomenclature is varied) are held together by the chronology and geography of the archaeology. Due to the vast size of the datasets involved, often developed over centuries, this approach to metal now requires carefully designed computerized databases, linked to specialized mapping and interpretation packages called Geographic Information Systems (GIS).

Key case studies and ideas

Atlantic Europe is both an ore-rich and metallurgy-rich part of the world. In each of its modern constituent countries (Portugal, Spain, France, Ireland, and Britain) there are ores for copper that were recognized and exploited in the Bronze and Iron Ages. It is important to distinguish between minerals, ores, extractive metallurgy, and metal use. The presence of metal-bearing minerals in a landscape does not necessarily mean that they were concentrated enough or recognized as 'ores' to be mined. Similarly, smelting of minerals to produce metal was not inevitably associated with potential ore sources, or indeed with large-scale metal use. The famous Bronze Age civilizations of Mesopotamia (corresponding mostly to present-day Iraq) for example had little access to local ores or extractive metallurgy, but were importers and users of metal on a tremendous scale. Rather than make assumptions about a linear trajectory of metal use (copper, through arsenical copper, on to bronze and then leaded bronze, and iron), modern research focuses instead on local patterns and traditions of material culture. Our case studies keep within this tradition. How can we use recent advances in interpreting the chemistry of copper alloy objects to define the character of each period? What do insights about their technology tell us about the metal-using people and the places involved?

Through combining the chemical data produced by the research groups highlighted above, along with several others, we can sketch out the overall character of copper used in Britain from the earliest metal artefacts to the onset of industrialization in the 1500s. By placing all the available data into the open copper space configuration, we can see which of the 16 chemical regions are populated. Rather than use an unwieldy design (such as Fig. 5.2) to summarize these patterns, the 16 regions are plotted in a table in Figure 5.4. This summarizes what percentage of each periods' assemblage have which combination of elements within its copper.

The chronological periods run from earliest at the top to the latest at the bottom, with each artefact being assigned a phase due to its shape, type, and associations

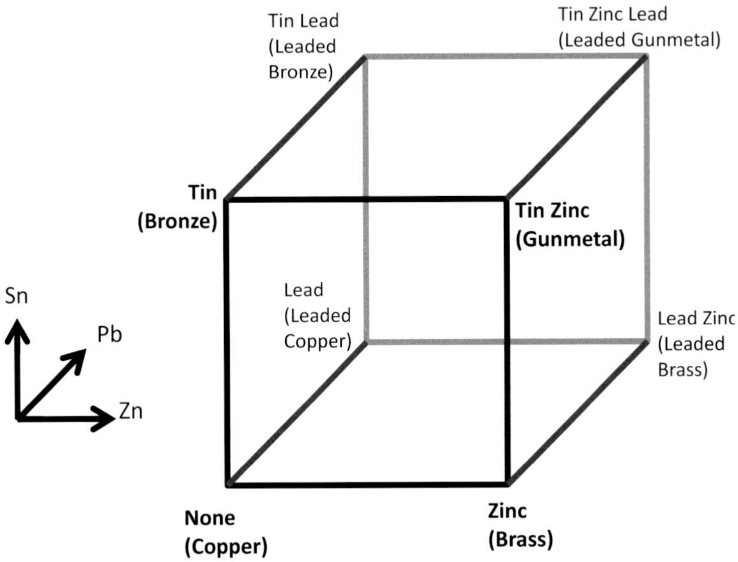

5.1. Schematic three-dimenisional representation of principal copper alloys. (image P. Bray)

(see above). The sequence of the Early Bronze Age (reckoning this as comprising approximately the years 2200 to 1500 BC) refers to Metalwork Assemblages (MA) as defined by Stuart Needham, with each division having specific kinds of axes and daggers. Metalwork Assemblage 1 and 2 being the earliest, with Metalwork Assemblage 6 finishing at 1500 BC; each row of data represents roughly 200 years. The Middle Bronze Age (*c.* 1500 to 1000 BC) data are mostly on palstaves (a type of axe), again with each group having a particular shape and time. During the Late Bronze Age (*c.* 1000 to 700 BC), dataset has been divided to highlight three key object types, late palstaves, the socketed axes, and swords. A similar process has been followed for the alloying elements (Fig. 5.1) used in British prehistory (Fig. 5.5), and then sets for Spain (Figs. 5.6 and 5.7).

These tables quickly give us a feel for the chemical dataset and allow us to make simple comparisons over long stretches of time and widely spread areas. It is only feasible through combining large volumes of data and creating a universal system to allow for this variety, rather than defining categories for each individual period. Regions of the chemical space that are empty for millennia can quickly become important, for example areas 3 (Sb) and 7 (Sb and Ag), suddenly become crucial to the Roman Empire after not appearing in the British assemblage for over 2000 years. This becomes more readily apparent if the scheme applied for the earlier periods notes absence as well as presence.

Though we are mainly concerned with the Atlantic region of Europe it is important to compare its patterns with bordering regions. This helps test our conclusions and puts them into a broader context. The rich Bronze Age of Denmark, with its large chemical dataset produced by Peter Northover, is an ideal comparison for the Atlantic seaboard countries. Figure 5.8 therefore zooms in on the areas of

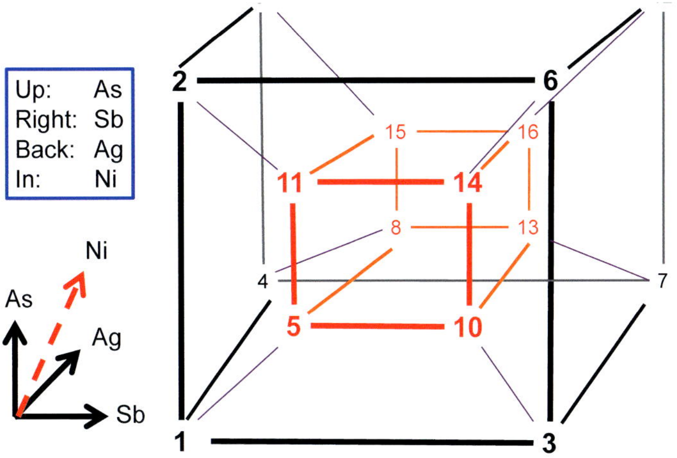

5.2. Schematic four-dimensional representation of elements commonly found as 'impurities' in copper alloys: arsenic (As), antimony (Sb), Silver (Ag), and nickel (Ni). (image P. Bray)

5.3. Defining the chemical impurity space for copper: arsenic (As), antimony (Sb), Silver (Ag), and nickel (Ni).

1	NNNN	No Minor
2	YNNN	As
3	NYNN	Sb
4	NNYN	Ag
5	NNNY	Ni
6	YYNN	As, Sb
7	NYYN	Sb, Ag
8	NNYY	Ag, Ni
9	YNYN	As, Ag
10	NYNY	Sb, Ni
11	YNNY	As, Ni
12	YYYN	As, Sb, Ag
13	NYYY	Sb Ag, Ni
14	YYNY	As, Sb, Ni
15	YNYY	As, Ag, Ni
16	YYYY	As, Sb, Ag, Ni

the copper space that are most significant for the Bronze Age, and places Britain and Spain alongside the Danish dataset. Aligning the regional chronologies within this larger area is not straightforward, and the offset rows attempt to reasonably represent how they correspond.

Chalcolithic and Early Bronze Age metallurgy

The earliest metallurgy on the Iberian peninsula in the early 3rd millennium BC predates the extractive metallurgy in Ireland by several hundred years. There is a longstanding debate over whether the adoption of metal within Iberian society represents a fully independent invention; however, the consensus has now moved to it being influenced and connected to the even earlier metal production of the Near East and Balkans. The fundamental character of this metal is that it is copper, but with significant amounts of arsenic, with no other elements found within the axes, daggers, halberds, Palmela points, and beads that comprise the assemblage (Figs. 5.6 and 5.7). This strong chemical signal that runs through much of Iberian prehistory was actually produced from a variety of mines, the apparent standardization caused by repeatedly using similar ores in different parts of the country, each mine largely (but certainly not exclusively) supplying the local region. Key excavated mining sites in the north are El Aramo, La Profunda, and El Milagro near the Bay of Biscay, and Sierra de Oriheula in the south near the Mediterranean Coast.

The model of a number of mines supplying interconnected regions coalesces into a wider circulation of the arsenic-rich copper. We can demonstrate this by comparing the chemical pattern in northern Spain with the contemporary copper objects in use in western France, the other side of the Bay of Biscay, and on into Britain (Fig. 5.4). Along this route, probably using coast-hugging sea journeys, we can see a trend of the importance of arsenic copper (Copper Space, CS 2) slowly declining. In Spain it contributes around 80% of the early assemblage, just over 50% in Atlantic France (less than 25% in the south and east of France), and around 15 to 30% in southern Britain (depending on the exact period subdivision that is examined). From a modern perspective it may be tempting to see this as valuable resource being traded directly to a range of markets. While certainly a precious material, the chemical evidence actually describes a series of shorter, more intimate exchanges, between neighbouring areas. With each region melting down some of the metal received in order to make new locally styled objects. This can be inferred as the average level of arsenic steadily drops as we move away from the north Spanish mines. Relatively close to the source the average Spanish arsenic level in the copper objects is 2.5%, for Atlantic France 1.6%, and in Britain 0.8%. If we compare that to how arsenical copper behaves in laboratory experiments, such as Tylecote's, we can see how the metal in Britain has possibly passed through several owners and was cast into new shapes before finally being deposited.

Metal moving in small steps from Spain is a relatively small contribution to the total amount of copper that was being used in Early Bronze Age Britain. Here, over half of all copper in the period 2200–1900 BC (MA 1, 2, and 3 in Fig. 5.4) shares a clear arsenic-antimony-silver signature, CS 12. Rather than in Spain where a number of mines used similar ores to produce arsenic copper, in Britain and Ireland the domination of the CS 12 chemical pattern is caused by the use of one mine at Ross Island, County Kerry, Ireland. William O'Brien has excavated the site and we are lucky to have direct evidence for Early Bronze Age mining activity, along with some of the associated work and living area. The miners were using Beaker-style pottery, a very distinctive type of ceramics that are associated with a wider package of behaviour across western and central Europe, including metalworking, individual burial, and archery sets. It is feasible that the discovery of Ross Island mine in the mid 3rd millennium was an act of deliberate prospection for new ore sources by metal-using people moving from elsewhere in Atlantic Europe, where copper had already been in use for several hundred years.

The distinctive chemical pattern of the Ross Island metal allows us again to follow the pattern of metal movement away from the mine in south-west Ireland. Similar to the drop in arsenic associated with melting and remelting found in Spanish arsenical copper as it was exchanged along coastal routes, we have the same pattern between Ireland (1% arsenic in the local CS12 axes) and eastern England (0.6% arsenic). Each region of Ireland and Britain tends to have distinctive axes and daggers at this time, and the raw material for their own metal objects appears to be the objects of their neighbours. This regional exchange of important copper artefacts, which then are melted to cast new objects, is very different to more modern directed trade of raw ingot metal. The chemical signatures help identify a style of metal use that binds societies together socially, rather than an economic system in which metal is stripped of an identity and commoditized.

Which objects were acceptable to be recast and which were retained is an exciting area of research. Across Early Bronze Age Europe, from their relative chemical signatures, it appears that axes were more likely to be remodelled, while smaller, perhaps personal objects such as daggers seem resistant to being recycled. To do this we compare the arsenic levels of axes and daggers that appear in the same region of chemical space (they share the same combination of impurity elements in the copper). The vulnerable arsenic and antimony tend to be lower in axes, indicating their metal is more likely to have been repeatedly melted. Is this difference in use due to the attachment and sentiment that accrues to special objects, or a more utilitarian employment of the larger lumps of metal locked up in axes? The former seems more likely when we compare the retention of daggers to other Early Bronze Age heirlooms such as well worn shards of pottery or beads that appear handed down over generations.

Though the Ross Island mine's chemical pattern dominates the earliest Irish and British artefacts, around half of known daggers from this period actually have high levels of nickel, which is commonly found in the Netherlands and northern Germany. It appears that these highly worn, small copper daggers, moved into Britain as personal possessions of some of the earliest migrant metal users from the continent. The daggers, perhaps after being handed down through further generations, were eventually buried with their last owner, often in a single interment in a round barrow. Meanwhile contemporary axes, overwhelmingly made from Irish metal that was melted and recast, were buried in hoards. These collections of axes were often highly ritualized and deliberate arrangements of objects in the landscape, which were kept away from human burials. Telling the social stories of metal locked into distinct shapes, with differing roles and influence, takes collaboration between chemistry, field archaeology, and new ideas on the role of material culture.

The Ross Island mine is a wonderful site for archaeologists for a number of reasons. From my selfish perspective as an archaeological chemist, the distinctive composition is extremely valuable; equally helpful is that the mine had a catastrophic end around 1900 BC due to flooding. This is especially useful as we have a clear cut off point for the characteristic arsenic-antimony-silver metal (CS 12 copper) entering into circulation. In Figure 5.4 the flooding occurs at the end of Metalwork Assemblage 3 (MA 3), and the high level of CS 12 copper quickly drops from over half of all British artefacts to just under 10%. In Ireland the drop is even more dramatic, falling from 77% just before 1900 BC, to 12% after, with much of that second figure being recycling of existing metal in the region around the mine. This gives us some insight into how long chains of metal recycling and retention were in the Early Bronze Age. After a sharp end to metal production from a particular mine, most of that copper will have been recast and entered the ground about three generations later.

Accompanying the cessation of the centuries-long route of copper moving east from Ireland is a major re-orientation of the metallic world in Britain. The arsenical copper (CS 2) from Spain, which was discussed at the start of

		CS 1	CS 2	CS 3	CS 4	CS 5	CS 6	CS 7	CS 8	CS 9	CS 10	CS 11	CS 12	CS 13	CS 14	CS 15	CS 16
Early Bronze Age	MA 1/2	6.7	4.5	0.0	2.2	1.1	3.4	7.9	0.0	3.4	0.0	7.9	53.9	0.0	7.9	0.0	1.1
	MA 3	5.7	11.4	0.9	0.0	0.4	7.9	1.3	0.0	3.9	0.0	8.7	55.9	0.0	1.7	0.9	1.3
	MA 4/5	26.6	32.4	0.6	2.3	2.3	1.7	0.0	0.6	5.8	0.0	13.9	9.8	0.0	1.7	0.0	2.3
	MA 6	22.7	18.3	0.0	0.4	0.4	9.6	0.0	0.4	3.1	0.4	12.2	6.1	0.0	11.4	2.6	12.2
Middle BA	"Group I" Palstave	0.0	1.9	0.0	0.0	1.9	0.0	0.0	0.0	0.0	0.0	84.6	1.9	0.0	3.8	5.8	0.0
	"Group II" Palstave	0.0	0.0	0.0	0.0	4.3	0.0	0.0	0.0	0.0	0.0	78.3	0.0	0.0	8.7	4.3	4.3
	"Group III" Palstave	0.0	2.0	0.0	0.0	0.0	0.0	0.0	0.0	0.0	0.0	74.5	0.0	0.0	17.6	5.9	0.0
Late BA	"Group V" Palstave	0.0	0.0	0.0	0.0	0.0	0.0	0.0	0.0	0.0	0.0	0.0	0.0	0.0	20.0	10.0	70.0
	"Late" Palstave	2.8	0.0	0.0	0.0	0.0	2.8	0.0	0.0	0.0	0.0	2.8	0.0	0.0	25.0	0.0	66.7
	Socketed Axe	4.5	17.0	0.0	0.0	3.4	5.7	0.0	0.0	2.3	0.0	10.2	3.4	0.0	13.6	3.4	36.4
	Sword	6.0	4.4	0.0	0.4	0.0	5.2	0.4	0.4	0.0	0.8	5.2	1.6	0.4	4.8	0.4	70.1
	Northover "Iron Age"	25.1	27.1	11.3	2.4	1.0	9.5	4.2	0.2	4.0	0.4	2.2	3.6	1.0	3.2	1.6	3.4
	Roman	9.6	0.0	64.9	4.3	0.0	1.1	20.2	0.0	0.0	0.0	0.0	0.0	0.0	0.0	0.0	0.0
	Early Saxon	2.1	0.0	28.1	2.7	0.3	3.2	49.9	0.0	0.3	1.1	1.1	4.8	0.5	2.1	0.8	3.2
	Middle Saxon	8.1	5.4	12.1	2.0	2.0	8.1	34.9	0.7	0.7	0.0	0.0	18.1	0.0	0.7	0.7	6.7
	Late Saxon	5.5	1.4	41.1	6.8	1.4	6.8	23.3	0.0	0.0	0.0	0.0	11.0	0.0	0.0	0.0	2.7
	Early Medieval	8.6	0.0	24.1	3.4	0.0	25.9	17.2	0.0	1.7	1.7	0.0	5.2	0.0	3.4	0.0	8.6
	Late Medieval	4.4	0.4	8.1	11.0	2.9	15.8	8.5	0.4	0.4	4.0	0.0	26.8	0.4	2.6	3.3	11.0
	Post Medieval	3.3	2.4	6.1	9.9	13.2	2.4	5.7	2.4	0.5	10.8	5.7	13.2	1.4	3.8	9.4	9.9

5.4. Table summarizing chemical character (see Fig.5.3) **of copper alloys in use in Britain from the Early Bronze Age to pre-industrial modern times.**

5.5. Table summarizing the use of various copper alloys in Britain from the Early Bronze Age through the Roman Period.

		Copper	Pb Copper	Bronze	Pb Bronze	Brass	Pb Brass	Gunmetal	Pb Gunmetal
Early Bronze Age	MA 1/2	96.2	0.0	3.8	0.0	0.0	0.0	0.0	0.0
	MA 3	4.0	0.0	96.0	0.0	0.0	0.0	0.0	0.0
	MA 4/5	1.4	0.0	98.6	0.0	0.0	0.0	0.0	0.0
	MA 6	0.3	0.0	99.7	0.0	0.0	0.0	0.0	0.0
Middle BA	"Group I" Palstave	0.0	0.0	55.1	44.9	0.0	0.0	0.0	0.0
	"Group II" Palstave	0.0	0.0	60.9	39.1	0.0	0.0	0.0	0.0
	"Group III" Palstave	0.0	0.0	78.0	22.0	0.0	0.0	0.0	0.0
Late BA	"Group V" Palstave	0.0	0.0	0.0	100.0	0.0	0.0	0.0	0.0
	"Late" Palstave	0.0	0.0	5.6	94.4	0.0	0.0	0.0	0.0
	Socketed Axe	0.0	0.0	11.9	87.1	0.0	0.0	0.5	0.5
	Sword	0.0	0.0	22.7	77.3	0.0	0.0	0.0	0.0
	Northover "Iron Age"	1.7	0.0	76.2	13.6	3.8	0.0	2.8	1.7
	Roman	1.2	0.2	14.1	22.5	10.9	1.3	16.6	33.1

this section, began to appear in Britain in much larger amounts. Crucially, the style of the objects cast from this copper became far more continental as southern Britain became more engaged with north French metalwork. Indeed the daggers from this period are called Armorico-British as those from Brittany and Britain are hard to distinguish. This fits extremely well with the chemical model that Spanish copper is moving from the production points near the mines in northern Spain, into Atlantic France, and then into southern England; with the metalworkers exchanging new ideas, shapes, and casting techniques along with copper.

A second dramatic change at the closure of the Ross Island mine comes with the opening of the first mines in Britain, mostly in mid and north Wales, with

5.6–7. Tables summarizing the use of various copper alloys in Spain from the Chalcolithic through the pre-Islamic Early Middle Ages.

	CS 1	CS 2	CS 3	CS 4	CS 5	CS 6	CS 7	CS 8	CS 9	CS 10	CS 11	CS 12	CS 13	CS 14	CS 15	CS 16
Chalcolithic	5.5	76.6	0.0	0.0	0.0	1.6	0.0	0.0	5.5	0.8	6.3	0.0	0.0	0.0	2.3	1.6
Early Bronze	6.7	82.0	0.0	1.0	1.0	0.5	0.0	0.0	3.6	0.0	4.6	0.0	0.0	0.0	0.5	0.0
Middle Bronze	13.4	52.2	1.5	6.0	1.5	4.5	0.0	0.0	6.0	0.0	9.0	1.5	0.0	3.0	0.0	1.5
Late Bronze	47.0	24.3	1.9	6.2	3.7	2.8	0.6	0.6	1.2	0.6	3.7	2.5	0.3	2.2	0.0	2.2
Iron Age 1	61.7	20.0	1.6	5.4	0.9	1.8	0.7	0.4	1.8	0.4	3.4	0.7	0.4	0.2	0.2	0.4
Iron Age 2	46.7	17.1	5.5	8.2	2.7	4.0	4.0	0.4	1.5	1.1	1.9	2.7	0.8	2.1	0.0	1.1
Roman	52.3	13.7	5.1	6.6	6.1	3.6	1.5	1.0	0.5	0.5	4.6	0.5	2.0	1.5	0.0	0.5
Visigoth	28.6	26.5	0.0	16.3	10.2	2.0	0.0	2.0	4.1	0.0	8.2	0.0	0.0	0.0	2.0	0.0

	Copper	Pb Copper	Bronze	Pb Bronze	Brass	Pb Brass	Gunmetal	Pb Gunmetal
Chalcolithic	97.0	1.3	0.9	0.8	0.0	0.1	0.0	0.0
Early Bronze	89.4	0.5	9.0	1.0	0.1	0.0	0.0	0.0
Middle Bronze	60.3	0.9	34.4	4.4	0.0	0.0	0.0	0.0
Late Bronze	11.2	2.6	51.8	34.4	0.0	0.0	0.0	0.0
Iron Age 1	7.0	3.5	44.6	44.5	0.0	0.1	0.1	0.2
Iron Age 2	7.3	1.8	28.7	60.8	0.7	0.2	0.1	0.5
Roman	7.8	2.3	12.3	45.3	9.9	3.6	4.3	14.5
Visigoth	4.3	0.7	3.8	32.1	16.5	9.7	4.1	28.7

BRITAIN

	CS 1	CS 2	CS 11	CS 12	CS 14	CS 16
MA 1/2	6.7	4.5	7.9	53.9	7.9	1.1
MA 3	5.7	11.4	8.7	55.9	1.7	1.3
MA 4/5	26.6	32.4	13.9	9.8	1.7	2.3
MA 6	22.7	18.3	12.2	6.1	11.4	12.2
"Group I" Palstave	0.0	1.9	84.6	1.9	3.8	0.0
Group II" Palstave	0.0	0.0	78.3	0.0	8.7	4.3
iroup III" Palstave	0.0	2.0	74.5	0.0	17.6	0.0
'Group V" Palstave	0.0	0.0	0.0	0.0	20.0	70.0
"Late" Palstave	2.8	0.0	2.8	0.0	25.0	66.7
Socketed Axe	4.5	17.0	10.2	3.4	13.6	36.4
Sword	6.0	4.4	5.2	1.6	4.8	70.1

SPAIN

	CS 1	CS 2	CS 11	CS 12	CS 14	CS 16
Chalcolithic	5.5	76.6	6.3	0.0	0.0	1.6
Early Bronze	6.7	82.0	4.6	0.0	0.0	0.0
Middle Bronze	13.4	52.2	9.0	1.5	3.0	1.5
Late Bronze	47.0	24.3	3.7	2.5	2.2	2.2

DENMARK

	CS 1	CS 2	CS 11	CS 12	CS 14	CS 16
Late Neolithic	5.4	7.1	5.4	14.3	5.4	57.1
Period I	10.2	30.7	10.2	5.1	11.7	13.1
Period II	7.0	17.1	31.6	0.6	26.6	2.5
Period III	6.4	11.9	34.9	2.8	14.7	5.5
Period IV	3.6	15.5	15.5	1.2	4.8	42.9
Period V	6.3	17.0	0.9	0.0	1.8	66.1
Period VI	3.7	11.1	3.7	1.9	5.6	66.7

5.8. Tables comparing the trace-chemical character of the copper alloys used during the Copper and Bronze Ages in Britain, Spain, and Denmark.

sites such as Cwmystwyth, Parys Mountain, and Nantyreira, but also English mines at Alderley Edge and Ecton. These show up as a dramatic change in the chemical character of the assemblage (Fig. 5.4, rows: MA 4/5 and MA 6). Alongside the rich arsenical copper of recycled Spanish metal, we now also have very pure copper (CS 1, no impurities) from mid Wales. There are also the first hints of the future importance of the largest Middle Bronze Age mine in northern Europe, the Great Orme on the northern coast of Wales, with its arsenic-nickel coppers (CS 11). Mining the small twisted seams of Welsh ore requires sophisticated understanding of water drainage, lighting underground, the use of fire and water to rapidly expand then crack rock, and the ability to feed and support seasonal workers. It is likely that the ability to do this spread across the same social networks that traded the smelted metal. The change in local economies, landscapes and social contacts was profound.

A challenging question then becomes whether the closure of Ross Island forced the maturing of connections between the regions of Atlantic Europe and the development of local British mines for the first time? Could flooding at just one mine create a cascade of changes that spurred significant social realignments and changes over a very broad area? Would these changes have occurred in the same way without the removal of such an important source of copper in Ireland? Within current archaeological research this kind of direct linking of cause and effect is seen as too deterministic. There were always important cross-Channel links, movement of people, ideas, and metal long before 1900 BC, and the Spanish–Atlantic French connections are older still. However these broader trends do not happen in a vacuum, and within a model of a very connected European Bronze Age it is tempting to see some of the exact patterns as reactions to specific historical events, such as Ross Island's closure.

Copper use does not happen in a vacuum either, and almost its entire history is bound up with tin. So far tin has not been discussed as the first two hundred years of British and Irish metallurgy was based around un-alloyed copper (MA 1/2 Fig. 5.5). Note that the arsenic, antimony, and silver in the Ross Island copper, or arsenic from the El Aramo mine, were small levels of 'impurities' in the ore that passed naturally into the metal. Spain and Portugal used unalloyed-copper for a much longer span of time than Britain, with tin alloys (bronze or leaded bronze) only becoming the majority in the Late Bronze Age (Fig. 5.7). Though tin ore (often cassiterite, tin oxide) is more rare than copper ores, it is still present in many of the modern countries we are discussing: Cornwall in Britain, Brittany in France, and north-western Spain. Atlantic Europe therefore has great potential for making bronze compared to other parts of the prehistoric world.

Bronze used to be seen as an inevitable step of technological progress as a harder, more lustrous metal than copper. It is also easier to cast. However, the shift from copper and high-arsenic coppers to tin bronze is not likely to have been as simple as observing the 'superior' properties of bronze. For one, high-arsenic bronzes, though more challenging to work with (particularly with retaining the arsenic during casting), are often as hard and tough as low-tin bronzes. Similarly arsenic also lowers the melting point of copper and aids casting like tin, and also causes attractive colour changes in the metal. Tin changes copper from deep reds towards amber then silver as the levels increase, while arsenic creates rose-red shades. In a world without modern scientific testing there is little dramatic difference between high-arsenic copper, as naturally produced in Spain, and low-tin bronze. The terminology used to describe bronze composition is often rather loose, but 'low' tends to refer to 2–7% tin, 'normal' or typical for 8–10%, with over this amount called 'high'-tin bronze. Overall, for people within long-held traditional rounds of agriculture, movement, trade, technology, and religion, there is perhaps little pull factor towards seeking and obtaining new types of alloy.

That is not to say that bronze was not a very attractive alloy if tin was readily available. Tin bronze had been in occasional use in the Near East before metallurgy had even begun in Atlantic Europe. Though this was always as part of a wider palette of metals and alloys, for example in mid 3rd millennium BC Mesopotamia we commonly see copper, arsenical copper, low-tin bronze, high-tin bronze, gold, and even solid antimony. This range (without the antimony) is also seen in Atlantic Europe in the late 3rd millennium BC (the Chalcolithic and start of the Early Bronze Age). The important exception is Britain, which quite dramatically switches to exclusively using bronze earlier than anywhere else, at around 2150/2000 BC. The primary explanation for this is the relative abundance of tin in Cornwall, where water erosion of cassiterite from the host granites creates rich placer deposits on stream banks. When combined with the pure copper coming from new mines in Wales, this produces a malleable, tough, easy to cast, attractive alloy. The difficulty of working the pure local copper may have been a technological push factor to go along with tin's attractive qualities and its (relatively) plentiful supply. Meanwhile in Spain, this total shift in deliberate alloying never occurred (Fig. 5.7), perhaps due to the properties of the local ore that when smelted became a natural high quality 'alloy' albeit with arsenic.

One likely way to produce bronze in prehistory was to melt solid tin metal with metallic copper. Alternatively, you could melt copper in a covered crucible over a fire and then pour in a mix of cassiterite and charcoal, this would reduce the tin ore to metal while mixing it with copper. Consequently there are three mechanisms that can create a trade in bronze: a) the movement of solid tin to a copper-using region and then local bronze making, b) the movement of tin in its ore form (tin oxide, cassiterite) to a region for local bronze making, or c) the movement of bronze itself. Smelting the two metals separately, then mixing them in the desired ratio may appear to be most straightforward from a modern perspective. It was certainly a common process for long periods of prehistory and tin ingots are well documented particularly in the Late Bronze Age of Atlantic Europe (see below), and earlier in the eastern Mediterranean.

The movement of bronze objects and then local recasting into new shapes can be demonstrated through combining the assemblage's alloy composition with the chemical impurity space pattern. Though we have stressed that Early Bronze Age Spain retained high-arsenic copper as its main metal, this is not the complete picture. In north-eastern Spain, bordering the south Pyrenees, there is some tin bronze use, out of step with the rest of Iberia. In Early Bronze Age Catalonia for example 41% of the Early Bronze Age objects are tin bronze, with 22% in Aragon. These tin bronzes are associated with the relatively high levels of CS 1 (pure, no impurity) copper found in this region. If we pull back we can infer a slow circular movement of metals around the seas and mountains of the modern Spanish-French border. To the west, in the Basque country and the Bay of Biscay we have a west-to-east movement of CS 2 arsenic copper into Atlantic France. Meanwhile from Mediterranean France into Aragon and Catalonia we have some movement of tin bronze comprising a mix of pure (probably west-Alpine) copper already mixed with tin (this gets far more speculative but potential sources include north Italy). The French Atlantic metalwork assemblage at the end of the Early Bronze Age can be broadly split into two: copper objects with arsenic and secondly tin bronze with no impurities. Identifying what social factors drove this trade is challenging, therefore a great deal of research currently focuses on what was passing in exchange for metal and why tin bronze was accepted in some parts of Spain and not others.

In Early Bronze Age Britain, with its dramatic shift to ubiquitous tin-bronze use, it may be expected that there was a substantial tin-smelting industry, perhaps a prehistoric version of the common medieval blowing houses. The evidence intriguingly points towards a very different style of technology based upon the trade of tin ore instead. There is a remarkable lack of evidence for mining, smelting, and metal smithing in the English south-west, aside from the large amount of tin bronze that was being deposited in Britain at the time. Often the best evidence for extractive metallurgy are waste residues such as smelting slags. These are extremely resistant to weathering or corrosion, and as they are of no value to the metalworkers are typically piled up on site and forgotten. The earliest tin-smelting slags, found under the Caerloggas Barrow, date to the British Middle Bronze Age. There are also no surviving tin objects from the British Early Bronze Age, with perhaps just one (now lost) bead from Sutton Veny. This absence of metallic tin or tin-smelting is completely at odds with the fact that tin is everywhere in Britain at this time, however, it is always locked up in, or joined to, something else.

Faience is an important key to understanding early tin use. Sometimes called the world's first synthetic material, it is made from ground up quartz or sand, to which is added plant ash or salt evaporates, and copper mineral colourants. These powders are then mixed with a binder such as water or egg white, moulded to shape and fired. At high temperatures, the salts and quartz combine to make glass, which fuses the body together (most of the quartz grains survive, glued together by glass). On the surface of the object a bright greenish blue glaze forms, coloured by the copper. It is most commonly associated with Ancient Egypt where it was famously used to produce blue and pale green ushabti figurines, along with a host of other decorative uses. In the British Early Bronze Age faience is typically used to make greenish beads, perhaps for necklaces or to be sown to clothing. Its presence in Atlantic Europe was often used to try and link Britain with the more 'civilized' states of the eastern Mediterranean and Near East. However scientific testing, using Neutron Activation Analysis (NAA) actually demonstrated that the British material was locally made. This extremely powerful analysis technique (which leaves the sample irradiated for several decades) shows that British faience, uniquely, contained tin, but at levels exceeding that expected from a bronze. Therefore it has been proposed that mixtures of cassiterite and copper-ore were added to the faience mix to produce a milky green glaze.

Further clues to early tin use are the several bronze axes from the British Early Bronze Age that have tinned surfaces. This would have produced a striking silver effect that would have particularly stood out again the red of unalloyed copper objects. Rather than this being a product of tin 'sweat', where the metal segregates from copper and accumulates at the surface, this effect was caused by deliberate fusing of tin to the surface. Through taking solid samples and imaging them under a scanning electron microscope it can be shown that the tin layer is thickly bonded to the bronze beneath. The process appears to have been applying a paste of cassiterite and charcoal to the surface of the bronze axe and then applying heat, essentially smelting tin onto the surface of the axe. This is reminiscent of the cassiterite reduction method of producing bronze, where a similar cassiterite charcoal mixture is poured over molten copper and reduced in a covered crucible. Overall the evidence may point towards tin ore, rather than tin metal, being at the heart of several early technological practices, from tin inlays and surfaces, glazes on beads, and the lack of tin objects or tin slags. Dense, black, hard cassiterite is certainly a plausible trade material, and one that could be easily overlooked during excavations unless it was specifically sieved for. Was cassiterite being traded in large amounts to be used to make bronze around Britain and Ireland? Research is ongoing to test these ideas and to see whether this cluster of technologies was employed elsewhere in Early Bronze Age Europe. Can we identify a pre-metallic-tin Bronze Age? This would certainly shake up assumptions that all bronze used in prehistory represents membership of one diffuse technological system.

Middle Bronze Age

There are several definitions of the Middle Bronze Age, each with particular relevance to one region or artefact class. Within Britain for example we begin to see field boundary systems emerge, perhaps indicating changing structures of land ownership and agriculture. For metallurgy studies the Middle Bronze Age has distinct axe forms known as palstaves, and extended daggers called rapiers. Overall, there is now more variety in the types of object made from metal, which is a nice contrast to the repetitiveness of their chemical composition. Figures 5.4 and 5.5 summarize how much of the British metal assemblage is essentially a monoculture for much of this period. Each row in Figure 5.4 represents one phase of the palstave-axe sequence, and for several hundred years the only signature is one of repeating arsenic and nickel impurities in the copper. In earlier periods there was a complex range of small active mines in Wales and England, and several important routes for metal being imported into Britain, all of which appear to cease. What replaced all that complexity was one of the largest known Bronze Age mines in Europe, the Great Orme, near Llandudno on the coast of north Wales.

Again the entire assemblage contains tin, but there is a technological shift towards the smelting of cassiterite to metal, then mixing of tin with copper. This is shown through small amounts of tin slag and solid metal beginning to appear in the record. There is also lead in some of the bronze for the first time in Britain, associated with particular sub-divisions of periods such as Acton Park. Often this lead is only around 1%, which is generally lower than the levels seen in Late Bronze Age Britain. This lead may have been incidentally added, as galena (lead sulphide) occurs within the complex mineralization at the Great Orme. Its presence would have been noted by metalworkers and users as lead affects the material properties of the bronze. Alternatively pockets of lead-ore smelting may have begun at this earlier time, however the evidence is tenuous and research continues. Either way these artefacts could be seen as a precursor to the more systematic exploitation and addition of lead to bronze in later periods.

The Great Orme mining area is on a remarkable scale, with extensive thin galleries of underground workings. It appears to have been active at the end of the Early Bronze Age (*c.* 1600 BC) and then continued through most of the Middle Bronze Age (to *c.* 1200 BC), with revivals of work in later periods. There are over 8 km of underground excavations chasing ores through the relatively soft dolomitic limestone host rock; many of the passages are so small they must have been excavated by children. Several thousand stone hammers and bone tools have been recovered, along with some rare bronze mining tools. Overall, this scale of mining alters the social activity of a wide area beyond its immediate limits, as well as dramatically affecting the landscape.

The repeating arsenic-nickel signature found in metalwork contemporary to activity at Great Orme in England and Wales matches that of the metal tools found underground, and also recent ore analysis produced by Alan Williams. Interestingly for several decades geologists had concluded that the Orme 'should' produce a very pure copper with no impurities, which again stresses the need for close collaboration between artefact specialists, field archaeologists, chemists, and geologists in characterizing ancient technologies.

To understand the flow of Great Orme metal out of north Wales we again need to consider the evidence on a series of levels. If we compare the chemical shape of elements within the assemblage of Wales to England we can see a trend of movement, use, and recasting of metal. By shape of elements we mean whether the arsenic levels tends to be high, low, dramatically skewed, or falling into a bell curve. Figure 5.9 plots the arsenic and nickel shape for Welsh and English palstaves from the period that we know the Great Orme was active. First compare the solid blue (Wales) and solid red (England) line for arsenic, we see a clear drop in the arsenic which is explained by Welsh metal being melted and recast after trading into a new region. Nickel is more resistant to oxidative loss and therefore the dashed lines (representing nickel's distribution in the assemblage) largely overlap for the assemblage of both areas. Some mixing with copper from the continent explains how some English artefacts have very low nickel levels. Overall the trend is clear that the Orme was a centre for prime copper production, which then gets changed and converted into locally styled objects as it gets traded.

The picture in the Spanish Middle Bronze Age is one of more gentle continuity rather than a move to a single dominant mine. The overall character, Figures 5.6 and 5.7, shows a longer, slow, trajectory of continued arsenic-copper (CS 2) use, but with increasing importance of tin bronze and pure copper sources. These pure copper (CS 1) artefacts will soon dominate the Iberian Bronze Age and reflect the opening and intensification of mining in the south-west of the Peninsula.

The seaborne connections within Atlantic Europe are intensifying in this period and coalesce into an Atlantic Complex. Specialists in metal typology can identify shifting provenances of tradition within broader western European links. Regional types of metalwork are commonly found away from their production centres, and evidence from shipwrecks becomes more common. In 1974 divers from the Dover Sub-Aqua Club began finding Middle Bronze Age artefacts in Langdon Bay, Kent. Over 350 artefacts, a mixture of weapons, tools, and ornaments dating to approximately 1100 BC have now been recovered. Though no wreck has been found, the collection appears to relate to a trading vessel that foundered just off shore. This collection therefore gives us a direct insight into nature of trade and exchange in metals at this time. The chemical character of the metal is almost entirely the arsenic-nickel that is associated with the Great Orme. While stylistically, experts have pointed to object types that are typically seen as French. This apparent contradiction requires more research to resolve, and leaves a series of questions. Was the vessel heading into or out of home port? Many of the objects appear to be scrap metal and there are no ingots in the assemblage. Could this collection therefore be French scrapped metal objects being traded back to the island where the prime metal was originally produced?

A possible sequence for the Langdon finds therefore becomes mining in Wales, metal smelting and casting, objects traded into France, remelting and casting to new French-style artefacts, which are eventually scrapped and traded back over the Channel towards southern England, where the boat sunk within sight of land. This complexity certainly fits with the more mobile, intense, and connected world of the Middle Bronze Age. Several archaeologists have proposed repeated movement between parts of Europe for individual people in the 'maritory' of the Atlantic Bronze Age. Of course such long itineraries are far easier for bronze, which can travel over several centuries. We often talk of the *potential* for bronze to be used and reused, and undergo complex lifetimes. Langdon may be an excellent example of such a material biography. The average chemistry of the Langdon Bay arsenic-nickel objects certainly supports a long sequence of casts, with relatively low arsenic levels of 0.2%.

On a broader scale we can see the influence that the Great Orme had on the flow of metal in the Middle Bronze Age (MBA). Figure 5.8 condenses a great deal of time and data, but aims to summarize quickly the character of British, Spanish, and Danish metal. The distinctive CS 11 Great Orme metal dominates most of the British MBA and up to a third of the Danish metalwork assemblage. In France we

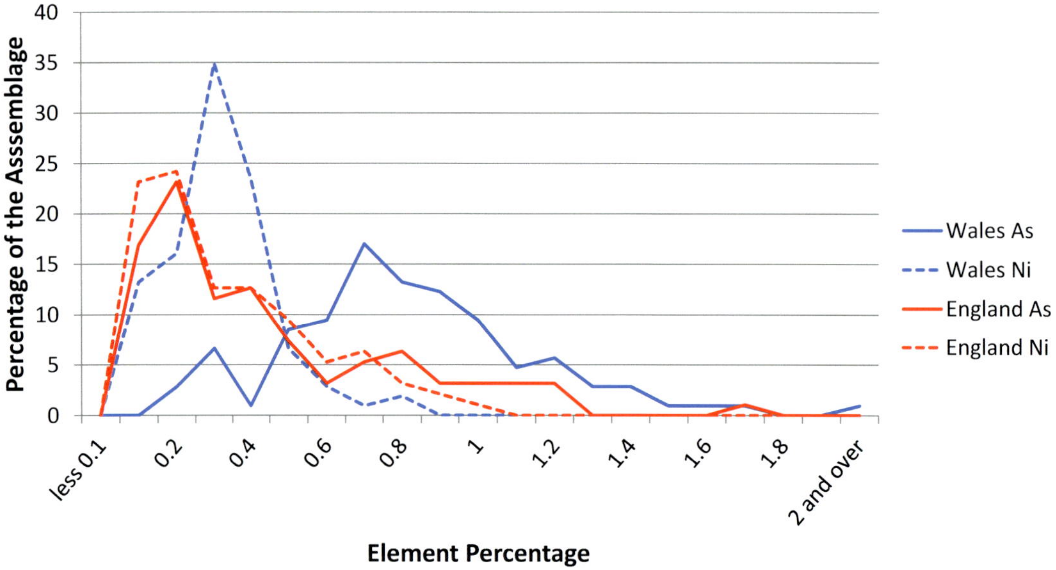

5.9. Middle Bronze Age palstaves from Wales and England with the arsenic–nickel (CS 11) impurity pattern.

see a similar pattern, where British metal becomes more important to bronze artefact casting than Spanish for the first time, roughly 20% compared to 10%. It is important to emphasize that new Alpine copper sources, largely from the Austrian mines, come to dominate central European metal and much of France and Denmark (the distinctive arsenic-antimony-nickel CS 14 pattern). Similarly there is evidence, mainly from lead isotope analysis, for mixing of metal from different sources at this time. The best ways to consider the chemical trends focus on where the bulk of the metal, the main signal, is coming from.

In northern and Atlantic Europe, the flow of metal out of Britain, across the Channel and around the North Sea is a remarkable pattern. This net outflow of metal means that Spanish arsenical copper does not appear to have been traded into Britain, but was of lasting importance in Denmark. The CS 2 (arsenic) signal stretches from the beginning of the Danish Bronze Age, through to its end in Period VI. The connection stretching along the north coast of continental Europe is seen in other archaeological evidence such as rock art, particularly the depiction of warrior élites in Portugal, Spain, Denmark, and most especially south-west Sweden. The hundreds of depictions of ships across Scandinavia is another reminder of how the sea was central to social connections, movement, and identity at this time. If metal was sweeping east (from Britain and Spain) and north (largely from the Alps) into Scandinavia, we can imagine furs, amber, and even timber moving back.

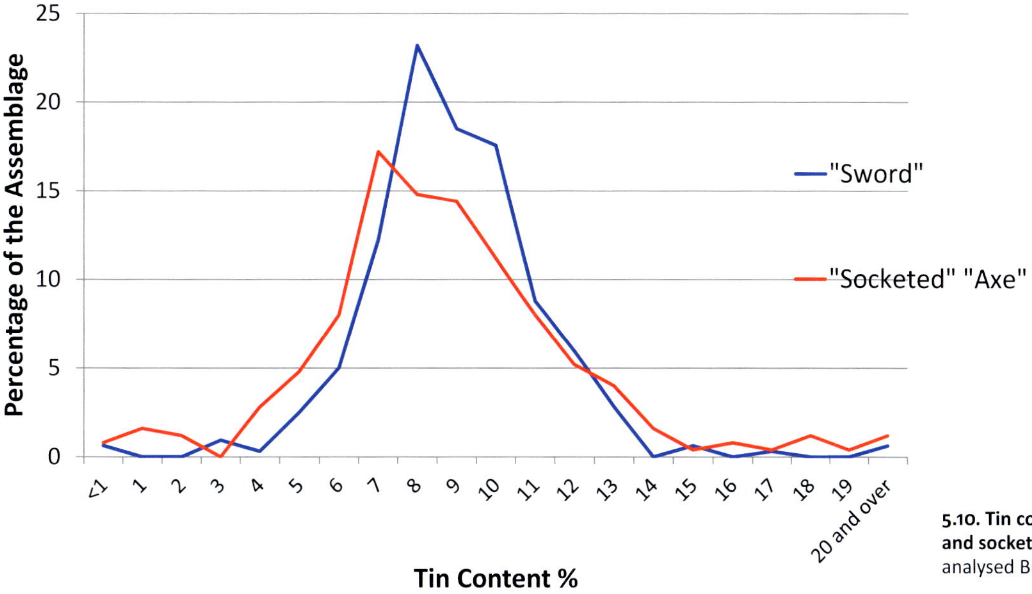

5.10. Tin content of swords and socketed axes: all analysed British artefacts.

Late Bronze Age

The iconic metal object of the Late Bronze Age is undoubtedly the sword. The romantic style of writing about the past, that was so common when archaeology was young, is now often reserved for evoking sword-bearing warrior élites. The same styles of sword stretch across Atlantic Europe, they are depicted in rock art with their owners, and are often large, intrinsically impressive artefacts. Swords therefore sit at the centre of models of how the Later Bronze Age world system worked. Steven Matthews and others describe them as underwriting powerful ruling élites, who used them as status markers, gifts, ritual sacrifices, as well as weapons. These powerful objects both represent a connected world, and also helped to actively glue it together through gifting and exchange.

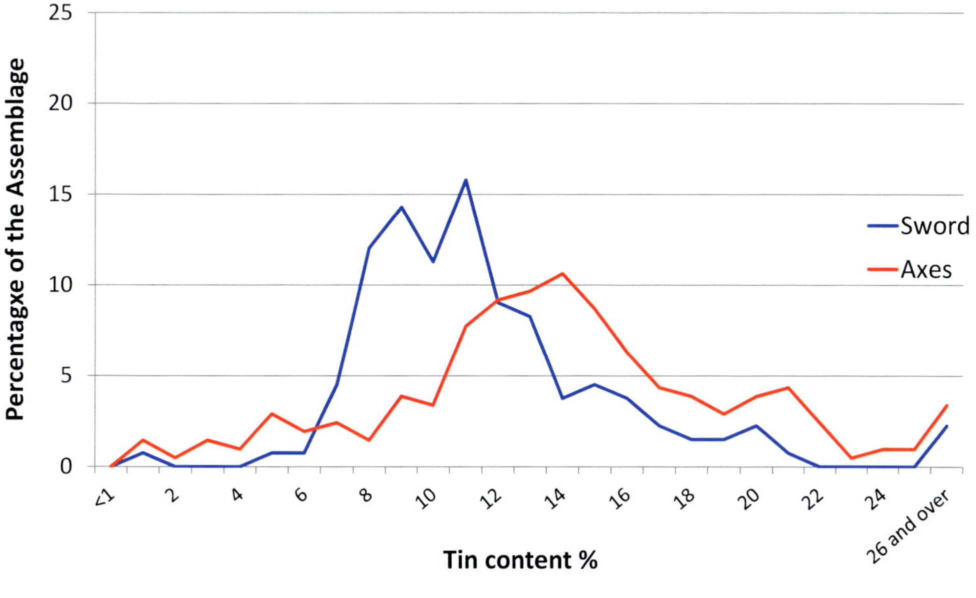

5.11. Tin content of Late Bronze Age Spanish swords and axes: all analysed Bronze artefacts

It has been often proposed that swords were a separate sphere of metalworking, outside of more commonplace, 'mundane' objects such as late palstaves or socketed axes. It is certainly challenging to cast a thin, long sword successfully, particularly compared to the simple flat axes of 1000 years before. Would this require fulltime specialist smiths in direct service to regional élites, or perhaps moving widely to sell their services on commission? Gordon Childe's concept of the respected, professional, wandering bronze smith is still part of current debates, even 90 years on from his key publications.

Characterizing the chemical composition can give a surprising contribution to this debate about special metalwork. Firstly we now have direct evidence for lead smelting in several parts of Britain, notably Somerset and Derbyshire. Ingots of copper and tin are also found, and represent a systematic, widespread trade in raw materials, with local mixing and casting. Again, the ship-wreck evidence is extremely helpful, with examples like the Salcombe Bay site showing the scale and range of metals trade at this time. This is all in complete contrast to the Early Bronze Age where the objects themselves often acted as ingots in Atlantic Europe, and metal moved largely through small-scale personal contacts.

Within this type of metallic diversity and availability it may be expected that specialist metalworkers could make their own mixtures to suit the objects being cast. From a naive perspective, the different requirements of an axe, spearhead, or sword may demand different alloying levels. In earlier periods the chemical composition can successfully reveal differing histories for classes of object, for example separate traditions of production for many Early Bronze Age copper daggers compared to the axes. However in the British Late Bronze Age the metal used for socketed axe and swords appears to come from exactly the same pool. Eighty percent of both swords and axes are made from leaded bronze, 20% bronze without lead, with the tin and lead profile for the sword and axes assemblages being statistically identical. Figure 5.10 shows the overall tin pattern for British finds. The two overlapping lines show no significant element of design in alloy composition, with both swords and axes being cast from the generally available pool of lead-tin-copper metal. This of course, does not rule out casting specialists or regional practice in the details of object production, and there were significant local trends. However, swords in Britain were not out of the normal flow of metal, even if they were used in a different social sphere to other objects.

The Spanish picture is more varied and perhaps does show design in the alloys used for different types of object. Here the swords are largely made out of bronze (85%) with the rest leaded bronze, while the Late Bronze Age axes are more evenly split: 55% bronze, 45% leaded bronze. Within the bronze objects there are also different styles of alloy, which are summarized in Figure 5.11. The bronze axes have a broader range of tin contents, with a higher average, than the swords which have a slightly more focused distribution of tin content, centred around 10%. These results condense a great deal of typological variety and regional traditions, but do show different pools of metal being used for contemporary objects.

If we are seeing alloys designed by specialists in order to produce specific objects, it may be in the Late Bronze Age of Iberia but not Britain. It is generally accepted that adding lead makes casting bronze easier. As lead remains liquid at much lower temperatures than bronze and does not dissolve into copper, it acts as a kind of lubricant as the alloy cools. Lead can also add weight to the metal, but can soften it, and at high levels added lead causes metal tearing. The apparent choice not to use lead while casting long, thin swords in Spain may indicate that unleaded bronze's sharpness, colour, and toughness were appreciated more than lead's advantages in casting.

One other key difference across Atlantic Europe is regional copper production. After the tremendous influence of the Great Orme in the Middle Bronze Age, it appears that Britain became a copper importer in the Late Bronze Age. Alongside local tin and lead smelting, much of the copper in its bronze contains a pattern that links it with the eastern Alps (CS 14, see Fig. 5.4). However this is only a small part of the system, as when the available LBA ingots are analysed they rarely match the artefact signatures. These ingots are often very pure copper with no impurities (CS 1). This points towards a highly recycled system, in which scrap, ingots, and reclaimed metal are being mixed, with lead and tin being added. You may notice that the actual dominant signal for British Late Bronze Age metal is CS 16, which contained all the diagnostic impurity elements: arsenic, antimony, silver, and nickel. The lead that was being smelted in Britain at this time actually contains low levels of silver, and almost all of the British objects are leaded-bronze. Therefore overall, pure copper ingots, mixed with imported arsenic-antimony-nickel bronze, mixed with silver rich lead, remelted to add tin, mixed with scrap and reclaimed metal would add up to a messy CS 16 'everything' chemical signature. Under this scenario it is not surprising that British swords, axes, and spearheads seem to be made from very similar metal. The Danish Late Bronze Age in Period V and VI has metal of similar character, dominated by CS 16 leaded-bronze (Fig. 5.8). Research continues into comparing metal practice from both sides of the North Sea to test what factors created these similarities. Is this, for example, the result of direct contact between Britain and Denmark (as seen in the MBA), or due to parallel processes leading to the same chemical end result?

Meanwhile Spain is still mining ore and smelting copper, however the mining areas have shifted and now are more commonly found in south-west Iberia, covering southern Portugal and overlapping the modern Portuguese-Spanish border. Particularly concentrated north of Huelva and Seville, over 80 small mines have been discovered and surveyed. Rather than the rich arsenic copper of earlier periods, the copper now is very pure and continues to appear in the sequence until the post-Roman Visigothic period, *c.* 500 AD This pure copper not only dominates the Iberian metal character but is also commonly found in France (34% of the Bronze Final III period), and may be the source of the pure ingots entering Britain. Perhaps this active metal production which was important to much of Atlantic Europe, gave local metalworkers more choice in raw materials and therefore led to more pronounced alloy traditions within the sword and axe casting (Fig. 5.11).

Final thoughts

If there is one theme to this chapter it is the importance of collaboration and communication. After several centuries of analysing, drawing, categorizing, and writing about Bronze Age metal objects, perhaps the main thing archaeologists have learnt is that no one specialism can work in isolation. Through combining ideas from a bewildering range of sources perhaps we can approach a more realistic understanding of past technologies and occasionally glimpse at the motivations of the people who were performing them. Bringing together different experts does not just fill in the gaps within an established picture, it often opens up brand new questions and areas of research.

The above account is patchy and biased towards the areas for which data and information is readily available. Despite the continuing three hundred year long chemistry experiment, we still have huge amounts of work to do and empty areas of the map to fill in. Aside from new data, it is often a struggle to get previously produced, legacy data available, and it has been a great pleasure to meet with several of the key analysts and help build archives of their work during this project. It is interesting to consider that most of the effort to understand early metallurgy has proceeded without any scholar having access to the entire chemical dataset. Then we must multiply that challenge by the difficulty of recording accurately the inventories of museums, objects in private hands, artefacts that have been found then lost, or are buried in the archives of various other institutions. Through digitizing records, and combining archives we are entering a very exciting period of research where for the first time everyone may be able to have equal access to the archaeological record. It will lead to radical new interpretations of ancient metal that more fully break down the artificial barriers between science and our understanding of past societies.

Further reading

Pioneers and Polymaths

A wonderful and detailed introduction to the history of archaeology is provided by **B. Trigger**, *A History of Archaeological Thought*, 2nd edn. (Cambridge, 2009). He blends changes in theory, practice and the wider historical context, and gives useful background to all sections in this chapter.

A. Pollard, C. Heron, & R. A. Armitage, *Archaeological Chemistry* (London, 2016) introduces both the history of science being applied to archaeology and also the details of the various techniques that were employed. This book also discusses the Provenance Hypothesis in detail. Again, this is a useful source for the entire chapter.

G. Pearson, 'Observations on some metallic arms and utensils; with experiments to determine their composition', *Philosophical Transactions of the Royal Society of London* 86 (1796) 395–451. This is a very readable account of early scientific practice as applied to Bronze Age metal.

A. Pollard, 'The first hundred years of archaeometallurgical chemistry: Pownall (1775) to von Bibra (1869)', *Historical Metallurgy* 49/1 (2015) 37–49. This article goes into more detail about the early laboratory work covered in this chapter.

J. Evans, *The Ancient Bronze Implements, Weapons and Ornaments of the British Isles.* (London, 1881) is one of the highpoints of Victorian archaeology. The hundreds of beautiful woodblock illustrations make this a valuable artistic achievement as well as an academic source. Freely available at: https://archive.org/details/ancbronzeimpleme00evaniala

Industrialization of Data

The multiple volumes produced by the *Studien zu den Anfängen der Metallurgie* project are often intimidating even to professional archaeologists; however, they are worth exploring for a real impression of the huge amount of data and the ambition of the team. Of particular importance to this chapter is: **S. Junghans** and colleagues 'Kupfer und Bronze in der frühen Metallzeit Europas', *Studien zu den Anfängen der Metallurgie 2* (Berlin 1968). A summary of their work and major conclusions are given by **A. Hartmann & E. Sangmeister** in 'The Study of Prehistoric Metallurgy', *Angewandte Chemie International Edition* 11/7 (1972) 620–9.

A more concise presentation of techniques and methods is provided by **H. Coghlan** and others, 'A Report Upon Analytical Methods, Presented by the Ancient Mining and Metallurgy Committee of the Royal Anthropological Institute', *The Journal of the Royal Anthropological Institute of Great Britain and Ireland* 92 (1962) 125–140. Contemporaries of SAM, this paper also summarizes the range of ideas that were competing in the mid 20th century.

The changing character of technology and material in archaeology

Christopher Hawkes, often working with his wife **Jacquetta**, produced a series of publications that pushed forward the role of materials within archaeology, while linking this work with laboratory science and fieldwork. We would highlight their short overview book *Prehistoric Britain* 2nd edn. (London, 1947). This set the stage for his later innovations and challenges, of which the 'ladder of inference' paper is most famous: **C. Hawkes**, 'Archaeological Theory and Method: Some suggestions from the Old World', *American Anthropologist* 56 (1956) 155–68. Equally compelling is his 1968 article: 'The proper study of mankind', *Antiquity* 42, 255–62.

Though thought to be inscrutable by many of his colleagues, the work of **David L. Clarke** is now recognized as preceding modern innovations in geographical information systems, and archaeological data science. In retrospect he was a leading thinker of the Processualist school. His most complete work is *Analytical Archaeology* (London 1968), particularly the unabridged first edition.

They do not fit into a neat box, but there are a wide range of interesting sources that debate the power, lifetimes, and agency of objects. Two useful edited volumes show much of this diversity. One from the beginning of the movement is **A. Appadurai** (ed.) *The Social Life of Things: commodities in cultural perspective.* (Cambridge 1986). **C. Gosden and Y. Marshall** edited the 2nd issue of the 31st volume of *World Archaeology* (1999). This collection, particularly their introduction, set the agenda for the next ten years: 'The cultural biography of objects', *World Archaeology* 31/2 (1999) 169–78.

Challenges to provenance models for metallurgy

H. Waterbolk and J. Butler provided a rapid response and thorough critique of the SAM project in 'Comments on the use of metallurgical analysis in prehistoric studies', *Helinium* 5, 227–51.

Fundamental work on the behaviour of metal and how this should be taken into account by archaeologists is provided by **H. McKerrell & R. Tylecote**, 'Working of copper-arsenic alloys in the Early Bronze Age and the effect on the determination of provenance', *Proceedings of the Prehistoric Society* 38 (1972) 209–18.

A more accessible overview of **Ronald Tylecote**'s work, which covered experimental casts, excavation, and analysis, is in *The Early History of Metallurgy in Europe* (London, 1987).

Peter Northover's work on Welsh Bronze Age metallurgy, which led to him developing his 'alphabet classification' is in **P. Northover**, 'The analysis of Welsh Bronze Age metalwork', *Guide Catalogue of the Bronze Age collections*, ed. H. Savory (Cardiff, 1982) 229–43.

Beyond provenance: People and processes hidden in the data

B. Roberts & C. Thornton (eds) *Archaeometallurgy in Global Perspective: methods and Syntheses* (London, 2014) is an excellent overview of both current analysis methods and regional archaeological studies on metal. **E. Pernicka** writes a strong defence of the traditional provenance model (239–68), which is challenged by **M. Pollard & P. Bray** (217–38). Other useful chapters include **T. Stöllner** on mining archaeology (133–61), and **D. Killick** on ore refinement and smelting (11–46).

More detailed explanations on the interpretive methods and concepts used in the rest of this chapter can be found in **P. Bray** and colleagues, 'Form and flow: The "karmic cycle" of copper', *Journal of Archaeological Science* 56 (2015) 202–9.

Key case studies and ideas

The regional chapters in **B. Roberts & C. Thornton** (eds) *Archaeometallurgy in Global Perspective: methods and Syntheses* (London, 2014), present the current state of the field. **R. Tylecote** *The Early History of Metallurgy in Europe* (London, 1987) is still of great use, and is more readily accessible to the non-specialist.

M. Barber, *Bronze and the Bronze Age. Metalwork and Society in Britain c. 2500–800 BC* (Stroud, 2003) focuses more on the social impact of metallurgy. While **W. O'Brien**, *Prehistoric Mining in Europe: 5500–500 BC* (Oxford, 2014) is an outstanding and thorough review of the complex field of ancient mines. This mostly discusses the copper mines, so for tin (often retrieved from placer surface deposits rather than from underground) the key text remains **R. D. Penhallurick**, 1986 *Tin in Antiquity* (London, 1986).

A. Harding & H. Fokkens (eds), *The Oxford Handbook of the European Bronze Age* (Oxford, 2013) contains a great deal of useful detail. Particularly relevant is **B. Roberts** and colleagues, 'Old Father Time: The Bronze Age Chronology of Western Europe'; **R. Bradley**, 'Hoards and the deposition of metalwork'; and **T. Keinlin**, 'Copper and Bronze: Bronze Age Metalworking in Context'.

Much of the remainder of this chapter is based upon **P. Bray**'s re-evaluation of the chemical datasets collected by generations of archaeological scientists. Many of the most important have already been mentioned: H. Coghlan, SAM, R. Tylecote, and P. Northover. To this list must be added **B. Rohl and S. Needham**'s *The Circulation of metal in the British Bronze Age: The application of lead isotope analysis* (London, 1998). Also we wish to highlight the generosity of **Ignacio Monteo-Ruiz** for allowing us to use his collated chemical dataset for Iberia, which builds upon his volume: *El origen de la metalurgia en el sudeste de la Península Ibérica* (Almería, 1994).

P. Budd & T. Taylor, 'The faerie smith meets the bronze industry: magic versus science in the interpretation of prehistoric metal-making', *World Archaeology* volume 27 (1995) 133–43, is a thought-provoking paper, which did a great deal to shake up traditional approaches to archaeological science.

Chalcolithic and Early Bronze Age metallurgy

Ross Island is one of the most important mining sites during this early period of metallurgy, published in detail by **W. O'Brien**, *Ross Island: Mining, Metal and Society in Early Ireland* (Galway, 2004).

Faience gives us a broader perspective of the uses of metallic minerals, and is covered in detail by **A. Sheridan & A. Shortland**, '"...beads which have given rise to so much dogmatism, controversy and rash speculation": faience in Early Bronze Age Britain and Ireland', *Scotland in Ancient Europe. The Neolithic and Early Bronze Age of Scotland in their European Context*, eds I. A. G. Shepherd & G. J. Barclay (Edinburgh, 2004).

Middle Bronze Age

S. Needham, D. Parham, & C. J. Frieman, *Claimed by the Sea: Salcombe, Langdon Bay, and other Marine Finds of the Bronze Age* (York, 2013) discusses in more detail the key wreck sites mentioned in this chapter.

Much of the primary science is contained within **M. Brown & A. Blin-Stoyle** 1959 'A sample analysis of British Middle and Late Bronze Age material using optical spectrometry', *Archaeometry* 2, supplement.

Late Bronze Age

Two key papers on the composition of Late Bronze Age swords are: **J. Northover**, 'The metallurgy of the Wilburton hoards', *Oxford Journal of Archaeology* 1 (1982) 69–109, and **J. Northover** 'Appendix 2: The analysis and metallurgy of British Bronze Age swords', *The Swords of Britain*, eds I. Colqhoun & C. Burgess (Munich, 1988) 130–46.

A more thorough discussion of the metal character of swords, the potential for design and specialization is in **P. Bray**, 'Metal, metalwork and specialisation: The chemical composition of British Bronze Age swords in context', *Celtic from the West 3: Atlantic Europe in the Metal Ages—questions of shared language*, Celtic Studies Publications 19, eds J. T. Koch, B. Cunliffe, K. Cleary, & C. D. Gibson (Oxford, 2016) 247–63.

Final Thoughts

Bringing together science, fieldwork, museum studies, and archaeological theory is not a fundamental problem akin to **C. Snow**'s *The Two Cultures and the Scientific Revolution* (Cambridge, 1959). Instead it is a matter of pragmatic problem solving, communication and collaboration. This is expanded upon in **A. Pollard & P. Bray**, 'A Bicycle Made for Two? The Integration of Scientific Techniques into Archaeological Interpretation', *Annual Review of Anthropology* 36 (2007) 245–59. Also see **K. Andrews & R. Doonan**, *Test tubes and trowels: using science in archaeology* (Stroud, 2003).

CHAPTER SIX

ONCE UPON A TIME IN THE WEST: THE ARCHAEOGENETICS OF CELTIC ORIGINS

Marina Silva[1], Katharina Dulias[1], Gonzalo Oteo-Garcia[1], Francesca Gandini[1], Ceiridwen Edwards[1], Maria Pala[1], Pedro Soares[2,3], James F. Wilson[3,4], & Martin B. Richards[1]

COMPARED to languages and cultures, genes evolve very slowly. Geneticists therefore tend to take the long view. Of necessity, we take our cue from Braudel and his idea of the *'longue durée'*—the rhythms of deep time and long-term historical processes. Please try to remember that, if you are inclined to feel short-changed at the end of this chapter.

The persistence of popular misconceptions about 'Celtic' ancestry was brought home to academics in the UK in 2015 by the confluence of a major British Museum exhibition, a prominent BBC Television series, and a book by one of the series' presenters. Whilst the exhibition presented an up-to-date view of the Celtic world, and the book displayed an awareness of modern academic views, the television programme (despite going out on BBC Two, which traditionally catered for a more critical audience) seemed unable to resist reinforcing popular stereotypes. Perhaps most jarring of all for scholars was the depiction throughout of 'the Celts' as a single people, from the British Isles to Turkey, equating the speakers of the Atlantic Celtic languages, the *Keltoi* or *Celtae* known to Greeks and Romans, and central European Iron Age archaeology, in a story that seemed to comprise little else but endless fighting, usually against Romans.

On the other hand, readers might be forgiven for thinking that the problem of Celtic origins, and the settlement history of the British Isles more generally, had already been solved by geneticists. After all, there have been quite a few books claiming to have done so in recent years, and even some academic publications. It may therefore come as

Institutional affilations of the authors:
[1]Department of Biological and Geographical Sciences, School of Applied Sciences, University of Huddersfield, Queensgate, Huddersfield, HD1 3DH, UK.
[2]CBMA (Centre of Molecular and Environmental Biology), Department of Biology, University of Minho, Campus de Gualtar, 4710-057 Braga, Portugal.
[3]Centre for Global Health Research, Usher Institute of Population Health Sciences and Informatics, University of Edinburgh, Teviot Place, Edinburgh EH8 9AG, Scotland, UK.
[4]MRC Human Genetics Unit, Institute of Genetics and Molecular Medicine, University of Edinburgh, Western General Hospital, Edinburgh EH4 2XU, Scotland, UK.

something of a surprise to realize that very basic aspects of the genetic history of the British Isles, such as the extent to which the modern populations are descended from the first postglacial settlers, at the end of the Ice Age around 12,000 years ago, or the impact of newcomers during the spread of farmers with the Neolithic, reaching Britain and Ireland around 6000 years ago, remain contentious.

There's a simple reason for this—it's an extremely difficult problem to address using contemporary genetic variation alone, which has been our main tool for the last 25 years. It's one thing to compare Africans with non-Africans, as when testing the 'out-of-Africa' theory for modern human origins. Even comparing Europeans with Near Easterners, when looking into the scale of the impact of farming, is much less complex—and even that led to endless controversy. It's a very different matter to tease out layers of settlement from patterns of present-day DNA for a small island on the edge of a continent across which genetic differences are very minor, and where contact with the potential source populations has quite likely been continuous for thousands of years.

Finally, though, the rate of progress has quickened. Recent technical advances in the recovery of ancient DNA (aDNA, i.e. DNA retrieved from prehistoric remains) are even now transforming this situation. Here we summarize what has been achieved so far, but bear in mind that the picture for the whole of the Atlantic zone of Europe remains murky at present. Yet at current rates of progress, any summary will doubtless have to be revised before the ink is dry.

How can genetics be used to explore Celtic origins?

It's not immediately obvious that genetics might have anything very much to offer on the subject of Celtic origins. Ethnic identity is fluid and tends to be fleeting, and in any case the references to Celts in the classical texts are ambiguous and even contradictory. So how can we approach this? The obvious answer is the one reached by scholars in other disciplines—to fix on language as the starting point. If we decide we're going to look into the ancestry of groups of people who today speak (or whose recent forbears spoke) what we now call Celtic languages, that might give us a bit more to latch onto than a few mentions of a possible ethnic identity in antiquity that may have meant rather little had they not been picked up on since the end of the seventeenth century. This approach also has the advantage of being of more direct relevance to those speakers today.

But how do we address questions of the origins of languages with genetics? There's nothing in the human genome that acts as a label for the language (or, more to the point, languages) a person speaks. We can look into the ancestry of the people who speak those languages today, of course. But languages are quite fluid and fleeting too, over the timescale of human evolution, so we need to take a bit of history and archaeology into account when we do that. In any case, broadly speaking, that's how geneticists, who until recently have been largely restricted to tracing the ancestry of present-day populations, have approached the subject of the Celts.

Text Box 6.1.

Genetic research of this kind began in the 1980s with the study of the mitochondrial DNA (or mtDNA). Most of the DNA in humans is found in the nucleus of the cell, in one of the 23 pairs of chromosomes. But the mtDNA is separate—a small circular piece of DNA, found in multiple copies in the mitochondria, which are the cell's power units and lie in the cytoplasm, outside of the nucleus. Partly for this reason, unlike most of the genome, which we inherit half and half from each parent, we only inherit our mtDNA from our mother—and therefore the variation of the DNA sequence from one person's mtDNA to the next can be used to trace the female line of descent. In a complementary way, only men have a Y chromosome—females have two X chromosomes whilst men have an X and a Y—so variation in the Y chromosome can be used to trace the male line of descent.

High-resolution analysis of the mtDNA has been possible for about fifteen years, whereas well-resolved Y-chromosome analyses, have only just started to appear in the last few years due to the much greater technical challenge of sequencing a whole chromosome (albeit, in the case of the Y, a very small one). But this has gone hand in hand with the genomics revolution of the last ten years, when technical advances in DNA sequencing mean it is possible to sequence whole human genomes in a matter of days, rather than the fifteen years or so that it took the Human Genome project to sequence the first one. Thus it is now possible to either sequence whole genomes or else to type 'genome-wide' variation across the chromosomes to a very high level of detail, covering most of the differences between one person and the next.

The same technical advances mean that it is often possible to extract a similar level of information from samples taken from prehistoric human remains as for modern samples. We are only just starting to reap the benefits of this revolution, but it may not be going too far to claim that many of the promises made twenty or thirty years ago about the potential of genetics for studying human history are finally on the cusp of being fulfilled.

The big picture from the genome

Although archaeologists moved beyond traditional core-periphery models in the 1970s, Britain and Ireland have often been considered by geneticists as part of an Atlantic far (or even wild) west margin of Europe, worlds away from the supposedly civilizing influences of the Near East. This was thought to be reflected in the overall genetic patterns, from the mitochondrial DNA and the Y chromosome to the rest of the genome. All show a broad pattern wherein Atlantic populations, including Iberia and western France as well as the British Isles, fall at one extreme of the continental genetic variation, the other being located at the gateway to south-west Asia. Thus, the picture has developed over the years of an Atlantic, perhaps 'Celtic', genetic façade that was relatively uninfluenced by developments emanating from the Near East. This was thought to go back to before the arrival of farming in the Neolithic, maybe even to the end of the Ice Age, around 12,000 years ago—albeit with indications of more recent Norse influence, especially in the Scottish islands, and continental, possibly Anglo-Saxon, influence in parts of England.

Yet parts of this picture now look to be quite wrong. A large part of the case for an ancient, pre-Neolithic Atlantic 'fringe' was based on the pattern of Y-chromosome variation. The focus was on a Y-chromosome haplogroup called R1b. A haplogroup is a cluster of lineages that all descend from a single common ancestor—in the case of mtDNA, a single sequence type in one particular woman who lived at some time in the past, and in the case of the Y chromosome, a single chromosome in one particular man. Haplogroup R1b is the most common male lineage cluster in western Europe, concentrated with its highest frequencies (getting on for 100%) in Ireland and the Basque region of northern Spain. Given that it was known archaeologically that south-west Europe had been a refuge area during the Last Glacial Maximum, when the Ice Age was at its peak around twenty thousand years ago, and was the source for the re-colonization of western Europe, it was proposed that R1b was a marker for this re-expansion. This was by analogy with the much less frequent mitochondrial haplogroup V (and it was also later proposed for the more common mtDNA lineages, H1 and H3, possibly H5, and U5b1).

However, as we point out in Text Box 6.1, Y-chromosome analyses were at the time only low resolution, and genetic dating for Y-chromosome variation in its infancy—in fact, it has only been set on a firm footing with the advent of whole-genome sequencing in the last few years. When this happened, researchers were in for a big surprise. Haplogroup R1b lineages in western Europe were, by and large, less than 5000 years old. A quite different explanation was called for, to which we will return in due course.

Genome-wide patterns have never been straightforward to date either. These patterns were initially the work of the great pioneer Luca Cavalli-Sforza and his colleagues, who more than anyone else founded the genetic study of Europe. They first described the distribution of the so-called 'classical' genetic markers—that is to say, non-DNA ones, before the technology for DNA sequencing was available—mainly blood groups, tissue compatibility antigens, and various enzymes. The picture was later augmented by studies (albeit at low resolution) of the 'non-recombining' mitochondrial DNA and Y-chromosome variation (so-called because they are inherited as a block, without the recombination that reshuffles variation in the rest of the chromosomes). The picture was, however, dramatically updated as the genomics revolution began to get underway in 2008. John Novembre and his colleagues used Cavalli-Sforza's method of choice, principal components analysis (PCA), to look into patterns thrown up by almost 200,000 genome-wide single-nucleotide polymorphisms or SNPs (that is, single-letter differences in the sequence of chemical bases, for example for A to G, or C to T) in the DNA of almost 1400 Europeans whose grandparents all came from the same country.

The resulting two-dimension plot (a *genetic* plot, remember) bore a striking resemblance to a geographic map of Europe. (A much more recent example, with ancient DNA samples included, is shown as part of Figure 6.7, below.) The fraction of variation explained by this pattern was admittedly extremely small—less than 0.5%—but a large body of work has subsequently confirmed that the overall pattern

Text Box 6.2.

In PCA (principal components analysis) we have a very traditional kind of visual analysis that can potentially be applied to an ultra-modern dataset. Another appealing approach is the 'STRUCTURE-like' family of analyses for individual ancestry estimation. These algorithms identify ancestral genetic clusters, and aim to reconstruct distinct ancestral source populations, seen in the present day as *K* distinct clusters, that have contributed to any particular individual's genome.

This is essentially estimating what population geneticists have long referred to as 'admixture'—the extent to which distinct genetic pools, which evolved separately and diverged over time, have been brought together in the more recent past. A simple example of admixture would be a marriage between a German and a Kenyan—the offspring would carry half the genome of each. A plot for such a situation would be a vertical bar in two colours, of about the same fraction each (i.e. 50/50)—representing the fraction of European and African ancestry in the individual's genome. In practice, what the algorithm is usually used for is to infer unknown ancestral population groups, with distinct genetic compositions.

PCA and ADMIXTURE both consider each position in the genome independently, as if they were being reshuffled in every generation. The fineSTRUCTURE approach accounts for the pattern of connections between these positions, allowing for the fact that despite the reshuffling many variants that are close to each other nevertheless tend to be inherited together for many generations as a 'haplotype block'. By accounting for these correlations across so-called haplotypes, or suites of variants that tend to be inherited together because they are close together on the chromosome, this thereby provides much more detailed resolution. The higher level of detail this affords is then, however, processed statistically to generate a clustering pattern which can be superimposed on a geographic map. In principle, a 'phylogeographic' approach, that made use of the genealogical relationships in the data, could be more powerful still, but this has yet to be attempted on anything like the genome-wide scale.

appears to be historically meaningful. In particular, British and Irish samples fall at one extreme in two dimensions, although they lie alongside other northern Europeans in the first component and other west-central Europeans in the second.

PCA remains one of the most popular visualization tools in human population genetics, alongside the 'STRUCTURE-like' family of analyses such as ADMIXTURE, which attempt to separate the genome of an individual into distinct clusters each of which is assumed to have its own historical trajectory (see Text Box 6.1). But these are approaches that, like every other procedure in population genetics, need to be taken with a certain amount of salt. Small and isolated populations, for example, that have undergone a lot of random genetic drift—that is, changes in the frequency of different variants due to chance—might have very different frequencies of particular markers from their neighbours despite recent ancestry, and sometimes give rise to

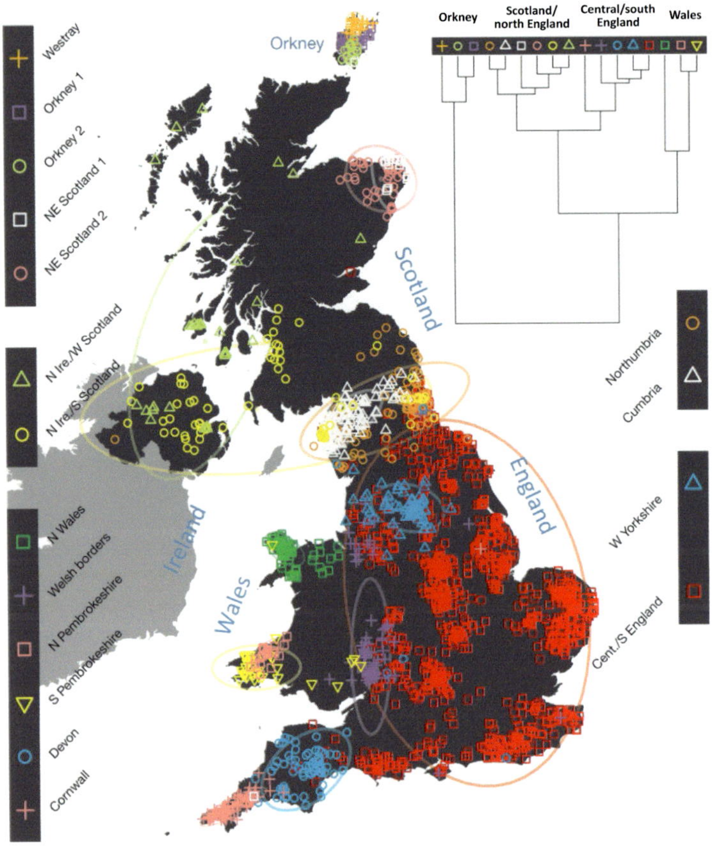

6.1. Genetic clustering of British individuals. Cluster names are in side-bars and ellipses give an informal sense of the range of each cluster. The tree (top right) depicts the order of the hierarchical merging of clusters.

(Source: S. Leslie et al., *Nature* 519, 309–14 (2015) doi:10.1038/nature14230, reproduced by permission)

their own, rather spurious, ancestry components. Moreover, even if we feel confident in attributing a certain set of ancestral pools to a particular population, their inferred frequencies can vary substantially depending on the dataset used, and the contextual data—the other populations included in the analyses—can lead to startling differences. As with other kinds of analysis, a huge amount of exploratory data analysis is needed before any given 'result' can be taken to be reliable. Nevertheless, the amount of data that goes into a typical PCA or ADMIXTURE analysis nowadays is huge, and moreover aDNA evidence has dramatically supported the existence of ancestral source pools inferred in modern Europeans, as we will discuss further later.

A genetic portrait of the British Isles

The genome-wide study of the British Isles was brought dramatically up to date with the publication of the Oxford 'People of the British Isles' (PoBI) project in 2015. As we mentioned earlier, it's now possible to test genome-wide variation on a scale—more than half a million variants (or SNPs), in this case—enough to represent all the common variation in the human genome (strictly, all those variants found in more than about 5% of the population). The PoBI project did this for about 2000 living people from Britain in the context of data from 6000 people from western Europe and Scandinavia—no aDNA was involved.

In practice, most of the British samples were from England and Wales, with many fewer from Northern Ireland and Scotland (outside Orkney)—and no representation from the Republic of Ireland—although the last of these has been remedied in more recent work. The team analysed the data using 'fineSTRUCTURE', which works in a rather different way to the STRUCTURE-like algorithms such as ADMIXTURE, or to PCA, and is much more powerful (see Text Box 6.2 for more details about these methods). It is important to emphasize again that all these approaches are blind to geography, so that the

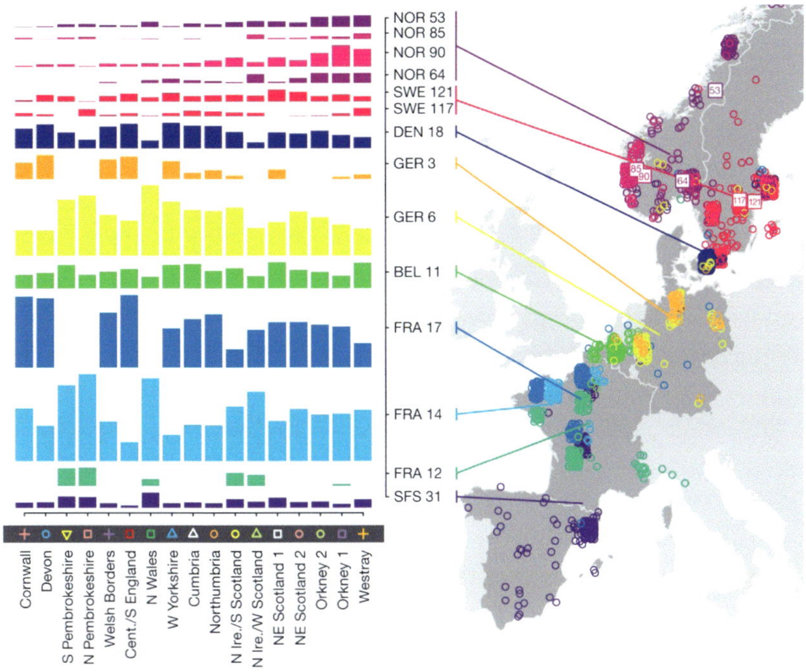

6.2. European ancestry profiles for inferred British clusters. Each row represents one of the 51 European groups (labels at right) inferred by clustering the European samples using fineSTRUCTURE. Each column represents a British cluster. Coloured bars have heights representing the proportion of the British cluster's ancestry best represented by that of the European group labelled with that colour. The map shows the location of the samples assigned to each European group.

(Source: S. Leslie et al., *Nature* 519, 309–14 (2015) doi:10.1038/nature14230, reproduced by permission)

clustering generated is purely on the basis of the genetic data. This means, again, that any geographic patterns that do emerge are likely to be meaningful. However, the clustering pattern that emerges is organized as a kind of population tree, and we have to remember that human populations have rarely evolved in a tree-like way—the processes that have generated the apparent splits are likely to have been many and various (Fig. 6.1).

For example, the deepest split was between Orkney and the rest of Britain. This certainly does not mean that Orkney and the rest of Britain were settled by two distinct ancestral populations, but reflects the fact that during its history Orkney received substantial additional settlement from Norwegian Vikings, who had in turn received input in prehistoric times from eastern Europe, differentiating Scandinavia from western Europe—as had already been clear from mtDNA and Y-chromosome variation.

In fact, though, the analysis was impressive for the degree of geographic structure that it captured. The next group of samples to split away were from Wales, with north and south Wales also highly differentiated from each other. After that, northern England and mainland Scotland split from central and southern England. At a shallower level, what was especially striking was that whilst there were many highly regionalized genetic clusters (which would be invisible to other analytical approaches, such as STRUCTURE or PCA), a single cluster predominated across lowland Britain, encompassing most of southern and eastern England, but with distinct English clusters in Cumbria and Northumberland (clustering with Scotland and Northern Ireland), West Yorkshire, Devon and Cornwall. Two closely related clusters seen in Northern Ireland were shared across the North Channel with western Scotland, and Orkney fell into three clusters belonging to different islands—a pattern already detected using PCA (Fig. 6.1).

Given that this was emphatically not a series of population splits, it is important to recognize what was going on here. The software picks up very fine differences between the populations, which may have arisen for a variety of reasons, and groups them together on the basis of overall similarity. Some of the differences may have arisen due to long-term isolation and random genetic drift, and others the result of immigration from elsewhere. A second analysis, therefore, included neighbouring continental populations in order to trace different ancestry components that may be due to migrations from different parts of Europe. The team performed a fineSTRUCTURE analysis of the European populations and, in this case, assigned them to one of 51 groups. The likely contribution of these clusters to each part of the British Isles sampled could then be estimated as shown in the chart in Figure 6.2. This step is crucial if we are to begin to learn anything about the regional settlement history of the British populations. We should bear in mind, though, that like any attempt to link groups back to source populations in population genetics, the outcome depends on the quality of the potential source sampling, and some continental regions were better sampled here than others.

The major contributors from the continent inferred by this procedure were two groups assigned to France (FRA14 and FRA17 in Fig. 6.2) and one each assigned to northern Germany and Belgium (GER6 and BEL11). (Note that the Netherlands was not sampled—a point that will become significant later on.) These were all found across every British population, with the exception of one of the major French clusters (FRA17), which was absent from Wales. This one reached its highest levels in central and southern England—including Devon and Cornwall. The authors assumed on the basis of this pattern that the more evenly distributed groups must be ancient and therefore pointing to a pre-farming, hunter–gatherer Mesolithic (or possibly early-farmer, Neolithic) ancestry. These groups amount to somewhat less than half of the ancestry in England, but around three-quarters in Wales.

In this sense, their interpretation was in line with earlier researchers who have usually attributed an ancient, pre-Neolithic ancestry to a large fraction of extant British variation. The assumption follows the tradition of Cavalli-Sforza's genetic geography, and has sometimes been adopted in phylogeography, too. The example of the Y-chromosome R1b lineages, however, shows that it does not always hold, even in relative terms. It tells us that there can be a huge and quite recent replacement of the majority of lineages in at least some genetic systems in a relatively short time. Admittedly the Y chromosome, slavishly tracking the alpha-males of history as it apparently does, can be somewhat idiosyncratic, but given that R1b predominates amongst male lineages in the British Isles and other parts of Atlantic Europe today despite arriving less than 5000 years ago, arguments that assume a high time depth for common markers need to be approached with caution. This emphasizes the need for a system with a molecular clock (such as the non-recombining markers, mtDNA and the Y chromosome) or, better still, aDNA from radiocarbon-dated samples.

There is no other clear-cut way to date the arrival of these groups from genome-wide data such as this, and if the assumption is incorrect then a very different history might be possible. As we will see below, early results from aDNA do indeed pose a major challenge to the interpretation of a deep Mesolithic, or even Early Neolithic, ancestry for much of the genetic variation in modern British populations. Still, the dataset here does provide an important baseline for future analyses, as well as some fascinating issues for immediate discussion.

For example, the frequent 'French' group (FRA17), that is nevertheless absent from Wales, is particularly intriguing. It captures between a third and a quarter of the ancestry in England and eastern Scotland, although substantially less in western Scotland/Northern Ireland. If the widespread groups did date to the Mesolithic, then this particular group might represent movements into Britain sometime between the arrival of agriculture and the Bronze Age—perhaps with the appearance of metals and Beakers. Intriguingly, a less frequent group from France (FRA12) has the reverse distribution, being largely restricted to Wales and western Scotland/Northern Ireland. There is also a group (SFS31) attributed to southern French/Spanish ancestry that is widespread, but again most frequent in the west, especially Wales (and, again, less so in Devon/Cornwall). It is worth noting that the low fraction of ancestry attributed to Iberia is unlikely to be an argument against a significant role for an Iberian refuge in the re-peopling of Atlantic Europe—rather, since this took place via France, the affinities there might be expected to be greater. The Iberian SFS31 component might then represent a more recent dispersal from the south-west.

It appears that one particular group (GER3) is largely responsible for the separation of central and southern England into a distinct cluster. This group seems to be otherwise largely restricted to Germany and Denmark, and the authors attributed it to Anglo-Saxon settlers, given that within the British Isles it is found mainly in England (including Devon and Cornwall). It is worth noting that despite its role in generating the widespread English cluster, it amounts to only about a tenth of the variation in these populations. A second more frequent Danish group (DEN18) has a similar, although more widespread, distribution in the British Isles, so that if this were also due to Saxon presence the total input from Saxon settlement would still amount to less than a quarter of English variation (although both are difficult to distinguish from Danish Viking influence)—the authors estimate a range of 10–40%. Norwegian influence is focused mainly on Orkney, as already noted, where it amounts to about a quarter of the overall ancestry.

There has been a tendency for genetic studies of Britain to emphasize either Anglo-Saxon or Viking settlement at the expense of the other—for example, in the early 2000s, rival Y-chromosome studies from competing groups based at UCL in London, led by Mark Thomas and Mike Weale in one case and David Goldstein and Cristian Capelli in the other, proposed a major influence from Anglo-Saxon settlement (almost amounting to replacement in England) in the former and Danish Viking settlement in the other (discussed below). The PoBI study falls into the

Anglo-Saxon camp, but as spelled out by Jane Kershaw and Ellen Røyrvik, the Anglo-Saxon and Danish Viking source regions overlap, and indeed the samples from northern Germany contributing to GER3 are closer to the likely source in Schleswig–Holstein/southern Jutland than the Danish DEN18 samples from Copenhagen. A partial Viking contribution might, they suggest, explain the poor fit of the estimated admixture date of around 860 AD with the Anglo-Saxon advent, which began in the 5th century AD and likely peaked in the 6th. They argue that up to about half of the GER3 cluster may be attributable to Danish Viking settlement, given the impact on archaeology (especially metalwork), place-names (especially in Yorkshire and the East Midlands), and the English language—much of which points to the settlement of family groups rather than a male military élite.

Nevertheless, the overall interpretation of the PoBI study was along similar lines to much previous research, suggesting a largely Mesolithic ancestry for the British Isles, with again rather small-scale Scandinavian and Anglo-Saxon arrivals, plus some mysterious settlers somewhere in between that might even have come with the Bell Beaker package.

One highly publicized finding was that the various pre-Saxon and pre-Norse clusters—what we might like to think of as 'Celtic' in some sense—were quite variable, with different clusters in different parts of Britain, with different continental sources. This led the authors to stress that there was no homogeneous pre-Saxon 'Celtic' population, but surely this is what would be expected from an ancient population, given some degree of geographical isolation over time. The long-standing suggestion of an Atlantic population that dates back to the Neolithic or even the Mesolithic remained unchallenged by this work.

Yet dating arrival times is very difficult for these kinds of data, as we have already said: we would need more detailed information from the mitochondrial DNA and Y chromosome, and aDNA from the rest of the genome, to be confident about when the different components first arrived. This has now begun to happen, with the first prehistoric British and Irish genomes having been published recently, and these will be discussed below.

The male and female lines of descent

The ideal situation is for genome-wide studies (involving the rest of the genome) to be complemented not only by aDNA work but also by studies of the male and female lines of descent, using high-resolution analyses of Y chromosome and mitochondrial DNA (mtDNA) variation. Low-resolution studies, although not in short supply, have varied from being rather uninformative in the case of mtDNA to occasionally generating rather more heat than light in the case of the Y, although some direct comparisons of the two systems have been intriguing. For example, such comparisons have suggested that Shetland and Orkney were both settled quite heavily from Norway in Viking times by roughly equal numbers of men and women (contributing almost half of extant lineages in the former and about a third in the

Text Box 6.3.

Both mitochondrial DNA and the Y chromosome are usually analysed by means of an approach referred to as *phylogeography*. This involves reconstructing a phylogenetic or genealogical tree of descent for the lineages being analysed and incorporating information about their geographical origin and the mutation rate so that lineages specific to a particular region can be dated, in order to set a lower bound to their time of arrival. This depends on the 'molecular clock' hypothesis, which argues that mutations accumulate at a measurable (if not necessarily constant) rate and hence that their number, across a phylogeny, can be converted into ages for each branching point expressed in thousands of years. By incorporating very large, geographically diverse sample sets, and using such a well-calibrated mutation rate or clock, this approach can be remarkably effective. In the case of mtDNA it was used to first demonstrate that modern humans evolved in Africa and spread across the rest of the world only relatively recently (around 60,000 years ago), and to map out the first colonization of the Americas and the Pacific. More controversially, it has been used to address the more complex story of the settlement of Europe, where aDNA evidence has been crucial to rounding out the details.

Phylogeography has sometimes been criticised as a 'story-telling' approach that relies only on a very small fraction of the genome at a time (usually mtDNA or the Y chromosome) and is not statistically robust. In fact, however, various statistical procedures for hypothesis testing have been developed for phylogeographic analyses and the incorporation of other markers—and especially aDNA—means that conclusions based on phylogeographic distributions have become more and more testable. For example, a recent, highly controversial phylogeographic hypothesis proposed that most of the mtDNA lineages in Ashkenazi Jews (Jews from eastern and central Europe) originated in prehistoric Europe, rather than the Levant, and were assimilated by conversions in the Mediterranean region (such as Rome) approximately 2000 years ago. Since many of the Ashkenazi male lineages seemed to have an origin in the Near East, this would be a good example of a strong sex-specific bias—women were mainly converted, whereas more men migrated from the Near East into Europe. Subsequent aDNA results showed that the most frequent and characteristic Ashkenazi lineage (haplogroup K1a1b1a) was indeed found in prehistoric Europe, in Middle Neolithic Spain, with a very closely-related lineage appearing in Iron Age England, dating to the 1st or 2nd century BC, substantiating the hypothesis.

latter), whereas the Western Isles carry a lesser Scandinavian signal and mainly on the male side (~15%). This has been interpreted to imply a family-based settlement model for regions closer to Scandinavia and mainly male settlement further afield.

Attempts to address the peopling of the British Isles using the male line of descent have also been made periodically for the past fifteen years. Until recently, the lack of genealogical resolution hampered the interpretations, but in the past few years, with the advent of high-throughput next-generation sequencing studies, this has finally changed.

There were a number of low-resolution studies of the Y chromosome in the early 2000s, which we referred to briefly earlier. One group, led by Mark Thomas and Mike Weale, studied Y-chromosome variation in a sample of about 300 men from seven British market towns, arranged on a transect between East Anglia and north Wales, and compared them with Dutch Friesland and Norway. Norway, or at least Scandinavia, had already been identified as the likely proximal source for Y-chromosome haplogroup R1a lineages in Shetland, Orkney, and the western coast and islands of northern Britain (see below). These researchers identified a distinction between England and Wales, reflecting a higher frequency in England of what are now referred to as haplogroup I lineages that form most of the remainder of British Y chromosomes, after R1b. From this, they inferred a mass-migration of Anglo-Saxons from the continent, with 50–100% replacement in central England. This estimate seemed to be at odds with the historical evidence, which estimated anything between a few tens of thousands of Anglo-Saxon immigrants (in a process analogous to the Roman and Norman conquests) and a settlement involving ultimately about a fifth of the population in England. The researchers subsequently proposed, therefore, the imposition of an apartheid system allowing the replacement of élite male lineages whilst the bulk of the population remained unchanged. Although this suggestion was criticized in its turn, some form of sex bias, as is increasingly being seen in the case of other dispersals within the last 5000 years or so, remains an appealing and plausible hypothesis.

This estimate for male Anglo-Saxon immigration was, in any event, reduced to below 40% for England overall in a much more comprehensive 'census' of British Y-chromosome variation led by Cristian Capelli and David Goldstein in 2003. This work had the added proviso that the admixture analysis could not distinguish Anglo-Saxon from Danish immigration, and the suggestion that the distribution might imply a higher fraction of the latter. Although it was also pointed out that much of the difference between lowland England and the rest of the British Isles might have been established much earlier, in the Mesolithic or Neolithic, this now seems less likely, as we will see shortly.

While this body of work addressed the issue of British Y-chromosome variation from the recent historical perspective of Anglo-Saxons *versus* an older, indigenous British or 'Celtic' population, others focused more on that seemingly more ancient heritage. These came in the wake of studies of mtDNA in the 1990s that had attempted to address the issue of the extent of Near Eastern migration during the Neolithic transition in Europe. The traditional model, put forward by Cavalli-Sforza and his colleagues in the 1980s, had suggested a large influx from the Near East at the start of the Neolithic and rolling wave of advance of Near Eastern farmers across Europe with continuous admixture at the wave-front. By contrast, the mitochondrial studies proposed a smaller-scale pioneer colonization for the earliest farmers in Europe and emphasized an important role for the later, gradual assimilation of indigenous hunter–gatherer lineages in the ancestry of European populations.

Several studies at the turn of the millennium focused on Y-chromosome variation in the British Isles, but they followed Cavalli-Sforza's reasoning by assuming that a high frequency of a given allele or lineage in a particular region, and a gradient of frequency moving away from that region, implied that that region was a likely source. This suggested that the west–east gradient in haplogroup R1b implied a very high level of Mesolithic survival in Atlantic Europe. It almost reached 'fixation' (i.e., 100%) in western Ireland and also reached levels of ~90% in Wales and the Spanish Basque country. The fly in the ointment at the time was the age of the R1b lineage—estimated for Ireland only at around 4200 years ago, and around 6800 years ago for the British Isles as a whole. Since the confidence intervals were very wide, however, the estimates did not seem unduly restrictive, and the suggestion of a very high level of Mesolithic survival in Atlantic Europe was taken up and elaborated using the similar geographic patterns in low-resolution mitochondrial and genome-wide data as well as a re-interpretation of the low-resolution Y-chromosome data several years later.

One study led by Jim Wilson focused on the settlement of the Orkney Islands, showing a very striking Y-chromosome signature in Orkney that was present at ~20% yet absent from adjacent areas in Britain and the continent, but present in Norway at ~22%. Moreover, this signature (now known to be a subgroup of haplogroup R1a, the sister group to R1b), was elevated in individuals with indigenous surnames. This suggested that the R1a lineage was a signature of Norse settlement following the annexation of the islands by Norway in the 9th century AD.

At the same time, however, the argument for a pre-Neolithic ancestry for R1b was also bolstered by the similarity of the British and Irish lineages to those of the Basques, which, on several grounds (including mtDNA analyses and the non-Indo-European Basque language) had been assumed to have a largely pre-Neolithic ancestry since the days when they had been shown to be European outliers by Cavalli-Sforza and his colleagues. This was despite a striking lack of diversity amongst this signature Atlantic lineage (implied in the age estimates above) that cast an additional shadow over the conclusions, since diversity accumulates over time.

R1b indeed turned out to be crucial, but not at all in the way that had been expected. The story began to be turned on its head in 2010, when one group of researchers proposed that the diversity patterns in the lineage suggested that it had been carried by the Neolithic expansion across Europe from the Near East, rather than representing a Mesolithic relict. This generated much discussion of the complexities of the R1b sub-cluster distribution within Europe, with George Busby and colleagues, for example, concluding that the dating was just too imprecise for clear conclusions. Now, however, some of these issues can be resolved, due to the huge increase in both genealogical resolution and dating precision possible from whole Y-chromosome data (or at least very large chunks).

The first tree published with such data focused on Sardinia, and although the new data clearly implied that there had been major Late Neolithic expansions involving both R1b and haplogoup I2, the impact was not immediate because of the restricted setting. But then two further groups of researchers, one including Y-chromosome data from the PoBI project that focused on Europe and the Near East (with several million bases of Y-chromosome sequence from 334 men), and the other with a

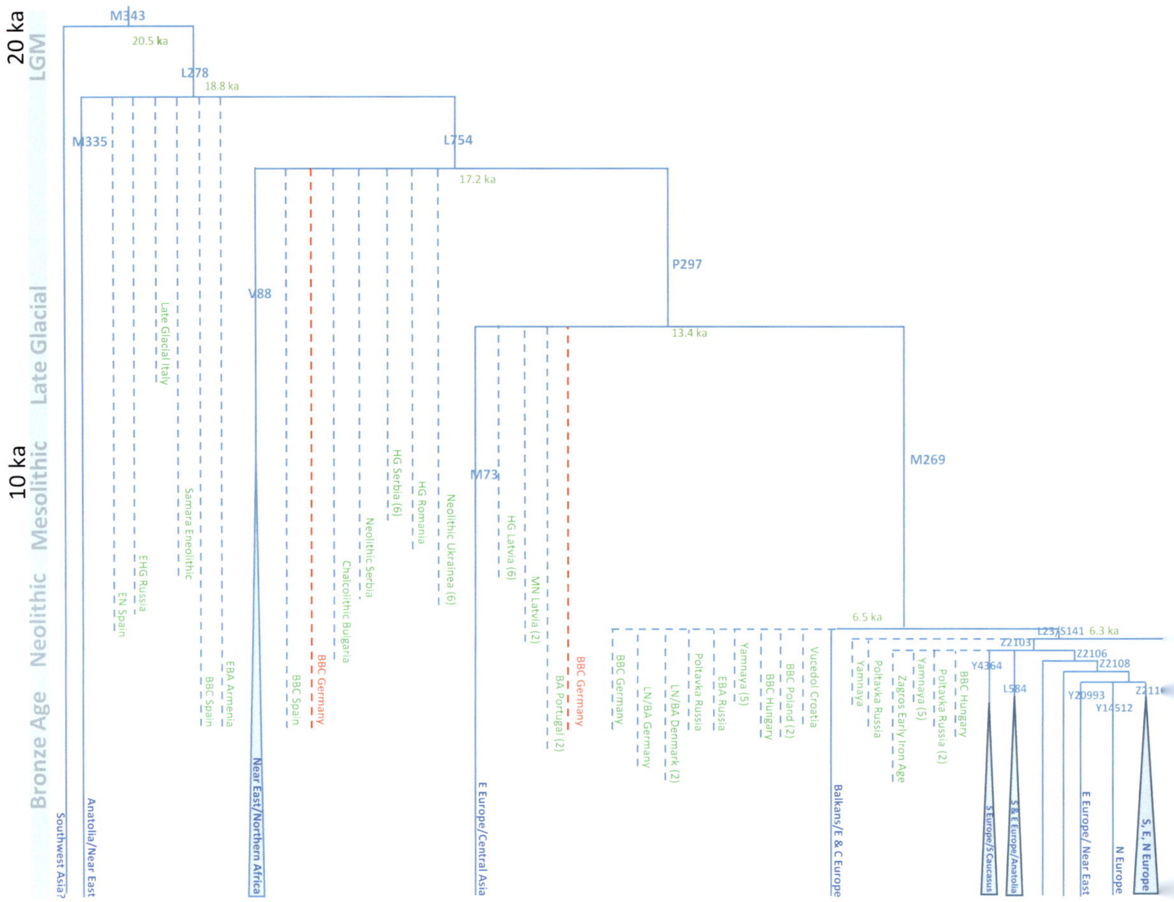

global dataset of 456 Y chromosomes, showed that this was a very widespread phenomenon—similar major Late Neolithic/Early Bronze Age expansions had taken place right across much of Eurasia. The first group dated the expansions, mainly in R1a, R1b, I1 and I2, to 2100–4200 years ago, whereas the second pointed more generally to expansions world-wide throughout the early to mid-Holocene (Fig. 6.3).

In the wake of the emerging aDNA evidence that we will discuss below, the first group, led by Mark Jobling and Chiara Batini and using the PoBI project dataset, explicitly made the link to the spread of Early Bronze Age innovations such as the emergence of élites and horse-riding, but both papers highlighted the extremely intriguing lack of a corresponding signature in the mitochondrial DNA—this appeared to have been a male-dominated phenomenon. These publications were followed up by a more comprehensive analysis led by Chris Tyler-Smith at the Sanger Institute in Cambridgeshire, where the first human genome had been sequenced, using 1244 world-wide Y chromosomes from the 1000 Genomes project. They cautiously suggested a possible link, in the case of R1b, to the spread of the

6.3. Schematic tree of Y-chromosome haplogroup R1b. (with facing page) Branching structure based on PhyloTree-Y, age estimates based on Batini et al. (2015), Karmin et al. (2015), Poznik et al. (2016) and YFull. Time scale and archaeological periods are shown on the left-hand side. Triangles represent major expansion clusters. Geographic ranges estimated from numerous published surveys of diagnostic markers. Ancient DNA lineages (in green)—taken from Lee et al. *American Journal of Physical Anthropology* 148:571–579 (2012); Mathieson et al. *Nature* 528: 499–503 (2015); Haak et al. (2015); Cassidy et al. (2015); Martiniano et al. (2016); Schiffels et al. (2016); Allentoft et al. (2015); Broushaki et al. *Science* 353: 499–503 (2016); and Fu et al. (2016)—are often included on dashed branches to highlight potential uncertainty in their position in the tree due to possible ungenotyped diagnostic sites.

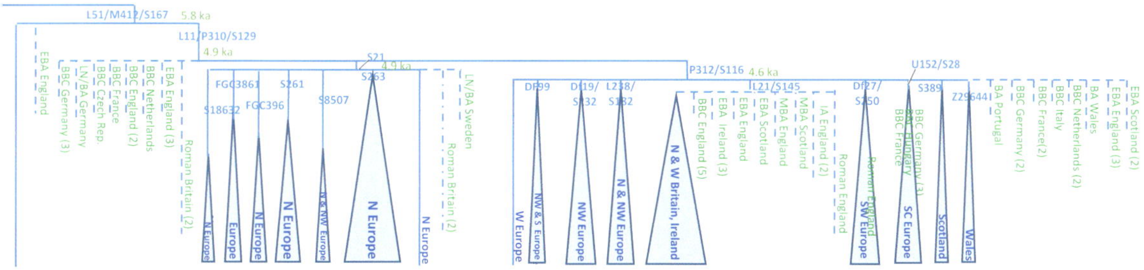

pastoralist Corded Ware at the end of the Neolithic, as well as a possible connection to the antecedent Early Bronze Age Yamnaya culture of the Pontic–Caspian steppe, and similarly a link in the case of R1a with the spread of Indo-European speakers into the Indian Subcontinent. When the results of aDNA analyses are taken into account as well, these links start to become compelling.

The wider European setting: New evidence from genomics and ancient DNA

As mentioned earlier (see Text Box 6.2), one of the most striking new statistical approaches to be applied to genomic datasets is the 'STRUCTURE-like' suite of algorithms for individual ancestry estimation, such as ADMIXTURE. These algorithms cluster genome-wide data into distinct components that potentially represent distinct ancestral genetic pools that combined in times past to contribute to present-day populations.

It is possible to estimate the optimal number of ancestral populations for a given dataset, and when this is done for European and Near Eastern populations using the ADMIXTURE programme, for example, set in the context of other Eurasian variation, they usually show three distinct source gene pools (Fig. 6.4). (Confusingly, the clusters tend to be portrayed as different colours in different publications, so we have numbered them here for clarity.) Cluster 1 is an indigenous European component, which predominates in Europeans, reaching its highest levels in the Saami of Scandinavia, the last remaining descendants of herding, non-farming populations in Europe. It is found at lower rates in other west Eurasian populations: in the Near East, the Caucasus, central Asia, and north Africa. Cluster 2 appears to be an Anatolian/Levantine component, which is most common around the north, east, and southern shores of the Mediterranean, the Caucasus and central Asia. Finally, Cluster 3 is most common in Iran, the Caucasus, central Asia, and western and northern south Asia. It occurs throughout the modern Near East and Arabia but barely in north Africa, and is found at low levels across Europe, although minimally in a few southern European outliers such as Basques and Sardinians.

Ancient DNA studies over the past couple of years, from teams led by researchers such as Wolfgang Haak in Jena, David Reich in Harvard, and Eske Willerslev in Copenhagen, have both dramatically supported the reality of these ancestral clusters and clarified their sources (Fig. 6.5). To date, Mesolithic Europeans belong almost entirely to Cluster 1, which is therefore indeed clearly indigenous to Europe and a signal of European hunter–gatherers and foragers after the last Ice Age, from Iberia in the west to Scandinavia in the north and Russia in the east.

Cluster 2 reaches almost 100% in Levantine Neolithic and the preceding (hunter–gatherer) Epi-Palaeolithic (or Natufian) individuals, around 90% of Anatolian Neolithic individuals, and 80–90% of Early Neolithic samples from central and northern Europe, and from Iberia. An ultimate source in the Levant therefore seems likely—we are not quite returning to Cavalli-Sforza style frequency-based arguments here, since the location of the highest frequency is also the oldest. It has therefore been proposed as the signature of the spread of Neolithic populations by direct migrations from the Near East, although the immediate source for the European Neolithic is not quite clear-cut, since there is little aDNA evidence from Mesolithic Mediterranean Europe. There is some evidence from both modern mitochondrial DNA and ancient genome-wide analyses to suggest that the Mediterranean region was repopulated by hunter–gatherers in the Late Glacial and postglacial, well before the earliest spread of the Neolithic, around 9000 years ago, and that these groups may have contributed to the spread of the Early Neolithic in Europe.

Cluster 3 reaches more than 80% in two Late Glacial and Mesolithic individuals from the southern Caucasus, and has therefore been conveniently dubbed the 'Caucasus hunter–gatherer' component by Dan Bradley and his colleagues in Trinity College, Dublin. It has recently been shown, however, to occur at similar—or even higher—levels in Mesolithic and Early Neolithic Iran, which is widely considered a more plausible source region because of the way it can be woven into a narrative about the spread of farming. Rather strikingly, the two ends of the Fertile Crescent, where farming originated in west Eurasia—essentially, the Levant and Mesopotamia—appear to have been genetically distinct at that time, around 10,000 years ago. It seems that before the Neolithic began, and during its early stages, there was little inter-breeding between these two very distinct groups despite farming developing across the whole area at around the same time. As the Neolithic progressed, however, and especially by the onset of the Bronze Age, there were major dispersals away from these source regions, so that Cluster 2 spread into Iran and the Caucasus, as well as into Europe, and Cluster 3 spread into the Levant and Anatolia, north across the Caucasus into the Pontic–Caspian steppe region, and also east and south into central Asia and south Asia—as well, again, as into Europe.

The role of aDNA has been absolutely critical here, because of the ability to chart the spread of the distinctive genetic signatures by radiocarbon dating. What has perhaps been most striking and surprising about these results is precisely the extent to which the theoretical model assumed by ADMIXTURE, of isolated gene pools subsequently combining, has been borne out. Moreover, whilst the existence of Cluster 1 in Europe and the spread of Cluster 2 with the Neolithic were not completely unexpected, the pattern for Cluster 3 came as a big surprise to many researchers, who had neither expected genetics (aside from the Y chromosome) to cast much light on later prehistory, nor to see such major genetic changes at such a late date. The distribution of these clusters, especially in dated archaeological remains, has revolutionized our understanding of west Eurasian dispersal and settlement history, and allowed us to test archaeological and linguistic models that had been fighting it out for decades.

The dispersal of Cluster 3 brings us back to the Y-chromosome story referred to earlier, and the question of the spread of the Indo-European language family, of which Celtic is a member. Cluster 3 is barely present in the Mesolithic of the Pontic–Caspian region of southern Russia, but is present at about 15–30% by the Copper Age and 40–50% by the Early Bronze Age. This calls to mind the suggestion for the origins of the burgeoning Yamnaya phenomenon of the Bronze Age steppe, characterized by distinctive burial mounds or kurgans.

As Barry Cunliffe has pointed out, there was a remarkable confluence of three huge cultural innovations in different parts of west Eurasia during the course of the 4th millennium BC. In the Near East there was population growth, the development of urbanism, writing, and trade. In south-east Europe (from the Carpathian Basin south to the plain of Thessaly), meanwhile, there was a late flowering of Neolithic village life, enriched by the production and exchange of copper and gold, stimulating demand for high-quality goods further north and east. On the steppe, there was an increasing reliance on domestic horses (although whether they were being ridden is debated) after around 6000 years ago, alongside the 'secondary-product' innovations of woolly sheep, ox-drawn carts, and covered wagons, leading to an increasingly mobile and pastoralist way of life. As each of these innovating centres gradually drew the others into its sphere of influence over the 4th millennium, the

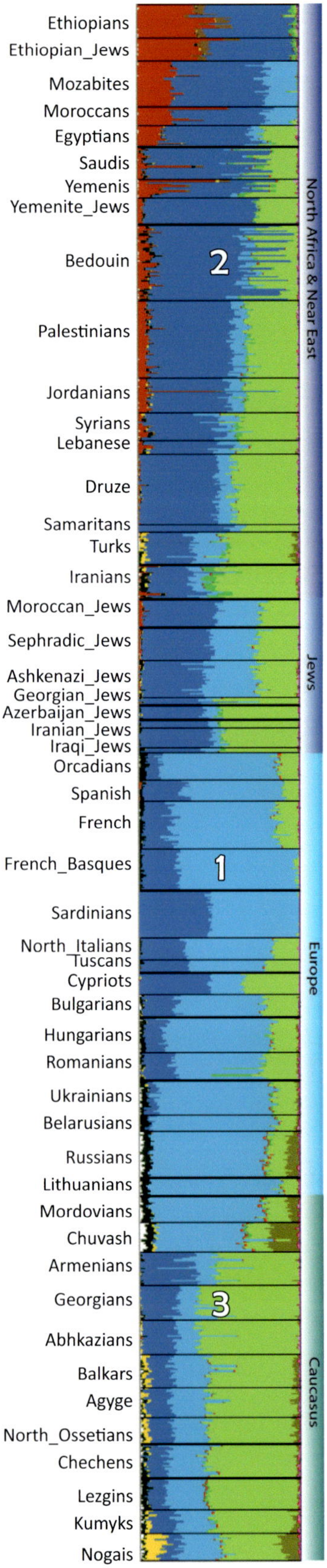

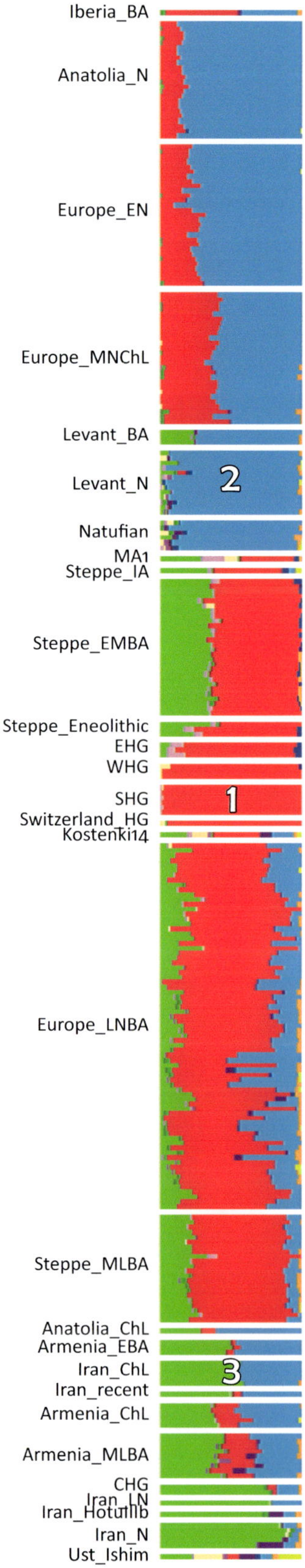

6.4. (far left) **Genome-wide SNP ADMIXTURE analysis of modern populations from Europe, the Near East, the Caucasus, and north and eastern Africa.**
1 = European hunter–gatherer component, 2 = Anatolian/Levantine hunter–gatherer component, 3 = Caucasus/Iranian hunter–gatherer component. *K* = 14

(Source: M. Pala, G. Chaubey, P. Soares, & M. B. Richards 2014 'The archaeogenetics of European ancestry'. *Encyclopedia of Life Sciences (eLS)*, Chichester, John Wiley and Sons, reproduced by permission)

6.5. (near left) **Genetic structure in ancient west Eurasian populations across time.** ADMIXTURE clustering analysis of present-day and ancient human samples; results shown only for ancient samples for *K* = 11.
E/M/L N = Early/Middle/Late Neolithic;
ChL = Chalcolithic;
BA = Bronze Age;
IA = Iron Age;
W/E/S/C HG = Western/Eastern/Scandinavian/Caucasus hunter–gatherers
HotuIIIb = likely Mesolithic Iran

(Source: I. Lazaridis et al. 2016 'Genomic insights into the origin of farming in the ancient Near East', *Nature* 536(7617), 419–24, reproduced by permission)

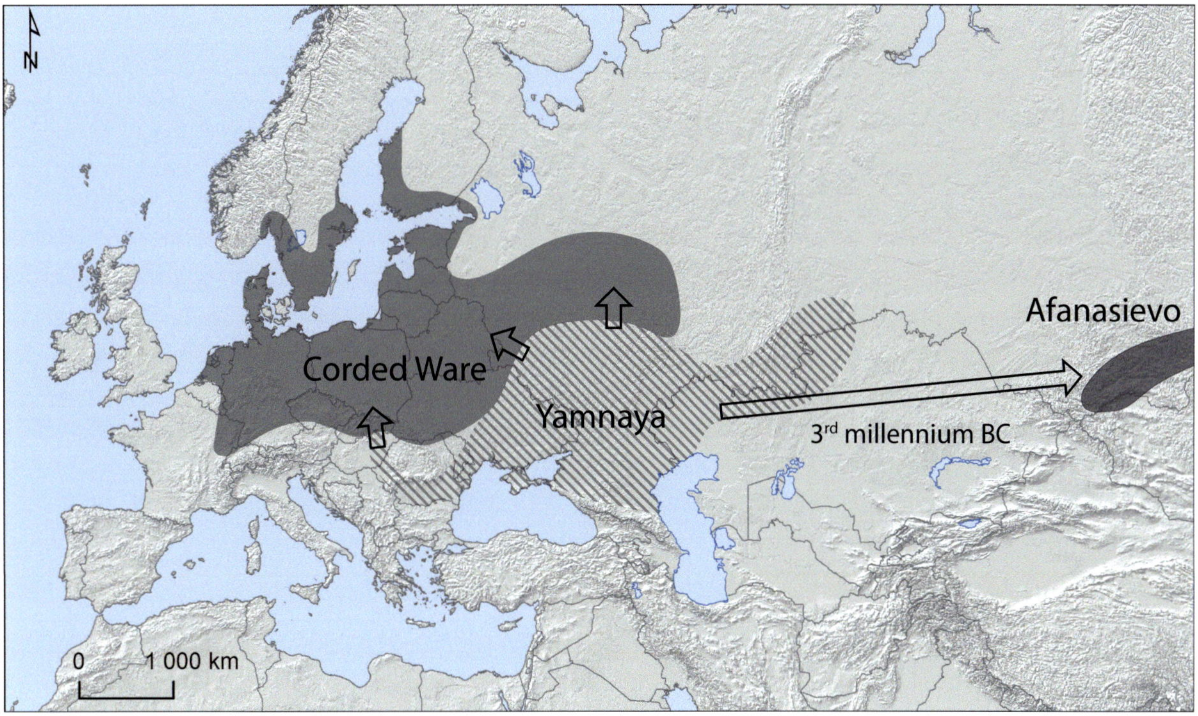

6.6. Distribution of Late Neolithic/Early Bronze Age cultures (Yamnaya, Corded Ware, and Afanasievo) with arrows showing the Yamnaya expansions.

(Source: M. E. Allentoft et al. 2015 'Population genomics of Bronze Age Eurasia', *Nature* 522(7555), 167–72, reproduced by permission)

stage was set for an earthquake in culture and society, the impact of which was ultimately to extend from the Indian Subcontinent to the Celtic West of Europe. The study of aDNA suggests that this whole transformation was to some extent accompanied by and likely mediated by gene flow—that is to say, the actual movement of people—across this vast region. Moreover, this is exactly the process suggested by historical linguists and archaeologists to explain the spread of the Indo-European languages.

With its distinctive pastoralist economy, the Yamnaya (or pit-grave) horizon may have had its roots in a well-known kurgan-burial and herder Maikop tradition of the western Caucasus, which was already characterized by very rich burials. Prestige goods such as decorated fabric, painted ceramics, jewelry, metalwork, and wine had been percolating around the Caucasus Mountains throughout the 4th millennium BC, from the highly urbanized Uruk culture in the south, centred on Mesopotamia. The Yamnaya were highly mobile herders who emerged in the vast swathes of steppe country to the north of the Caucasus around 5300 years ago, as the steppe recovered from the impact of an environmental crisis in the preceding millennium. By this time, copper use was widespread, joined by bronze-making technologies 300 years later. Yamnaya pastoralism rapidly expanded over a huge area, penetrating the lower Danube and Great Hungarian Plain in the west by 4800 years ago, and extending eastwards towards central Asia—with an increased emphasis on warriors, weapons, and warfare—at around the same time (Fig. 6.6).

As we have implied already, it is not only the broad genome-wide patterns that point to migration from the steppe at the end of the Neolithic to Early Bronze Age. Y-chromosome phylogenies have begun to provide quite precise molecular-clock dates and suggest a similar chronological story. Haplogroup R1b has been confirmed to have been present in Europe since Late Glacial times—the haplogroup as a whole dates to the Last Glacial Maximum, and there are deep pre-Neolithic and Copper Age south Russian branches at the root of modern lineages in the Near East. Similarly deep-rooting lineages have also been identified in a sample dating to Late Glacial Italy, 14,000 years ago, and to 7000 years ago from Early Neolithic Spain. But amongst modern Europeans, these ancient lineages are vanishingly rare. The vast majority belong to branches that post-date the onset of the Neolithic, with the deepest shared branch (R1b-M269) dated to around 6500 years ago and the major expansion clusters (R1b-L11, and R1b-S116 nested tightly within it) to around 4900 and 4600 years ago respectively—the time of the expansion of Corded Ware pastoralists in northern Europe (Fig. 6.3).

Moreover, apart from two individuals belonging to I2a, all of the Yamnaya samples tested to date (and, although fewer, all those from the Poltavka culture that succeeded the Yamnaya in the middle Volga region) fall close to the root of the European R1b-M269 cluster, found today mainly in the Balkans and eastern and central Europe, its immediate R1b-L23 sub-cluster, or the next-derived R1b-Z2103 sub-cluster (Fig. 6.3). The Z2103 lineages, it should be noted, are not directly ancestral to the major Late Neolithic/Early Bronze Age European expansion clusters, but predominate in the Near East, the Balkans and the Mediterranean, although one sub-cluster, R1b-Z2110, expands into northern Europe. This may well imply that the simplest models, which argue that Late Neolithic Corded Ware groups derived directly from Yamnaya pastoralists (transmitting Indo-European languages ultimately to almost all Europeans, including the ancestors of Celtic speakers in the west) might fail to capture the full picture. Given that the earliest split in the Indo-European language tree separates the Anatolian branch from the remainder, and that this branch is thought by linguists to have entered Anatolia via the Balkans, it is particularly intriguing that the present-day focus of underived M269 lineages is in the Balkans, with the early divergence of the Z2103 Yamnaya cluster in both southern and eastern Europe, Anatolia and the Near East—and with the derived (but fairly minor) sub-cluster, Z2110, and several other lineages spreading soon afterwards through Europe. This is seemingly well before the main radiation across Europe of the L11 sub-cluster that is found in the majority of central and, especially, west European men today.

The origins, early dispersals, mode of spread, and even the precise source of the European lineages are therefore likely to be more complex than the current aDNA analyses have suggested. Nevertheless, despite very limited sampling of Yamnaya so far, the outlines of a model are at least starting to materialize. Moreover, R1b also predominates in samples from the subsequent steppe Middle Bronze Age and has also been found in Corded Ware samples from Scandinavia and Germany, and potentially in all of the German Bell Beaker samples so far tested—although these belong to the much more derived R1b-S116 cluster that predominates in present-day western Europeans.

Although this new picture for R1b came as a surprise to many, its sibling haplogroup, R1a, had already been widely mooted as a possible marker for the spread of Indo-European languages on the basis of its modern distribution, which straddles Europe (especially the north) and the Indian Subcontinent (again, especially in the north). In fact, many would have expected to see R1a in the Yamnaya, rather than R1b, which again suggests that the situation might be more complex than sometimes suggested, and remains currently dependent on small and potentially unrepresentative aDNA datasets. Although not so far identified in the Yamnaya, R1a was found in human remains across north and central Europe, ranging from a Mesolithic sample from Russia up until the Bronze Age across the region, and is notably frequent amongst the Corded Ware samples, although these too are still few in number. We have already mentioned R1a in the context of the Norse settlement of Orkney—it is uncommon elsewhere in the British Isles, but reaches 10–20% in Scandinavia and central Europe, rising to more than 50% in eastern Europe to the north of the Black Sea, from Poland to western Russia. Intriguingly, the modern distribution of R1a led some researchers to posit that its early diversification took place somewhere between eastern Anatolia and Iran. In the Indian Subcontinent, meanwhile, where most of the R1a variation is restricted to a small number of shallow sub-clusters dating to less than 4000 years ago, the frequency varies from 30–60% in the north to none in some parts of the south.

Moreover, R1a has also been found in the great majority of remains analysed to date from the Bronze Age Sintashta culture (east of the southern Ural Mountains) and the Sintashta-derived Andronovo horizon in central Asia and Srubnaya culture on the western steppe. These samples now number dozens in total. R1a is overwhelmingly predominant in kurgan burials in south-central Siberia, dating from the Middle Bronze Age Andronovo horizon and continuing to the Later Bronze and Iron Ages. These are the groups proposed as potential source populations for Bronze Age expansions of Indo-Aryan speakers south into the Indian Subcontinent, replacing the Neolithic Indus Valley civilization, 4000–3500 years ago.

Present-day South Asians also carry the 'Caucasus hunter–gatherer' Cluster 3 genome-wide component at varying frequencies. Whilst a fraction of this may be the result of Early Neolithic dispersals into the Subcontinent from the Iranian pole of the Fertile Crescent, David Reich and his colleagues have used the Iranian Neolithic and Yamnaya gene pools as sources for an admixture analysis to estimate that the Yamnaya steppe component was as great or greater than the Neolithic fraction from Iran for many Indian and Pakistani populations. On the mitochondrial side, however, the signal for dispersal into the Subcontinent is much weaker, highlighting the extent to which the process of Indo-European expansion was male-dominated. A similar sex bias appears to be emerging for the spread across Europe.

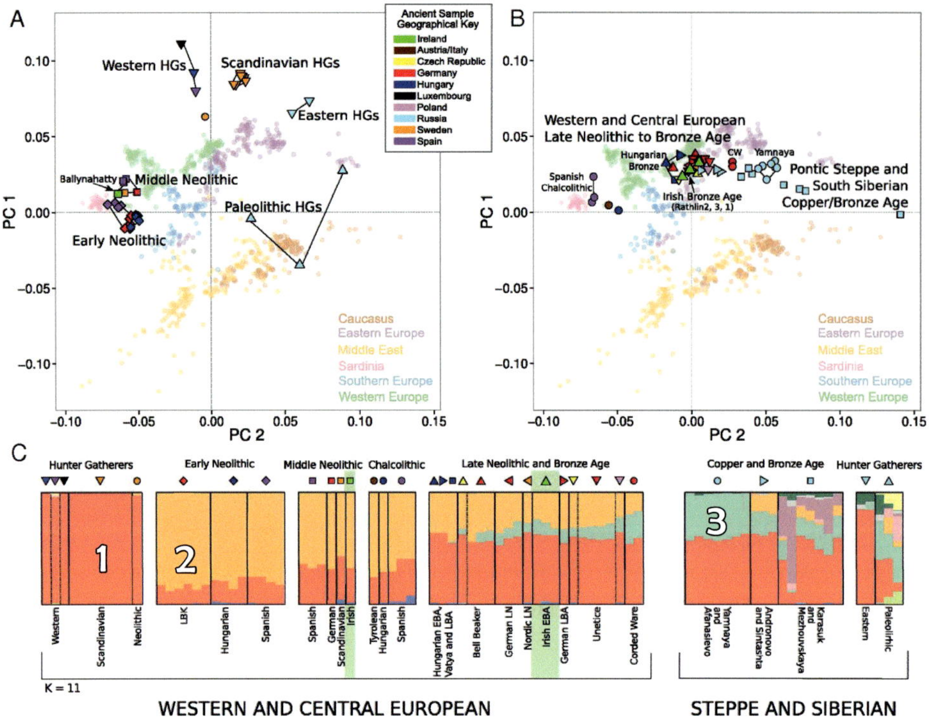

6.7. Genetic affinities of ancient Irish individuals. (A and B) Genotypes from ancient samples are projected onto the first two principal components from Eurasian populations. (A) PCA projecting ancient Eurasian hunter–gatherers and Neolithic farmers, where they separate clearly into Early Neolithic, MN (including the Irish Ballynahatty genome), and several hunter–gatherer groups. (B) PCA projection of Late Neolithic, Copper, and Bronze Age individuals where the three Rathlin genomes adopt a central position within a large clustering of European Bronze Age individuals. (C) ADMIXTURE ancestry components ($K = 11$) of these same ancient genomes. In west and central Europe, ancient individuals are composed almost entirely of two dominant strands of ancestry, linked to hunter–gatherer (red) and early farmer (orange) populations, until the Late Neolithic. At this point, a third (green) Caucasus component features. Previously, this component was only seen in ancient steppe and Siberian populations such as the Yamnaya. The three Rathlin genomes each display this Caucasus strand of ancestry whereas the Irish Neolithic does not. HG = hunter–gatherers

(Source: Lara M. Cassidy et al., *PNAS* 2016; 113:2:368–73, reproduced by permission)

The first ancient DNA results from the British Isles

There have been four substantial studies to date of aDNA from the British Isles, three from Britain and one from Ireland, and already they are transforming our understanding of ancestry and settlement history of the region.

Lara Cassidy and her colleagues in Dan Bradley's group in Dublin were the first to focus directly on earlier prehistory, carrying out whole-genome analysis on one Middle Neolithic female, dating to around 5200 years ago, from Ballynahatty, County Down, and three Bronze Age males, dating to around 3600–4000 years ago, from Rathlin, an island off the northern coast of County Antrim, close to Scotland. The genome-wide ADMIXTURE and PCA profiles revealed two striking features (Fig. 6.7). Firstly, the Neolithic individual closely resembled other Middle Neolithic remains from Germany and Spain, with a large fraction of the 'Neolithic' Cluster 2 (estimated at ~58%) in the ADMIXTURE analysis and a smaller fraction of the 'Mesolithic' Cluster 1 (~42%). This Mesolithic element is, by the way, consistently represented at higher levels on the continent in the Middle Neolithic than in Early Neolithic remains, whether they be from Germany, south-east Europe, or Spain, implying a pioneer colonization model for the Early Neolithic followed by assimilation of hunter–gatherer populations in the later stages of the Neolithic across continental Europe, as suggested previously from both mitochondrial and archaeological studies. It is worth noting that whilst the process of pioneer colonization is often described by geneticists

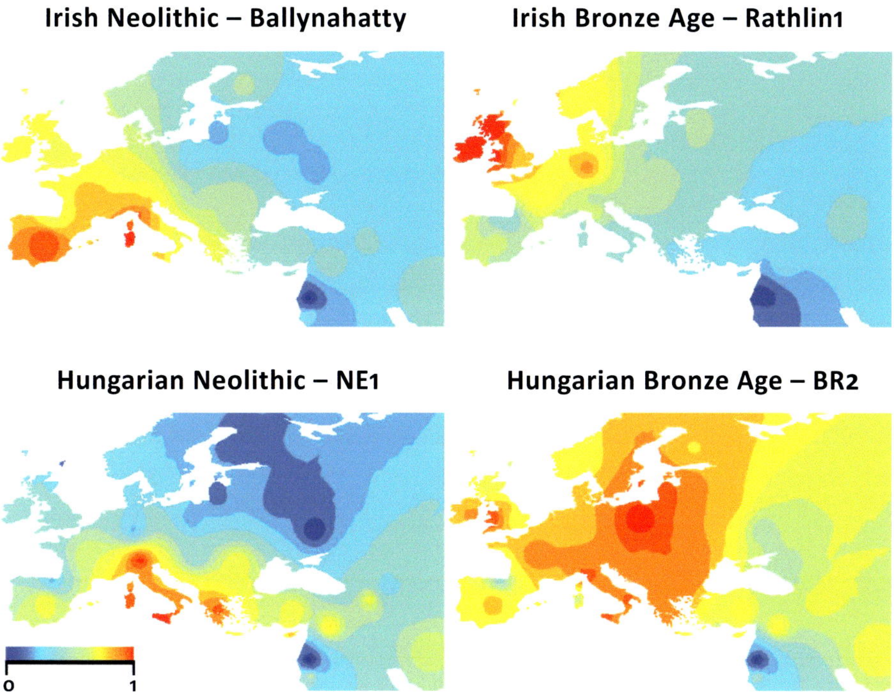

6.8. Comparison of Irish and central European ancient genomes for haplotype-based affinity to modern populations. Interpolated 'heat maps' comparing relative haplotype donations by Irish and Hungarian Neolithic and Bronze Age genomes.

(Source: Lara M. Cassidy et al., *PNAS* 2016; 113:2:368–73, reproduced by permission)

as 'replacement', this is a complete misnomer. If a new group arrives in the midst of an indigenous population but remains apart from it, it will inevitably appear completely distinct. But that hardly means that the entire genetic landscape has changed—just that the surrounding groups have not been sampled. Even if they are invisible at the time, their continued existence can be inferred from the fact that they become visible later as they are assimilated into the farming groups.

On the other hand, although we might assume that this assimilation also took place within the British Isles, in fact the result is rather surprising. It is striking how extremely similar the Ballynahatty woman appears to the other Middle Neolithic remains sampled so far from across Europe. This would make sense in terms of pioneer migration, given that the Early Neolithic only reaches the British Isles by the time it is coming to an end in central Europe, so that the Mesolithic fraction ancestry in this individual (about a third of her genome) might have a largely or even entirely continental source.

In any case, the three Bronze Age samples from Rathlin are markedly different, and consistent with other Late Neolithic/Early Bronze Age remains from across northern and central Europe. They closely resemble one another genetically, although the dating makes it very unlikely that they were all members of a contemporaneous family group. These samples carry a majority of the Mesolithic European Cluster 1 (almost two-thirds), a smaller fraction of the Neolithic Cluster 2 (about a quarter), and they also (unlike the Middle

Neolithic woman) carry the third 'Caucasus hunter–gatherer' cluster, which makes up roughly 10% of their genomes.

As we noted above, Cluster 3 is very widespread amongst modern Europeans, but did not appear in northern and central Europe until the end of the Neolithic, with the appearance of the pastoralist Corded Ware culture. It is then also seen in the slightly later Bell Beaker Complex in Germany, but remains largely absent from the Copper Age of southern Europe. It has been seen at its highest levels in Mesolithic samples from the Caucasus and Iran, and subsequently in remains from the Early Bronze Age Yamnaya culture on the Pontic–Caspian steppe. The Yamnaya share it roughly equally with the European Mesolithic cluster and lack the Mediterranean Cluster 2 altogether. It has therefore been interpreted as reflecting immigration at the end of the Neolithic by pastoralists from the Pontic–Caspian steppe, very likely speaking an early form of Indo-European, in line with archaeological models that have inferred an important steppe Yamnaya influence on the formation of the Corded Ware in northern Europe.

Since the Yamnaya carried Cluster 1 as well as Cluster 3, Cassidy and her colleagues estimated that about a third of the Irish Bronze Age genomes trace directly back to the steppe populations. Again, the high degree of similarity with other European remains of similar age is striking, and once again, although immigration and assimilation within the British Isles/Ireland might seem the most plausible scenario, the genomes could perfectly well represent new arrivals and heavy replacement from the continent. In other words, a possible implication was that these samples may have almost no local Irish ancestry whatsoever.

Comparisons of the affinities of several ancient genomes with modern genomes from across Europe by Cassidy et al., using the fineSTRUCTURE approach previously employed in the PoBI study, also provided some very striking results. The Irish Middle Neolithic genome had closest affinities with modern Iberians (and Sardinians, whose genomes seem to more closely resemble those of Early Neolithic Europeans than any other modern population), which would make sense in terms of the source of the Atlantic Neolithic (although also if the woman had recently arrived from France, say). By contrast a Hungarian Neolithic sample had closest affinities with modern south-east and south-central Europeans (Fig. 6.8).

On the other hand, the Irish Bronze Age genome (one of the three was analysed to high resolution) has its closest affinities with modern people from the north and west of the British Isles and, after those, to north-west Europeans and Scandinavians, consistent with a major Corded Ware influence. The burial of the three individuals in stone cists, including in one case with a Bowl Food Vessel, is typical of Ireland and Scotland at the time. By contrast with this, a Hungarian Bronze Age sample most closely resembled genetically modern east-central Europeans. This pattern could imply further assimilation of Middle Neolithic individuals into the dispersing Late Neolithic population as it spread into north-west Europe, before the move into the British Isles. This is also consistent with the closer similarity of Corded Ware individuals sampled in Germany to the Yamnaya than seen in Bell Beaker, Bronze Age, or modern northern Europeans.

On the Y chromosome, all three Bronze Age individuals belong to the R1b-L21/S145 sub-haplogroup (within R1b-S116—see Fig. 6.3), which reaches its highest global levels in modern Irish populations and dates to less than 4000 years ago in molecular-clock analyses of modern lineages. Since the Bronze Age individuals date to around 3800 years ago, this suggests that their lineage had only recently arisen from its immediate ancestor. Those particular lineages are now found across western and northern Britain and Brittany, and reach almost 80% in modern Ireland, but have been heavily displaced in south-east England—reflecting the pattern we referred to earlier, first identified more than fifteen years ago. As we noted earlier, all Yamnaya Y-chromosome lineages tested so far from the Pontic–Caspian steppe, and their Poltavka descendants, belong to R1b-M269 and most, to date, to its nested sub-cluster, R1b-L23, lying close to the root of almost all extant European R1b lineages or, within them, the derived cluster R1b-Z2103; and the latter seems likely from its modern distribution to have had an origin somewhere in European Russia or the Balkans around 6000 years ago (Fig. 6.3). Both the Neolithic and high-coverage Bronze Age samples also carried a common haemochromatosis variant. Hereditary haemochromatosis (or 'iron overload') also occurs at a higher rate in modern Ireland than anywhere else in the world, with one in five members of the population carrying the risk variant, and has been referred to as the 'Celtic disease'. By contrast, the lactase persistence variant, which allows many Europeans to drink milk into adulthood, appears only in the Bronze Age sample.

The mtDNA from the Middle Neolithic sample, at the time the oldest known lineage from north-west Europe, was interpreted by the authors as having been brought from south-east Europe with the spread of the Neolithic. This interpretation came from recent aDNA analyses, but it disregarded work on the distribution in modern populations. This lineage (now called HV0), although found across western Europe at less than 5%, has been elevated to very high levels in the Saami of Scandinavia—around 40%—and dates back to the Late Glacial. It had therefore previously been attributed to a postglacial expansion from south-west Europe. If this were the case, then it might represent a surviving trace of assimilation of hunter–gatherers within the British Isles (or, at least, within Atlantic Europe) during the Neolithic. Some low-coverage, as yet unpublished, data from Mesolithic England and Scotland lends some tentative support to this suggestion.

The Bronze Age mtDNAs belong to three further distinct lineages, including two distinct branches of one of the most ancient haplogroups in Europe, U5. U5a1 dates to around 8500 years ago, and before the Chalcolithic is only seen in eastern Europe and Scandinavia. It flourishes in the Eastern European Bronze Age (appearing in kurgan graves in several cases), appears in the Corded Ware and Beaker cultures of north-central Europe, and then appears in the Netherlands and Britain with the Beaker culture, and into the Bronze Age. Today this lineage represents less than 0.5% of the British mtDNA pool, but it nevertheless looks like an authentic snippet of female Yamnaya ancestry. The second lineage is U5b, which, like HV0, is also common in the Saami and still looks likely to be a marker for Late Glacial, Late

Magdalenian expansion from the south-west European glacial refuge at the end of the Ice Age—the particular branch concerned dates to around 11,000 years ago. Finally, there is also J2b1a, which has been proposed as a marker for the spread of the Neolithic in Atlantic Europe from the Mediterranean. Again, this dates to around 11,000 years ago, and it may have been part of a dispersal into the European Mediterranean from a Near Eastern glacial refuge area at the end of the Ice Age, before the Neolithic spread through southern Europe. A closely related lineage has recently been identified in Mesolithic Sardinia.

Thus, of the three Bronze Age maternal lineages, only one (U5a1) can plausibly be attributed a Yamnaya origin, whereas all three paternal lineages seem likely to have a closely related eastern-European steppe source—once again, very likely reflecting a strong male bias in the Late Neolithic dispersals from the east, as we noted earlier for the spread of the Indo-Aryan languages into the Indian Subcontinent.

The authors tentatively proposed that this may have been the point at which languages ancestral to modern Celtic languages may have been introduced. Their overall conclusions have been dramatically supported and strengthened by a more recent—and much larger—study by Iñigo Olalde and colleagues, in a huge collaboration across research groups including Harvard, Jena, Copenhagen, Barcelona, and the Natural History Museum in London. This has provided the most complete overview of British genetic prehistory to date, with a special focus on the Bell Beaker period. They analysed 166 new individuals from west and central Europe, including 80 ancient British individuals spanning the Neolithic and Bronze Age, dating from around 6000 to 3000 years ago, and compared them with previously published samples from continental Europe (including more than 640 samples in total).

They achieved this much larger database by taking a different approach from Cassidy et al., by enriching and capturing a very large fraction of the genome (more than a million SNPs) rather than undertaking whole-genome sequencing—allowing for a more 'industrial-scale' of data generation. They confirmed that the earlier Neolithic individuals in Britain (52 samples from across Britain), as well as France (but only four samples in this case), had affinities primarily with the Iberian Early Neolithic rather than central Europe, but the new data suggested that the Mesolithic component was similar across the British Neolithic and across Britain and higher than the Early Neolithic on the continent—more similar to continental Middle Neolithic levels, reflecting the later arrival of the Neolithic in the British Isles (Fig. 6.9). The assimilation, which includes all of the British Neolithic samples carrying the Mesolithic Atlantic forager Y-chromosome haplogroup I2, may of course have taken place *en route*, rather than within the British Isles. The effectively 100% assimilation of forager lineages on the male side contrasts with about a fifth to a quarter of forager mtDNAs on the female side (judging from the level of U5b, U5a2, and possibly also HV0) and about 45% forager lineages in the genome as a whole. This suggests a dramatic sex bias in the spread of the Neolithic into north-west Europe which might reflect the pattern of interaction across Marek Zvelebil's 'agricultural frontier,' where dispersing Neolithic groups from the south would

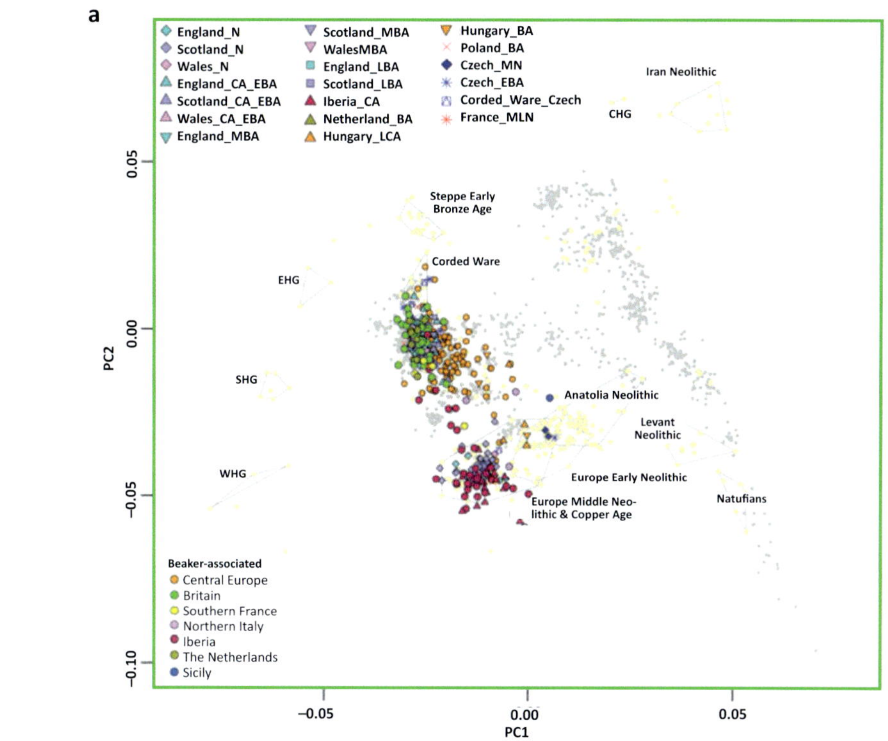

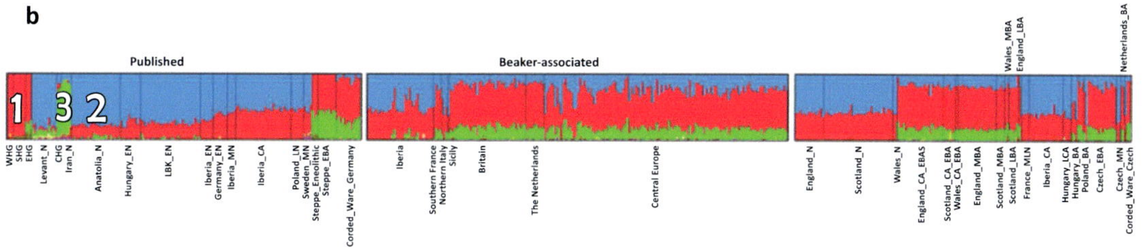

6.9. Population structure of ancient Britain, in European context.
(a) PCA including 990 modern individuals (grey), previously published ancient (yellow) and new British ancient individuals projected onto first two components. (b) ADMIXTURE clustering with $K = 8$, showing ancient samples. E/M/MLN = Early/Middle/Middle–Late Neolithic; W/E/S/CHG = Western/Eastern/Scandinavian/Caucasus hunter–gatherers.
(Source: I. Olalde et al. 2018 'The Beaker phenomenon and the genomic transformation of northwest Europe', *Nature* 555(7695), 190–6, reproduced by permission)

encounter high-density populations of sedentary foragers in the northern Atlantic zone, with women from farming groups moving across the frontier much more readily than men. This seems to be the reverse of the situation we see at the other end of the Neolithic.

By contrast, the nineteen British Beaker remains had affinities to central European Bell Beaker remains—especially to the (just nine) samples from the Netherlands (Fig. 6.9). The big genetic break in England therefore coincided with the Chalcolithic and the appearance of the Beaker Complex, and the new genetic pattern was maintained into the Bronze Age, with only slight indications in the genome-wide patterns of assimilation from indigenous British farming groups. Amongst nine male samples, eight belonged to the highly derived form of the Y-chromosome haplogroup R1b we discussed earlier (Fig. 6.3), and only one to the indigenous haplogroup I2a found in the Neolithic samples. On the other hand, the picture for the female line is not so clear—whilst a few eastern lineages appear, and there is an evident new influence from the former Early Neolithic LBK zone in central Europe—which were presumably assimilated during the expansion of

Corded Ware—many of the same Atlantic Neolithic and Mesolithic lineages seem to persist from the Neolithic through to the Bronze Age and indeed to the present-day.

The authors themselves estimated the level of genome-wide replacement between the Middle Neolithic and the end of the Middle Bronze Age at more than 90%—turning the previous thirty years of assumptions about the genetic history of Britain on their head at a stroke. But perhaps again there was a considerable male bias to these new arrivals. In any case, it is ironic that, due to the high levels of forager assimilation during the Neolithic in eastern Europe, it is at this point that the British Isles, and central Europe, return to a predominance of European hunter–gatherer lineages in their genomes (roughly 70%)—albeit in part brought by post-Neolithic migration from the east.

Several additional studies over the past couple of years have augmented this picture. From the Dublin group, Rui Martiniano and his colleagues published analyses of seven Roman burials, one Anglo-Saxon burial, and one Late Iron Age burial from northern England. As we have already seen, whilst the work of the Harvard and Copenhagen groups and their colleagues is widely recognized, the work of this group has also been pioneering. Firstly, they established the use of petrous bone for DNA recovery from ancient remains, which has been the biggest boost to aDNA research since the development of next-generation sequencing; as its name implies, the petrous portion of the temporal bone in the inner ear is one of the densest parts of the human skeleton, greatly increasing the chances of DNA survival. Moreover, they also developed the imputation of missing variants in ancient genomes (that is, estimation of missing variants using databases of high-quality sequences) and its use in generating haplotype data for the kind of high-resolution analyses (such as fineSTRUCTURE) used by the PoBI team for modern data.

Six of the Roman burials appeared to be indigenous to Britain, as they closely resembled both the Iron Age samples—and also modern Welsh, Irish, and Scottish genomes—with one being an immigrant from from the eastern Mediterranean. Moreover, the Anglo-Saxon individual had particular affinities to modern East Anglians and Dutch, therefore likely carrying rather more continental ancestry. All of the Roman individuals with indigenous genomes also carried west European R1b Y chromosomes (all R1b-L11, including both R1b-U106/S21 and R1b-S116). This lends weight to a model of continuity between the Iron Age and Roman period, and to some intrusion during the Anglo-Saxon period from the continent, as well as to the idea that the Celtic-speaking (or formerly Celtic-speaking) areas are the best modern representatives of the prehistoric British population.

A further paper rather strikingly featured both researchers *and* aDNA sequences from the Sanger Institute—some of the remains studied had actually been discovered during archaeological excavations prior to the construction of the laboratories. Stefan Schiffels and his colleagues analysed whole genomes from ten East Anglian burials: three from the Late Iron Age (from the last few centuries BC), four from the early Anglo-Saxon period (late 4th to mid 6th century AD) and three from the Middle Anglo-Saxon period (7th to 9th centuries AD). Again, the two Iron Age males carried R1b Y chromosomes (both R1b-L21/S145, the sub-cluster of R1b-S116 that predominates in the British Isles). The genome-wide analyses suggested that modern British samples, including those in England, were closer to those from the Iron Age than to the Anglo-Saxon remains, estimating that modern eastern England has around 30% Saxon ancestry, and Wales, and Scotland around 20%. They argued that two of the early Anglo-Saxon samples were genetically immigrant, with a third indigenous and the fourth admixed between the two communities. Interestingly, this is hard to reconcile with the concept of apartheid and segregation proposed earlier on the basis of low resolution Y-chromosome analyses by Mark Thomas and his colleagues at UCL, although once again some kind of male-sex bias remains plausible.

Celtic from the West?

Following on from the archaeological critique of traditional views of Celtic origins, from J. R. Hill's *Rethinking the Iron Age* in 1989 to Simon James' *The Atlantic Celts* a decade later, one of the most influential re-evaluations of Celtic origins has been Barry Cunliffe and John Koch's 'Celtic from the West' model. They point out a striking correspondence between what is known of the ancient distribution of Indo-European languages in western Europe and the archaeological extent of the Atlantic Late Bronze Age, around 1250–1100 BC. An important strand of this suggestion argues that the Celtic languages were spoken as a lingua franca across Atlantic Europe by the end of the Bronze Age, rather than originating in the Urnfield–Hallstatt–La Tène trajectory of west-central Europe—in fact, the spread of the famous 'Celtic' Gündlingen swords is now thought to have been from Britain towards central Europe. In one version of this model, the ultimate source might rather have been in Copper Age or Bronze Age Iberia, as Koch has argued on the basis of south-west Iberian Early Iron Age 'Tartessian' inscriptions—implying that the Proto-Indo-European from which Celtic evolved might have been dispersed by the Beaker radiation into western and central Europe around 4500 years ago. What does the new genetic evidence mean for the recent re-evaluations of Celtic language and archaeology that associate them with an origin and dispersal from Iberia?

Regarding the big picture from genetics, the two major post-Mesolithic dispersals identified in the genome-wide data correspond to the two main views on the spread of the Indo-European languages. The earlier view, to which most linguists subscribe, was detailed vividly from the 1950s onwards by the Lithuanian archaeologist Marija Gimbutas, and was initially known as the 'Kurgan hypothesis'. This view, significantly refined by James Mallory and David Anthony in particular, has strong support from most historical linguists, as a recent series of devastatingly critical blogs and subsequent book by Asya Pereltsvaig and Martin Lewis make clear.

Gimbutas posited an origin on the Pontic–Caspian steppe of Ukraine/south Russia, amongst the 'Kurgan culture'. Not surprisingly, geneticists and archaeologists working together have suggested that the people who brought the 'Caucasus

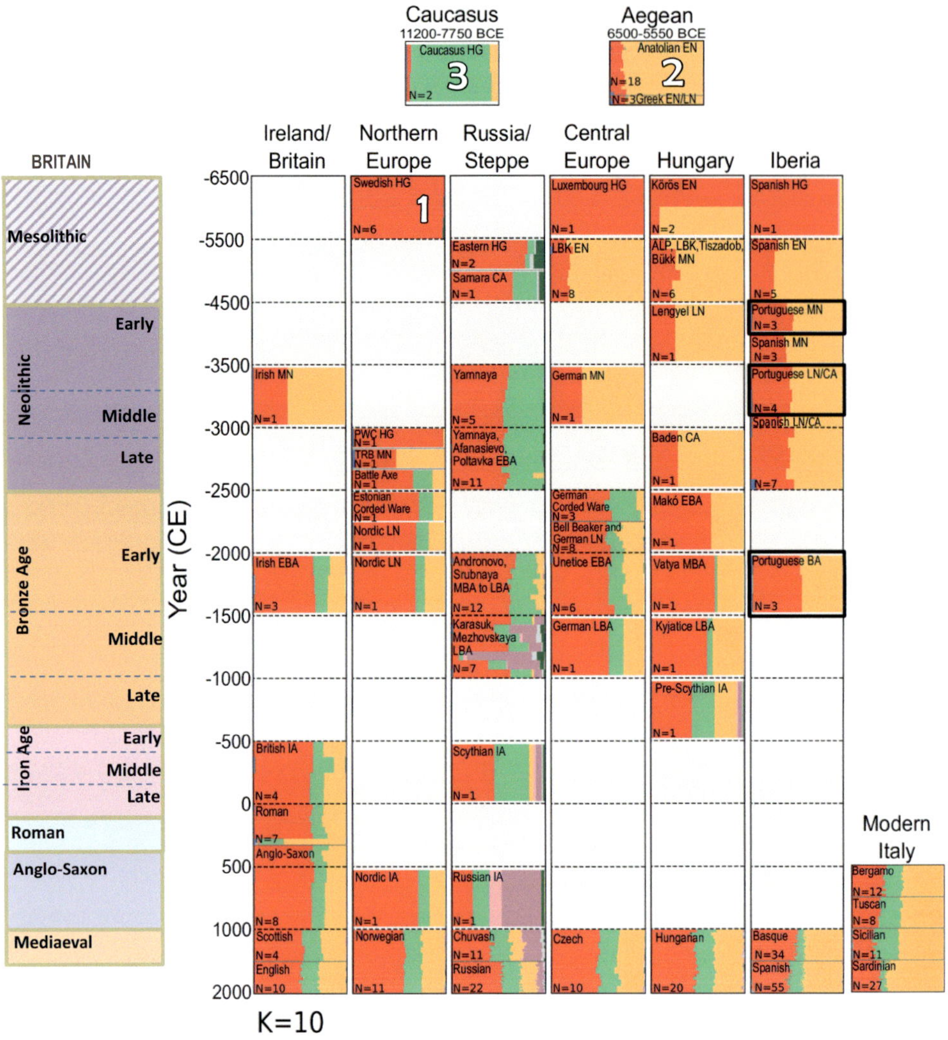

6.10. ADMIXTURE analysis with *K* = 10 of 176 ancient and almost 2000 modern Europeans. Note that the fractions are plotted horizontally rather than vertically so they can be displayed on an approximate time axis.

(Source: R. Martiniano et al. 2017 'The population genomics of archaeological transition in west Iberia: Investigation of ancient substructure using imputation and haplotype-based methods', *PLoS Genet* 13(7), e1006852, reproduced under Creative Commons licence. We have added a British time-line to the left-hand side.)

hunter–gatherer' Cluster 3 genome-wide component, along with eastern European variants of the Mesolithic Cluster 1 and Y-chromosome lineages belonging to R1a and R1b, to Europe at the Neolithic–Chalcolithic–Early Bronze Age transition (as well as, later in the Bronze Age, to south Asia) may also have brought the Indo-European languages with them, in line with the traditional steppe model. Given the major change in the gene pool and the shift to a more pastoral economy, the chance that language was involved too seems likely.

But what about the pioneer Early Neolithic farmers who leap-frogged across Europe much earlier? They very likely carried their languages with them too. Could they not also have been Indo-Europeans, as famously suggested by Colin Renfrew and supported by some well-publicized computational analyses of word lists? Is a hybrid, two-step model that incorporates both Early Neolithic farmers and steppe pastoralists possible?

Some reconstructions of the Indo-European language tree would make this implausible, but others make it seem possible, and there is still no overall consensus on the shape of the language tree. So perhaps Celtic, along with the Romance languages (their clustering seems to be one of the few reasonably well-established facts about the tree), were the result of a spread along the Mediterranean with early farming, whereas Germanic and Slavic have a more direct source in the steppe, via the Corded Ware Complex. In that case, perhaps Celtic might have arisen more gradually in Iberia, independently of the steppe arrivals—'cumulative Celticity', as Renfrew described it, using Christopher Hawkes's term—and spread from there around 4500 years ago, forming hybrid archaeological cultures as they met the newcomers from the east in central Europe?

This looks increasingly unlikely, given the scale of the replacement across Europe by R1a and R1b of the male lineages associated with the Neolithic. It is greater than in south Asia, for example, where the Dravidian languages seem likely to have been spread as a result of the dispersal of the Early Neolithic from the north-west, with Indo-European overlaid during the Bronze Age—although the scale of the sex bias in both cases points strongly to a highly male-dominated, patriarchal social formation, as suggested by Helsinki linguist Asko Parpola. More plausibly, there was substantial interaction from an early date, around 6500 years ago, between steppe pastoralists and the Balkans. Early Indo-European may have developed as a result of these earlier interactions between the steppe and the Balkans, with important processes taking place in Late Neolithic south-eastern, south-central and Mediterranean Europe, for which we so far have little genetic evidence. But this is really still the steppe model in another form.

All this suggests that the ultimate ancestor of the Proto-Indo-European that became the Celtic languages arrived in western Europe only about 4500–4000 years ago, from the north-east. This is clearly something that we need to take into account if we wish to argue that Celtic languages arose in Iberia amongst early copper metallurgists and spread into western and central Europe from there, only a few hundred years later.

Two main lines of genetic evidence have so far been invoked in this discussion, the Y-chromosome variation and the genome-wide picture. These markers suggest that, unlike in central and northern Europe—especially Britain—there was a high degree of population continuity in Iberia from the Neolithic, through the Chalcolithic and into the Bronze Age. During the Neolithic, Y-chromosome haplogroup R1b lineages in western Europe, whilst present, were infrequent, and have left few descendants. The Neolithic variation in Iberia comprises lineages that were likely inherited from local forager ancestors (mainly I2a) alongside some that arrived from further east along the Mediterranean with the Early Neolithic (G2a). R1b predominates in present-day Iberia, but most of its diversity belongs to more recently derived lineages that entered much later, from the Beaker period onwards—Iberia seems to have been largely a recipient of male gene flow at around this time.

However, whilst R1b-M269 lineages (and the modern western sub-cluster, R1b-S116) do appear in the Beaker period and the Early Bronze Age, it seems that, in contrast to the British Isles, there was no major, large-scale steppe influx at that time. The earliest male Beaker burial sampled in Iberia to date carries Y-chromosome haplogroup I2a, and the derived form of R1b (and the genome-wide Cluster 3) only begins to trickle into the north-east around 4500 years ago. It is a minority in Beaker burials, and not seen at all in other Chalcolithic remains of similar age. It is clearly intrusive, appearing to arrive late from the north. Similarly, the genome-wide Cluster 3 only begins to appear sporadically at around this time. The overall picture across Europe through time is summarized in Figure 6.10, a figure from the Dublin group.

There are therefore two possible kinds of explanation for the emergence of the increasingly hierarchical, gendered, and individualist ethos of the Copper Age that accompanied the rise of copper-working and the use of Beakers in Iberia from around 4800 years ago. It may have been a local development, arising from the social and economic forces created by the control of copper working. Or it may have been due to a male-dominated élite, arriving ultimately from the Yamnaya steppe, via central and Mediterranean Europe, rather than the larger-scale movements we see in northern Europe.

Harrison and Heyd defined a 'Yamnaya package' that spread from north of the Black Sea into the Balkans and further west after 4900 years ago, with eleven clearly recognizable components, including individual burial mounds often marked by large anthropomorphic stelae, wooden wagons placed in graves, new techniques for gold and copper metallurgy, a pastoral economy with domesticated horses, distinctive material culture items including gold or silver hair rings, and cord-marked pottery. The Yamnaya orbit extended at this time as far as the Aegean, the Adriatic, and well into central Europe. Not all elements always spread together, however, beyond the core area of the Danube. For example, it is difficult to directly derive the Late Neolithic European Corded Ware from the Yamnaya. Parpola has suggested an earlier steppe origin amongst Copper Age pastoralists, possibly beginning as early as almost 7000 years ago, involving infiltration of Copper Age Balkan communities and giving rise to both the Corded Ware and Yamnaya horizons when it broke up around 5400 years ago. Several sporadic instances of steppe ancestry in Copper Age Bulgarian remains are in fact seen as early as around 6600 years ago, in the early days of the famously wealthy (and socially stratified) Varna culture.

At high resolution the whole process starts to look quite heterogeneous, with little sign of a single over-arching 'mass migration'—although it has been estimated that Corded Ware individuals have around 75% Yamnaya genome-wide ancestry. Elements of the Yamnaya package also spread into the Alps and towards the Mediterranean. For example, the trail of anthropomorphic stelae stretches from the Black Sea to Iberia, via the Aegean, Alps, Italy, and France, carrying markers of individuality and a new distinctiveness between the genders, including an emergent warrior male identity.

A similar individual- and status-based ideology and warrior ethos can be seen developing in the far west. Iberia shows signs of a similar transformation from a communal to a more individual-oriented and hierarchical ideology from the first half of the 3rd millennium BC. Around 4800 years ago, large fortified settlements began to appear in Iberia, with Maritime Bell Beakers appearing alongside copper-working and a 'proto-Beaker package' in this context, probably first in central Portugal. Nevertheless, whilst the new way of life seems to have been sweeping across Europe, it is not at all clear that developments in Portugal were directly influenced by the cultures further east. Does the line of stelae reflect the spread of Yamnaya males, as Jean Manco has suggested? Almost a quarter of Beaker-associated individuals from Iberia (mostly sampled from Spain rather than Portugal) carry a small amount of the genome-wide Cluster 3, and a few of these (all from Spain and dating to 4500 years ago or later) carry R1b-M269. So we can at least say that the steppe influence was not very dramatic, as it was in central Europe, and the jury is still out on whether it was there at the start, in central Portugal 4800 years ago. The deepest origins of the Beaker culture remain mysterious until more work is carried out on Neolithic and Chalcolithic Iberia.

It already seems likely though that the genetic shift in Iberia was largely male-dominated—the genome-wide Cluster 3 only reaches roughly half the levels of central and northern Europe, whereas R1b-M269 is seen at levels only exceeded in north-western Europe—intriguingly, within Iberia, reaching very high levels (65–70%) in central Portugal and eastern Spain and virtually 100% in the Basque country, where the rise in frequency was likely helped by the small size and isolation of the population—despite the genome-wide Cluster 3 being almost undetectable there. These high levels may have been due to further immigration during the Bronze Age, but perhaps more likely is that they were due to males with those lineages leaving successively more descendants from the Copper Age onwards due to their dominant position in society.

The process of dispersal of the Beaker culture out of Iberia remains even more enigmatic in the wake of the new genetic data. The Beaker culture spread rapidly around 4500 years ago across Spain and into southern France, and onwards to a patchwork of territories across north-central Europe (ultimately as far as Poland), where it encountered the Corded Ware culture directly, and into the British Isles. As we have seen, the spread into Britain was almost certainly a large-scale migration from the region of the Low Countries.

But a major conclusion of Olalde and his colleagues was that there was no detectable expansion out of Iberia as the Bell Beaker Complex spread. Let's assume that the Beaker culture really did originate in Portugal—and if the radiocarbon dating is somewhat equivocal, even after the increase in dates that has accompanied the DNA data, there remain some other good reasons to think this may be so, as shown by John Koch in Chapter 3. Then the means by which they might have dispersed north and east remains enigmatic.

Paul Brotherton, Wolfgang Haak, and their colleagues had previously suggested that there was an expansion of maternal lineages, in particular belonging to members of the widespread European mtDNA haplogroup H1, and possibly other sub-clusters of H, such as H3, from Copper Age Iberia. But in genome-wide profiles,

Beaker groups in central Europe resemble more a mix of the adjoining Corded Ware and preceding local Late Neolithic groups than they do Beaker groups from the south-west. The high frequency of haplogroup H in central European Bell Beaker groups is striking by contrast with its much lower frequencies in Corded Ware samples (only about a third, and they completely lack H1 and H3). But this is a legacy of the Atlantic and west Mediterranean Neolithic, where H1, H3, and H overall were all strongly represented, in contrast with the impoverished haplogroup H palette of the steppe.

Intriguingly, early Bell Beaker burials from Germany, dating to around 4500 years ago, not long after the first appearance of the Corded Ware in this region, were the first people to carry both R1b Y chromosomes, which spread from the north-east, and a high frequency of mtDNA haplogroup H lineages, including H1, most likely hailing substantially from the south and west, suggesting once again a mixed, sex-biased ancestry—female farming lineages from the Mediterranean, but male pastoralist lineages originating on the steppe. Again, the contrast with central European Corded Ware samples, which have mainly Y-chromosome haplogroup R1a rather than R1b, and a higher genome-wide steppe component, is very striking.

In any case, it was most likely dispersals from the east that first brought the Indo-European languages to central and western Europe, perhaps opening up channels for the flow of material culture in the reverse direction. This might fit a version of Sangmeister's 'reflux hypothesis,' based on archaeological evidence, of a meeting of Corded Ware and incipient Bell Beakers (the latter spreading from Iberia), in a central European melting pot, followed by dispersals in many directions, including to the British Isles and back south again towards Iberia.

On the face of it, this would seem to imply that Beaker dispersals from Iberia are unlikely to have mediated the spread the Celtic languages. If the genome-wide Cluster 3 and paternal R1a/R1b-M269 can be taken as markers for the spread of 'Old European', or an undifferentiated Late Proto-Indo-European dialect continuum, into central and western Europe, dispersal of Proto-Celtic dialects out of Iberia with the Beaker culture only a few hundred years later seems unlikely. This has led some commentators, such as Jean Manco, to suggest that Celtic languages really did form where the traditional model proposed, in west-central Europe.

However, this unfairly caricatures the 'Celtic from the West' model. Proto-Indo-European would likely have developed gradually into Proto-Celtic over many centuries, well into the Bronze Age, even if the process began in the Copper Age. This may have been over a wide area that may have encompassed much of western Europe (arguably the core Beaker and subsequent Atlantic Bronze Age area), where it served as a lingua franca, as argued by Barry Cunliffe. Proto-Celtic could even have still plausibly formed in Iberia (or southern/western France) due to élite dominance during the course of the Bronze Age, spreading further in the Late Bronze Age as a lingua franca, via the Atlantic coastline and the continental river system.

John Koch has suggested that this formation might have taken place quite rapidly, due to the influence of indigenous substrata, from local non-Indo-European languages such as the Iberian and Palaeo-Basque local languages (which were present in southern and western France, as well as Iberia), and a few hundred years later perhaps even Phoenician, on the incoming Late Proto-Indo-European. The importance of multiple substratum effects would be consistent with the genetic evidence that Indo-European newcomers in Iberia would have been in a minority. Koch has also pointed out that if Proto-Celtic were subsequently to replace Late Proto-Indo-European or Proto-Italo-Celtic as it expanded across France, the linguistic change needed would not have been very great.

The overall situation from the Late Neolithic to the Early Bronze Age is clearly extraordinarily complex, involving multiple spheres of interaction across Europe that may or may not have been linked by gene flow. If the spread of the new language and ideology was mediated by conversion to a new religion (or set of ritual practices) for example, as may have been the case for the Austronesian language family's expansion into the Pacific, as well as for more recent examples such as the spread of Arabic with Islam, only a small number of widely travelled proselytes might have been needed to seed the new society in some places. Even where there was substantial gene flow, testing the details of the models with genetic data will require the careful analysis of a great many stratified samples from throughout the Copper and Bronze Ages, both in Iberia and more widely, including across the Mediterranean where little ancient DNA has hitherto been successfully recovered.

Of course, there will always remain the issue that even if we can determine the most intimate details of the genetic structure of people who lived thousands of years ago, we can never be sure what language they spoke. When languages appear to have been transmitted through cultural networks and minor gene flow involving a few individuals, rather than by discrete movements of large groups of people, this seems even more true.

But we have suspicion that this concern might gradually evaporate as further evidence comes in, and a wealth of detail is revealed about human movements around the continent. The pace of advance in archaeogenetics at the moment is absolutely unprecedented. This is likely to continue more and more in years to come as, for example, the phylogeographic techniques applied in the past only to the mtDNA and Y chromosome start to be applied to chunks of whole human genomes as well. If this continues, we may well have a convincing and highly detailed model for the spread of people alongside archaeological cultures and technologies within the next few years, to complement and embed within our knowledge of the ancestry of present-day peoples.

At the very least, that gives us a much firmer demographic base on which to place discussions of the origins and spread of languages. The rest, as they say, is history. But if genetics can provide the basis for a detailed reconstruction of the settlement history of western Europeans in general, that relates the ancestry of modern Atlantic Europeans to the peoples of the British Isles, France, and Iberia in antiquity, then perhaps that's as close to a genetic history of the Celts as we're ever likely to get.

ACKNOWLEDGEMENTS

We warmly thank John Koch, Catriona Gibson, and Kerri Cleary for their careful reading and valuable comments on an earlier version of the manuscript, and Iñigo Olalde for his suggestions for Figure 6.3. M.S., K.D., and G.O.-G. are supported by a Leverhulme Trust doctoral scholarship programme awarded to M.B.R. and M.P. P.S., M.B.R., and M.P. acknowledge FCT support through project PTDC/EPH-ARQ/4164/2014 partially funded by FEDER funds (COMPETE 2020 project 016899). P.S. is supported by FCT, European Social Fund, Programa Operacional Potencial Humano and the FCT Investigator Programme and acknowledges FCT/MEC for support to CBMA through Portuguese funds (PIDDAC)—PEst-OE/BIA/UI4050/2014.

Further reading

How can genetics be used to explore Celtic origins?

By far the best textbook covering archaeogenetics is *Human Evolutionary Genetics* by **Mark Jobling, Ed Hollox, Matthew Hurles, Toomas Kivisild, & Chris Tyler-Smith** (Oxford, Garland Science, 2nd edn., 2013). Inevitably, even this is now very out of date. The most authoritative and up-to-date popular account of recent work in ancient DNA is **David Reich**'s *Who We are and Where We Came From* (Oxford, OUP, 2018). Beware, however, that Reich presents little that is not his own group's work, and in the process ignores much of the history of the subject—with a particular blind-spot on the non-recombining marker systems, especially the mtDNA. A broader overview is **Adam Rutherford**'s *A Brief History of Everyone Who Ever Lived* (London, Weidenfeld & Nicolson, 2016). A vivid account of the development of ancient DNA studies can be found in **Svante Pääbo**'s *Neanderthal Man: In Search of Lost Genomes* (New York, Basic Books, 2014).

Highly readable and engaging primers on Celtic identity can be found in **S. James** 1999 *The Atlantic Celts: Ancient People or Modern Invention?* London, British Museum Press, and **B. Cunliffe** 2004 *The Celts: A Very Short Introduction.* Oxford, Oxford University Press. **J. D. Hill**'s (1989) 'Rethinking the Iron Age.' *Scottish Archaeological Review* 6, 16–23, is also seminal.

The big picture from the genome

A summary of the genetic situation as it stood in 2008, and an indication of how far things have moved on, can be seen in **M. Richards, C. Capelli, & J. Wilson** 2008 'Genetics and the origins of the British population', *Encyclopedia of Life Sciences (eLS)*, Chichester, John Wiley & Sons, Ltd. Cavalli-Sforza's pioneering work was **A. J. Ammerman & L. L. Cavalli-Sforza** 1984 *The Neolithic transition and the genetics of populations in Europe*, Princeton, New Jersey, Princeton University Press. John Novembre's new portrait of Europeans using genome-wide SNPs is in **J. Novembre, T. Johnson... M. Stephens, & C. D. Bustamante** 2008 'Genes mirror geography within Europe', *Nature* 456, 98–101.

A genetic portrait of the British Isles

The main PoBI project publication is **S. Leslie, B. Winney... P. Donnelly, & W. Bodmer** 2015 'The fine-scale genetic structure of the British population', *Nature* 519(7543), 309–14. The Irish updates are in **E. Gilbert, S. O'Reilly... J. F. Wilson, & G. L. Cavalleri** 2017 'The Irish DNA atlas: Revealing fine-scale population structure and history within Ireland', *Scientific Reports* 7(1), 17199 and **R. P. Byrne, R. Martiniano... D. G. Bradley, & R. L. McLaughlin** 2018 'Insular Celtic population structure and genomic footprints of migration', *PLoS Genet* 14(1), e1007152. The Viking issue is pursued by **J. Kershaw & E. C. Røyrvik** 2016 'The 'People of the British Isles' project and Viking settlement in England', *Antiquity* 90(354), 1670–1680.

The male and female lines of descent

Human mitochondrial phylogeography is introduced in **V. Macaulay & M. B. Richards** 2013 'Mitochondrial genome sequences and their phylogeographic interpretation', *Encyclopedia of Life Sciences (eLS)*, Chichester, John Wiley & Sons, Ltd, and the story of Ashkenazi Jews is told in **M. D. Costa, J. B. Pereira... L. Pereira, & M. B. Richards** 2013 'A substantial prehistoric European ancestry amongst Ashkenazi maternal lineages', *Nature Communications* 4, 2543.

Scandinavian Y-chromosome lineages in Orkney, as well as the possibility of sex-biased dispersal, were first demonstrated by **J. F. Wilson, D. A. Weiss... N. Bradman, & D. B. Goldstein** 2001 'Genetic evidence for different male and female roles during cultural transitions in the British Isles', *Proceedings of the National Academy of Sciences of the United States of America* 98, 5078–5083. Family-based settlement was suggested by **S. Goodacre, A. Helgason... R. Ward, & B. Sykes** 2005 'Genetic evidence for a family-based Scandinavian settlement of Shetland and Orkney during the Viking periods', *Heredity* 95/2, 129–35. The predominance of R1b is Ireland was first shown by **E. W. Hill, M. A. Jobling, & D. G. Bradley** 2000 'Y-chromosome variation and Irish origins', *Nature* 404(6776), 351–2, and the suggestion that it represented the pre-Neolithic population of the British Isles was taken up in **S. Oppenheimer** 2006 *The origins of the British*, London, Constable.

The early-2000s debate over the Anglo-Saxon Y-chromosome contribution to Britain began with **M. E. Weale, D. A. Weiss... N. Bradman, & M. G. Thomas** 2002 'Y chromosome evidence for Anglo-Saxon mass migration', *Molecular Biology and Evolution* 19, 1008–1021, and was played out in **C. Capelli, N. Redhead... N. Bradman, & D. B. Goldstein** 2003 'A Y chromosome census of the British Isles', *Current Biology* 13, 979–84; **M. G. Thomas, M. P. Stumpf, & H. Harke** 2006 'Evidence for an apartheid-like social structure in early Anglo-Saxon England', *Proc Biol Sci* 273(1601), 2651–2657; and **J. E. Pattison** 2008 'Is it necessary to assume an apartheid-like social structure in Early Anglo-Saxon England?' *Proc Biol Sci* 275(1650), 2423–2429; discussion 2419–2421.

The Y-chromosome next-generation revolution is well represented by **C. Batini, P. Hallast... B. Winney, & M. A. Jobling** 2015 'Large-scale recent expansion of European patrilineages shown by population resequencing', *Nature Communications* 6, 7152; **M. Karmin, L. Saag... R. Villems, & T. Kivisild** 2015 'A recent bottleneck of Y chromosome diversity coincides with a global change in culture', *Genome Research* 25, 459–66; and **G. D. Poznik, Y. Xue... C. D. Bustamante, & C. Tyler-Smith** 2016 'Punctuated bursts in human male demography inferred from 1,244 worldwide Y-chromosome sequences', *Nature Genetics* 48(6), 593–9.

The wider European setting: New evidence from genomics and ancient DNA

There is an accessible introduction to European archaeogenetics in **M. Pala, G. Chaubey, P. Soares, & M. B. Richards** 2014 'The archaeogenetics of European ancestry'. *Encyclopedia of Life Sciences (ELS)*, Chichester, John Wiley and Sons, although, given the pace of discovery since 2014, this is already dated in several respects. We cover the European background further in **M. Pala, P. Soares, & M. B. Richards** 2016 'Archaeogenetic and palaeogenetic evidence for Metal Age mobility in Europe', *Celtic from the West 3: Atlantic Europe in the Metal Ages—questions of shared language*, Celtic Studies Publications 19, eds J. T. Koch, B. Cunliffe, K. Cleary, & C. D. Gibson, 351–84, Oxford, Oxbow Books. An excellent review of the ancient DNA evidence up to this point is **G. Brandt, A. Szecsenyi-Nagy... K. W. Alt, & W. Haak** 2014 'Human paleogenetics of Europe—the known knowns and the known unknowns', *Journal of Human Evolution* 79, 73–92. The pre-Neolithic background from the perspective of female lineages is charted in **C. Posth, G. Renaud... A. Powell, & J. Krause** 2016 'Pleistocene Mitochondrial Genomes Suggest a Single Major Dispersal of Non-Africans and a Late Glacial Population Turnover in Europe', *Current Biology* 26(6), 827–33; and the issues are summarized in the accompanying despatch, **M. B. Richards, P. Soares, & A. Torroni** 2016 'Palaeogenomics: mitogenomes and migrations in Europe's past', *Current Biology* 26, R229–R246.

Spearheading the new wave of genome-wide ancient DNA work were **W. Haak, I. Lazaridis... K. W. Werner Alt, & D. Reich** 2015 'Massive migration from the steppe is a source for Indo-European languages in Europe.' *Nature* 522, 207–211, and **M. E. Allentoft, M. Sikora... K. Kristiansen, & E. Willerslev** 2015 'Population genomics of Bronze Age Eurasia.' *Nature* 522(7555), 167–72, although the notion of a Bronze Age wave from the east was prefigured in **G. Brandt, W. Haak... A. Cooper, & K. W. Alt** 2013 'Ancient DNA reveals key stages in the formation of central European mitochondrial genetic diversity', *Science* 342, 257–61. The high frequency of cluster 3 in the Caucasus was shown in **E. R. Jones, G. Gonzalez-Fortes... R. Pinhasi, & D. G. Bradley** 2015 'Upper Palaeolithic genomes reveal deep roots of modern Eurasians', *Nature Communications* 6, 8912; and the likely Levantine and Iranian provenance of clusters 2 and 3 was demonstrated in **I. Lazaridis, D. Nadel... R. Pinhasi, & D. Reich** 2016 'Genomic insights into the origin of farming in the ancient Near East', *Nature* 536(7617), 419–24.

Evidence for a pre-Neolithic dispersal from the Near East into Europe is provided by both mtDNA (**J. B. Pereira, M. D. Costa... L. Pereira, & M. B. Richards** 2017 'Reconciling evidence from ancient and contemporary genomes: a major source for the European Neolithic within Mediterranean Europe', *Proceedings of the Royal Society Series B* 284(1851), 20161976) and perhaps also genome-wide ancient DNA (**Q. Fu, C. Posth... S. Paabo, & D. Reich** 2016 'The genetic history of Ice Age Europe', *Nature* 534, 200–5).

Cunliffe's grand synthesis of 4th-millennium developments is in **B. Cunliffe** 2015 *By Steppe, Desert, and Ocean: The birth of Eurasia*, Oxford, Oxford University Press. A clear and detailed overview of Yamnaya innovations and their complex relationship with the Bell Beaker culture is given in **R. J. Harrison & V. H. Heyd** 2007 'The Transformation of Europe in the Third Millennium BC: the example of "Le Petit-Chasseur I + III" (Sion, Valais, Switzerland).' *Prähistorische Zeitschrift* Band S, 129–214, and the whole subject of Indo-European origins is dealt with compellingly in **D. W. Anthony** 2007 *The horse, the wheel, and language: how Bronze-Age riders from the Eurasian steppes shaped the modern world,* Princeton, Princeton University Press.

The modern R1a distribution is well summarized in **P. A. Underhill, G. D. Poznik... T. Kivisild, & R. Villems** 2014 'The phylogenetic and geographic structure of Y-chromosome haplogroup R1a', *European Journal of Human Genetics* 23, 124–31; and its male-dominated Bronze Age epansion into the Indian Subcontinent is suggested in **M. Silva, M. Oliveira... M. B. Richards, & P. Soares** 2017 'A genetic chronology for the Indian Subcontinent points to heavily sex-biased dispersals', *BMC Evolutionary Biology* 17, 88.

The first ancient DNA results from the British Isles

The first Irish prehistoric genomes are described by **L. M. Cassidy, R. Martiniano... B. Hartwell, & D. G. Bradley** 2016 'Neolithic and Bronze Age migration to Ireland and establishment of the insular Atlantic genome', *Proceedings of the National Academy of Sciences of the United States of America* 113(2), 368–73, and the big British study is **I. Olalde, S. Brace... C. Lalueza-Fox, & D. Reich** 2018 'The Beaker phenomenon and the genomic transformation of northwest Europe', *Nature* 555(7695), 190–6. The two early

English studies are **S. Schiffels, W. Haak... A. Cooper, & R. Durbin** 2016 'Iron Age and Anglo-Saxon genomes from East England reveal British migration history', *Nature Communications* 7, 10408 and **R. A. Martiniano, A. Caffell... M. J. Collins, & D. G. Bradley** 2016 'Genomic signals of migration and continuity in Britain before the Anglo-Saxons', *Nature Communications* 7, 10326.

Celtic from the West?

B. Cunliffe & J. T. Koch, eds (2010) *Celtic from the West*, Celtic Studies Publications 15, Oxford, Oxbow Books, has been followed by two further volumes, both of which are also essential reading, in particular **J. T. Koch** (2013) 'Out of the flow and ebb of the European Bronze Age: Heroes, Tartessos, and Celtic', *Celtic from the West 2: Rethinking the Bronze Age and the Arrival of Indo-European in Atlantic Europe*, Celtic Studies Publications 16, eds J. T. Koch & B. Cunliffe, 101–146, Oxford, Oxbow Books. The first modern statement of the steppe model is **J. P. Mallory** 1989) *In search of the Indo-Europeans*, London, Thames and Hudson. The most up-to-date and widely based critique of Indo-European origins is A. Pereltsvaig & M. W. Lewis (2015) *The Indo-European Controversy: Facts and Fallacies in Historical Linguistics*, Cambridge, Cambridge University Press. On Celtic specifically, see **C. Gibson & D. S. Wodtko** 2013 *The background of the Celtic languages: Theories from archaeology and linguistics*, Aberystwyth, University of Wales Centre for Advanced Welsh and Celtic Studies.

The evidence for a 6th-millennium steppe penetration of south-east Europe is presented in **I. Mathieson, S. Alpaslan-Roodenberg... R. Pinhasi, & D. Reich** 2018 'The genomic history of southeastern Europe', *Nature* 555(7695), 197–203. Christopher Hawkes's 'Cumulative Celticity' was adapted by Renfrew in his classic statement of the Anatolian model, which remains a rewarding read despite the model no longer being viable: **C. Renfrew** 1987 *Archaeology and Language*, Harmondsworth, Penguin Books. Jean Manco discussed the ancient DNA data relating to Celtic and Indo-European origins in **J. Manco** 2015 *Blood of the Celts: The New Ancestral Story*, London, Thames and Hudson Ltd. The trail of the anthropomorphic stelae is described there and also in **C. Broodbank** 2013 *The Making of the Middle Sea: A History of the Mediterranean from the Beginning to the Emergence of the Classical World*, London, Thames & Hudson, as well as in detail in Harrison & Heyd, *op. cit.* The first major genome-wide ancient DNA study of Iberia was **R. Martiniano, L. M. Cassidy... A. M. Silva, & D. G. Bradley** 2017 'The population genomics of archaeological transition in west Iberia: Investigation of ancient substructure using imputation and haplotype-based methods', *PLoS Genet* 13(7), e1006852. **A. Szecsenyi-Nagy, C. Roth... W. Haak, & K. W. Alt** 2017 'The maternal genetic make-up of the Iberian Peninsula between the Neolithic and the Early Bronze Age', *Scientific Reports* 7(1), 15644, focuses on the maternal line of descent at low resolution, but includes a large volume of data.

An excellent introduction to the evolution of languages in general as well as in the Indian Subcontinent in particular is **A. Parpola** 2015 *The Roots of Hinduism: The Early Aryans and The Indus Civilization*, Oxford, Oxford University Press.

CHAPTER SEVEN

A DIALOGUE AT THE CROSSROADS

Barry Cunliffe & John T. Koch

WHEN the project began in 2008 it was clear that we had to address the potential contributions of three quite different sets of data, archaeological, linguistic, and genetic. The quantity of archaeological data was already massive and was growing at an exponential rate. Not only were hundreds of excavations underway but scientific methods of analysing the artefacts and ecofacts recovered were proliferating, opening up new ways of viewing past societies—their belief systems, their technical achievements, and the processes by which they shared knowledge. It is no exaggeration to say that the rate at which information is being extracted from the detritus of the past has never been greater. New data brings with it new complexities and the greater its amount the more nuanced and intricate our interpretations have to become.

The linguistic database is quite different in that it is strictly circumscribed consisting of the spoken Celtic languages, a scattering of place-names of Celtic origin and a restricted number of short texts surviving from the pre-Roman and Roman world. No doubt more texts will be found and more place-names identified but at a comparatively slow rate. For real advances to be made in our understanding of the Ancient Celtic languages we must look to new methods of analysis which, to be of lasting value, must be evidence-based and testable. Advances are being made. Witness, for example, the phylogenetic methods developed by scholars like Grey and Atkinson, but their approach is not without its critics. Given that the dataset for Ancient Celtic and Indo-European languages will always be limited, major new understandings will depend on progress in the theory and methods of historical linguistics, and this will come gradually.

The potential of genetic evidence is different yet again. When our project began much energy was being expended in studying and mapping the DNA of modern populations in attempts to display geographical variations. One of the most ambitious and sophisticated of these projects was the 'People of the British Isles' project (PoBI) undertaken by an Oxford-based group. It produced a detailed map showing hitherto unsuspected variations in genetic composition, especially in the northern and western parts of the country, but the map was achronic—that is it had no time depth. While it undoubtedly reflected the formative mobility pervading Britain over the last 10,000 years, the processes leading to the present-day snapshot were undiscoverable. To take one example, over much of the south-east of Britain the population displayed a marked degree of genetic homogeneity. It was tempting to conclude that this was the result of an influx of population in the Anglo-Saxon period at the time when historical sources record arrivals from continental Europe. But the archaeological evidence shows that the south-east of Britain had been receiving successive incomings of population from as early as 4000 BC. In other words, the genetic mix reflected in the modern population of the south-east is likely to be the aggregate of 5000 years of connectivity.

It was widely recognized that to be able to make real advances in understanding population movements it was necessary to characterize the genetic structure of ancient populations which could be accurately dated. The study of ancient DNA (aDNA), having faced some initial technical problems, finally began to show its real potential with a series of publications beginning in 2015 (above pp. 167–73). The results published to date have far-reaching implications. There can be no doubt that the method has huge potential to contribute to our understanding of population dynamics and, carefully used, will enable a more nuanced prehistory to be written. These are exciting times.

The study of aDNA is now rapidly overcoming obstacles, and costs are coming down. Where we now have hundreds of samples, we will soon have thousands, and with wider coverage of the genome. We await the next round of results with a backlog of unanswered questions. There are, on the other hand, some serious limitations that may never be overcome. For example, in warm climates, aDNA degrades. This is a particular problem on the southern edges of the Celtic world towards the Mediterranean. Another obstacle across wide areas of Atlantic Europe is acid soil, causing human remains to brake down completely. There were also periods when the dead were cremated or disposed of with rites leaving no trace. To fill these gaps, 'diagonal comparisons' can be made linking high-quality modern DNA, like the PoBI database, with ancient genomes from the places and times these were preserved.

Working together

Genetics, linguistics, and archaeology are three very different disciplines with their own distinctive evidence bases, methods of analysis, and constraints on interpretation. At best they can work side-by-side respecting each other's integrity. This means avoiding the temptation to cherry-pick data or provisional conclusions from one discipline to support a theory generated in another and being prepared to wait until the database is robust enough and tested against the consensus of a kindred discipline before rushing into print. Given these strictures, how can we best work together? One way is for one discipline, using its own discrete database and rigorous methods of analysis, to offer an hypothesis which the kindred discipline then sets out to test using its own methods. The result could vary from confirmation, encouraging a broad acceptance of the hypothesis, to doubts or disagreements leading to its recasting or rejection.

A good example has recently been presented with the publication of a paper by Olalde et al 2018 which, using aDNA evidence, suggests that 90% of the population of Britain was replaced in the Beaker period as the result of incoming migrations from the lower Rhine, the Low Countries, and northern France. Archaeologically it has long been accepted that there was a significant influx of population from the adjacent continent at this time bringing about significant cultural change. But a 90% replacement of population needs thinking about. How could this physically have happened? Would it not require genocide far outstripping the worst excesses of the 20th century or a plague many times more virulent than the Black Death of the 14th century? And could these disasters, if they had occurred, have ramified into every corner of the British Isles? Questions of this kind will lead to a fascinating debate that cannot fail to be revealing. To begin to address them far more aDNA samples will be needed and archaeologists will have to look again at their evidence and challenge their cherished beliefs and assumptions.

The key to identifying the immigrant population was the recognition of strong genetic markers derived from their steppe ancestry. New evidence now indicates that this steppe component had declined in south-east Britain by Roman times and probably already in the Iron Age. This raises new questions. There is more than one possible explanation, but it is tempting to deploy this finding to calibrate the hard to believe 90% population replacement, seeing here descendants of British Neolithic people who had remained undetected in Bronze Age samples thus far.

Before reaching pessimistic conclusions about the prospects for forging an integrated approach for Celtic origins (and for later prehistory in general), we should ask to what extent the barriers are inherent in the evidence and proven methods for dealing with it and to what extent specialists in different disciplines have succumbed to incompatible intellectual fashions. In presenting their findings to archaeologists and linguists, geneticists confront listeners uncomfortable with 'migrations' and 'populations' as concepts and as words. But you can't do genetics without these. The aversions are not inherent in archaeology and linguistics *per se*, but arise from a heightened awareness of the misuse of archaeology and philology to support various modern injustices and horrors, Nazism most obviously.

In the mid 20th century, it had been more common for linguists and archaeologists to work together in Celtic studies. The orthodox Hallstatt and La Tène account of Celtic origins is a legacy of this period. The subsequent breach that began to develop can partly be seen as an inevitable outcome of expanding bodies of information leading to specialization. But it is also the case that an idea took hold in archaeology that made no sense to linguists. This is anti-migrationism, for which Graham Clark's 'The Invasion Hypothesis in British Archaeology' (1966) can be cited as a manifesto. For Celtic linguists, this seemed to amount to an impossible model in which a new language was introduced without new people in an age before writing. At the International Congress of Celtic Studies in Galway in 1979, the archaeologist Stuart Piggott and the linguist David Greene joined in a symposium taking on the subject 'The Coming of the Celts to Britain and Ireland'. Greene's talk included the rejoinder: 'As linguists, however, we must say that it is very difficult to conceive of cumulative Celticity, except in the sense in which we might speak of the cumulative Anglicisation of Ireland, as a process spread over many centuries; in the latter case, however, we know that it began with an invasion, and that nobody was ever in any doubt as to which of the languages he was speaking.' With the archaeogenetics revolution, migrations are back in archaeological explanation. So at least this one factor that caused linguists and archaeologists to talk past each other is now gone.

While it is not difficult to see how real and exciting advances in knowledge can be made by geneticists and archaeologists working closely together and informing and constraining each other, it is not easy to visualize similar partnerships involving linguists. How can we set out to demonstrate whether a specific ancestry can be correlated with a particular language group? We can offer hypotheses but they are untestable, at least not in ways easily recognized by researchers in other fields. At best, geneticists and archaeologists (whose databases are potentially unlimited) can generate evidence-based hypotheses and invite response from linguists, asking 'can this be contained within your existing understanding of language and if not could you generate a new hypothesis consistent with it?' This is not to belittle the value of the discipline and the weight of scholarship it has generated, it is simply to recognize that linguistic hypotheses can seldom, if ever, be brought into direct engagement with the archaeological or genetic evidence to create a stronger degree of certainty.

Linguistics, especially the historical-comparative linguistics used in this project, is science. But it can be frustrating to try to use linguistics to build straightforward tests for hypotheses formulated by archaeologists or geneticists. The history of a language and its relationship to another is defined by scores of sound laws and grammatical changes and hundreds or even thousands of etymologies. But these are not all of equal weight. A sound law, i.e. a change of one sound to another operating systematically across a language at a particular time, can be significant or trivial. In other words, it can be unusual, and so represent a 'smoking gun', or it can occur so frequently in the languages of the world as to be inconclusive. Significant-to-trivial is a sliding scale and hard to quantify. With etymologies, some are very secure. Other words are thought probably related, but then discovered not to be. Or words look like inherited vocabulary shared between related languages, but an early loanword is actually involved.

One reason some linguists have been reluctant to embrace the new phylogenetic approaches is that it is based on retention of inherited vocabulary using short lists of words. A few dubious etymologies will throw the result off. Some linguists also reject the idea that languages change—or specifically lose inherited words—at a regular rate over time. Not long ago, earlier attempts to establish a kind of 'half life' for linguistic change became highly unfashionable at many linguistics departments. It was drummed into students that 'glottochronology', as that earlier technique was called, was simply wrong. Nevertheless, Chang et al. 2015 found the phylogenetic method credible enough to try to improve it. Their result differed from Grey and Atkinson's by reducing the overall time depth of the Indo-European family tree, bringing it into line, they concluded, with steppe-homeland theory. The matter did not come to an end there. Continued refinements of the phylogenetic approach are being pursued by the multidisciplinary team of the Max Planck Institute for the Science of Human History in Jena, Germany, with results tending back towards greater time depth.

Be all that as it may, the centre of gravity of historical linguistics lies elsewhere, that is, not in short lists of cognate words, but in the complex totalities of grammars, vocabularies, and sound systems evolving over time. None of that lends itself to distillation as statistics, charts, or phylogenetic tree diagrams that could give a quick 'yes' or 'no' to hypotheses arising from archaeology and genetics. On the other hand, what is lacking in crispness might be made up in solidity. We can ask whether a proposal is broadly compatible or incompatible with the vast body of linguistic evidence for a fully attested language family.

The spread of Indo-European

The original Celtic from the West hypothesis, summarized in Chapters 1 and 2, suggested that the Celtic language might have developed as a lingua franca along the Atlantic seaboard of Europe, beginning perhaps as early as the Neolithic period. This is predicated on the assumption that Indo-European was introduced into Europe with the spread of farming from Anatolia between 7000 and 5000 BC, a view put forward by Colin Renfrew in his book *Archaeology and Language* published in 1987. Renfrew's hypothesis challenged the orthodoxy of the time, most energetically championed by Marija Gimbutas, which argued that Indo-European first entered Europe from the Pontic–Caspian steppe in the 3rd millennium and contributed to the Corded Ware Complex of northern Europe. This model, usually referred to as the Kurgan hypothesis, has gathered strong support from more recent writers like James Mallory and David Anthony. If Indo-European was first introduced through this vector, then the argument that the Celtic language began to develop in the Atlantic zone as early as the Neolithic period cannot be sustained (though its later development in the region remains a possibility).

Today Renfrew's theory tends to be remembered simply as Proto-Indo-European spreading from Anatolia with the first farmers beginning about 8500 years ago. That is the strand challenged by the aDNA evidence published in 2015 and what's been made of it. But for Celtic studies there was a second revolutionary dimension. Renfrew envisions Indo-European reaching Atlantic Europe as Proto-Indo-European and then evolving into Celtic there, *in situ*. There was no secondary homeland about the sources of the Danube and Rhine and no secondary swarm issuing from that secondary hive. In essence, this was the forerunner of Celtic from the West. And stripped down to this, this model of Celtic origins can be explored while keeping agnostic about the Indo-European homeland—5000 years ago on the Pontic-Caspian steppe or 8500 in Anatolia.

When our project began in 2008, the Indo-European homeland debate appeared to be at a stalemate and that stalemate appeared distant from our immediate Celtic subject. New arguments were not changing committed minds. Celtic was relatively marginal and the bulk of its written evidence relatively late, certainly when compared to Hittite, Greek, and Sanskrit. So it did not seem likely that a decisive answer to the Indo-European question could come from Celtic.

In 2015, we were caught by surprise. It was not that we had not known that aDNA evidence was on its way. What we had not expected is that it would reveal migrations and population changes so stark that they almost surely brought changes of language.

It is in nobody's interest now, even those with a prior investment in the steppe hypothesis, for the Anatolian hypothesis to be summarily abandoned in an episode of bandwagonism. This would result in a fragile version of the steppe hypothesis prematurely anointed as the new orthodoxy, anchored only to a few points confirmed by aDNA with vast remaining gaps glossed over. Much better that the weaknesses of the archaeogenetically enhanced steppe hypothesis be rigorously probed against alternatives. With the rapidly expanding datasets now at our disposal—archaeological as well as genetic—we can surely do better than merely to choose between two 20th-century models. If something like the steppe-homeland hypothesis prevails, it will not be Marija Gimbutas's Kurgan hypothesis, but a much stronger theory explaining a wide range of unforeseen discoveries.

The coming on stream of new aDNA data has greatly enlivened the debate. At a simple level it has demonstrated that the spread of Neolithic life-styles to Europe involved the movement of people and that Near Eastern genes contributed to the gene pool of Atlantic Neolithic communities. It has also shown that there was a significant inflow of steppe genes into northern Europe in the Late Neolithic and Early Bronze Age. This second observation has been taken by some as proof of the Kurgan hypothesis. But this need not be so. As Martin Richards and his colleagues have shown in their carefully balanced review of the aDNA data currently available 'the overall situation from the Late Neolithic to the Early Bronze Age is extraordinarily complex involving multiple spheres of interaction across Europe that may or may not have been linked to gene flow'. They go on to advise 'even where there was substantial gene flow, testing the details of the models with genetic data will require careful analysis of a great many stratified samples' (above, p. 187). In other words they are warning that, given the complexity of the situation and the paucity of samples, it is too early in the debate to make headline-grabbing generalizations. That said, aDNA will eventually enable a finely textured picture of human mobility to be presented.

So how is all this likely to reflect on the spread of Indo-European to peninsula Europe? Perhaps the most obvious point that needs to be made is that the Anatolian and Kurgan hypotheses are not necessarily opposing alternatives. It is conceivable, indeed even likely, that the spread of Indo-European was a multi-phased process taking place over an extended period of time with episodes of convergence and divergence as communities interacted. Developing this idea, at a very simplistic level it could be argued there may have been at least two phases of introduction, one at the time of the expansion of farming in the period 7000–5000 BC, the other as a result of incursions from the steppe *c.* 3500–2500 BC. For this hypothesis to be credible it requires Indo-European to have been spoken in Anatolia by 7000 BC and on the Pontic–Caspian steppe by *c.* 3500 BC. Here the work of geneticist David Reich promises to throw light on the problem. Based on aDNA results so far obtained Reich has suggested that the cradle of Indo-European lay south of the Caucasus, in present Iran and/or Armenia. His argument rests on the observation that 'ancient DNA from people who lived there matches what we would expect for a source population for both the Yamnaya [on the steppe] and for ancient Anatolians'. Further, he says that the aDNA data shows that there was a steady influx of people from south of the Caucasus to the Pontic–Caspian steppe during the period 5000–3000 BC. If this is correct it would allow that the steppe pastoralists acquired their Indo-European language from south of the Caucasus rather than requiring it to have developed on the steppe as some writers have assumed.

A model which could contain these new insights together with both the Kurgan and Anatolian hypotheses would be to accept that Indo-European was spoken by the farmers who, around 7000–6000 BC, moved into Greece and the Balkans and that, over the next millennium, the language spread from there with farming by way of the middle European rivers and through the Mediterranean reaching the Atlantic coast *c.* 5500–5000 BC (the Anatolian hypothesis). Over the next two millennia people moving northwards through the Caucasus introduced new technologies and their Indo-European language to the Pontic–Caspian steppe. It was from there that aspects of steppe culture, together with Indo-European, began to impact on northern Europe in the 3rd millennium (the Kurgan hypothesis). Those arriving at this time would have found people already speaking an Indo-European language.

This simple model is consistent with both the archaeological and aDNA evidence, as far as it is at present understood. But, even if it is broadly correct, the situation is likely to have been far more complex. We know, from archaeological sources, that contacts developed between the Balkans and the Pontic steppe over a considerable period of time before the advent of the Yamnaya culture. Around 5200 BC aspects of settled farming began to spread eastwards from the Carpathian region into the forest steppe zone eventually reaching as far as the Dnieper. Later, around 4200 BC, pastoral groups from the lower Dnieper valley, adopting the Kurgan burial rite, moved westwards penetrating the lower Danube valley. Over and above these local and regional developments was a complex super-regional exchange network in copper goods known as the Carpatho-Balkan Metallurgical Province which embraced

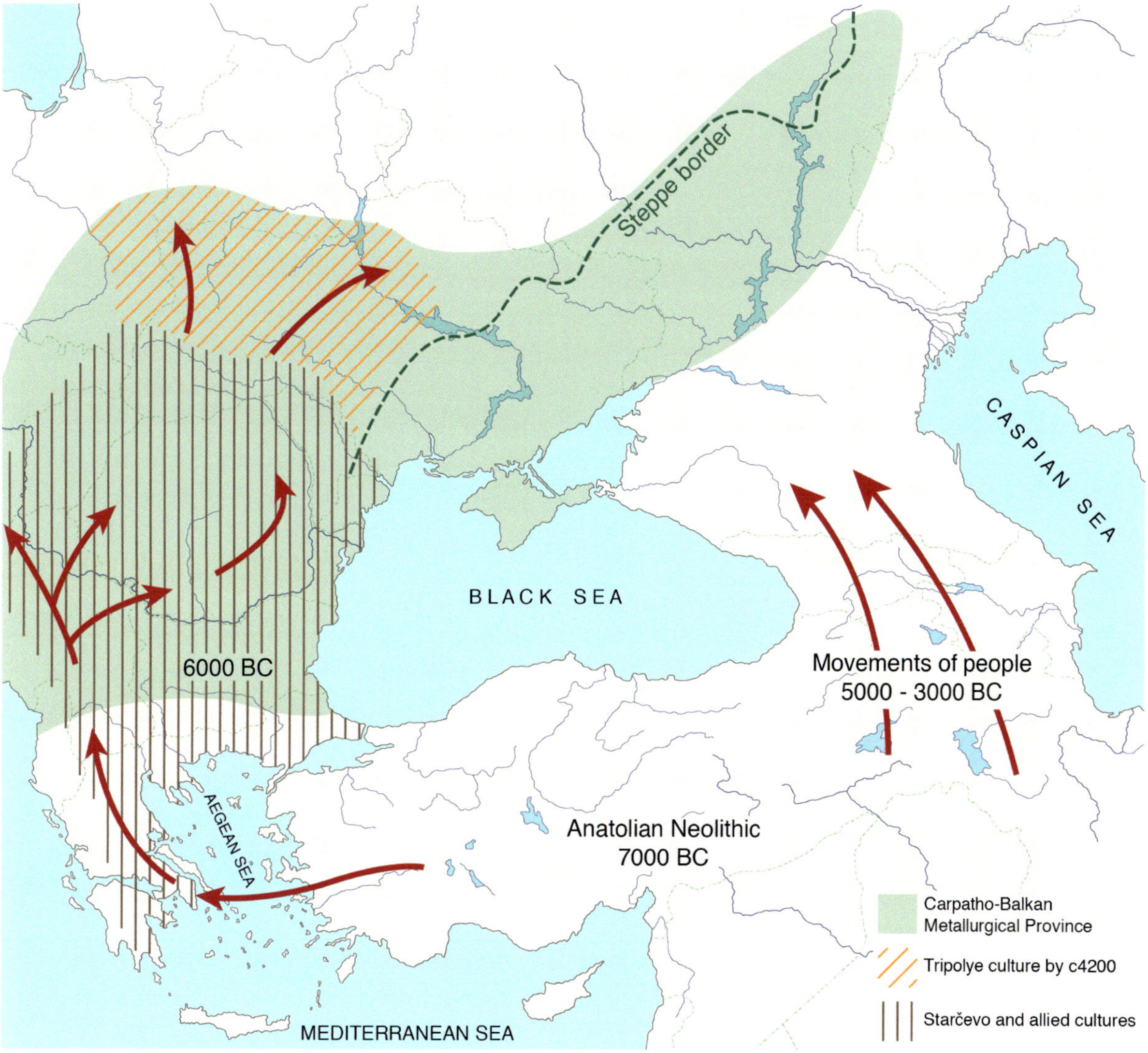

7.1. A hybrid hypothesis of the homeland and expansion of Indo-European, synthesizing elements of the Anatolian and steppe hypotheses, taking into account movements from Anatolia westwards into the Balkans and northwards across the Caucasus to the Pontic–Caspian Steppe.
(map B. Cunliffe)

the zone from the Carpathian Basin to the river Volga in the period 5400–3800 BC and is characterized by the use of sophisticated tools and weapons manufactured from Balkan ore. These complex networks in operation over more than two millennia can be identified in the archaeological data and there is sufficient evidence to suggest that some movements of population were involved in both directions. Clearly, then, there is a far more nuanced story to be told about the *longue durée* interactions between the steppe and the Balkans than the simple narrative of the expansion of Yamnaya pastoralists into the Great Hungarian Plain and beyond in the early 3rd millennium. There is much here for geneticists to elucidate: their work has hardly begun.

Insofar as all this impacts on the Indo-European question, might there not be another hypothesis to consider? Could it be that Indo-European was introduced into the Balkans about 6500–6000 BC along with farming, as the Anatolian hypothesis suggests, and that it was from this region, as well as from south of the Caucasus, that the pastoralists on the Pontic–Caspian steppe absorbed the language over a period of several millennia? It would be a difficult hypothesis to test but a preliminary would be to explore the extent, direction, and intensity of human movements over these crucial three millennia using aDNA.

One huge question that has yet to be answered is the origin of the Anatolian branch of Indo-European. Its best known representative is Hittite, spoken in central Anatolia in the 2nd millennium BC. It is the only branch retaining the archaic 'laryngeal' sounds, a system of genders predating the feminine, and a simpler verbal system. Everyone agrees that Anatolian is the most archaic of the branches, the first to split off. The status and origin of Anatolian lie at the root of Indo-European studies. In the current state of aDNA discoveries, the case can be made that the rest of Indo-European, i.e. post-Anatolian Proto-Indo-European, is to be identified with the Yamnaya horizon of the Copper Age Pontic–Caspian steppe. Anatolian surely branched off earlier than that. Was it always south of the Caucasus? Did its speakers have the steppe component, i.e. a mix of DNA from south of the Caucasus and 'eastern hunter–gatherers' (EHG) from north-east Europe? Were they related to the first farmers who spread from Anatolia across the northern Mediterranean and up the Danube? To get this right we will have to work out not only the relationship of the Anatolian speakers to the other Indo-Europeans, but also to speakers of the non-Indo-European languages that survive in the Caucasus to this day and ancient ones spoken in Asia Minor alongside Hittite, including Hattic and Hurrian. How much future theories of Indo-European origins owe to the Anatolian hypothesis will depend a lot on the answers to these questions.

On 4 May 2018, Harvard archaeogeneticist Iosif Lazaridis summed up the ongoing state of play: 'In the next few years this lingering mystery will be solved: either Anatolian speakers will be shown to possess steppe-related ancestry absent in earlier Anatolians (largely proving the steppe PIE hypothesis), or they will not (largely falsifying it, and pointing to a Near Eastern PIE homeland).' As if to dramatize the dizzying pace of discoveries, an answer, at least the beginnings of one, came back in five days (9 May 2018), rather than a 'few years', with 74 ancient whole genomes sequenced at the Copenhagen Centre for GeoGenetics, published in de Barros Damgaard et al. That study showed no steppe or EHG ancestry in Bronze Age people from Anatolia, including five individuals deemed probably Hittite speakers. Caution is in order. Five is not many. We can at best only guess what language(s) a person probably spoke from the archaeological context of their bones. The Hittites ruled an expansive empire, so many people without deep Anatolian-speaking ancestry probably learned the Hittite language and passed it on to their children. Nonetheless, if this new evidence holds up and is confirmed by further samples from Hittite and Luwian contexts, the result would falsify the steppe hypothesis according to Lazaridis's formulation.

Back to the Atlantic

The archaeological evidence leaves little doubt that the Atlantic seaways provided a corridor of communication throughout much of the Neolithic and Bronze Age, 5000–900 BC, during which time technological skills, cosmological knowledge, and belief systems were shared by communities living along the Atlantic face of Europe from Portugal to the Shetland Isles. Intensity of contact varied from place to place and from time to time. For the most part interactions would have been between neighbours with information passing 'down the line'. But from time to time people may have made longer journeys driven by curiosity or the desire to acquire rare commodities. This seems to have been the case in the middle of the 3rd millennium when the search for metals was at its height and Beaker prospectors were involved in developing copper mines in Brittany and south-west Ireland. Archaeologists have worked long and hard studying these networks and, as we have shown in Chapters 4 and 5, the huge range of varied data reflecting on the intricacies of connectivity provides a detailed and convincing picture of the systems at work. That the communities of the Atlantic façade shared in a flow of knowledge leading to similarities in culture over some four millennia is not in doubt. It is not an unreasonable hypothesis that over this time one of the region's local languages was adopted and adapted to facilitate information transfer and so became Atlantic Europe's lingua franca.

So far aDNA has had comparatively little to add to this theme largely because samples from Iberia and western France are few but what little we know is that throughout much of the Neolithic period the genetic composition of the Atlantic Neolithic population reflects their Mesolithic hunter-gatherer ancestry with an input from the Near East which probably represents incomers, using the Mediterranean route, setting up farming communities in the mid 6th millennium. What is needed now is a thorough study of the aDNA of the Neolithic and Maritime Bell Beaker population of the Atlantic zone. This will enable us to provide an additional test for the belief that the Maritime Bell Beaker Complex was an indigenous Atlantic phenomenon developing in Portugal *c.* 2800 BC and spreading rapidly by sea and river across much of western Europe.

By the middle of the 3rd millennium the picture has become more complex. What the archaeological evidence shows is that contact developed across the north of France, linking the lower Rhine valley, the Seine, and the Loire, along which material culture and value systems spread in both directions. In this way amber from the north began to reach the Atlantic communities while Grand Pressigny flint from the Loire valley was transported in some quantity to the lower Rhine (Fig. 1.3). The preference for the rite of single burial beneath a barrow—a characteristic of the Rhine region—began to spread to the west while the form and decoration of the Maritime Bell Beaker was adopted in the Rhine valley adding to the local repertoire. More recently Stuart Needham has developed the concept of the corridor across northern France convincingly arguing that it was from here that Beaker colonists spread to most parts of Britain in the period focusing on 2300–2100 BC.

Ancient DNA studies have confirmed and amplified this picture by identifying a significant steppe component in the genes of the north-European Beaker population deriving from an influx of people ultimately originating in the Pontic–Caspian steppe and transmitted either directly or through the Corded Ware culture extending across the North European Plain. The dramatic demonstration that the aDNA of the Beaker population of Britain showed a high steppe component has led to the suggestion that the influx of Beaker immigrants from the continent caused a 90% replacement of the indigenous British population. The full implications of this still have to be thought through (above p. 194). The absence of aDNA samples from central and western France means that, at present, it is not possible to model the impact of people with steppe ancestry on Atlantic Europe although samples from Iberia, only small numbers published so far, indicate the existence of a steppe component by the Bronze Age.

That the aDNA data is broadly consistent with the archaeological evidence is reassuring. Archaeologists have long been aware that the Beaker period was a time of mobility, not only of materials but also of people. The genetic evidence is now beginning to allow the intensity and direction of population movement to be modelled on an empirical basis.

The demonstration that there was a significant steppe component in the genes of the population of northern Europe in the 3rd millennium encouraged some commentators to claim that this proved the Kurgan hypothesis—that it was an incursion from the steppe that first introduced Indo-European into peninsula Europe. It does no such thing. While it is likely that those with a high component of steppe genes spoke an Indo-European language, where and when that language developed is, as we have seen above (pp. 197–200), a complex issue that still has to be resolved. The introduction of a form of Indo-European through the north European Corded Ware vector by no means precludes the possibility that Indo-European languages had already been introduced into the European peninsula much earlier. It was, however, probably through this later infusion that words related to horses and wheeled vehicles were introduced into the vocabulary of the west. Clearly there is much to debate but what most will agree is that the time for simplistic assertions is past.

If we allow that there were multiple routes along which, over time, Indo-European was introduced into peninsula Europe, what does this mean for the way in which we view the conventional language tree? It need no longer be seen as a simple dendritic structure. Many linguists would agree that Italo-Celtic branched off from Proto-Indo-European earlier and that Balto-Slavic and Germanic separated somewhat later. Could it be that Italo-Celtic developed from the Indo-European introduced via the Mediterranean with the initial spread of the Cardial ware Neolithic sometime in the 6th millennium when enclaves of Neolithic farmers were establishing themselves around the coasts of the west Mediterranean and along the Atlantic coasts of Iberia and France? It was from this base that the Italic (whence Romance) and Celtic languages were subsequently to develop. It could then be argued that the Balto-

Slavic and Germanic languages were a separate development arising from the Indo-European introduced with the spread of the Neolithic Linearbandkeramik (LBK) in the 6th millennium augmented and modified by the Indo-European spoken by subsequent incursions originating in the Balkans/steppe zone.

The mobility of population, so evident in the Beaker period in the second half of the 3rd millennium, created a situation in which language is likely to have developed rapidly, in some areas converging, in others diverging. It would have been at this time that the lingua franca of the Atlantic zone (if our case that there was one is not disproved) was impacted upon by the dialects spoken by the Beaker population emerging from the lower Rhine region. Could this, perhaps, be the beginning of the divide between the Celtic spoken in Iberia and that spoken in Gaul and the British Isles?

There are two strong points favouring a lingua franca in Atlantic Europe in later prehistory. First, there is the archaeological evidence for intensity of contacts across the region, the sharing of values and know-how, based on complex information. Secondly, when the languages of this region appear to us in the pre-Roman Iron Age, many of them are similar and belong to the same branch of Indo-European—Celtic. As the Palaeohispanic languages become better known and are studied more closely, we will gain a better idea as to how different Hispano-Celtic was from Gaulish, Brythonic, and Goidelic, although getting a date of separation out of that degree of differentness might hinge on a method still viewed by some linguists as a newfangled glottochronology.

It is not unlikely that the genetic and cultural diversity of the Beaker phenomenon created subsystems that were eventually reflected in the main dialect divisions of the Celtic languages. It is striking, for example, that near what appears to have been the cradle of the Beaker Complex by the lower Tagus, a unique Italo-Celtic language emerged that linguists call Lusitanian (see above, pp. 27–30). In the Roman period, this language was used to commemorate pre-Roman gods.

Sociolinguistics would lead us to expect that so long as intense contacts prevailed across Atlantic Europe, dialects that had been mutually intelligible to begin with would have remained so. Today's great lingua francas—such as English, Spanish, and Arabic—have dialect divisions going back many centuries, but because they are increasingly used as world languages, the dialects are converging: young people from Texas and Glasgow have less difficulty communicating than their grandparents. For our hypothetical Proto-Celtic lingua franca circumstances would have maximized mutual intelligibility until *c.* 900 BC, at which time Iberia—at least most of it—left the Atlantic Bronze Age as the Phoenicians became the dominant maritime traders in the region. The steep decline of contact that followed would have favoured Hispano-Celtic becoming a fully separate language, rather than a dialect (albeit possibly an ancient one) of Proto-Celtic.

Whatever time depth and Indo-European homeland scenario we're considering, we mustn't forget the non-Indo-European languages. Basque is still with us today. An ancient form of Basque or something very similar to it had been widely spoken in one of Caesar's three parts of Gaul, Aquitania. Iberian was once spoken widely in what is today the Valencian Community and Catalunya, continuing into Mediterranean France. In what is now Italy, there was Palaeo-Sardinian, Etruscan, and Rhaetian in the Alps, which seems to have been a relative of Etruscan. Where did these come from? If Cardial ware came to the Iberian Peninsula together with the Proto-Indo-European that became Celtic, does that mean that Basque/Aquitanian and Iberian descend from the language(s) of hunter–gatherers? That is not *a priori* impossible. Some Basques think it should be so. Bearing that possibility in mind, we will want to see, as further aDNA samples are reported, whether these regions show elevated levels of pre-Neolithic hunter–gatherer genes. Alternatively, we will also want to resift the residues of pre-Indo-European languages in Anatolia and Mediterranean Europe to determine whether that evidence supports the case that Basque descends from the language of the first farmers.

We began this research in what seems now to have been an age of innocence with a few simple questions. During the course of the programme we have been overtaken by the tsunami of aDNA that has not only introduced an entirely new set of data but has raised a set of questions we could hardly have conceived of a decade ago. What has emerged from all this is a glimpse of the tantalizing complexity of it all and the realization that simple answers are likely to be wrong or at best misleading. We have raised some of these issues in this brief chapter in the hope of expanding the debate and moving to a new level of understanding. This, after all, is what research is about.

Further reading

Phylogenetic approaches to the time depth of Proto-Indo-European

The seminal paper putting forward this new approach to dating prehistoric languages is **R. D. Gray & Q. D. Atkinson** 2003 'Language-tree divergence times support the Anatolian theory of Indo-European origin', *Nature* 426, 435–9, https://www.nature.com/articles/nature02029. Continuations of this methodology, which also support the deeper chronology of the Anatolian hypothesis of Indo-European origins, include **Q. D. Atkinson, G. Nicholls, D. Welch, & R. D. Gray** 2005 'From Words to Dates: 'Water into Wine, Mathemagic or Phylogenetic Inference?' *Transactions of the Philological Society* 103, 193–219 http://dx.doi.org/10.1111/j.1467968X.2005.00151.x; **M. Pagel & A. Meade** 2006 'Estimating Rates of Lexical Replacement on Phylogenetic Trees of Languages', *Phylogenetic methods and the prehistory of languages*, ed. P. Forster & C. Renfrew, 173–82, Cambridge, McDonald Institute for Archaeological Research; **R. Bouckaert, P. Lemey, M. Dunn, S.J. Greenhill, A. V. Alekseyenko, A. J. Drummond, R. D. Gray, M. A. Suchard, & Q. D. Atkinson** 2012 'Mapping the Origins and Expansion of the Indo-European Language Family', *Science* 337, 957–60. http://dx.doi.org/10.1126/science.1219669 ; **R. Bouckaert, P. Lemey, M. Dunn, S.J. Greenhill, A. V. Alekseyenko, A. J. Drummond, R. D. Gray, M. A. Suchard, & Q. D. Atkinson** 2013 'Correction to: Mapping the Origins and Expansion of the Indo-European Language Family', *Science* 342, 1446. http://dx.doi.org/10.1126/science.342.6165.1446-a; P. Heggarty 2014 'Prehistory by Bayesian Phylogenetics? The State of the Art on Indo-European Origins', *Antiquity* 88, 566–77. http://antiquity.ac.uk/ant/088/ant0880566.htm. A key paper explaining why many linguists are reluctant to estimate dates for prehistoric linguistic events and states is **A. McMahon & R. McMahon** 2006 'Why Linguists Don't Do Dates: Evidence from Indo-European and Australian Languages', *Phylogenetic Methods and the Prehistory of Languages*, eds P. Forster & C. Renfrew, McDonald Institute Monographs, 153–60, Cambridge, McDonald Institute for Archaeological Research. A project seeking to improve the linguistic methodology of Atkinson and Gray, with conclusions closer to the Kurgan hypothesis, is published in **W. Chang, C. Cathcart, D. Hall, & A. Garrett** 2015 'Ancestry-Constrained Phylogenetic Analysis Supports the Indo-European Steppe Hypothesis', *Language* 91/ 1, 194–244.

Anti-migrationism in archaeological explanation

A seminal statement is **G. Clark** 1966 'The Invasion Hypothesis in British Archaeology', *Antiquity* 40, 172–89. Implications of anti-migrationism for the question of Celtic origins are confronted in **C. F. C. Hawkes** 1973 '"Cumulative Celticity" in Pre-Roman Britain', *Études Celtiques* 13, 607–28, and **D. Greene & S. Piggott** 1983 'The Coming of the Celts to Britain and Ireland', *Proc. 6th International Congress of Celtic Studies, Galway, 1979*, ed. G. Mac Eoin, 131–48, Dublin, Dublin Institute for Advanced Studies.

The Anatolian homeland hypothesis of Indo-European origins

For the original formulation of the idea and the principal arguments in its favour, see **C. Renfrew** 1987 *Archaeology and Language: The Puzzle of Indo-European Origins,* London, Pimlico, 1998, first published, London, Cape. On the eve of the archaeogenetics revolution, Renfrew published a concise update of his hypothesis, including an overview of alternative hypotheses and their implications for Celtic from the West: **C. Renfrew** 2013 'Early Celtic in the West: The Indo-European Context', *Celtic from the West 2: Rethinking the Bronze Age and the Arrival of Indo-European in Atlantic Europe,*

Celtic Studies Publications 16, eds J. T. Koch & Barry Cunliffe, 207–17, Oxford, Oxbow Books. For an argument favouring the Anatolian hypothesis from a linguistic perspective, see **P. Heggarty** 2013 'Europe and Western Asia: Indo-European linguistic prehistory', *The Encyclopedia of Global Human Migration*, eds I. Ness & P. Bellwood, 157–67, Oxford, Wiley-Blackwell.

Archaeogenetics

Two key 2018 papers discussed in Chapter 7 are **I. Lazaridis** 2018 'The evolutionary history of human populations in Europe', https://arxiv.org/abs/1805.01579v1 [q-bio.E], and **P. de Barros Damgaard**, ... **E. Willerslev** 2018 'The first horse herders and the impact of early Bronze Age steppe expansions into Asia', *Science* 10.1126/science.aar7711/. Fuller annotated lists of breakthrough publications in this fast-moving field are included in the Further Reading sections in Chapters 3 and 6 (above pp. 75, 188–91).

Early responses from archaeologists to archaoegenetic papers

The following have advised caution before adopting sweeping conclusions that appear to contradict recent archaeological thinking: **M. Vander Linden** 2016 'Population history in third-millennium-BC Europe: assessing the contribution of genetics', *World Archaeology* 48, 714–28; **V. Heyd** 2017 'Kossinna's smile', *Antiquity* 91, 348–59; **L. S. Klejn, W. Haak, I. Lazaridis, & N. Patterson** 2018 'Discussion: Are the Origins of Indo-European Languages Explained by the Migration of the Yamnaya Culture to the West?' *European Journal of Archaeology* 21/1, 3–17.

For the subject of the **Lusitanian** language and its implications for the origins of Celtic, see the Further Reading section for Chapter 2 (p. 36).

GENERAL INDEX